ECONOMIC DIPLOMACY BETWEEN THE EUROPEAN COMMUNITY AND JAPAN 1959 – 1981

For Fumi Dan

Economic Diplomacy between the European Community and Japan 1959 – 1981

ALBRECHT ROTHACHER
London School of Economics

Gower

Published by
Gower Publishing Company Limited,
Gower House, Croft Road, Aldershot, Hants., GU11 3HR, England.

British Library Cataloguing in Publication Data

Rothacher, Albrecht
    Economic diplomacy between the European Community and Japan 1959–1981
    1   European Economic Community–Japan
    2   Japan Foreign economic relations–European Economic Community
    I   Title
    337'.094   HC241.25.J/

ISBN 0-566-00532-8

Printed and bound in Great Britain by
Biddles Ltd, Guildford and King's Lynn

Contents

List of diagrams   viii

List of tables   ix

Preface   xi

Abbreviations   xiii

Japanese expressions   xvi

1 Introduction: the interaction between developed
   countries — theory and conceptualisation
      Theories on relations between developed countries   1
      A working hypothesis, variables and the research
         design   7
      References   10

PART I
   The institutional framework for policy decisions on
   bilateral relations

2 The structure for foreign policy decisions in the
   European community
      Variables for EC foreign policy decisions   15
      The institutional Community framework   17

                                                                 v

National policies   34
Actual foreign policies   40
References   42

3 The structure for foreign policy decisions in Japan
The power structure of post-war Japan   50
Institutions of foreign policy decision making   57
The conduct of Japan's foreign policies   67
Conclusion   75
References   76

PART II
The empirical development in bilateral relations
and trade policies

4 Euro—Japanese relations 1950—68: the prelude to the common
commercial policy and the gradual emancipation of Japan
The theoretical interest in the 1950—68 period   83
The chronology of Euro—Japanese post-war relations   85
Euro—Japanese communication and decision making
1950—68   117
The economic dimension in bilateral relations   125
Evaluation   132
References   134

5 EC—Japan relations 1969—75: the beginnings of a common
commercial policy and the liberalisation of imports in Japan
The chronology of EC—Japanese relations   146
The economic dimension in bilateral relations   183
Decision making in bilateral relations   197
Conclusion   200
References   203

6 EC—Japan relations 1976—80: cyclical crises and high
politics co-operation
The empirical development in EC—Japan relations
1976—80   218
The economic dimension in bilateral relations   277
Decision making in Euro—Japanese relations   287
Conclusion   297
References   300

7 Conclusion: explaining and forecasting EC—Japan relations
The quality of EC—Japan relations   317

Bureaucratic politics in EC—Japan relations   320
A multivariable explanation   323
Options and forecasts   330
References   335

Bibliography

Books and monographs   337
Articles   344
Newspapers, periodicals and agency dispatches   354
Archive and PR materials   355
Interviews   356

Subject index   358

Diagrams

1.1 Theories on the management of the developed international system   3

1.2 A model for 'normal' interactions between developed countries (DCs)   8

5.1 Japanese commercial representation in the EC versus EC representation in Japan   184

7.1 EC–Japan relations, 1980   319

7.2 Bureaucratic decisions versus political decisions   322

7.3 EC–Japan trade 1959–80   326

Tables

4.1 Euro–Japanese trade by countries (1956–68) — 126

4.2 Japanese trade with the EC in its relative shares (1960–68) — 127

4.3 Main Japanese exports to the EC (1960–68) — 129

4.4 Main EC exports to Japan (1960–67) — 129

4.5 EC import restrictions (1962–65) — 130

5.1 Euro–Japanese trade by countries (1969–75) — 185

5.2 Japan's trade with the EC in its relative shares (1969–75) — 186

5.3 Major EC exports to Japan (1971–75) — 187

5.4 Major Japanese exports to the EC (1970–75) — 188

5.5 World market shares of Japanese export products (1971) — 190

5.6 Japan's import liberalisation — 193

5.7 Japanese investments in Europe (1951–73) — 195

5.8   Companies with European participation in the top 50
      list of companies with foreign equity in Japan   196

6.1   European–Japanese trade by countries (1976–79)   278

6.2   Japan's trade with the EC in its relative shares (1976–79)   279

6.3   Major EC exports to Japan (1976–79)   280

6.4   Share of chemicals and machinery and equipment in EC
      exports to Japan (1979)   280

6.5   Share of luxury items in EC exports to Japan (1979)   281

6.6   Major Japanese exports to the EC (1976–79)   281

7.1   Tasks in the foreign policy management   322

Preface

This book attempts to analyse the development of EC—Japanese relations over a considerable span of time. At the outset, for theoretical reference, the medium range theories relevant to the interaction between developed countries are outlined: functionalism (Mitrany), bureaucratic politics (Allison—Halperin), power politics (Morgenthau) and trilateralism (Brzezinski).

In the first part decision structures for foreign economic policies are reviewed within the EC — both at Community and at national levels — and in Japan. With weak political decision centres in both, there is a structural bias towards complex and slow bureaucratic decision making oriented primarily at achieving domestic consensus.

The second part analyses in great detail the development of EC—Japanese diplomatic and economic interactions through the various stages of bilateral relations: Japan's search for international recognition and emancipation 1955—63, the EC attempting to initiate a common trade agreement with Japan 1969—72 and the cyclical bilateral crises of 1976—77 and 1980—81.

A final summary offers a multivariable explanation for past and likely future developments. Most significant are structural variables: the changes in Japan's economic system and the relative stagnation in the EC's industrial structure. Then there are organisational variables on both sides supporting the notion of predictable bureaucratic exchanges as the dominant mode for official interactions and policy decisions. As a consequence events associated with negotiations or with the associated policy issues were prevented from becoming politicised. External variables

— policies pursued by the superpowers and by the oil exporting nations — strongly affected Euro—Japanese relations. Cognitive factors, the role of mutual perceptions, were rated less important compared to the effects of structural, external and organisational variables on EC—Japan relations.

As a longitudinal policy analysis, this book complements earlier studies of Euro—Japanese relations. Hanabusa (1979) largely focussed on the economic side of these relations. Sir George Sansom (1950) analysed the historical development in bilateral cultural contacts and perceptions until the 1980s. These lines were continued by Wilkinson (1981) with their implications for the present. To these cultural and economic perspectives this book adds a third dimension: the political economy side of EC—Japan relations.

I started research on this study in October 1978 and finished writing in June 1981. I spent the academic year 1978—79 at the London School of Economics, familiarising myself with the subject matter, collecting materials and reading on the EC's foreign policies. In 1979—80, thanks to an extremely generous dissertation grant from the Japan Foundation, I was able to visit the Far East and to spend nine months in Tokyo. In the International Christian University's Social Science Research Institute I found a suitable and rewarding place to do further research work both on foreign economic policy decisions in Japan and on EC—Japanese contemporary diplomatic exchanges. I also did most of my interviewing in Tokyo.

Upon return to London I spent most of the summer 1980 in the formidable press library of Chatham House. In 1980—81 I had the splendid opportunity to spend one year as a researcher at the European University Institute in Florence. Here I found sufficient time and encouragement to analyse my collection of materials and to write most of this book.

I am most grateful to Professor Michio Morishima and to the late Professor Andrew Shonfield, without whose help — enabling me to work in Tokyo and in Florence — this book could not have been written. I am greatly indebted to my supervisor at the LSE, Paul Taylor, for his valuable and encouraging comments on my manuscripts. At the ICU my thanks go to Professors Tsuneo Nakauchi and Tadashi Fujita who encouraged and aided my stay and research work in Japan. Among the many Japanese who unfailingly made efforts to explain the mysteries of Japan's society and way of life to an ignorant 'gaijin' my friends Issei Suzuki, Akira Nakazato, Katsumi Yokobori and Ms Yasuko Wachi deserve special mentioning.

The tedious job of editing this manuscript was undertaken by Peter Kennealy who executed it with almost professional efficiency. Any mistakes remaining are, of course, solely the author's responsibility.

Firenze, July 1982   Albrecht Rothacher

Abbreviations

ACP	African, Caribbean and Pacific Countries
ADD	Anti-dumping Duty
Art. 35	Article XXXV (GATT), providing for Most Favoured Nation treatment
ASEAN	Association of South East Asian Nations
AWES	Association of Western European Shipbuilders
BDI	Bundesverband der Deutschen Industrie
BIAC	Business and Industry Advisory Committee to the OECD
BL	British Leyland
BMW	Bundesministerium für Wirtschaft
BOJ	Bank of Japan
BPA	Bureaucratic Politics Approach
CAP	Common Agricultural Policy
CCMC	Committee of Common Market Automobile Constructors
CCP	Common Commercial Policy
CDU	Christlich Demokratische Union (Conservative party in Germany)
CEBLS	Council of EC Builders of Large Ships
CET	Common External Tariff
CIPI	Interministerial Committee for Industrial Policy (Italy)
CNPF	The French Patronat
Com. 113	Committee 113, assisting the Commission in external negotiations
Coreper	Committee of Permanent Representatives
DAC	Development Assistance Committee of the OECD

DC	Developed Country
DG	Directorate General in the Commission
DGB	Deutscher Gewerkschaftsbund
DGES	Directoraat General voor Europese Samenwerking in the Dutch Foreign Ministry
DOT	Department of Trade (UK)
DSP	Democratic Socialist Party of Japan
ECSC	European Community for Steel and Coal
EDC	European Defence Community
EFTA	European Free Trade Area
EMS	European Monetary System
EP	European Parliament
EPA	Economic Planning Agency (Japan)
EPC	European Political Co-operation
FBI	Federation of British Industries (later CBI)
FBR	Fast Breeder Reactor
FCO	Foreign and Commonwealth Office
FEBMA	Federation of European Bearing Manufacturers
FTC	Fair Trade Commission (Japan)
GATT	General Agreement on Tariffs and Trade
GNP	Gross National Product
GSP	Generalised System of Preferences (on LDC imports)
HI	Heavy Industries
HLC	High Level Consultations between the Commission and the Japanese government
IBRD	International Bank for Reconstruction and Development
IMF	International Monetary Fund
JAMA	Japan Automobile Manufacturers Association
JCP	Japan Communist Party
JETRO	Japan External Trade Organisation
JFTC	Japan Foreign Trade Organisation
JSP	Japan Socialist Party
LDC	Less Developed Country
LDP	Liberal Democratic Party (the Conservative Party of Japan)
LTA	Long Term Agreement on cotton textiles
MAFF	Ministry of Agriculture, Fisheries and Forestry (Japan)
MEP	Member of the European Parliament
MFA	Ministry of Foreign Affairs (Japan)
MFN	Most Favoured Nation
MHW	Ministry of Health and Welfare (Japan)
MITI	Ministry of International Trade and Industry (Japan)
MOF	Ministry of Finance (Japan)
MOT	Ministry of Transport (Japan)
MP	Member of Parliament

MTN	Multilateral Tariff Negotiations
NATO	North Atlantic Treaty Organisation
NIC	New Industrialised Country
NPT	Non Proliferation Treaty
NTB	Non Tariff Barrier
OAD	Official Aid for Development
OAPEC	Organisation of Arab Oil Exporting Countries
OECD	Organisation for Economic Co-operation and Development
OEEC	Organisation for European Economic Co-operation (the predecessor for the OECD)
OPEC	Organisation of Oil Exporting Countries
PCI	Partito Communista Italiana
PLO	Palestine Liberation Organisation
PMO	Prime Minister's Office (Japan)
PR	Public Relations
PRCh	People's Republic of China
SAJ	Shipbuilders Association of Japan
SALT	Strategic Arms Limitation Agreement
SC	Safeguard Clause
SCAP	Supreme Commander Allied Powers (the US administration in occupied post-war Japan)
SGCI	Secretariat General du Comité Interministerial (the French government's central co-ordination bureau)
SMMT	Society of Motor Manufacturers and Traders (UK)
TA	Trade Agreement
TCN	Treaty of Commerce and Navigation between Britain and Japan
TUC	Trades Union Congress (UK)
UAR	United Arab Republics (Egypt)
UN	United Nations
UNCTAD	United Nations Conference on Trade and Development
UNICE	Industrial Association of the EC
VSR	Voluntary Self Restraints on exports
VW	Volkswagen
WP 6	OECD Working Party 6 (on shipbuilding)
WW II	The Second World War

Japanese expressions

Amakudari   'Descendants from heaven', post-retirement business careers of senior government officials

Awase   Syncretist ('Japanese') thinking

Domei   Association of (mostly) blue collar unions in Japan

Doyukai Keizai   'Committee for Economic Development', association of (more liberal) industrialists

Erabu   Analytical ('Western') thinking

Gaimusho   Foreign Ministry

Gyokai   Sectoral industrial interests

Keibatsu   Family and marriage ties in the administrative, political and business elites

Keidanren   Industrial Association of Japan

Keiretsu   Post-war business conglomerates, centring on the national banks

Kigyo	Individual companies' interests
Kokumin kyokai	Keidanren's funding organisation for the LDP
Komeito	Buddhist party (affiliated with the sokko gakkai sect)
Nemawashi	Sounding out one's superior's consent
Nikkeiren	Employers' Association of Japan
Nissho	Japanese Chamber of Commerce and Industry
Ringi sei	Standard drafting procedure in Japanese administration
Sogo shosha	General trading companies
Zaibatsu	Pre-war business conglomerates (family-owned)
Zaikai	'Financial circles', the network of elites of the organised financial and industrial interests in Japan
Zenno	National Federation of Agricultural Co-operatives
Gaijin	Foreigner (from the West)

1 Introduction: the interaction between developed countries – theory and conceptualisation

International relations as the system of systems with their metacomplexity are a complicated subject matter for both theory and research. Small wonder if the state of the art still frequently resembles what C. Wright Mills once criticised as the unrelated coexistence of grand theory and abstracted empiricism.[1] This book has to come to grips with this dilemma. Its focus is an empirical one. And for this theories of an intermediate level are more relevant. These concepts are frequently criticised for their lack of solid metaphysical and epistemological references.[2] Be that as it may, only medium theories in international relations so far appear suitable to be operationalised, and possibly modified and improved by empirical research

In order to demonstrate this proposition this chapter will discuss the relevant theories as they apply to the interaction of developed countries and thereafter will outline the working hypothesis and research design used in this book.

Theories on relations between developed countries

Relations between developed countries (DCs) can theoretically be viewed from two perspectives. One concerns the predominant *political quality* of their relations, namely whether either low politics (sectoral economic or technical issues, i.e. peripheral national interests) or high politics (matters of national security or strategic importance, i.e. core national interests) characterises their interaction.[3] The delineation problem of where and when an economic dispute has spilled over from a mere sectoral affair of low politics to a matter of high politics depends in the final instance on the decision makers' responses, i.e. their definition of the situation. Under the heading of high politics theories in international relations one has to mention also a Marxist school dissenting from the academic mainstream.

The second perspective refers to the *structural potential* of their relations, determined by assumptions about the nature of the international economic and political order. Interactions are viewed either as taking place in a neomercantilist zero sum game in which conflict is the prevalent mode of relation, or in a neoclassical positive sum game in which — proper management capacities provided — co-operation can prevail.

Following this scheme the common theoretical approaches to relations between developed countries — seen in their ideal types in the Weberian sense — can be classified as shown in Diagram 1.1.

Trilateralism†

Certainly, there has never been any theoretical claim in trilateralism nor was there ever an attempt to formulate in a systematic fashion the theoretical assumptions and concepts it stands for. Nevertheless, in spite of the loose and diverse character of the Trilateral Commission's membership, there is no doubt that a coherent cognitive and normative conception on the working of the international system guided Brzezinski's, Rockefeller's and the Commission's work.

As is evident in the major Trilateral publications, the basic and long term interests of the US, Japan and Western Europe (and of the multinational corporations as well) are seen as identical:[4] all share common democratic values and experiences, and as open and developed societies have a common interest in the maintainance and survival of these values and the societies representing them.

In economic terms this means a vital interest in the stability of a liberally structured world economy, which is seen as threatened by the proliferation of protectionist regimes, by excessive North—South discrepancies, by curtailed supplies of raw materials and energy sources, by possible social upheavals at home and by Soviet expansionism abroad.[5]

Given the assumptions of common interests and of challenges which best could be mastered by common and co-ordinated action, the prac-

† An article of mine which deals in greater detail with trilateralist theory and method, entitled 'Der Trilateralismus als internationales Politikmanagement', is published in *Aus Politik und Zeitgeschichte*, B 6/81, 7.2.1981, pp. 25—30.

Economic Quality		Political Quality		
		Low Politics	High Politics	
			Conventional IR	Marxist IR
Co-operation (positive sum)	Free Trade (neoclassicism)	Functionalism (Mitrany)	Trilateralism (Brzezinski–Rockefeller)	Ultraimperialism (Kautsky–Poulantzas)
Conflict (zero sum)	Protectionism (neomercantilism)	Bureaucratic Politics* (Allison–Halperin)	Power Politics (Morgenthau–Kennan)	Imperialism (Lenin–Mandel)

* The reasons for labelling 'bureaucratic politics' here roughly as 'conflict' and 'low politics' are explained on p. 320

Diagram 1.1 Theories on the management of the developed international system tical consequence appears plausible: the management of relations between developed countries is seen purely as a question of proper communication and co-operative organisation between the policy deciding elites in the trilateral regions.

Though sometimes endorsing functionalist stands,[6] trilateralism aims at high politics (security, detente, relations with OPEC, and global economic relations: commodity trade, monetary issues, the North—South dialogue) and at the implementation of institutionalised Western high politics co-ordination;[7] and hitherto in operational terms it has exclusively relied on the concept of elite socialisation (via trilateral conferences, discussions, publications and mutual informal contacts).[8] The trilateralists reject explicitly the position of 'power politics', which takes the opposite intellectual position.[9]

Power politics

Trilateralism assumed international relations to be a positive sum game in which mutual co-operation would yield a maximum of benefits to the largest number. Power politics takes the opposite view.

International relations are a zero sum game in which, in Morgenthau's notion, nations pursue the maximisation of their national interest as defined in terms of power,[10] a strategy which if successful necessarily has to succeed at the expense of others. Power is thereby the means and end in international politics and the behaviour of nations is explainable only as struggle for power. Mutual distrust, therefore, is the basis for interstate behaviour in this Machiavellian world.[11]

Since the global allocation of power is inherently unstable, continuous conflicts and threats of war must prevail, according to power politics, only to be temporarily and superficially adjusted by diplomatic action. Harmonious and possibly increasingly co-operative policies in trilateral relations are, therefore, a dangerous illusion according to this Realist school.

The core of the national interest is national survival, usually defined in strategic and geopolitical terms (i.e. high politics). All other interests are considered subservient to this.[12]

Imperialism — ultraimperialism

The debate between Realists and Trilateralists has long since had its parallel on the Marxist side.

Lenin's theory of imperialism assumes that the monopolisation of national industries has reached such degrees that during cyclical crises,

4

due to overproduction and underconsumption, the larger companies, having eliminated their national competitors, are then forced to push for overseas markets. Here national monopolies, with the assistance of their governments, confront each other in the struggle for imperialist spheres of influence (captive overseas markets and cheap sources of raw material supply). This tendency inevitably leads to intraimperialist wars.[13]

Mandel modified this theory slightly: in Europe the degree of monopolisation and internationalisation of production had outgrown the limits of narrow national territories. Thus today the allied European bourgeoisies battle against their US and Japanese counterparts. Increased competition on the world markets and political tensions between the imperialist rival blocks follow on this.[14]

Kautsky's theory of ultraimperialism reflects a more trilateral logic: the monopolisation and internationalisation of capitalist economies gradually leads to such a degree of corporate mergence and concentration that in the end a single world trust essentially runs the international economy. On the political side, international integration — or, for that matter imperialist subjugation — proceeds in an analogous fashion: only one world-dominating metropole is left managing an imperialist chain of one client state exploiting the next further down the pecking order. Nicolaus and Poulantzas agree that the dominant metropole will be (is already) the US.[15]

Seeking to choose between these two positions East German party Marxists found the coexistence of both centrifugal and centripetal tendencies in the capitalist world — a discovery which they immediately diagnosed as a new contradiction in the capitalist mode of production. They assert: 'dass sich objektiv die Bestrebungen des Monopolkapitals zur Vereinigung seiner Kräfte verstärken, dass aus den Grundlagen der kapitalistischen Produktionsweise aber zugleich die Tendenzen erwachsen, die diesem Zusammenschluss zuwiderlaufen'.[16]

Though the degree of abstraction renders this statement meaningless the authors finally go on to predict that increasing global competitiveness and protectionist tendencies would make trade wars more likely. At the same time however capitalists would close ranks in order to combat jointly the advance of socialism and the interests of the developing countries.[17]

In our terminology this would imply the coexistence of low politics conflicts with high politics co-operation (though in Marxist logic which sees the state as the agent of the monopolists, economic conflicts would immediately spill over into the high politics realm).

Functionalism

Functionalism not only applies to integration processes, but also, arising out of its concern with the working of international organisations, to the working of the international system.

Mitrany observed the growth of technical problems and of the non-political tasks of governments which in an increasingly interdependent world make necessary ever more co-operation of specialists at the international level. The growing international concern with non-controversial technical problems — away from divisive political issues — would gradually lead to the mutual recognition of the need also for co-operation in related fields (spill over).

Functionalism, in consequence, offers an alternative to the nation state: the gradual creation of a global transnational web of economic and social organisations and the furthering of mass attitudes towards international integration.[18] Groom and Taylor assert: 'The nation state . . . is thought to promote values in high politics and national prestige at the expense of public welfare'[19] and with reference to low politics: 'The range of technical difficulties within countries as in relations between them demands more the knowledge of experts than the judgements of politicians'.[20] The functionalists' preference for the technocratic way of handling international affairs presupposes that technical and economic problems in national and international bureaucracies are actually handled by *experts*, who in addition also care about the issues of their professional concern in purely functional terms. Bureaucratic politics contests those two assumptions.

Bureaucratic politics

Halperin and Allison both developed their bureaucratic politics scheme with the analysis of typical high politics decisions: the US decision to deploy an anti ballistic missile system and the US—Soviet handling of the Cuban missile crisis. These issues which according to an 'objective' definition would doubtlessly rank as 'high politics' were, however, according to Allison and Halperin more or less subjected to a low politics treatment.[21]

Bureaucratic mechanisms determined even the most crucial foreign policy decisions. The observation that 'each government consists of numerous individuals, many of them working in large organisations . . . Constrained . . . by the shared images of their society, these individuals nevertheless have very different interests, very different priorities, and are concerned with very different questions', is therefore essential for foreign policy.[22] Thus foreign policy decisions are made in a process

6

of 'pulling and hauling'. The implementation of these decisions is watered down by the same bureaucratic process.

In the final instance, bureaucratic politics have a universal claim: all foreign policy is bureaucratic politics. Policies are decided in intra-bureaucratic squabbles, characterised by departmental rivalries, information deficiencies, intrigues, organisational inertia, routines, back-staging, 'leaking', ambitions for personal careers and conformist and opportunist orientations ('where you stand depends on where you sit').[24] It follows from this that the prospects should become remote for an adequate consideration of shared interests with some foreign nation (or rather foreign bureaucracy). Domestic interests count most in this intra-administrative power wrangle[25] — conflicts with one's overseas partners and allies are the likely consequence.*

Bureaucratic politics have been criticised for over emphasising organisational conflicts; and on methodological grounds their decision analysis is ahistorical and immediate; considering the pressures on office holders ('pulling and hauling') Steiner argues that organisational factors cannot be the sole explanatory variable in international relations.[27]

Freedman states 'that it concentrates attention on the immediate fragmentary bureaucratic battles rather than the underlying power structure'. [28] It is this power structure from which the definition of the national interest emerges. In the process of its definition, *tactical* aspects have to be distinguished from *strategic* ones. While the tactical elements are of use in the immediate bureaucratic battles, the strategic elements are more significant: they are the capacity to define the broad objectives of policy and to co-ordinate the individual policies accordingly.[29] In this context Freedman quotes Robert McNamara: 'Vital decision making . . . must remain at the top. This is partly, though not completely, what the top is for'.[30]

A working hypothesis, variables and the research design

From their theoretical plausibility among developed countries we expect low politics to follow bureaucratic politics (here modified as a complementary rather than an exclusive model) and high politics to follow trilateralist lines. This is illustrated graphically in Diagram 1.2. We would expect the line BT to represent the normal pattern of interaction between developed countries. Only in special cases would we expect, for example, a line FT (such as in case of successful supranational

---

* This has been shown convincingly on a genuine low politics issue (Japanese textile imports to the US), by Destler, Fukui and Sato (1979). (See reference 26.)

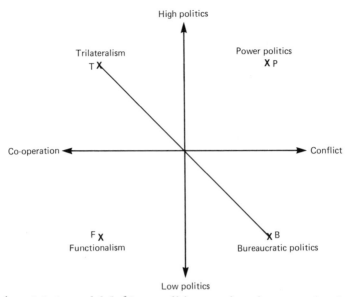

High politics

Trilateralism
T X

Power politics
X P

Co-operation ← → Conflict

F X
Functionalism

X B
Bureaucratic politics

Low politics

Diagram 1.2 A model for 'normal' interactions between developed countries (DCs)

integrations), or a line BP (in case of warlike crises between two DCs). In the case of relations between the EC and Japan, which are neither at war with each other nor attempting to initiate some form of regional integration, we should therefore investigate the coexistence of trilateralism and bureaucratic politics as our central hypothesis.

With reference to EC–Japan relations Galtung advocated a curious hypothesis: [31] 'Whether protection [of EC industries] takes the form of cross-investment or barriers against Japanese exports into the EC remains to be seen. *Most likely,* in our mind, *is the OECD directorate hypothesis, together with the other regulating mechanisms of the capitalist world*' (my italics). Earlier he had defined the OECD as the executive organisation for the economic triumvirate EEC, Japan and USA.[32] In a way this would correspond to our idea of trilateralism.

The testing of our hypothesis could be done best by a 'longitudinal policy analysis'. This approach attempts to view the historical development of policies and analyses their genesis, their conditions and consequences beyond the narrow focus of decision analysis.

For the development of EC–Japan relations over time the following set of variables seems relevant to explain variance (see also: Chapter 2, introduction) and ought to be examined:

1 *External variables* (of the international system): external demands, world events and trends of global significance.
2 *Structural variables* of the domestic socio-economic systems.

3 *Organisational variables*: the working of the bureaucratic system, the role of political leadership.

4 *Sociological variables*: the impact of ideologies, cultural perceptions, professional experiences, motivations, and of personalities involved.

5 *Policy variables* concerning the issue under review: policy objectives, decisions and their implementation.

6 *Incidental variables* of the bilateral bargaining—negotiating situation and its feed-back on policy decisions in the domestic system.

My empirical research will focus on institutional (organisational) and incidental variables (see also Chapter 4, introduction). External and structural variables will be referred to by using secondary sources. As the next chapter explains, there are severe data problems impeding a satisfactory analysis of policy and sociological variables.

For my longitudinal policy analysis I selected the development of EC—Japan relations since the early post-war years. These relations grew from mutual insignificance to reach dimensions of some importance: the interaction of the first and the third world trading powers. As the title of this book suggests, their interrelation was largely determined by economic diplomacy and thus could be suspected of being purely low politics. However, shared high politics interests were evident as well from the very beginning: first, as fraternal Cold War warriors, and later, being jointly faced with intemperate LDC demands. In addition, as we shall see, Japan in the early sixties treated her policies towards Europe in terms of high politics. With the second oil crises, the political instability in the Gulf area and the revitalisation of Soviet imperialism since 1979 a significant amount of bilateral high politics interaction has been evident between Japan and Western Europe as well. Thus their relations provide a fairly convincing test case for our hypothesis.

My methodological approach is basically that of a contemporary historian: to reconstruct the relevant events and their circumstances in order to collect the data of our variables. Because of the thirty-year rule all archives remain closed. Thus we have to look for sources elsewhere. First there is the obvious starting point of trade statistics and the academic literature in the field. However, the latter is scarce and is neither very analytical nor theoretical in focus. My main additional sources are reports in newspapers (as they are collected in the Press Library of Chatham House) and in specialised magazines, materials available in reference sections (such as the fairly extensive selection of documents in the EC delegation in Tokyo), and about thirty interviews with mostly middle-level officials in the institutions involved in bilateral relations in Tokyo, London and Brussels.

Part I of this book, Chapters 2 and 3, refers to the institutions and decision procedures on foreign economic policies in the EC and in Japan. Part II, Chapters 4 to 6, offers an analytical account of the development of bilateral relations. The final chapter (7) summarises our empirical findings in the light of the theoretical claims made in this introduction. In this context it will also offer some predictions on the likely development of future relations between Japan and the European Community.

References

1 Mills, C. Wright. *The Sociological Imagination.* London: Oxford University Press. 1977 (1959), p. 25.
2 Steiner, Miriam. The Elusive Essence of Decision. *International Studies Quarterly 17,* 1973, 147–74.
3 Adapted from his 'Classification of national interest' in : Northedge, F.S. *The International Political System.* London: Faber & Faber 1976, p. 195; and see also: Rosenthal, Glenda Goldstone *The Men behind the Decisions.* Lexington, Mass.: Lexington Books 1975, p. 3.
4 Ullmann, Richard H. Trilateralism: Partnership for What? *Foreign Affairs 55,* 1976, 1–19, p. 5; Kiichi Miyazawa, in: *Trialogue* No. 24, 1980, p. 6; and Graham Allison, in: *Trialogue* No. 22, 1980, p. 42.
5 Frieden, Jeff. The Trilateral Commission: Economics and Politics in the 1970s. *Monthly Review 29,* 1977, 1–18, p. 6; and : *Trialogue* No. 23, 1980, p. 11.
6 Cooper, Richard N., Karl Kaiser and Masataka Kosoka. *Towards a Renovated International System.* The Triangle Papers No. 14. New York, Tokyo, Paris: The Trilateral Commission. 1977, p. 32; and: Hosoya, Chihiro, Henry Owen and Andrew Shonfield. *Collaboration with Communist Countries in Managing Global Problems: An Examination of the Options.* The Triangle Papers No. 13. New York, Tokyo, Paris: The Trilateral Commission. 1977.
7 Ortona, Egidio, J. Robert Schaetzel and Nobuhiko Ushiba. *The Problem of International Consultations.* The Trialogue Papers No. 12. New York, Tokyo, Paris: The Trilateral Commission. 1976, p. 20.
8 Smith, Gerald L. The Vital Triangle. *The World Today 30,* 1974, 142–50, p. 149.
9 Duchêne, François, Kinhide Mushakoji and David D. Owen. *The Crisis of International Cooperation.* The Triangle Papers No. 2.

Brussels, New York, Tokyo: The Trilateral Commission. 1974, p.16.
10   Dougherty, James E., Robert L. Pfaltzgraff, Jr. *Contending Theories of International Relations.* Philadelphia PA: J. B. Lippincott Co. 1971, p. 15.
11   Ibid., p. 74.
12   Ibid., p. 80.
13   Lenin, V.I. *Der Imperialismus als höchstes Stadium des Kapitalismus.* Ostberlin: Dietz Verlag. 1975 (1917).
14   Mandel, Ernest. *Die EWG und die Konkurrenz Europa—Amerika.* Frankfurt: Europäische Verlagsanstalt. 1968.
15   Nicolaus, Martin. The Universal Contradiction. *New Left Review* No. 59, 1970; and: Poulantzas, Nicos. The Internationalization of Capitalist Relations and the State. *Economy and Society 3,* 1974, 145—79.
16   Autorenkollektiv. USA, Westeuropa, Japan — imperialistische Zentren der Rivalität. *IPW Forschungshefte 11,* 1976, 5—138, p. 12.
17   Ibid., p. 114.
18   Dougherty, 1971, op. cit., p. 280.
19   Taylor, Paul and A.J. Groom. Introduction: Functionalism and International Relations. In: Groom, A.J.R. and Paul Taylor (eds.) *Functionalism — Theory and Practice in International Relations.* London: University of London Press. 1975, p. 1.
20   Ibid., p. 4.
21   Halperin, Morton H. *Bureaucratic Politics and Foreign Policy.* Washington D.C.: The Brookings Institution. 1974, p. 293; Allison, Graham T. *Essence of Decision.* Boston, MA: Little, Brown and Co. 1971, pp. 162.
22   Halperin, 1974, op. cit., p. 311.
23   Ibid., p. 312.
24   Quoted in: Allison, 1971, op. cit., p. 176.
25   Halperin, 1974, op. cit., p. 67.
26   Destler, I.M., Haruhiro Fukui and Hideo Sato. *The Textile Wrangle — Conflict in Japanese American Relations, 1969 — 1971.* Ithaca, N.Y.: Cornell University Press. 1979.
27   Steiner, 1977, op. cit., p. 391.
28   Freedman, Lawrence. Logic, Politics and Foreign Policy Processes: A Critique of the Bureaucratic Politics Model. *International Affairs 52,* 1976, 434—49, p. 437.
29   Ibid., p. 448.
30   Ibid., p. 443.
31   Galtung, Johan. *The EC: A Superpower in the Making.* Oslo: Universitetsforlaget. 1973, p. 62.
32   Ibid., p. 59.

PART I

The institutional framework for policy decisions
on bilateral relations

2 The structure for foreign policy decisions in the European Community

Variables for EC foreign policy decisions

With respect to the academic treatment of European integration it has
been observed that American studies mainly offer theoretical models
of the integration process, while European authors usually prefer more
substantive and policy-oriented approaches – historical, empirical and
descriptive studies.[1] With respect to analyses of the EC's external relations this development has produced a dilemma: the unrelated coexistence of highly abstract models of analysis (inspired by grand system
theory) and the largely descriptive mass of studies on the EC's foreign
relations.

What is needed, therefore, is to apply these models to empirical reality. It may be more suitable to assemble a slightly more modest framework of European decision making and to list its relevant variables
(hereby the EC specifics require some variation from the more general
scheme in Chapter 1).

For our purposes there are already several, partially conflicting, partially complementary models, frameworks, conceptual schemes and
variable sets offered in the literature to analyse EC foreign policy making and its behaviour as an international actor. Soldatis,[2] Rosenthal,[3]
Torrelli,[4] and Sjöstedt[5] have developed such analytical schemes suitable
for decision analysis.

Decision analysis itself does not reveal socio-economic structures.
The effects of the international environment are felt only indirectly.
Its basic concern is the working of bureaucratic politics: it is essentially

15

an inside perspective. The task is to be aware of this limitation and to put appropriate variables in a structured framework which one can then follow in order to show the working of the EC's foreign policy formulation.

An EC decision framework may vary according to the nature of policies concerned. In case of foreign policy decisions the following variables should explain most variance under Community conditions:

1 *External variables* (of the international system): external demands, initiatives. Present, past or anticipated international negotiations. International crises, policy changes. World economic trends.

2 *Structural variables:* characteristics of the socio-economic system. Societal conflicts, stability. Political legitimacy. Working of the economic system.

3 *Community variables:* policies of national administrations. Public pressure: lobbies, parties, media, public opinion. European interest groups. Formation of supra-national coalitions.

4 *Institutional variables:* formal—informal initiatives. Co-operative structures between Community institutions. Intra-bureaucratic frictions, rivalries. Role of political leadership.

5 *Sociological variables:* sources of information. Political ideologies, cultural perceptions. Motivation, qualification of staff. Role of personalities involved.

6 *Policy variables* concerning the issue under review: policy objectives. Perception of problems. Evaluation of alternatives. Planning of strategies and their evaluation.

It is evident that our data base does not allow for the full investigation of all these variables and their components. Not knowing the Commission's inside story, for example, we have to largely ignore sociological variables. Similarly we have only scant knowledge of which policy alternatives were available to policy makers at the time of their decisions. A great deal of external demands are made informally and discreetly and will escape our attention as well. It would also appear overly ambitious to attempt a full-fledged socio-economic analysis of the EC here. For the purpose of this book it is more essential to focus on the complex institutional set-ups and interactions in the Community from which the EC's foreign policies emerge. This chapter therefore aims at clarifying the working of their institutional framework.

Legal foundations

The legal basis for the EC's external relations is provided by the articles 110–116, 228, 238 and the fourth part of the Treaty of Rome, by Chapter XI of the Euratom Treaty and Chapter X and Part 2 of the transitional provisions of the ECSC Treaty.[6] The following gives a short review of the most essential provisions.

Art. 110 recommends the abolition of restrictions in intra-Community trade.

Art. 111 for the transitional period (intended to last until 1970) demands the co-ordination of commercial policies towards non-member countries in order to prepare for the future implementation of a common trade policy. It asks for the gradual adjustment of national tariffs towards the Common External Tariff (CET) and for uniform lists of liberalised products. It further defines the proceedings for the Commission to negotiate on a Council's mandate with third countries.

Art. 112 demands the harmonisation of subsidy measures for exports to non-member countries.

Art. 113 defines the provisions for the Common Commercial Policy (CCP) after the transition period has ended. It transfers the instruments of traditional trade policy to the Community level: ' . . . the common commercial policy shall be based on uniform principles, particularly in regard to changes in tariff rates, the conclusion of tariff and trade agreements, the achievement of uniformity in measures of liberalisation, export policy and measures to protect trade such as those to be taken in case of dumping or subsidies'.

Art. 115 allows temporary import restrictions for individual member states in case of troublesome imports.

Art. 238 regulates the conclusion of Association agreements, i.e. countries forming a free trade area with the EC without participating as members. Direct Commission contacts to international organisations, such as the UN and its agencies, GATT, and the Council of Europe and OECD are granted by Art. 229. After the transition period had ended, member states in international economic organisations were only required to proceed by common action in matters of relevance to the Community (Art. 116). The common commercial policy functionally implied the active and passive right of legation – the right to set up and to receive permanent diplomatic missions – in order to enable adequate diplomatic communication – though the Treaties did not provide for it explicitly. In 1960 the Council accepted the EC's passive right of legation and subsequently around 150 diplomatic missions of third countries were accredited in Brussels. However, it was not until 1971 that France agreed to the Community's active right of legation, i.e. to set up diplomatic representations ('delegations') in third countries.

The Common External Tariff was to be established as the arithmetical average of the original national tariffs in order to confirm with GATT provisions for customs unions (Art. XXIV GATT). In 1960 the Council of Ministers planned subsequent adjustments of national tariffs in certain stages. The harmonisation of external tariffs was later accelerated and the Customs Union was even realised one and a half years ahead of schedule in 1968.

During this transition period the treaty making powers of the Community were rather limited, since commercial policies remained within the member states' competence until 1970. Then in 1970 a Commission—Council controversy on the interpretation of Art. 113 emerged. Drafted in 1957 Art. 113 defined a 'trade policy of the first generation',[7] argued the Commission. After two major GATT rounds of tariff reductions commercial policy had become less concerned with regulating commodity flows through duties and quotas and more with the promotion and creation of commodity exchange in general. This 'second generation' policy, therefore, should focus on economic co-operation agreements. The Council proved quite hesitant in accepting this extensive and updated interpretation. Only in 1976 the EC—Canadian co-operation treaty achieved a breakthrough allowing the Commission to expand its scope from limited foreign trade policies towards more comprehensive foreign economic policies.[8]

The basic institutional features of the Treaty of Rome for decision making on the EC's external relations provide for four Community institutions: (a) the Commission as the initiating body, (b) the Committee of Permanent Representatives (Coreper) as the transmitting preparatory organisation to the Council, and (c) the Council of Ministers — in case of foreign relations: the assembled Foreign Ministers (General Council) — institution for Community decisions. An intergovernmental working party, (d) Committee 113 (during the transition period: Committee 111) had the task to supervise the implementation of the mandate given to the Commission by the Council. The European Council — the meeting of the heads of states or governments — formally institutionalised itself as the supreme European decision maker at a European summit in 1974 (de facto it had already exercised this role since 1969).

Goodwin interprets the provisions of the Treaty of Rome as giving the EC's external activities a clearly subordinate role to its internal integrative development. During the years this has led to the traditional EC introspection: Customs Union and CAP were largely realised without due regard for their external effects.[9]

18

The need for a more comprehensive and active European foreign policy beyond economics was soon felt. The European Political Co-operation (EPC) was intended to alleviate this deficiency. The EPC was set up by the European Council as an intergovernmental consultation procedure on high politics foreign policies. So far it has no legal basis, except for the Council's approval of the Luxembourg Report (later renamed Davignon Report) in 1970, and of the Copenhagen Report three years later which proposed slight procedural modifications of the EPC mechanism.

The Commission

Functions. The Commission has the following functions relevant to the conduct of its external relations: [10]
- to supervise the working of the Treaty of Rome and to take violators to the European Court of Justice,
- to draft and to apply statutory instruments (delegated legislation),
- to propose initiatives on commercial policies,
- to decide on tariff quotas, customs duties, transport subsidies, anti-dumping measures etc.,
- to exercise control powers to ensure competitive trade,
- to apply agricultural regulations, including import rules,
- to conduct its relations with other international organisations, and
- to negotiate commercial treaties according to a mandate of the Council.

As its basic role among the Community institutions the Commission in general represents 'le conservatoire de l'esprit communautaire' [11] in the community process.

Administrative units. The division of labour within the Commission is illustrated by the organisational chart of its directorate-generals (DGs).[12] Directly concerned with foreign relations are:

1 *DG I — External relations* — which holds the following directorates:*

    (a) — International organisations; commercial questions of agriculture and fisheries; South Africa.

    (b) — North America, Australia, New Zealand, Japan.

    (c) — Developing countries in Latin America and Asia (except

---

* In 1967 'external trade' was split off from DG I and was made a separate unit as DG XI. Both were merged again in 1973–74. Nevertheless during their separation both units expanded considerably in administrative terms reflecting the development of the CCP. (See reference 13.)

Middle and Far East); UN economic agencies; co-ordination with DG VIII.

(d) — General questions and instruments of external economic policy; commercial questions of industry and energy.
(e) — Textile agreements; generalised tariff preferences.
(f) — Non-member countries in northern, central and southern Europe.
(g) — Negotiations with Greece.
(h) — CSCE; state trading countries.

2 *DG VIII — Development* — containing the directorates:

(a) — General development policy; co-ordination with DG I.
(b) — Africa, the Caribbean and the Pacific.
(c) — Projects.
(d) — Operations.
(e) — Finance and Administrations.

On relations with developed countries DGs III (Internal Markets and Industrial Affairs), IV (Competition), VI (Agriculture) and VII (Transport) are also strongly involved whenever their sectoral interests are affected.

The Treaties of Rome require that all of the Commission's formal decisions, regulations and proposals to the Council have to be agreed upon by all Commissioners jointly (Kollegiales Prinzip), that Commissioners should not be ministers (Ressortminister) of their directorate generals. [14]

Most formal decisions are made by circulating drafts among Commissioners which are then considered accepted if no veto has been cast. [15] These drafts are in turn handled by the cabinets which each Commissioner maintains. There are about 14 officials in each cabinet (1972), usually sharing their Commissioner's nationality. With these cabinets, then, the respective national member state administration keeps close connections. [16] The meeting of the chefs du cabinet works as a 'substitute cabinett' (Ersatzkabinett) under the chairmanship of the Commission's Secretary General. They decide the agenda for the Commissioners' meetings.

This preparation implies the definition of most drafts as 'point A' proposals — i.e. non-controversial issues which require only routine approval by the Commissioners. [17]

The *General Secretariat of the Commission* is considered the 'nerve centre' for Community initiatives. [18] All official communications between the Commission and other Community institutions and the national governments must pass through it. With its co-ordination function for the Commission's DGs (being the sole effective means of liaison between them) it plays an essential role in the preparation of the sessions of both the chefs du cabinet and of the Commissioners. The General Secretariat is also Coreper's negotiating partner. It consequently has to fulfil an important function in co-ordinating the external policies of the Commission. The General Secretariat also serves as a liaison body to EPC institutions. Its Secretary General or his deputy represents the Commission at those EPC meetings that take place below the minister level (i.e. Political Committee meetings in particular).[19] The Secretary General can initiate ad hoc inter-DG working groups whenever the need arises. On international negotiations (e.g. the GATT rounds) such high level working groups, then, were able to decide more efficiently on urgent issues.[20]

Within the Commission its *President* finally exercises the ultimate responsibility for external relations and is also its chief representative in external affairs.

Evaluation. Allen interprets the Commission's political role as 'a bureaucracy with policy making competence and an executive body that acts as a legislature', but lacking political leadership.[21] McGeehan and Warnecke consider the effects of disunity in the Councils and the Commission's organisational deficiencies (especially of effective policy co-ordination between the DGs) as responsible for the Community's foreign policy shortcomings.[22] They conclude that the Commission's role simply reflects the fact that its external relations are not based on sufficient internal consolidation or on effective institutions for decision making.[23]

Poullet and Deprez' analysis seems to concur with this conclusion. For the decline of the Commission's general influence they hold responsible:[24]

— the tendency towards intergovernmentalism, as evident in the unanimity rule of the Council and in Coreper's growing influence; and
— the lack of leadership abilities among Commissioners who have proved inept at organising effective coalitions of interest in order to strengthen the Commission's role and the Community's interest.

This lack of leadership also led to a dysfunctional bureaucratisation which increasingly inhibited inter-DG co-operation in the Commission — as evident in the unchecked 'Agrarimperium' of a powerful and rigid DG VI.[25] As diplomatic agent of the Community the Commission suffered from the lack of overseas offices and from understaffing in DG I: foreign diplomats accredited in Brussels commonly complain that the Commission has no time for them.[26]

The Foreign Ministers of the Nine meet more than ten times annually as the Council of Ministers (General Council) in order to decide on the Commission's proposals on foreign relations.

The Foreign Ministers also have to decide on institutional questions and on issues left unresolved by other ministerial Councils.[27] These other Councils are the meetings of the heads of the Nine's ministries for agriculture, economics and finance.[28] In the traditional community cycle major decisions are taken at great marathon sessions in December and to a lesser degree at the end of June or in early July.[29] Their agenda is prepared by the Council's two supportive institutions: Coreper and the Council's Secretariat.

The Council is the place of confrontation between Community interests and national interests. In respect to the EC's commercial policy Dahrendorf observed: 'The Foreign Ministers see the Council as the place to represent national, even sectoral interests . . . The Council permits its individual members to hide behind the skirts of collectivity in dealing with third countries'.[30]

Its membership makes the Council the least coherent community institution with divergent interests and loyalties. Frequent changes in its composition — as national governments change — and the twice-yearly rotation of its presidency — following the alphabetic order of the member states — inhibit the continuity of its work. Conflicting conceptions on Europe's future and the effects of 'bureaucratic politics' contribute to a diminished decision making capacity.[31]

The Council's frequent marathon sessions ('le processus de décision typique d'un système en crise permanente')[32] are caused by decisions that have to be made and which cannot be delayed further. The multitude of issues in conflict created a new mode of community method: the 'package deal', in which the perceived disadvantages of national interests on some issues are skilfully balanced against anticipated benefits on others, i.e. different policies are tied together. Another community method regularly practised by the Council is to postpone decisions whenever conflicts do arise.[33]

The Council's workload is aggravated by its policy of keeping the Commission under tight supervision and control. On external relations this has led the Council to formulate extremely narrow negotiating mandates for the Commission which, in turn, under the dynamics of the negotiating process usually require modification, that is: redefinition and rediscussion by the Council.[34]

With the Luxembourg compromise in January 1966 voting hardly ever takes place in the Council any more, not even on minor issues. This created a tendency towards intergovernmental compromise and unanimity which required less mediation by the Commission.[35] The ministers prefer to be accompanied by large delegations of their own staff which then works over compromise proposals during the sessions.[36] Because of its complexity and secrecy it is nearly self-evident that parliaments are excluded from participating in the Council's decision making. There appears to be no effective public control.

The Secretariat of the Council. In co-operation with Coreper, the Secretariat of the Council has to support the Council's work.[37] It is headed by a general secretary presiding over six general directorates. Among these General Directorate E is in charge of external relations and ACP countries. GD E is subdivided into three directorates, of which one is in charge of trade and OAD. This directorate in turn has three departments of which one deals with trade policy. Here we find one subdepartment concerned with: 'relations to non-European developed countries'.[38]

The Council's Secretariat has to recall earlier Council decisions in the policy process with the Commission, and to support and to produce reports for Coreper and its Council's working groups.

Finally it provides a legal service that screens all proposals submitted by the Commission. (The General Secretariat of the Commission has a similar legal service which screens all Commission proposals going out to the Council.)[39]

The European Council

De facto the European Council had already started in The Hague in 1969, but officially only a European summit in 1974 created it as a new Community institution. Its participants decided to rename themselves the European Council and to meet regularly to discuss EC as well as EPC issues.[40] This institution of the heads of governments is essentially intergovernmental. As such it outranks the Council of Ministers and soon assumed a more decisive role in the decision process. The European Council thus does not need to bother about formal competences. It is free on programmatic questions, for instance interpretations of the Treaties. In addition the European Council serves well the publicity needs of the heads of governments.[41]

Its position also enabled the European Council to take over the Commission's initiative on major policy issues. Questions of enlargement, of major decisions on CAP, on allocations of regional and social fund resources and the EMS are now essentially initiated and decided by the European Council which may give the Commission a mandate to proceed. Though the President of the Commission may now participate at the Council's sessions — after original French objections had been waived — the Community's institutional framework is largely bypassed by this new 're-diplomatisation' of the European policy process.[42]

This illustrates both Councils' institutional deficiencies. As Ayberk observed: occasional meetings do not make a coherent foreign policy.[43] The Commission however possesses this institutional ability.

Coreper

The Committee of Permanent Representatives (Coreper) constitutes a link between the national administrations and the Commission. Coreper thus plays a decisive role (precouncil) in the EC's decision process. It consists of delegations from the national administrations with diplomatic status who are concerned with all the activities of the Commission. Coreper's task is to prepare the Council of Ministers' meetings and to carry out their instructions, a function that necessitates 'negotiation permanent'[44] with the Commission. Coreper officials have to refer back to their capitals and in case of conflicts work out preliminary compromises with the Commission as well as with their home administrations.

Another task is to serve as co-ordinating link between the Community and the associated countries. [45]

Coreper's national delegations — each about 20–50 officials strong — are made up of around 30 to 50 per cent of people from the Foreign Ministries, the others coming from ministries of trade, economics, agriculture, social affairs etc.[46] Poullet and Deprez report strong infighting within national administrations on adequate ministerial representation within the national Coreper delegation which the foreign ministries want to keep under their control. [47]

According to Wallace, the Dutch, French and Belgian delegations were very efficient teams, while she found the German delegation with dispersed individual responsibilities, engaging only in formal interactions.[48]

Coreper's contacts are particularly well established towards those units in the national administrations specialising on EC issues. Thus its officials are, to some extent, able to participate in the co-ordination of national EC policies as well. They usually have long term assignments in Brussels which aid the maintenance of informal contacts with both Community and national administrations.[49] This position of considerable influence is counterbalanced by their dependency on the capitals and their having to follow their administrations' guidelines and policies. The degree of rigidity and precision of these instructions varies according to national administrative tradition, expertise, issues or personalities involved.

In order to prepare the Council's sessions Coreper clears the agenda of insufficiently prepared issues, i.e. the most controversial ones. Others — mostly technical matters on which common agreement had been reached — are presented to the Council as 'point As' and then are usually approved as a matter of routine. In case of unforeseen disagreement on the part of the ministers or the Commission during the session, the respective issue reappears as 'point B' to be debated at the next session.

Urgent administrative matters on which agreement has been reached between Coreper and the Commission are decided by 'procedure écrite': approval is asked from the capitals in written form without a formal meeting of the Council. [50]

Coreper also plays its role in the elaboration of the above-mentioned package deals, though there is a tendency to circumvent Coreper as a bottleneck by involving the Secretariat of the Council.

We may illustrate Coreper's working in the simplified course of a Commission proposal through the European decision making apparatus: (1) the Commission submits a proposal* to (2) the Coreper session, which delegates it to (3) a Coreper working group which starts discussing it with the national administrations and the Commission officials concerned. (4) Results are presented to the Coreper session. (5) Commission and national administrations are informed again and their reaction is collected. In case of persistent disagreements (6) the Secretariat of Coreper's Presidency negotiates for a mutually acceptable compromise. (7a) In the case of a common agreement: (8a) the draft appears as 'point A' on the Council's agenda. (7b) In the case of continued disagreement: (8b) re-negotiation, withdrawal of the proposal or ultimately: (9b) point B on the Council's agenda. In case of point B the Council will not consider the Commission's draft any more and will only discuss the compromise proposals forwarded by Coreper. [51]

Coreper's presidency — rotating like the Council's presidency — has an important role to play. Presiding over the Coreper sessions it decides which working group(s) is to deal with the Commission's proposal, often a major factor in determining its fate.

In case of troublesome negotiations it may also intervene with its 'compromis de la presidence' to facilitate a compromise draft.[52] Coreper meets at two levels: 'Coreper 1' is made up of the deputy heads of the national delegations and mainly deals with technical and routine issues. 'Coreper 2' meets at the ambassadorial level and deals with high grade political, institutional or foreign relations questions. Coreper then organises working groups which deal with the Commission proposals in greater detail. About ten of them handle trade questions, such as general trade policy, GATT, tariff preferences etc. [53]

These working groups may establish permanent or ad hoc sub-groups. Though nobody really keeps track of number and activity, Sasse in

* They are formally addressed to the Council.

1975 estimated 70 working groups and 90 subgroups.[54] In these working groups officials from the national governments, from Coreper and from the Commission may participate.

The two-fold function of Coreper 'comme agent national et comme agent communautaire'[55] frequently created problems of loyalties among its personnel to their conflicting national and community roles. [56] In the final instance, however, Coreper officials are bound by their instructions which imply the defence of the Council's and the national administrations' competences. [57]

According to Noël the efficiency and initiative of the Commission was able to prevent the development of Coreper to the status of a 'third executive'. [58] This may also have been due to Coreper's relatively small staff and to the increased complexity of issues. It is more likely that Coreper's overwork with an ever increasing amount of Commission drafts strengthened the position (particularly during intensive international negotiations) of another intergovernmental institution with foreign relations' competence: the Committee 113.[59]

The Committee 113 (during the transition period: Committee 111)

This committee is made up of national officials — mainly from the foreign ministries, but also from the ministries of economics and agriculture. As defined by Arts. 113 and 111 (Treaty of Rome) its function is to assist with the Commission's external relations and to clarify the Council's mandate whenever necessary. [60]

Committee 113 may meet at titular level or at deputy level. Its titular members are high ranking national officials holding positions with significant competence on foreign trade policies in the national administrations. Since they hold their positions usually for a considerable time (and attendance of Com. 113 is an integral part of these positions), Com. 113 is able to operate in a continuous fashion. At the titular level again the more political questions of the EC's foreign economic policies are dealt with whereas the deputy level focusses on the technical aspects. Both meet according to need and during important negotiations (such as during GATT rounds) almost daily among themselves and with Commission officials.

Com. 113 operates independently from Coreper, but during intensive international negotiations their work usually overlaps when both have to prepare the Council's session dealing with the agenda of these negotiations. However, frequently these issues are too detailed and time pressures too great for Coreper to deal adequately with them and so as to offer a suitable compromise deal for the Council's agenda, Com. 113 then sometimes does this directly. When such negotiations end, Coreper again resumes its foreign relations' precouncil function. As is easily conceivable, the doubled work creates considerable frictions between the two bureaucratic bodies. [61] In this contest Ayberk attests more expertise and a higher degree of Community mindedness to Com. 113 as compared to Coreper, which he found tied by strict directives to represent member states' interests.[62] This happens when the Commission requests the modification of a mandate given by the Council to negotiate with a third party:

1 In case of Com. 113 agreeing and Coreper agreeing as well: the draft containing a modified mandate will land as 'point A' on the Council's agenda. The Council then (hopefully) will confirm it.

2 In case of disagreements within Com. 113 (the Commission will only submit drafts that have already *some* national support), Coreper will then give compromise another try. If unsuccessful and an urgent matter the draft will appear on the Council's agenda as 'point B' awaiting discussion and possible resolution. If the Council cannot agree, the Commission's negotiations will either be interrupted or fail altogether.

Other community institutions

The European Parliament (EP). Until 1979 it consisted of 198 parliamentarians (EMPs) delegated from their national parliaments. After the first European elections in June 1979 the EP was enlarged to 410 seats. The EP does not yet exercise actual power, except for the right to dismiss the whole Commission by a two-thirds majority.

Generally the EP serves as an ally rather than as a controller of the Commission.[63] Its function on foreign relations is limited to issuing general and non-committal proposals and resolutions, to staging debates and to asking questions of the Commission. In this context it is not seldom that one finds a detailed and elaborate two-page parliamentary question being answered by the Commission by a laconic and evasive ten-line note one year later.

Although not required by the Treaties the Commission keeps the EP's External Relations Committee informed about current activities, partly in order to make use of the Committee members' connections to the national Parliaments and parties for a greater understanding of the Commission's positions.[64] Nevertheless, the characteristics of the EC's external relations procedure hardly permit any effective parliamentary control or participation at present.

The Economic and Social Committee (ESC). It was established as an advisory body to the Commission made up of representatives of relevant organised societal groups. The ESC supposedly is the least influential institution in the community process. [65] The Commission sometimes considers it politically useful to inform the ESC on its initiatives — including foreign relations — in order to stimulate the ESC's channels to national interest groups hoping to initiate lobbying efforts on the Commission's behalf in the member states. [66]

The European Court of Justice. Its function is to defend and to enforce the Treaties and their subordinate instruments created in virtue of the Treaties. Since to some observers the provisions of the Treaties seem vague and the question of the sources for their interpretation as hardly settled, the judges appear to have a wide range of freedom in deciding these matters. [67] The Court then wields considerable political power.

The European Political Co-operation (EPC)

The EPC scheme basically follows the lines of the Fouchet plans (1961 —1962), which proposed a framework to co-ordinate European foreign policies by creating a council at the level of the heads of states and governments. They would have met every four months and decided on the co-ordination of foreign and defence policies. Its political secretariat was supposed to be established in Paris, composed of senior foreign ministry officials. [68] But the plan died due to German and Dutch opposition which resented its Gaullist intergovernmental features.

   The Fouchet plans were revitalised in 1969 by the Davignon plan and its essential features were adopted by the summit in Luxembourg in October 1970, when impending British membership allowed perspectives for significant future common foreign policies. [69]

   The EPC's aim is to harmonise the 'high' foreign policies of the member states and — if possible — to permit common action. Its method is a regular consultation procedure which is not, however, mandatory and neither are decisions made by majority rule. There are three levels of co-operation:

1 Meetings of the Foreign Ministers, initially on a twice-yearly basis, then (after 1972's Copenhagen report) every four months, later even more frequently.
2 The Political Committee — the heart of the EPC, composed of the political directors of the foreign ministries, meeting for two days each month — among other things prepares for their ministers' meetings.
3 Study groups of officials from the national ministries, set up by the Political Committee. There was, for example, an ad hoc committee of officials from the Middle East sections of the foreign ministries. [70]

28

Already in November 1970 the embassies of the Six in third countries and at international organisations were instructed to co-operate. Their embassies in other member states had to designate a liaison officer to the host countries' foreign ministry in order to institutionalise regular political contacts.[71] Plans of integrated missions in third countries — particularly in the small, newly independent nations — have not yet materialised.

The issue of where to locate the EPC's projected co-ordinating secretariat soon became controversial. While France insisted on Paris, other governments proposed Brussels in order to facilitate a later merger with Community institutions. As a compromise the Presidency — which again rotates twice-yearly — now assumes the secretarial functions. Some observers note the difficulty of pursuing a coherent policy — which also implies tasks of long term studies and planning — without a regularly operating secretariat.[72] Others stress the advantages of its absence in that it could create an urge for 'direct integration' of the foreign ministries.[73]

In the early years of EPC France insisted on a clear-cut segregation of Foreign Ministers meetings discussing EPC affairs and Council of Ministers sessions arguing on EC commercial policies. Thus on 23 July 1973 the same ministers met in Copenhagen — the seat of the presiding country — as the EPC body in the morning and in the afternoon they met in Brussels — as the seat of the Community authorities — as the Council of Ministers.[74] Since 1974 both the Council of (Foreign) Ministers and the EPC Ministers' session takes place in an integrated fashion.[75] The tendency to overlap and often interrelate high and low external policies blurred the distinction between the two institutions.

Similar problems arose when competences had to be delineated between the Political Committee — which has to prepare the EPC Ministers' meetings — and Coreper — which has to prepare the Council's meetings. This slight organisational chaos surprisingly aided the Commission's role because its officials are the only ones attending both meetings.[76] The Commission's General Secretariat — responsible for the co-ordination of the DGs policies — and the Commissioner of DG I or his Director General may be present at both the relevant Coreper and Political Committee meetings.[77] Since the President of the Commission is entitled to attend the Foreign Ministers' sessions (since 1974 he speaks only on issues concerning EC matters) and Council of Ministers meetings the Commission's General Secretariat serves as co-ordination and information body to and between these institutions.

As examples of successful European Political Co-operation are usually mentioned the following: the CSCE conferences, the Middle East declaration of 1973, the Euro—Arab dialogue, the Cyprus diplomacy, the stabilisation of Portugal and the second enlargement.[78] Failures were highlighted during the 1973 oil embargo against the Netherlands, the disagreement on UNCTAD issues, the disunited response to the Soviet invasion of Afghanistan 1979—80 and by the EPC participants' obvious hesitation to go beyond non-committal declarations as well as the failure to actually implement or back them by joint actions. A further significant deficiency is the non-consideration of defence issues.

Other criticisms mention the EPC's secretive operation without public control and its weak link to those Community institutions dealing with the EC's commercial and development policies. [79]

Interest groups

With the establishment of the Commission in 1958 interest groups were organised at the European level. Among employers the main association is UNICE. Hundreds of more specialised sectoral interest groups were also set up. For UNICE which serves as an umbrella for most of the industrial producers' associations this creates an arduous task of coordination. Similarly the unions and the agricultural lobby are organised in Brussels.

Meynaud and Sidjanski distinguish the indirect sections of European interest groups from direct ones. Under direct actions they consider the use of Commission hearings, of issuing statements when asked by the Commission to comment on certain projects, and the exchange of information during informal meetings with officials in Brussels. Indirect actions, such as attempts to mobilise public opinion, are used only as a last resort and a complementary means at the European level. [80]

For decision analysis, then, the difficulty arises that the less significant indirect actions are far easier to follow than the direct ones. [81] Among the top interest groups, such as UNICE, a daily working contract is established with the Commission's leadership.[82] Access to the Councils, Coreper, the Committee 113 and the Political Committee by contrast is considered difficult. Interest groups, then, will have worked already on their usual national channels, well before their concern is brought up at the Council level. A sole exception are agricultural marathons during which COPA's opinions are asked on certain compromise proposals.[83]

There is every indication that on European issues lobbying at the national level has proved to be more successful. [84] There, contacts to the political parties and to the bureaucracy are already well established and it is possible to exercise leverage in the electoral processes. [85]

Conflicts arise in European interest groups when the positions of their national associations disagree on certain issues. The resulting cross pressures then might paralyse the whole organisation temporarily. The loose confederal structure of most European interest groups, however, allows survival of such incidents. [86]

In general one should assume that foreign relations, in contrast to most domestic issues, are too political to be affected by lobbying efforts in a significant manner. But also on external policies the expertise of interest groups is needed (e.g. on sectoral export—import conditions, changing market and employment situations, etc.). Prior to major international negotiations (such as GATT rounds) the Commission, therefore, regularly consults with the larger European associations. At a later negotiation stage when issues have been narrowed down the information input of more specialised interest groups grows in importance. [87] Still, even then their influence appears limited. In her decision analysis Rosenthal found considerable lobbying efforts at both the national and the European level, but none of them was able to overcome the determined political will of a concerned elite network within the Commission or well-orchestrated intergovernmental co-operation on foreign policy issues. [88]

The human factor

It would be extremely valuable to have results of systematic research on the socialisation of the European foreign policy elites ready at hand. In the US for instance, few elite groups are better investigated than those shaping US foreign policy. But in Europe, unfortunately, the quality of the data is less well grounded.

In organisational sociology the concept of a curve of influence has been validated: it rises with the hierarchical ranks, but drops shortly before reaching the top organisational positions underlining the power-yielding function of the men second in line. Their advisory role and expertise should be expected to affect decisions usually to a larger extent than the views of the presiding personalities do. This may be particularly true for the European foreign ministers, who are occupied by a multitude of highly demanding full-time functions: 'little time is left for essential routine work, preparation for meetings or thinking out policies', [89] and: 'ministers are unlikely to read more than a page or two on all but the most vital subjects'. [90] Thus, in implementing routine foreign policy as well as in their role as innovators and foreign policy planners the foreign ministries' senior officials may assume decisive influence. This might be even more true on issues — such as the EC's external relations — which lie at the fringes of the media's and the general public's attention and on which the political parties hardly ever formulate a coherent programme.

Thus we can expect the political socialisation of the European senior ministry officials to have a considerable impact on the conduct of European foreign policies. In the following paragraphs the few empirical investigations are summarised.

Feld and Wildgen (1975), for example, found no evidence for allegations that anti-EC attitudes existed among national civil servants which might lead them to sabotage the integration process.[91] In the same study, however, ideological support for the European integration in the national administrations appeared to be of an ephemeral nature at best.[92] There were also indications that diplomats in the capitals dislike the EC's slow and relatively overt foreign policy making and prefer the EPC's secretive scheme with its wider range of negotiating initiatives.[93]

Feld (1972) pursued the question to what extent Coreper officials with their twofold functions — their national as well as their Community role — become 'Europeanised' during their long term assignments in Brussels. Interacting with Community officials on a daily basis — far more frequently than with their own home ministries' colleagues — he saw them adopting the Brussels' working style and acquiring strong positive orientations and attitudes towards 'European values'.[94] Wallace (1973) and Ayberk (1978) contest this view. They found Coreper's national loyalties unaffected by their jobs in Brussels.[95]

Feld's interviews revealed that Coreper officials consider themselves playing a more important role for the EC's foreign relations than the people in DG I whose administrative abilities they supposedly disrespect.[96] Eurocrats themselves similarly perceived an assignment to the Secretariat of the Council of Ministers as a promotion compared to the same position within the Commission. In addition, the staff of the Political Committee think of themselves as exercising more significant functions than Coreper does — due to the broader range of issues they are dealing with — and are perceived as a threat and an unwanted competition by the Commission's personnel. It is not surprising that Feld observed 'a high degree of competition and jealousy' between the three institutions.[97] If we follow the sketchy evidence then some change in the Commission's working morale took place over time. In 1970 Coombes still characterised the typical Eurocrat working with a ' . . . desire to participate in a new and interesting undertaking, and to be given the opportunity to take some initiative in the policy making process'.[98] He then praised the Commission's administrative style as free-wheeling, informal and pioneering in most DGs.[99] Ten years later the *Japan Times* quoted an EC official commenting on Sir Roy Denman's (Director General of DG I) public remarks that officials in the Commission followed alcoholic and promiscuous pursuits during office hours: 'Progress is often slow and that leads to frustration. Frustration then sometimes leads to laziness' and: 'It is difficult to remain idealistic when you see so much of your work just disappear into a drawer'.[100]

Other criticisms refer to the frequent change of Community and national officials dealing with the EC's external relations, leading to inconsistencies in its foreign policies. [101] It is also alleged that senior DG I officials are so frequently and in such numbers absent from Brussels on business that the decision process became at times severely inhibited.[102]

In her analysis of EC decisions Rosenthal found as a positive aspect of informal interactions in the Commission the small elite networks co-operating efficiently in informal but nevertheless well organised groups pursuing vigorously their policy objectives in the Community's administration. In the two foreign relations cases Rosenthal examined (the Maghreb agreement and the GSP decision) the mentioned elite network factor of officials working in the Commission and efficiently employing their various contacts to the national administrations and to the other Community institutions was found to be more decisive than intergovernmental politics or interest groups or parliamentary pressures. She concludes: 'It is the men who govern the processes, and not the processes that govern the men. In other words, although time, subject matter, external pressures, and personalities are all extremely important variables, the last carries the greatest weight'.[103]

The evaluation of the organisational structure

'We believe that the mechanism of a Commission negotiating for the Community, and referring back to the Council of Ministers whenever necessary, may turn out to be highly effective, and for once the Community may be described as a model in so far as its decision-making procedure is concerned'.[104] This positive statement — made by Dahrendorf (1973) — is quite rare among those evaluating the Community's decision-making system.

One of the major arguments to justify the establishment of the EPC had been that the complexity and slowness of the Community procedure was unsuitable for fast common European reactions to changes in the international system. [105] The Commission's tendencies to react in a legalist, piecemeal and frequently incoherent fashion were considered increasingly inept for innovative policies.

It is equally evident that the multitude of intermediary bodies in the Community process offers plenty of opportunities for dilatory national policies whenever obstruction is considered a suitable tactical means on certain issues. [106] A trimming and streamlining of this organisational maze would reduce the opportunities for national obstruction. From the very beginnings of the Community a shift of power to the Council became manifest. The Commission had to consult the national authorities at a very early stage for consultation. It had to compromise already *before* submitting its proposals to Coreper and the Council in order to facilitate their approval. This weakened the Commission's capacity for independent decision making as well as the role of the European Parliament: the elaborate compromises finally submitted to the EP for 'advice' hardly allowed any amendment.[107]

The emergence of the EPC and the dominating role of the European Council increasingly replaced the Commission's original role as 'motor' and 'initiator' in the Community. On all major policy decisions the European Council now issues the Commission a mandate to proceed, i.e. to work out detailed proposals for submission to the Council of Ministers according to the European Council's guidelines.[108]

It is doubtful whether the relatively strong position of the Commission's General Secretariat is able to counterbalance the growing dominance of intergovernmentalism.

Third parties generally view the EC as a difficult negotiating partner. In the Community procedure the EC's bargaining positions are elaborated as complex compromises — which makes later changes quite unlikely. In addition, the outcome of these complex internal EC decision procedures — particularly those emanating from package deals — is difficult to comprehend and often surprising for the EC's external partners.[109]

Rigid EC bargaining was particularly successful against smaller countries, whose protests when being subjected to unilateral EC decisions affecting their exports to the Community, could not shake up the Community process. Prior to 1970 only the US proved strong enough to warrant the revision of a mandate given by the Council.[110]

The US, in addition, treated the EC very skilfully in tactical terms: whenever it was thought useful they made significant statements or other bargaining moves immediately before Council sessions. This threw the carefully prepared Commission—Coreper—Committee 113 packages on a mandate into the desired disarray. This would either divide the Council or influence its decision ad hoc in a more welcome direction.[111]

National policies

The nature and the contradictions of European intergovernmentalism

The coalition concept of European co-operation, the rise of intergovernmentalism and the decision procedure of the Community itself clearly indicate that member governments remain the ultimate source of power and decision. National governments even decide effectively on most of the Commission's budget and on the Commissioners' appointments. On external matters they decide which issues are to be regulated through traditional diplomatic channels, summits, or Community institutions.

The integration process has not yet reached the point of no return. However, all existing EC governments find necessary further participation and even a further deepening of European integration.

In spite of this general European commitment several inhibiting features have emerged or intensified as matters of concern during the 1970s, a period of slower economic growth and persistent high unemployment levels:

— narrow national interests dominating high policy objectives,
— increased European discrepancies in economic development and political stability,
— member states (with governmental assistance) competing for external markets, raw materials and energy supplies,
— a stiffening of anti-EC sentiment in the political organisations representing those strata in Europe that feel disadvantaged by the present mode of integration (e.g. the British and French working classes and small entrepreneurs).

At the same time the features of the European political system inhibiting integrative progress remained intact:

— different macropolitical perspectives due to distinct historical experiences (Great Depression, WW II, inflations, decolonisation, German division etc.),[112]
— differing assessments of the international system (in respect to NATO, the role of the US, detente, the new economic order),
— different ruling national economic philosophies: planification versus neoliberalism, free trade versus protectionism, monetarism versus welfare state,
— disagreement on internal features of the EC (CAP, EMS, Economic and Monetary Union).

At the same time, basic strategic, economic and functional needs (see 'Actual foreign policies', page 40) are effective in making necessary closer European integration.

The European working of the national administrations

This section will review the procedures and major institutions within the national administrations as they formulate and transmit European policies to Brussels.

National decision making on EC matters will appear as quite varied. It ranges from tight co-ordination in a central governmental secretariat in France to informal and largely unexaminable interministerial deals in Italy. [113]

France. The coherence of the French administrative top layers is renowned: common grand ecole and grand corps education created ties and a common outlook which cut across formal organisational structures.[114] This facilitates considerably interministerial co-operation on EC policies. Contacts here are particularly close between the Ministry of Foreign Affairs (Quai d'Orsay) and the External Economic Relations Directorate at the Ministry of Finance and Economics (Quai Branly).[115] The rule applied is that the Quai d'Orsay defines, negotiates and co-ordinates foreign economic policies while the Quai Branly is in charge of their implementation.[116] The Quai d'Orsay is also, in principle, in charge of EC policies. Their actual co-ordination however is done by the Secretariat General du Comité Interministeriel (SGCI). SGCI has about 100 officials and negotiates mainly on routine and administrative matters. But still all instructions to Coreper and to the French officials sent to special committees (such as Committee 113) go through SGCI. [117]

Political decisions affecting the EC's external relations are made at cabinet or presidential level. Then only SGCI's secretarial services are used. EPC is managed by the Quai d'Orsay directly, but SGCI remains informed as well. [118]

The effect of this tight co-ordination is a confident and efficient conduct of negotiations in the Community process. The specifics of French administrative training contribute to a treatment of European questions as apolitical, technocratic issues where, in case of conflicts, French national interests always supersede the interests of the Community.[119]

Britain. Foreign economic policies in Britain are decided in a triangular fashion between the Foreign and Commonwealth Office (FCO), the Bank of England, and the Department of Trade (DoT). [120] With its close links to British business DoT is formally in charge of foreign trade policies[121] but the Foreign Secretary usually participates in the EC's Council of Ministers sessions on trade policy. [122] After the British EC entry a strong interministerial co-ordination scheme was established: [123]

1 The European Section of the Cabinet Office: A staff unit in charge of issuing instructions to Coreper.

2 The European Unit: An interministerial planning body at the Cabinet Office. Its task is to develop long term perspectives in Britain's EC policies.

3 The Official Committee for Europe: An interministerial body working under the chairmanship of the Cabinet Office. It discusses Coreper issues and the agenda of Council meetings and its task is

thereby to resolve controversial questions before they are put before the Ministerial Committee.

4 The Ministerial Committee for Europe: Ministers of State meet under the chairmanship of the Chancellor of the Duchy of Lancaster (who is in charge of European questions) to deal with unresolved EC high politics.

5 The European Integration Department in the Foreign Office: It exchanges informations with the British Coreper delegation and co-ordinates FCO policies on EC matters.

Germany. The Economics Ministry (BMW) is formally in charge of European affairs. Its 'Division E' elaborates and sends the German instructions to Coreper. However, since the other ministries may also directly instruct their officials working in Coreper's or the Council's subgroups, the German position in Brussels usually has already been defined before the issue is taken up at Coreper so that Division E's instructions, then, are too late. [124] Foreign economic relations, in principle, are the Economics Ministry's domain while their political aspects are dealt with by the Foreign Office. This distinction also applies to their competence on the EC's foreign relations.[125] Also on more general EC policies both ministries have to co-operate (especially BMW's Division E and the Foreign Office's divisions for trade policy and political affairs).

On routine problems Division E (BMW) informally contacts the relevant desk officers in other ministries and then sends instructions to Coreper. On a more formal level officials meet at a interministerial 'Ausschuss der Europabeauftragten' for policy co-ordination on EC issues.

On the political level the secretaries of state (from the Chancellery, the Foreign Office, BMW, and the Ministries for Finance and Agriculture) meet under the chairmanship of the Foreign Office's Minister of State who is also in charge of attending the EC's (General) Council of Ministers. [126]

On the Cabinet's agenda 'Europafragen' figure regularly as well. German policies on foreign trade issues so far have been fairly consistent: both BMW and the Foreign Office subscribe to liberal principles. An influential Foreign Trade Advisory Council to BMW represents a strong majority of institutions with free trade interests (the major banks and export oriented companies).[127] On other European questions, however, Sasse found German EC policies frequently incoherent, poorly co-ordinated between the ministries and thus often unpredictable. [128]

Italy. The Foreign Ministry is in charge of both Italy's EC policies and of the instructions to Coreper. The six economic ministries (Treasury, Budget, Finance, Industry, Trade and State Participations) are too fragmented to exercise this function.[129]

Due to perennial intra-coalition rivalries the co-ordination of EC policies at the political level hardly exists, but on the administrative level (Riunione dei Direttori Generali) undisputed issues can be co-ordinated. On important and potentially controversial issues however the ministries represent their positions in Brussels themselves in order to safeguard their competences.[130] Since the Italian central administration is noted for its susceptibility to powerful interest groups, cross pressures often accumulate on decisions concerning foreign economic relations which prevent the formulation of coherent policies.[131]

In case of lacking or contradictory instructions Italian experts or Coreper officials in Brussels are free to take the necessary decisions themselves.[132] Still, during Council of Ministers sessions the final Italian position often is left unresolved and unknown until the last minute.[133]

The Netherlands. Similar to Germany in the Netherlands competence for both foreign economic relations and EC matters are distributed between the Foreign and the Economics Ministry. When consequently frictions developed between the respective divisions, namely the Economics Ministry's 'Buitenlandse Economische Betrekkingen' and the Foreign Ministry's 'Directoraat General voor Europese Samenwerking' (DGES), the dispute was settled in the latter's favour.[134] DGES is now in charge of appointing and instructing the Dutch Coreper officials and organising the co-ordination of EC policies. There are again three interministerial co-ordination levels:[135]

1 meetings of desk officers, arranged by DGES, which handle the bulk of all EC issues,
2 politically more sensitive problems are handled by monthly meetings of senior officials (including Coreper officials), the 'Coordinatie Commissie voor Europese Integratie en Associatie Problemen' chaired by the Foreign Ministry's Secretary of State,
3 finally, a Cabinet committee (Raat voor Europese Zaken) meets with the Prime Minister presiding.

Dutch administrative style is considered fairly informal, flexible and functional. On foreign economic policies both in the foreign and economics ministries a liberal 'Rotterdam school' is dominant.[136] This also reflects the interest of Dutch business as represented by the industrial federation and by the three major Dutch MNC: Royal Dutch Shell, Philips and Unilever, 'qui peuvent assez facilement attendre le niveau ministeriel pour exprimer leurs idées'.[137]

Political co-operation with fellow Benelux countries is 'plus un esprit qu'une réalité pratique'. The Dutch thereby consider the francophone Belgian administrative style as the main barrier.[138]

Belgium. Officially the Foreign Ministry is in charge of EC matters,[139] and both on the Cabinet level and on the senior official level co-ordinating institutions were created. These institutions were dealing with both domestic economic as well as with European problems thus inhibiting their effectiveness.[140]

Informal high level consultations and the direct involvement of Coreper in the Belgian administrative process — both operating in Brussels — soon effectively substituted for the more formal procedures.[141]

Luxembourg. The size of Luxembourg's national administration and their geographical proximity to Brussels facilitates both informal co-operation — desk officers can consult their ministers directly — and enables effective working relations with Coreper.[142]

The 'Direction des Relations Economiques Internationales' in the Foreign Ministry is in charge of both EC policies and of Luxembourg's foreign trade.[143] Among EC issues officials have to concentrate on problems of immediate interest to Luxembourg, such as steel, which is seen as nearly identical with the national interest. All other questions are delegated to the Belgians, who together with the Dutch do most of Luxembourg's overseas diplomatic representation as well.[144]

Denmark. The Foreign Ministry's division for foreign economic relations is in charge of EC policies and issues instructions to Coreper.[145] More important for actual decision making is an interministerial EC Officials' Committee, which has formed subcommittees for each of the Commission's DGs. In these subcommittees the respective ministries in charge of the issues preside. They issue the instructions to officials in the corresponding working groups in Brussels.[146] The Foreign Ministry prepares the Danish positions for the European Council meetings. Its political department — like in all other EC countries — is in charge of EPC.

Ireland. EC affairs are the Irish Foreign Ministry's main concern and Brussels constitutes its largest overseas mission.[147] The Foreign Ministry's EC section issues the instructions to Coreper, while national officials attending working groups in Brussels receive instructions from their own ministries. Informal, ad hoc interministerial co-ordination is frequent, as are Irish cabinet sessions devoted to European affairs.[148]

We can summarise this section by saying that national EC policies (and the EC's external relations) in Italy, Belgium, Luxembourg, Denmark and Ireland are most clearly a Foreign Ministry domain. In Germany and in the Netherlands responsibilities are divided between the Economics and the Foreign Ministries, while in France and in Britain an interministerial body above—between the ministries is in effective charge of EC policies.

39

Actual foreign policies

The following outline is intended to give an impression of the EC's foreign policy orientation. It may also serve to support the notion that — in spite of its complex decision-making structure — the Commission's foreign policy has so far achieved more productive results than the numerous solemn declarations of the EPC.

Having listed a variety of inhibiting factors in the discussion of intergovernmentalism in an earlier section it may be useful to mention those common strategic and long term common orientations that are capable of eventually outweighing divergent particular interests and of enabling the common pursuit of both CCP and EPC:

- Security from Soviet military threat; continuation of detente and disarmament talks; increase of autonomy from US influence.
- Secure supplies of energy, of raw materials; the guarantee of markets for European products; outlets for European capital.
- A system of international trade and monetary relations operating predictably and enabling an uninhibited flow of trade — with possible emergency checks in those cases where imports are seen as harmful to the interests of European producers.
- Maintainance of traditional ties to Third World countries in Africa and the Mediterranean.
- As a long term goal ('Toujours y penser, jamais en parler'): the desired end of Soviet domination of Eastern Europe under peaceful conditions.[149]

As functional and as external pressures for a common policy orientation the following factors are effective for a joint EC foreign economic policy:

- The Customs Union requiring a common commercial policy. The conduct of the CCP with its network of international agreements then evidently creates strong foreign policy effects.
- The expectation of third countries of being able to deal with the EC as a whole (whose CCP and CET they experience), or their perception of the EC as a 'civilian power' as a possible and desirable partner in counterbalancing the influence of the superpowers.[150]
- US pressure (particularly during the Nixon—Kissinger era) to assume more 'responsibility' in a 'pentapolar' world order.
- Finally the declining US imperial power constituting an urge for European co-operation on security issues. Effective European military integration, then, would presuppose the creation of a European federation.[151]

Genscher writes that against the superpowers, against coalitions like OPEC and the Group of 77, a European national state on its own is incapable of protecting its vital interests sufficiently. The European shock of realising its impotence during the fourth Middle East war and the oil crisis in 1973 signalled the 'hour of birth' of co-ordinated European foreign policies.[152]

After the failure of the EDC project in the 1950s and of the Fouchet plans in the early 1960s the EC developed its inward-looking perspective. It was fully occupied implementing the two pillars of integration: CAP and the Customs Union. Though the Commission successfully negotiated at the Kennedy Round, it was not until the Den Haag summit in 1969 that the heads of government decided to co-operate externally beyond limited technical and trade issues. The decisions for the economic and monetary union and the first enlargement (1969) consequently led to the EPC decision (1970).[153] Strong external stimuli to develop a common foreign policy have already been mentioned: the Arab world, South American and other LDCs seeing the EC as an alternative to diversifying their external relations from their dependency on the superpowers. China wished a strong Europe as the Soviet Union's neighbour. The EC had to defend itself against the Nixon administration's pressures on CAP's protectionist rules and on the preferential agreements with the ACP countries. During Kissinger's year of Europe (1973) Atlantic relations hit their post-war low when Europe collectively had to put off the US design for a New Atlantic Charter which would have contained a combined military and economic 'co-operation' formula. It was perceived in Europe as mere blackmail: the US trying to trade military protection for economic concessions.[154] As a new feature in the international economic system during the early 1970s bloc negotiations started replacing bilateral negotiations. The two oil crises and the UNCTAD's challenge to the unequal North—South distribution of wealth and resources demanded a responding common policy.

The EC — whose actual state of integration in the 1970s was grossly overestimated by its overseas partners — had, however, no conception of its world role except for the maintainance of the status quo.[155] This role reflected adequately the member states' national policies, which up to then proved to be incapable of providing any substantial positive input into a major international policy initiative.

The sole exception to this performance was Britain's initiative on Zimbabwe 1979—80. Its success illustrated the European states' foreign policy potential and thus rather forcefully highlighted the gap between this potential and their actual foreign policies.

The US initially had been a strong supporter of the EC, hoping for a junior partner in securing US foreign policy goals. High EC tariffs were either considered as a necessary political price for burden sharing or of a temporary nature. After the US became disillusioned on both, its frustration grew.[156]

Similarly the EC failed to fulfil the expectations of the ASEAN,

South American and other non-ACP developing countries.

In institutional terms, in spite of organisational frictions and resentments of national decision makers, the Commission was able of extending its commercial policy towards more comprehensive foreign economic and development policies.[157] Due to its economic leverage the EC is now able to promote (as possibly in case of some ACP countries) or to inhibit (as with Argentina or New Zealand) economic welfare in third countries. Consequently the EC's policy measures are seen in highly political terms from outside, but at the same time it lacks all necessary response mechanisms and forms 'a paradox of considerable strength and deplorable weakness'.[158] Or as Dahrendorf put it: there is a 'wide discrepancy between the effects and the actions' of the EC.[159]

In addition to their policy response deficiency the essence of the EC's foreign policies itself is still judged as being 'characterised by their miscellaneous and unpurposive quality, by their passive nature . . . and by the frequent cases of incoherence or even incompatibility between their component parts'.[160]

Given the present state of European intergovernmentalism with its bureaucratic maze in foreign policy co-operation this criticism can hardly come as a surprise.

References

1   Morgan, Roger P. Introduction: European Integration and the European Community's External Relations. *International Journal of Politics 5,* 1975, 3—10, p. 3.

2   Soldatis, Panayotis. La théorie de la politique étrangère et sa pertinance pour l'étude des relations extérieures des Communautés Européennes. *Etudes Internationales 9,* 1978, 7—42, p. 17.

3   Rosenthal, Glenda G. *The Men behind the Decisions.* Lexington, Mass.: Lexington Books. 1975, p. 3.

4   Torrelli, Maurice. L'élaboration des relations extérieures de la C.E.E. *Revue du Marché Commun.* No. 167, 1973, 328—40, p. 329.

5   Sjöstedt, Gunnar. *The External Role of the European Community.* Farnborough, Hants: Saxon House. 1977, p. 86.

6   See: *Sweet and Maxwell's European Community Treaties.* (3rd ed.) London. 1972.

7   Dahrendorf, Ralf. It is not easy for a Community to have a Foreign Policy. *International Journal of Politics 5,* 1975, 11—28, p. 21.

8   Pentland, Charles. Linkage Politics: Canada's Contract and the Development of the European Communities External Relations.

International Journal 32, 1977, 207—31, p. 229.

9 Goodwin, Geoffrey L. The External Relations of the European Community — Shadow and Substance. *British Journal of International Studies 3,* 1977, 39—44, p. 39.

10 See also: Pickles, William. Political Power in the EEC. In: Carol A. Cosgrave and Kenneth J. Twitchett (eds.). *The New International Actors.* London: Macmillan. 1970, 201—21, p. 206.

11 Cartou, Louis. Le role de la Commission. In: Pierre Gerbet and Daniel Pepy (eds.) *La décision dans les Communautés Européennes.* Brussels: Presses Universitaires de Bruxelles. 1969, 3—11, p. 3.

12 European Community. Commission. *Directory of the European Communities* (January 1979). Luxembourg: Office for Official Publications of the EC. 1978, p. 21.

13 Ayberk, Ural. *Le méchanisme de la prise de décisions communautaires en matières de relations internationales.* Bruxelles: Bruylant. 1978, p. 437.

14 Poullet, Edouard, and Gerard Deprez. *Struktur und Macht der EG Kommission.* Bonn: Europa Union Verlag. 1976, p. 49.

15 Ibid., p. 53.

16 Wallace, Helen. *National Governments and the European Communities.* London: Chatham House/PEP. 1973, p. 57.

17 Poullet, 1976, Op. cit., p. 53.

18 Coombes, David. *Politics and Bureaucracy in the European Community.* London: Allen and Unwin. 1970, p. 249.

19 Allen, David. Foreign Policy at the European Level: Beyond the Nation-State? In: William Wallace and W.E. Patterson (eds.). *Foreign Policy Making in Western Europe.* Farnborough, Hants.: Saxon House. 1978, 135—54, p. 145.

20 Ayberk, 1978, Op. cit., p. 97 and p. 105.

21 Allen, 1978, Op. cit., p. 146.

22 McGeehan, Robert and Steven J. Warnecke. Europe's Foreign Policies: Economics, Politics or Both? *Orbis 17,* 1974, 1251—79, p. 1260.

23 Ibid.

24 Poullet, 1976, Op. cit., p. 80.

25 Ibid., p. 40.

26 Ayberk, 1978, Op. cit., p. 428.

27 Ibid., p. 398.

28 Sasse, Cristoph. *Regierungen, Parlamente, Ministerrat — Entscheidungs prozesse in der Europäischen Gemeinschaft.* Bonn: Europa Union Verlag. 1975, p. 198.

29 Rosenthal, 1975, Op. cit., p. 135.

30 Dahrendorf, 1975, Op. cit., p. 18.

31 Nöel, Emile and Henri Etienne. Quelques aspects des rapports et

de la collaboration entre le Conseil et la Commission. In: Gerbet et al. (eds.). 1969. Op. cit. 33–55, p. 33.

32 Alting von Geusau, F.A.M. Les sessions marathon du Conseil des Ministres. In: Gerbet et al. (eds.). Op. cit. 1969. 99–107, p. 99.

33 Lindberg/Scheingold (1970) as quoted by: Rosenthal, 1975 Op. cit., p. 135.

34 Ayberk, 1978, Op. cit., p. 400.

35 Wallace, H., 1973, Op. cit., p. 7.

36 Ayberk, 1978, Op. cit., p. 120.

37 Vignes, Daniel. Le rôle du Secretariat des Conseils. In: Gerbet et al. (eds.). Op. cit., 1969. 75–81, p. 75.

38 Europäische Gemeinschaften. Generalsekretariat des Rates. *Leitfaden der Rate der Europäischen Gemeinschaften.* Brüssel. 1979.

39 Poullet, 1976, Op. cit., p. 57.

40 Sasse, 1975, Op. cit., p. 210.

41 Ibid.

42 Goodwin, 1977, Op. cit., p. 50.

43 Ayberk, 1978, Op. cit., p. 409.

44 Salmon, Jean J. A. Le rôle des représentants permanents. In: Gerbet et al. (eds.). 1969. Op. cit., 57–73, p. 66.

45 Ayberk, 1978. Op. cit., p. 410.

46 See lists of officials and their functions in: EG. Generalsekretariat des Rates. 1979. Op. cit.

47 Poullet. 1976. Op. cit., p. 128.

48 Wallace, H. 1973. Op. cit., p. 63.

49 Noël, Emile. Le comité des représentants permanents. Institut d'Etudes Européennes. Université Libre de Bruxelles (ed.). *Institutions Communautaires et institutions nationales dans le développement des Communautés.* Bruxelles: Editions de l'Institut de Sociologie. 1968. 9–49, p. 47.

50 Noël, Etienne. 1969. Op. cit., p. 45.

51 Poullet, 1976. Op. cit., p. 131.

52 Salmon, 1969, Op. cit., p. 72.

53 Sasse, 1975. Op. cit., Annex.

54 Ibid., p. 167.

55 Salmon. 1969. Op. cit., p. 58.

56 Feld, Werner. Diplomatic Behaviour in the European Communities: Milieus and Motivations. *Journal of Common Market Studies 11,* 1972, 18–35, p. 30.

57 Ayberk, 1978. Op. cit., p. 415.

58 Noël. 1968. Op. cit., p. 47.

59 Ayberk. 1978. Op. cit., p. 149.

60 Ibid., p. 418.

61 Ibid., p. 420.

62 Ibid., p. 422
63 Pickles. 1970. Op. cit., p. 203.
64 Ayberk. 1978. Op. cit., p. 445.
65 Pickles. 1970. Op. cit., p. 202.
66 Feld, Werner. *The European Common Market and the World.* Englewood Cliffs, N.J.: Prentice Hall. 1967, p. 27.
67 Pickles. 1970. Op. cit., p. 218.
68 Feld. 1972. Op. cit., p. 24.
69 Rhein, Eberhard. Die Europäische Gemeinschaft auf der Suche nach einer gemeinsamen Aussenpolitik. *Europa Archiv 31,* 1976, 171—80, p. 173.
70 Allen. 1978. Op. cit., p. 148.
71 Hansen, Niels. Politische Zusammenarbeit in Westeuropa. *Europa Archiv 26,* 1971, 456—64, p. 458.
72 Mackintosh, John P. Gemeinsame Europäische Aussenpolitik. *Europa Archiv 27,* 1972, 365—76, p. 374.
73 Staden, Berndt von. Politische Zusammenarbeit der EG Staaten. *Aussenpolitik 23,* 1972, 200—9, p. 209.
74 Bridgford, Jeff. European Political Co-operation and its Impact on the Institutions of the European Community. *Studia Diplomatica 30,* 1977, 393—411, p. 396.
75 Genscher, Hans-Dietrich. Notwendigkeit und Möglichkeit einer europäischen Aussenpolitik. *Europa Archiv 31,* 1976, 427—34, p. 432.
76 Allen. 1978. Op. cit., p. 150.
77 Bridgford. 1977. Op. cit., p. 378.
78 Genscher. 1976. Op. cit., p. 429.
79 Hansen. 1971. Op. cit., p. 463.
80 Meynaud, Jean and Dusan Sidjanski. L'action des groupes de pression. In: Gerbet et al. (eds.). 1969. Op. cit., 133—48, p. 136.
81 Sidjanski, Dusan. Pressure Groups and the European Economic Community. In: Cosgrave et al. (eds.). 1970. Op. cit., 222—36, p. 229.
82 Meynaud. 1969. Op. cit., p. 139.
83 Ibid., p. 142.
84 Feld. 1967. Op. cit., p. 34.
85 Meynaud. 1969. Op. cit., p. 144.
86 Ibid., p. 146.
87 Ayberk, 1978. Op. cit., p. 195.
88 Rosenthal. 1975. Op. cit., p. 47 and p. 51.
89 Cardozo, Michael. *Diplomats in International Co-operation.* Ithaca, N.Y.: Cornell Univ. Press. 1962, p. 105.
90 Wallace, William. *The Foreign Policy Process in Britain.* London: The Royal Institute of International Affairs. 1975, p. 68.

91 Feld, Werner and John K. Wildgen. National Administrative Elites and European Integration: Saboteurs at Work? *Journal of Common Market Studies 13,* 1975, 244–65, p. 264.
92 Ibid., p. 266.
93 Allen. 1978. Op. cit., p. 150.
94 Feld. 1972. Op. cit., p. 30.
95 Wallace, H., 1973. Op. cit., p. 81, and: Ayberk. 1978. Op. cit., p. 472.
96 Feld. 1972. Op. cit., p. 32.
97 Ibid., p. 33.
98 Coombes. 1970. Op. cit., p. 215.
99 Ibid.
100 *Japan Times,* 13.5.1980.
101 Ayberk, 1978. Op. cit., p. 17.
102 Personal interview.
103 Rosenthal. 1975. Op. cit., p. 14.
104 Dahrendorf, Ralf. The Foreign Policy of the EEC. *The World Today 29,* 1973, 47–57, p. 53.
105 Staden. 1972. Op. cit., p. 200.
106 Coombes. 1970. Op. cit., p. 190.
107 Alting von Gesau. 1962. Op. cit., p. 196.
108 Goodwin. 1977. Op. cit., p. 50.
109 Ayberk. 1978. Op. cit., p. 465.
110 Ibid., p. 206.
111 Ibid., p. 460.
112 See: Morgan, Roger P. *High Politics, Low Politics: Towards a Foreign Policy of Western Europe.* London: Sage Publications. 1973, p. 21.
113 Sasse. 1975. Op. cit., p. 19.
114 Zysman, John. The French State in the International Economy. In: Katzenstein, Peter J. (ed.). *Between Power and Plenty: Foreign Economic Policies of Advanced Industrial States.* Madison: University of Wisconsin Press. 1978. 255–93, p. 266.
115 Wallace, H. 1973. Op. cit., p. 42.
116 Tint, Herbert. *French Foreign Policy since the Second World War.* London: Weidenfeld & Nicolson. 1972, p. 221.
117 Sasse. 1975. Op. cit., p. 23.
118 Ibid., p. 22.
119 Gerbet, Pierre. La préparation de la décision communautaire au niveau national français. Gerbet et al. (eds.). 1969. Op. cit., 195–208, p. 195.
120 Wallace, William. The Management of Foreign Economic Relations in Britain. *International Affairs 50,* 1974, 251–67, p. 256.
121 Wallace, W. 1975. Op. cit., p. 177.

122 Wallace, W. 1974. Op. cit., p. 266.
123 Sasse. 1975. Op. cit., p. 58.
124 Schwarz, Hans-Peter. Die Bundesregierung und die Auswärtigen Beziehungen. In: H.P. Schwarz (ed.) *Handbuch der deutschen Aussenpolitik.* Munchen: Piper & Co. 1975. 43–111, p. 73.
125 Wallace, H. 1973. Op. cit., p. 30.
126 Sasse. 1975. Op. cit., p. 27.
127 Kreile, Michael. West-Germany: The Dynamics of Expansion. In: Katzenstein (ed.). 1978. Op. cit., 191–224, p. 201.
128 Sasse. 1975. Op. cit., p. 38.
129 Wallace, H. 1973. Op. cit., p. 23.
130 Sasse, 1975. Op. cit., p. 42.
131 Posner, Alan R. Italy: Dependence and Political Fragmentation. In: Katzenstein (ed.). 1978. Op. cit., 225–54, p. 239.
132 Olivetti, Marco M. La préparation de la décision communautaire au niveau national italien. In: Gerbet et al. (eds.). 1969. Op. cit., 209–27, p. 227.
133 Wallace, H. 1973. Op. cit., p. 25.
134 Baehr, Peter R. The Foreign Policy of the Netherlands. In: J.H. Leurdijk (ed.). *The Foreign Policy of the Netherlands.* Alphen aan den Rijn: Sijthoft & Noordhoff. 1978. 3–27, p. 11.
135 Sasse. 1975. Op. cit., p. 47.
136 Bruin, Robert de. La préparation de la décision communautaire au niveau national néerlandais. In: Gerbet et al. (eds.). 1969. Op. cit., 239–55, p. 253.
137 Ibid., p. 254.
138 Ibid., p. 249.
139 Wallace, H. 1973. Op. cit., p. 27.
140 Sasse. 1975. Op. cit., p. 54.
141 Mahieu, Marie-Paule. La préparation de la décision communautaire au niveau national belge. In: Gerbet et al. (eds.). 1969. Op. cit., 183–94, p. 194.
142 Muyser, Guy de. La préparation de la décision communautaire au niveau national luxembourgeois. In: Gerbet et al. (eds.). 1969. Op. cit., 229–35, p. 230.
143 Sasse. 1975. Op. cit., p. 57.
144 Personal interview.
145 Sasse. 1975. Op. cit., p. 72.
146 Ibid.
147 Keatinge, Patrick. *The Formulation of Irish Foreign Policy.* Dublin: Institute of Public Administration. 1973, p. 116.
148 Sasse. 1975. Op. cit., p. 74.
149 Morgan. 1973. Op. cit., p. 50.
150 Allen. 1978. Op. cit., p. 143.

151 Rhein. 1976. Op. cit., p. 179.

152 Genscher. 1976. Op. cit., p. 434.

153 Allen. 1978. Op. cit., p. 143.

154 McGeehan. 1974. Op. cit., p. 1254.

155 Dahrendorf, Ralf. International Power: A European Perspective. *Foreign Affairs 56*, 1977, 72–88, p. 86.

156 McGeehan. 1974. Op. cit., p. 1253.

157 Genscher. 1976. Op. cit., p. 431.

158 Rieber, Roger A. The Future of the European Community in International Affairs. *Canadian Journal of Political Science 32*, 1977, 207–31, p. 210.

159 Dahrendorf, Ralf. Possibilities and Limits of the European Community's Foreign Policy. *The World Today 27*, 1971, 148–61, p. 152.

160 Morgan. 1973. Op. cit., p. 9.

3 The structure for foreign policy decisions in Japan

After a six-month research stay in Japan, Brzezinski concluded in his
Fragile Blossom that the Japanese elite perceives world events with American eyes: ' . . . taking foreign events into account by first calculating
their impact on America and on American—Japanese relations'.[1] Nothing
could be further from the truth. The Japanese elite views world events
with Japanese eyes and in a Japanese perspective only. Brought up in a
strong ethnocentric culture they also seem to expect the rest of the
world to perceive international events in the Japanese way, perhaps repeating Brzezinski's mistake. The foreign policies of Japan emerge both
from quite distinct ideas of her international environment and a unique
domestic political set-up. Thus it seems to be useful to spend a chapter
on the ways Japanese foreign policies are decided upon and to reflect
on the set of domestic and external factors and restraints which affect
Japanese policies towards Europe.

This chapter will first deal with the political power structure of Japan
which consists of an uneasy coalition of big business groupings, the government bureaucracy and the factions of the conservative ruling party.
Then the institutions in Japan's foreign policy structure will be discussed with reference to their political stands and interests: the Foreign
Ministry (MFA), the Ministry for International Trade and Industry
(MITI) and the other economic ministries, the role of the Prime Minister, the Diet and the political parties, the general trading companies
(sogo shosha) and the business community. The basic features of Japan's
foreign and foreign economic policies will be dealt with briefly. Then
case studies and a summary on how foreign policy decisions are made

in Japan will be followed by a section on Japan's international negotiating style which reflects domestic cultural traits that render Japanese diplomats quite handicapped on the international scene.

The power structure of post-war Japan

The ruling conservative power coalition

'Japan Inc.' is the most catchy description of the close and co-operative relations between Japan's political, administrative and economic power centres. Pickert views Japan's international behaviour as not unlike the working of a giant multinational corporation:[2] government and business are linked in every aspect of business abroad, reinforcing a web of interpersonal indebtedness among Japanese bureaucrats, businessmen and politicians. Yanaga in an extensive study also underlines the importance of cross-cutting loyalties, personal ties and cliques as a prime means for big business control of Japan's government.[3] The emphasis on harmonious interpersonal relations and consensus-oriented decisions in Japanese culture prevents autocratic one-man rule. Thus it is hardly possible to identify the individuals exercising ultimate power in Japan, but it is quite feasible to identify the groups through which power is channelled and applied, both formally and informally. Yanaga reports a general agreement on the proposition that 'The nation is governed jointly by organised business, the party government and the administrative bureaucracy'.[4] Most influential in this coalition is zaikai, the 'power centre of Japan's business'.[5] The membership of zaikai is not clearly delineated, but what is usually meant are those company presidents and business leaders who are active in the top four economic organisations, Keidanren, Nikkeiren, the 'Council for Economic Development' and the Japanese Chamber of Commerce and Industry. They are the elder statesmen of Japan's big business, industry and finance, and according to Yanaga, they more or less decide on who becomes Prime Minister.[6] It would be more plausible to assume that zaikai could exercise veto powers on such matters. Within the obvious broad conservative, pro-business, low-welfare expenditure consensus in zaikai a wide variety of economic interests and political convictions is represented and these also stretch into incompatible foreign trade stands particularly on trade liberalisation and on exchange rate policies.

The stronger in-group ties and institutional identifications are cherished the stronger usually is the rejection of non-group members so that communication gaps, inter-organisational rivalry and hostility are likely consequences. The severity of competition among Japanese companies on the domestic market is equally noted as are intra and inter-ministerial hostilities, e.g. MITI versus MOF, MAFF versus MITI and MOF versus MAFF and so on. The factional infights within political parties are equally notorious among the conservatives and the socialists. Clark, who therefore claimed that 'Japan Unincorporated' would better characterise Japan's political system, also cited the historical Army versus Navy rivalry which greatly helped accelerate Japan's defeat in WW II.[7] Curtis[8] finally rejects Japan Inc. as vulgar and recites 'instances of zaikai's inability to control the LDP presidential election . . . [which] are evident as instances where zaikai has allegedly manipulated the election'.[9] Patrick and Rosovsky assert a 'pluralist distribution of power in economic decision making'.[10] There is a representation of big and small business interests, of farmers, of labour, the government bureaucracy and the media. There are also consumers, urban residents and environmentalists with varying alliances and interests. Though the LDP financially depends on business contribution, it equally, at least, depends on voters' support and therefore needs to develop alternatives to the opposition parties' proposals.

While to most observers there is no doubt that government — business relations are closer in Japan than in most developed Western countries,[11] at the same time the over-simple monolithic or monopoly-capitalist type assumptions do not reflect the complexity and diversity of Japan's political economy.

The bureaucracy

The consensus orientation of Japanese decision making has already been mentioned. On most controversial issues it is considered essential to reach some sort of compromise even if majorities are clear in order not to alienate the minority and to avoid serious threats of splits in the organisation. This principle inevitably leads to a painful slowness in decision making, to endless conferences and to often deliberately vague final agreements which can be ambiguous and puzzling even to participants. The two standard administrative procedures are similarly intended to be conducive to intra-organisational harmony. These are *ringi-sei*, a drafting procedure for routine decisions, and *nemawashi*, the subtle search for acceptance of a potentially more controversial draft with one's superiors and at other departments through informal approaches. Both procedures, in theory, generate from the hierarchical bottom, upwards. Ringi-sei means documents circulating from department to department up the bureaucratic ladder, each consenting official affixing his seal for approval. Due to the flood of drafts from bureau chief onwards seals are affixed usually without reading. The ideal Japanese decision model requires that 'as many people as possible are duly consulted and not a single dissident voice remains at the end of the final decision'.[12] Consequently, after all means of compromise are exhausted, strong social pressure is exerted upon dissenters to either accept the final version and to silence their protest or to leave the organisation eventually. In reality subordinates will have sounded out their bosses' consent on issues on which they might disagree, and will have changed their drafts accordingly. In fact, many of the 'consensus finding' conferences are only staged pro forma and serve to legitimise already made decisions.

The effects of Japanese style decision making are that Japanese organisations lack strong and dynamic leaderships at the top — a result of the permanent accommodation and consultation requirements — which may clearly prove dysfunctional in times of crises. It follows that middle-level officials (heads of divisions) exercise strong influence in Japanese bureaucracies. After the arduous decision procedure, implementation is usually extremely swift since consensus is established, information distributed and the organisational working climate is in harmony.

For decision analysts the Japanese way constitutes a nightmare because responsibility is utterly diffused. At the core of political decision making are evidently government officials and cabinet ministers with party notables and concerned business representatives trying to pull their strings. Since at the top echelons of Japan's political establishment close and informal co-operation is practised, it is hard to determine which institutions, arguments or personalities were most influential; and records are not kept for their more decisive discussions in the teahouses of Akasaka.

Decision by accommodation and domestic consensus encourages pragmatic and necessarily ad hoc policy responses while discouraging long term thinking on foreign affairs. It creates passive, reactive policies and inflexible bargaining positions, since negotiators have to delay decisions in order to allow a new consensus to build at home. Finally the requirements of co-ordination alone among the many ministries and agencies involved in the conduct of Japan's external relations creates policy-lags which could be lethal in case of serious international crises.[13]

Officials in Japan's national bureaucracy enjoy wide powers of discretion with only a minimum of control from the politically appointed top level.[14] Japanese laws are not only drafted in the ministries themselves prior to submission to the Diet, but are also worded in an extremely vague fashion which leaves a wide freedom of action to the ministries to draft, to announce and to implement and control regulations. The practice of administrative guidance, of giving informally fairly compelling 'advice' combined with a set of incentives and possible sanctions to key industries in bypassing the Diet signifies the bureaucracies' power. The political leadership (ministers and parliamentary vice-ministers) changes at a fast pace — at least every second year — and is not expected to meddle in the affairs of its more qualified and experienced staff. Japanese officials' self-image and social prestige exceeds even those enjoyed by officials in continental Europe: a Confucian tradition valuing governmental service, graduation from usually the most prestigious universities, preferably the University of Tokyo's Law Faculty, and excellent prospects for post-retirement managerial posts in semi-governmental agencies, the private economy or for political careers. There is not only an extremely competitive civil service entrance examination to be passed, but still a second examination ahead to qualify for promotion to higher career posts.

After their entry young officials are rotated from department to department every two or three years to enable them to acquire the desired generalist qualification and outlook. It is an unwritten rule that no official can ever serve under a colleague from the same or even a junior entrants' class. Promotions follow roughly according to seniority. Special achievements or talents are honoured only with special assignments. On higher levels cliques begin to flourish: they may be based on the old boy network of common graduation from the same university, on family ties or origin in the same prefecture. The closer and more personal cliques are formed by people with common career experiences and interests or shared leisure activities. Stretching across bureau and ministry lines, such cliques facilitate the needed informal consultation and help to overcome the effects of inter-bureaucratic jealousies and communication failures.[15] Japanese officials cannot be expected to serve under a superior with equal or even fewer years of service in the ministry. When the time comes for promotions to scarcer bureau chief level jobs for one generation of entrants (the class of, let's say, 1955) then the unsuccessful candidates of this class will be assigned to head prefectural offices or respective posts in the vast array of associated governmental or semi-governmental agencies, which they then hold for one or two years at most until the next class comes up to inherit their positions. The highest civil service position, the administrative vice-minister, is held at most for two to three years by each incumbent and most officials retire in their early 50s. Thus the retired officials are still in their best years and due to their qualifications and connections (particularly with their previous subordinates now rising to influential middle or senior positions) they are usually in high demand for managerial or advisory posts for those industries or businesses with which they and their ministry had dealt most. Former MOF officials are recruited by the major banks, MOT officials to the transportation industry and to the national railways, MITI officials to the trading companies, the steel, engineering and chemical industries and the other economic ministries to their respective client industries. This 'amakudari' (descendants from heaven) practice evidently affects bureaucratic policies considerably — officials have to care both for future — and usually very lucrative — post retirement jobs for themselves and also to treat their former bosses in the related businesses nicely since their real or assumed bonds of loyalty to them are expected to continue.

The lavish entertainment funds of Japanese companies and the intense liking of Japanese men for endless night-time drinking and dining sessions serve as a further lubricant to maintain business — bureaucratic friendships which frequently result in the exchange of entertainment pleasures for governmental favours. Foreign businessmen with tighter expense accounts and possibly less preference for permanent nightlife activity face a considerable non-tariff barrier when neglecting relations with a powerful and at times pedantic and slowly working bureaucracy.

A further element of co-operation between government and business is the vast bulk of advisory commissions and councils (shingikai) attached to the Prime Minister's Office and the other ministries. Their agenda is controlled and their members are appointed by ministry officials.[16] Most of the members come from the businesses concerned, others are respected journalists and academics or represent economic federations or institutes. The recommendations of these councils are highly influential.

Still, this close government—business collaboration does not exclude conflicts (e.g. between commercial banks with MOF on discount rates or the internationalisation of the Yen) nor is administrative guidance accepted by all industries at all times.

The conservative party (LDP)

Apart from the short-lived Socialist-led coalition government of 1947–1948, all of Japan's post-war government was under conservative party rule. The Liberal Democratic Party was formed in 1955 as a merger of the equally conservative Liberal and Democratic Parties, whose historical antecedents reached back to the Meiji period from which they inherited their traditional rural power base. In the pre-war years the alliance with the zaibatsu, oligopolist business conglomerates, was added, and continued to be maintained with their dismantled post-war successors. The LDP remained largely a coalition of a varying number of intriguing, feuding and allying factions, which have only faint programmatical differences and are maintained by highly personal leader—follower ties. Each faction has its own fund-raising system which is used by the factional leader to finance the campaigns of his followers. Factional strength in the Diet and in the (poorly organised) party organisation depends on the faction leader's political influence, the consequent monetary supply (donations) and his ability to maintain his faction. The financial requirements to cultivate relations with followers in the constituency and for successful election campaigning are immense: in 1979 the costs for a successful conservative campaign were estimated at about 300m Yen per constituency. Therefore, pressure mounts on faction leaders to expand their influence in order to attract more business contributions and to provide for more government posts for their men in the Diet — who after many years of faithful service feel entitled to a short stint as at least a parliamentary vice-minister, where they usually after one year's service resign in order to give way for other meritorious senior backbenchers. Top LDP politicians and faction leaders usually are retired bureaucrats, who still maintain their links to their former ministries and in positions of power take care of their former subordinates' interests. Their unyielding loyalty is expected in return. The local party organisation is usually weak and disorganised and divided into hostile former Democratic and Liberal party followers.[17] Most LDP Diet seats are based in rural constituencies in which the agricultural co-operatives maintain the electoral and organisational backbone for the LDP. In return government projects are distributed over the area and strict agricultural protectionism maintains farms with microscopic acreage on price levels many times above the world level.

The source of most of Japan's trouble with agricultural exporters, such as the US, Australia and the EC, lies in this electoral pay-off. Though also courting the rural vote the opposition parties with urban and consumer constituencies could be expected gradually to reduce food prices and protectionism.

Japanese top politicians are typically pragmatic power-broker types with a great propensity towards compromise and backstaging to accommodate the perennial interfactional strive. They usually lack charisma, are often considered corrupt and held in low public esteem.

The LDP's capacity for policy innovation and decision making is limited. Substantial policies are worked out in co-operation with the respective bureaucracies taking into account the interests of sponsoring businesses.

Big business

Keidanren, the 'Federation of Economic Organisations' is the representative organisation for big business. It exercises strong political influence by organising and allocating the political donations of its members. These donate to Kokumin Kyokai (People's Association), which has the exclusive function of channelling funds to the LDP.[18] The Kokumin Kyokai monies then are distributed among the various factions according to a prearranged key. Apart from that individual companies are free to support candidates or factions of their choice, to sponsor opposition parties as well or set up independent candidates of their own (usually popular sportsmen or TV singers) who later are to join conservative ranks.

The four major economic federations whose policy recommendations frequently have to be elaborated as a compromise of countervailing membership interests practise a specific division of labour. Keidanren is the representative of big business, the major corporations and their trade and industry associations. *Nikkeiren,* the 'Federation of Employers' Associations', is in charge of industrial relations and the labour unions' national negotiating counterpart. *Nissho,* the Japan Chamber of Industry and Commerce, articulates also small and medium business interests. *Keizai Doyukai,* the 'Committee for Economic Development' has individual memberships, often overlapping with Keidanren. Its policy concerns are traditionally of more long term nature and it usually takes slightly more progressive stands than its fellow associations.[19]

All of them have professional research staff and conduct unending series of conferences; they are — except for Nikkeiren — engaged in private economic diplomacy and their views — especially on basic issues like stimulating macroeconomic policies and tax reforms when reflecting business consensus — are bound to find political responsiveness.[20] On the other hand, they are not always successful in forays into foreign policy making or attempting to settle intra-LDP faction fights.[21]

Zaikai members, of course, have direct access to politicians. There is a variety of exclusive clubs which the Prime Minister and other leading politicians maintain to keep their business connection. They meet regularly — and are named accordingly (e.g. Itsukakai: 'fifth day of the month club') — in an informal setting, preferably in geisha restaurants in downtown Tokyo. Since a great many managers and top politicians graduated from the leading universities or are retired bureaucrats, old boys' networks are working[22] and sometimes also far reaching family ties (keibatsu). It is still common for senior officials in MOF to act as go-betweens for their young and promising subordinates (Japan's most desired marriage partners) and to match them with available daughters of the economic or political elite.[23] This secures both able recruitments for the Japanese elite and prospects of a brilliant career for the young official. In interviews with 50 presidents of Japan's leading companies at least 11 were reported to be in some way part of the econo-political elite keibatsu marriage system,[24] to which after the Crown Price's marriage the imperial family is also tied.

To sum up, in Japan an unusually close elite interaction is maintained between big business, top politics and the national bureaucracy. At the same time it is not entirely clear who dominates whom: a monopoly capitalist type of business domination of the government, or a 'Japan Inc.' where the bureaucrats enslave the nation's industries. Kaplan's case studies on government intervention in the car, steel and computer industry found: 'Diet and Keidanren involvement with MITI has varied considerably from case to case'.[25]

Conflicts of interests were evident in repeated confrontations between ministries and or bureaus in the pursuit of their sectoral functions or in the interest of their client industries. In the mentioned case studies MITI thus clashed successively with MOT, MOF, the Bank of Japan (BOJ) and the Fair Trade Commission (FTC).[26]

Institutions of foreign policy decision making

In supplementation of what has already been outlined on Japan's power structure the institutions of Japan's foreign policy structure will be discussed here in more detail. These are MFA, MITI, the various domestic economic ministries, the Prime Minister and his Office, the political parties and the Diet, the business community and the general trading companies (sogo shosha). While such a listing suggests considerable pluralism, to some observers on the essential policy choices the Japanese power elite has the final say: 'A conservative coalition linking key elements of Japanese government, big business, and big finance has carried out a foreign economic policy aimed at maximising that coalition's interpretation of Japan's national interest'.[27] Others reject the idea of a 'Japan Inc.' type foreign policy formulation and see a passive consensus working: government, the ruling party and big business co-operating with mutual veto powers.[28] After the discussion of the role of each foreign policy institution this latter notion will appear as more convincing.

Gaimusho — the Ministry of Foreign Affairs (MFA)

Gaimusho employs 3,400 officials and is thus the second smallest Japanese ministry; about half of its staff is regularly on assignments abroad. It is subdivided into nine bureaus and the ministry's secretariat. The secretariat handles the overall co-ordination and the personnel management of the ministry. Planning and policy analysis are additional tasks. Among the bureaus, the four geographical bureaus deal with bilateral issues: Asian Affairs, American Affairs, European and Oceanic Affairs, and Middle Eastern and African Affairs. The European and Oceanic Affairs Bureau covers Europe, including the Soviet Union, as well as Australia and New Zealand. It is divided into the First (in charge of the old 6 EC countries) and the Second West Europe Divisions (in charge of all other Western European countries), the First and the Second East Europe Division and the Oceania Division. The functional bureaus are concerned with multilateral issues: the Economic Affairs Bureau is in charge of international trade issues and their appropriate international organisations, such as OECD and GATT. This bureau suffers from overlapping competences with more powerful ministries (MITI, MOF and EPA).[29] The Economic Co-operation Bureau (equally in competition with a more powerful MITI bureau) deals with the distribution of OAD and therefore enjoys the largest budget among Gaimusho's bureaus. The Treaties Bureau advises all bureaus on legal matters and is thus involved in most current affairs. The United Nations Bureau handles UN matters, other international organisations and co-operation on nuclear energy. The Public Information and Cultural Affairs Bureau finally is in charge of cultural exchange and international and domestic PR work.[30]

Without a domestic constituency and as the second smallest ministry in terms of budget and personnel, Gaimusho clearly lacks all the prerequisites that make up a powerful ministry in Japan. As one sogo shosha manager put it: 'Gaimusho is there to make nice words to foreigners'.[31]

All foreign embassies in case of commercial problems formally are supposed to report to Gaimusho only. In reality they will contact directly the respective desk officer at MITI and for politeness sake will inform Gaimusho about it. Compared to other ministries Gaimusho officials have relatively little influence on the Foreign Minister's or the Prime Minister's decisions on important high politics foreign policy issues. These often listen to other sources of information and advice and may decide against Gaimusho's recommendations. Its direct influence on the LDP or the Diet is also smaller than for example those of MITI or MOF. Bitter fights with MITI on interministry jurisdictional and policy matters have in addition weakened Gaimusho's position.[32]

While routine decisions are made in bureaucratic channels, high level issues are decided politically (e.g. the normalisation of relations with PRCh, the recognition of the PLO). Most of the 'EC issues' certainly fall into the routine category — since all foreign non-OPEC representatives, dignitaries and delegations visiting Japan complain about Japan's trade surplus and express their desire for stepped up Japanese imports, for Japanese capital, OAD and know-how. On the ministerial level they are all assured that the matter will be studied and one will try to do one's best to resolve the issue. When Giscard during the Tokyo summit 1979 asked Ohira for tax concessions for French cognac imports, this not only angered the Commission and fellow Europeans but also amazed the Japanese. The issue was clearly considered a routine matter, which should not be dealt with at the top level. After Ohira had uttered some reassuring noises, the matter went straight down to the First West Europe Division (which is in charge of France) in MFA's European and Oceanic Affairs Bureau. The head of the division put one of his junior officials in charge of the matter. This desk officer then drafted a mutually acceptable document in co-operation with two colleagues from MOF and MITI. Then the formal ringi-sei procedure for circulating the draft started. Such routine decisions are usually approved at division chief level. Bureau chiefs (or rather their deputy chiefs) intervene actively only in case of severe inter-divisional or inter-bureau disagreements. In rare cases the Permanent Vice-Minister, the most senior career official, settles the issue. The political heads never intervene.

In 1970 22.5 per cent of MFA's officials had passed the Higher Foreign Service Examination which is the key for speedier promotions. Those who do not pass cannot be promoted above the position of a deputy division head.[33] Obviously this division of people who otherwise do the same work creates considerable tensions and resentments. Apart from this, Fukui believes, there are no strong cliques or ideological disputes among MFA people who work in a pleasant, conformist and non-competitive atmosphere.[34] While theoretically officials accept the official view that politicians decide and bureaucrats implement, in reality they resent the incompetence, ignorance and corruption of politicians.

There was a strong orientation favouring the alliance with the US and 'high priority' given to democratic countries of Western Europe among MFA officials, who at the same time — during interviews 1971—73 — displayed distrust towards the PRCh and the USSR.[35] Assignments to west of Burma (West Asia, Middle East, Africa) are strongly disliked, while those to the larger Western developed nations enjoy highest prestige. Yet among younger Gaimusho officials there is a gradual change towards pro-Asian and pro-Chinese attitudes and towards a more sceptical assessment of the US.[36] Among the geographical bureaus each division cultivates sympathies towards its assigned country or world region. The same emotional effects usually happen in the careers of Japanese diplomats during their first overseas assignments. Only the rotation scheme of Gaimusho's generalist training can prevent serious biases. Among the MFA officials who occupied top positions in the late 1970s those who started their careers in the 1940s in the German group with assignments in Berlin until 1945 were Yoshino, former Deputy Vice-Minister for Foreign Affairs,[37] and Ushiba, former External Economic Affairs Minister.[38] The next generation of MFA top officials is likely to have started in the post-war American group. It should be kept in mind, however, that on routine decisions the middle echelon division and deputy division heads are more important. On very sensitive and controversial issues the permanent vice-minister, one or two bureau heads, and some counsellors and division heads form an ad hoc group. However, both the vice-minister and the bureau chiefs have extremely limited time preventing them from familiarising themselves with the details.[39] There is only one formal horizontal liaison within MFA: an executive council (Kanbukai), attended by the Permanent Vice-Minister, the Deputy Vice-Ministers for Foreign Affairs and for Administration and the latter's assistant. It is however not clear what this Council does.[40]

There is also a parliamentary vice-minister, who is frequently a senior LDP backbencher enjoying the fruits of decades of loyalty for a year prior to retirement. As in all other ministries he is nicknamed a walking tape recorder. His sole business is to read prepared statements to parliamentary questions in the Diet.

Diplomats on assignment abroad are not involved in decision making; their main function is to gather information. But when involved in negotiations with a foreign party the ambassador and his senior staff are quite influential.[41] Like most foreign ministries, Gaimusho is criticised by academics for the neglect of long term planning and for the pursuit of isolated interests in a piecemeal fashion. To counter these criticisms in 1971 a Planning Section has been established within the Research Division. As a potential critic it is viewed with dislike by other departments[42] and so its policy impact can be expected to remain quite marginal.

The Ministry of International Trade and Industry (MITI)

MITI employs 10,900 officials and ranks second in the hierarchy of Japan's ministries. During the 1960s when international interest in the working of Japan's economic miracle awakened, MITI quickly acquired a notorious image for its pursuit of protectionist import and expansionist export policies. Its potential for administrative guidance added to its alleged role as the conspiratory centre of Japan Inc. Today MITI is far from being a monolithic fortress, the front line between free traders and the few remaining protectionists runs straight through MITI along bureau lines: the international bureaus acting as allies of foreign importers, the domestic industries' bureaus resisting when it is felt necessary and following their clienteles' protectionist interests.[43]

The most powerful among MITI's bureaus is the Industrial Policy Bureau which is in charge of industrial policies, such as restructuring, economic planning goals and the reform of the distribution system. The head of this bureau holds the second highest administrative position within MITI, junior only to the Vice-Minister, to whose position he traditionally succeeds.[44] The International Trade Policy Bureau is headed by a second Deputy Vice-Minister and deals with the general co-ordination of planning and the enforcement of trade policies, the negotiation and implementation of trade agreements such as the Tokyo Round, and with OAD policies. It is made up of the following divisions: the General Affairs Division, the Americas—Oceania Division, the West Europe—Africa—Middle East Division, the South East Asia—East Europe Division, the North Asia Division and the International Trade Research Division. There are four more divisions working on international economic affairs and on development assistance policies.[45] The more concrete aspects of import—export policies are handled by the International Trade Administration Bureau, which works on trade promotion, emergency import programmes, export insurance, export control and guidance etc. The Industrial Location and Environmental Protection Bureau was set up in 1973 when the lack of regional planning and environmental destruction became a major public concern. The Basic Industries Bureau, which looks after iron, steel, non-ferrous metal and chemicals production, and had been well known in its advocation of growth policies in the 1960s, lost these functions in the same year.[46] The Machinery and Information Industries Bureau handles engineering, data-processing, electronics, aircraft and car production. The Consumer Goods Industries Bureau, finally, is in charge of textile, fibre, paper, pulp and household goods production and it further deals with the housing and recreation industries.[47]

MITI's minister has traditionally been one of the LDP's bigwigs, such as Sato, Tanaka, Miki, Komoto and Nakasone. This often proved to be a disillusioning honour for the ministry's officials. As one former MITI official, Ito put it:[48] 'We kept getting these people who did not know the first thing about economic problems. . . . the will to work and the theoretical basis of work is lost when you work under people who speak nonsense.'

There are three types of regular meetings within MITI: on the highest level, the administrative Vice-Minister meets with his bureau chiefs once a week. They talk on matters of general importance such as the budget and new laws. They do not however ordinarily handle concrete issues.[49] The minister rarely attends but is kept informed through his Vice-Minister, who knows the political wishes of his minister. Twice a week the division chiefs confer in each bureau, and so do the staffs of each division. In general, vertical co-ordination is well developed while the horizontal links appear poorly institutionalised.

In MITI as in all other ministries there is a regular annual cycle: from June to August each year policies for the next fiscal year (starting on 1 April) are prepared. The budget proposal then is presented to MOF in August; in negotiations with MOF the draft budget is settled by December. By March the decisions concerning planned revisions of laws have been finalised. When things are planned so carefully, they appear as inflexible: 'as a rule, if something is not in the budget by August, it must wait one more year'.[50] It came as a considerable shock to Japan's bureaucrats when in spring 1980 the opposition parties for the first time ever imposed last minute changes on the budget during Diet deliberations.

MITI has close relations with its fellow economic ministries EPA, MOF, MAFF, and with MFA. On important issues, then, high level liaison meetings may take place on demand. Twice weekly, the administrative Vice-Ministers of each ministry meet to discuss new laws, important law revisions and policy changes.[51]

The Ministry of Agriculture, Forestry and Fisheries (MAFF)

MAFF is in general charge of promoting the welfare and economic basis of its rural clientele. Because of the ruling LDP's dependency on rural votes and its need for organisational backing from the agricultural co-operatives, the political power base of MAFF is considerable: 70 to 80 LDP Diet members regularly endorse the views of Zenno, the National Federation of Agricultural Co-operatives.[52] The rural lobby within the LDP maintains a powerful Overall Agricultural Policy Research Council, headed by a former MAFF vice-minister who also wields great political clout within the ministry.[53] This political influence and the strategic importance assigned to autarchy in basic food production keep Japan's agriculture alive and well. Due to its small-sized lots and the adversity of nature, Japanese agriculture is the developed world's most inefficient, pushing Japanese food prices about threefold above world market levels. These exorbitant price levels with their handsome profit expectations naturally attract food exporters, particularly from the US, Australia, New Zealand, Argentina and the EC. On beef imports notorious scandals have developed: a 'meat mafia' of MAFF officials and LDP politicians share large bribes in exchange for exclusive quotas allocated to certain importers.[54] While accepting that there are legitimate reasons for subsidising Japan's disadvantaged agriculture to a certain degree, pressure from food exporting nations led MITI and MFA to lobby for more liberalised agricultural import regulations in order to protect Japan's industrial exports. MAFF responded by setting up a vice-ministership for general affairs devoted to negotiations with foreign countries. In addition MAFF's Economic Affairs Bureau handled the agricultural issues in Japan's delegation at the Tokyo Round. Japanese concessions in this sector therefore remained minimal.

The Ministry of Transport (MOT)

MOT controls shipbuilding, ports, railways, aviation, airports, tourism and road safety. Two of its bureaus are of significance to international negotiations. The Ships' Bureau which supervises Japan's shipbuilding industries participates in the OECD sponsored talks on reductions in world surplus construction facilities. The Road Transport Bureau, in rivalry with MITI, which is in charge of automobile production, carved out its competence for car safety and pollution control. Its testing requirements and application procedures were rightly felt as an NTB by foreign car importers. Their removal proved a difficult procedure as 'three special characteristics of MOT are: (1) an obsession with the vertically-divided administration system which has very few horizontal interrelationships, (2) a need for a huge number of permission and authorisation rights, and (3) high susceptibility to political pressures'.[55] The immediate source of power which bureaucracies possess is their capacity to grant approvals or to refuse them. ' . . . MOT boasts the largest number of such permission and approval rights of all the Japanese government ministries and agencies'.[56] Its officials, even by Japanese standards, are noted for their bureaucratic rigidity and adherence to petty details. At the same time MOT has been involved in an endless string of corruption affairs since the post-war years, culminating in the Lockheed scandal in 1976. Demands for inner reforms were building up to alter the ways of what in Japan is called the second rate ministry.[57]

The Ministry of Finance (MOF)

MOF as elite of the elite enjoys most power and prestige among Japanese ministries. Its basic function is public finance: to collect taxes and to redistribute them in the annual national budget. The priorities set up in the budget reflect important policy decisions. Therefore, the post of MOF's Budget Bureau director is considered as the most important among all ministries' bureau directorships. Apart from taxes and budgets, supervision of banking activities and monetary policies are MOF responsibilities. International monetary relations are managed by the International Finance Bureau; it watches over speculation on the foreign exchange markets deciding about possible interventions there, and handles the co-ordination with other major currency countries. MOF's Customs and Tariffs Bureau handles Japan's customs system and is represented on these matters in Geneva's MTN.[58]

The responsibilities of MOF are widely reflected in its political influence and recruitment patterns. Even if one is well advised to be hesitant in distributing elite attributes on the grounds of simply passing competitive examinations and to working in prestigious organisations, still as one observer put it: 'the typical MOF bureaucrat tends to be very highly educated, quick thinking, and highly aggressive. He is also adept in handling people, and . . . tends to be a very strong drinker'.[59] Small wonder, that after their retirement in their early fifties, MOF officials are in high demand for careers as banking executives or in politics and enjoy excellent prospects up to even the Prime Minister's position. The higher a retiring official ranked in MOF the better are usually his career prospects in his second professional life. The exceptional 'amakudari' positions of former MOF people further enhance the ministry's influence on Japan's political and financial institutions. MOF also maintains intimate ties with the Japanese media, is known to embark upon subtle media campaigns and is often successful in winning over editors in order to gain public support for certain policy objectives.[60]

The Prime Minister and the Prime Minister's Office (PMO)

PMO is in charge of intragovernmental co-ordination, of distributing decorations, of the government pension system and the compilation of national social indicators. The co-ordination task is handled by the Prime Minister's Secretariat. Its ability to do so is seriously marred by both the shortage of funds and personnel. The Secretariat has only 422 workers (0.09 per cent of all government employees) so the most it can do for interministerial co-ordination is to gather representatives from other ministries and agencies and hold conferences.[61] The PMO's efforts to enlarge the Secretariat's co-ordination potential so far appear to bestalled by the concerted resistance of all its fellow ministries. The Prime Minister's role is itself shaped by the fact that in spite of continued one-party rule he is the leader of an uneasy coalition of warring factions: he 'seems to perceive his role as one of establishing accommodation among the differing views of the various leaders and agencies concerned in order to secure their maximum support, rather than the assertion of his own priorities'.[62]

The search for compromise and consensus evidently takes time; fast and assertive US-style foreign policy changes are therefore unthinkable in Japan. In addition, the Prime Minister does not have his own foreign policy staff which could help him in circumventing Gaimusho's or MITI's bureaucracy with more expertise. Tsurutani claims that ' . . . his ability to evaluate, modify or reject the policy recommendations from the Foreign Ministry is critically limited, if not entirely nonexistent'.[63] This appears as exaggerated particularly on such high politics issues on which other ministries, the media, LDP factions, the opposition parties and the business community have already forwarded their views. Although Gaimusho's position in this concert is certainly not the strongest, it is at the same time correct that the Japanese Prime Minister's ability to conduct foreign policies is far more limited and the bureaucracies' influence stronger than it would be in presidential systems of the US or the

French type.

The political parties and the Diet

The Diet is the stage for the approval of treaties and the discussion of foreign policy issues. Yet most observers consider the Diet's influence as secondary, with an impact at most on public opinion. Baerwald claims that the Foreign Affairs Section of the LDP's Policy Research Council actually decides the foreign policy position which the LDP will finally endorse in the Diet.[64] Among the opposition parties the respective party headquarters are assumed to decide on the vote of their Dietmen on foreign policy issues.[65] The influence of party headquarters is certainly stronger among Communist and Komeito deputies while LDP, JSP and DSP are too split on ideological and—or personal lines to make this assumption plausible. The Diet's Foreign Affairs Committee exercises only marginal influence: its power base is small, its members are party or faction controlled and hardly possess any foreign policy expertise. There are also no informal ties to the Gaimusho.[66] In any case, significant foreign policy initiatives do not emerge from the Diet. A Japanese diplomat, Hanabusa, when asked, could cite only one example of such an initiative: a protectionist bill against silk imports.[67] When a new policy issue crops up, politicians usually watch how the argument goes on in the media, among the general public what steps organised groups and lobbies take and then jump on the bandwagon.[68]

Since 1976, Wakaizumi observed a growing consensus among Japanese parties towards middle of the road foreign policy positions: JCP and JSP reduced their public fervour for the abrogation of the Security Treaty, while Komeito and DSP came a long way in accepting the existence of the Japanese armed forces, thus enabling consensus on foreign policy issues in a possible middle parties coalition.[69]

The business community and the sogo shosha

One of the myths of Japan Inc. is the notion of monolithic business interests. But there are even a few powerful business leaders who oppose the LDP's rule, others who want more government expenditure for social infrastructure etc.[70] Still, there are mainstream business policies that can be identified with at least the first two of the following three groups: (a) *zaikai*, the leaders of the major economic organisations and big business conglomerates; (b) *gyokai*, representing specific industrial interests, such as steel, electricity, banking etc.; and (c) *kigyo*, the policy stands and interests of individual companies.[71] Because of this diversity most business associations, such as Keidanren, contribute financially for continued LDP reign without being able to issue specific demands. During intra-LDP squabbles zaikai intervenes to settle these factional disputes which are harmful to its political interests.

In a case study, Ogata investigated business influence on Japan's decision to normalise relations with China. While as gyokai, the fertilizer and steel industries showed the greatest interest to secure a share in the Chinese market via normalisation, the intensity of pluralism and diversity of attitudes and interests and tactical manoeuvring among Japanese companies caught in their Peking–Taipeh dilemma paralysed any effective common initiative. A decision came about only through external events: China's opening after the cultural revolution and the sudden US de facto recognition of the PRCh created faits accomplis which the Japanese business community accepted with some relief.[72]

On more low key and less controversial issues Keidanren, the foreign policy representative of Japan's business, is usually able to work out a consensus and to present policy recommendations to the government. In 1968 there were 26 standing committees within Keidanren to work out such consensus-based recommendations. The decision to adopt a certain position or to return the proposal to the committee lies with Keidanren's president and his eight vice-presidents. Approved papers are transmitted to government agencies and to the press. Evidently prior to such visible steps intensive consultation with higher level ministry officials has already taken place. A retired former MFA official for instance serves as full-time liaison officer to the Gaimusho for Keidanren. Keidanren's international activities are co-ordinated by its International Economic Affairs Department. Policy questions on certain issues are handled by standing committees − e.g. one on Internationalisation Promotion.[73] A unique feature in Japan's conduct of foreign relations is the extensive use of private economic diplomacy. Businessmen in semi-official missions conduct usually informal and exploratory talks with foreign parties abroad and report their impressions and results back to both the Gaimusho and Keidanren. Private economic diplomacy may take the form of economic missions, of roving ambassadorships, and may take place in joint bi- or multilateral economic committees or in international economic conferences. After consultations with the major business organisations the Gaimusho appoints the business leader of the mission. He selects his fellow mission members who must be acceptable to both the business community and the government. Upon return from their mission a final report is issued with policy recommendations.

Private economic diplomacy is welcomed by the Gaimusho: it helps to widen domestic consensus and to gain more domestic support for certain foreign policy positions.[74] Thus it was only after a Keidanren study mission to Europe in autumn 1976 led by its president Doko, that Japanese business and the public suddenly became aware of the severity of European criticism against Japan's trade expansion in Europe.

In Japan, the most powerful vested interests in liberalised trade and stable international trade relations are represented by the general trading companies, and their top nine in particular, the sogo shosha. Handling about 50 per cent of Japan's exports and 60 per cent of her imports they are in a strategic position in a country with vital import dependencies on foodstuff and raw materials. The sogo shosha are linked with the zaibatsu successor conglomerate groups (keiretsu), handling most of their groups' domestic and international supply and marketing needs. Usually they are one of the keiretsu's major companies. Via the intra-keiretsu 'old boy network' and through regular presidential conferences (e.g. named kinyokai — Friday conference — at Mitsubishi) business strategies can be co-ordinated.[75] Evidently the same channels can be employed to synchronise trade policy views. Four times annually the top 14 sogo shoshas' presidents meet as the Trading Companies' Presidents' Club (Boeki Shosha Kai), which Eli believes, has decisive influence on Japan's foreign trade and domestic economic policies.[76] According to the situation further ad hoc meetings are arranged and formal policy recommendations issued for the government. Though formally and sometimes actually fierce competitors, twice per month the directors (bucho) of these sogo shosha meet to decide upon more concrete measures of co-operation.[77]

As formal governmental advisory council on foreign trade and investment issues the Japan Foreign Trade Council (Nihon Boeki Kai) is most influential. As the German Chamber of Commerce in Tokyo observed: '. . . it is only natural that the work of the JFTC is largely determined by the sogo shosha'.[78]

The conduct of Japan's foreign policies

Basic orientations of Japanese foreign policy

Official declarations on the goals and priorities of Japan's foreign policies appear usually as pretty empty and well sounding statements: to bring about the lowering of international tensions, to maintain international peace while furthering Japan's foreign economic and security interests at the same time. The truth of the matter is, that these propagandist idealisations are actually not far from the mark. When Halliday and McCormack tried to prove contemporary imperialist Japanese policies,[79] they could present plenty of data on Japan's foreign investments being concentrated on South East Asia — typically exploiting its raw material wealth and cheap labour there — but were unable to give evidence of one single instance of Japan's businesses or government influencing their alleged client states' policies beyond bribery on limited individual projects. Rather the Japanese and their economic activities serve as an excellent scapegoat and rallying motive for the nationalist appeals of the area's autocratic rulers.

There are several external and internal restraints on Japan's foreign policies preventing any imperialist grand design — or any well planned long term foreign policy for that matter:

1 The *war experience* in which Japan's military might and her imperialist pan-Asian ambition suffered a lethal defeat. Today a strong and highly emotional pacifism is part of the 'consensus' political culture in Japan: 'Japan ranked consistently the most pacifist of all nations included in world poll studies'.[80]

2 The US imposition of a *peace constitution,* which explicitly forbids the maintenance of armed forces, which however has been interpreted since 1951 (when the Self Defence Forces were established) as merely forbidding overseas engagement of Japanese troops and limited Japan's defence spending to 0.9 per cent of the GNP.

3 Consequently strong dependency on the US nuclear 'umbrella' as deterrent against possible threats from Japan's northern superpower neighbour. A result was the 1951 *Security Treaty* with the US, which basically stipulates US military guarantees for Japan in exchange for Japan conceding military bases to the US. This facilitated US operations during the Korean and the Vietnamese wars.

4 *Geo-strategic military deficiencies:* the vulnerable nature of the Japanese islands: literally all population, industry, traffic and communication lines are concentrated on small, densely populated coastal plains stretching from Tokyo down to Kyushu which appear as entirely indefensible against any major air or naval attack. Japan's essential supply lines are similarly vulnerable, their most vulnerable spots, the Malacca Straits and the Straits of Hormuz being far outside the reach of any Far Eastern middle power's military potential.

5 *Domestic constraints* are not only posed through the vertical divisions in Japan's foreign policy bureaucracy but also by the hostile jealousies in Japan's ruling coalition. When taking controversial foreign policy stands two prime ministers, Hatoyama and Kishi, were overthrown by their own party rivals, after, at least in Kishi's case, popular uproar had indicated a massive erosion of consensus.

These restraints correspond to a more positive description of Japan's foreign policy aims: in the absence of an imperial grand design a multitude of various usually short- and middle term security and economic interests dominate.

Security interests are pursued:
- in the alliance with the US which takes priority over eventually conflicting interests,
- in co-operative and friendly policies towards the PRCh (culminating in the friendship treaty of November 1978),
- in policies of distance and cautious detente with the USSR with which territorial and fishery disputes are kept at low profile level,
- in distributing OAD, joint venture projects and good will missions among those countries whose raw material supplies are essential for the survival of Japan's economy,
- in shy and so far unsuccessful attempts to somehow acquire the role of a honest broker in the Korean and the various Indochinese conflicts.

Economic interests: to secure raw material supplies and outlets for manufactured exports. It was from this perspective that Japan conducted most of her post-war relations with Europe. A favourite contemporary Japanese scheme, the Pacific Basin Community, a free-trade area comprising all major non-oil raw material suppliers to Japan: Australia (iron ore, coal, wool and meat), Indonesia (oil, timber), the Philippines (timber, copper), Thailand (rubber) as well the Asian NICs, Hong Kong, Singapore, Korea and possibly Taiwan as workshops with cheap labour for Japan's export industries, and the Pacific nations of the Americas, is suspected of serving purely Japanese economic interests in the first place.

Besides economic and security interests Langdon lists international recognition as a third Japanese foreign policy goal in the sixties.[81] With Japan's full-fledged and sometimes leading membership in all global international organisations and major international negotiations, such as GATT, OECD, UN, UNCTAD, the Western summits etc., this desire seems to have been satisfied in the seventies at least as far as official policies are concerned. As the only non-Western industrialised nation Japan's public opinion still perceives itself as the odd man out and reacts strongly to any form of foreign criticism (hence the disproportionate amount of publicity to foreign complaints against Japanese exporters in the Japanese media) and all forms of alleged economic, cultural or racist discrimination. Persistent US pressures and Chinese suggestions for stronger Japanese rearmament have reinforced domestic pressures particularly from the depressed steel, aviation and shipbuilding sectors on the Japanese government to increase defence spending to counter the build-up of the Soviet Far Eastern fleet. With the long term implication that strong rearmament would include the military again in Japan's consensus decision making process — from which they had been eliminated in 1945 — the Japanese government has hitherto appeared extremely reluctant to increase military spending by massive margins. On both the

1979—80 Iranian and Afghanistan crises Japanese and European interests were identical in their pursuit of moderation and detente vis à vis
US policies and in spring 1980 led to the rare spectacle of Euro-Japanese
high politics co-operation (or rather: Japan, after consultations, following European policies).

Case studies on foreign policy decisions in Japan

There are quite a few excellent analyses of Japanese foreign policy decisions during certain crisis situations which required significant changes
of policies — situations for which Japan's slow working decision ma chin-
inery is particularly inept. Hellmann[82] analysed Japanese decisions during the 1956 peace negotiations with the Soviet Union. Juster[83] examined Japanese policy responses during the 1974 oil crisis. Duncan[84] described the US—Japanese automobile dispute 1967—71, and Destler,
Fukui and Sato[85] analysed both US and Japanese decisions and negotiating interactions during the textile wrangle 1969—71. Kimura[86] examined the Soviet and Japanese negotiating behaviour during the 1977 fisheries' talks.

On the Soviet peace treaty as a high politics issue the Prime Minister
was negotiating in Moscow, thus inviting the neglected Gaimusho's obstruction which resented his amateurish negotiating style,[87] which put
emphasis on establishing personal trust, focussing rather on personal relations than on issues, a typical domestic Japanese technique for conflict resolution. On the planned peace treaty there had not been any debate either in public or in the Diet and neither were the business community and the ministry officials in charge duly consulted.[88] Hatoyama's
departure from prior consensus-building fuelled renewed factional infights which harmed the Prime Minister's negotiating stand. He was soon
absorbed in the ensuing domestic power struggle (in which he was later
defeated), leading to a paralysed 'immobilisme' in Japanese bargaining
which prevented positive stands, swift decisions, clear-cut policies or
flexible changes to use sudden advantages.[89] Japan, consequently, did
not succeed in obtaining any significant Soviet concessions.

In 1973 Japan was surprised by the threat of an Arab oil boycott and
was forced to abandon her hitherto neutralist Middle East policies (she
used to vote for both pro-Israel and for pro-Arab resolutions in the UN).
At the time the ministries' Middle East sections and the Japanese embassies in the area were neglected and understaffed, leading to serious information deficiencies and initial surprises at the event, the timing and
the extent of both the oil boycott and the subsequent price rises.[90]

When in November 1973 the oil cutbacks continued, panic started in
Japan fearing a national economic collapse. The Gaimusho with its powerful American Affairs Bureau usually taking a pro-US line was confused

and temporarily paralysed. Its then recently organised Middle East Division was able to mobilise and with a proposal for a pro-Arab shift tried to take control of the issue. MITI with its International Trade Policy Bureau and the National Resource and Energy Agency initially was only interested in maintaining good relations with the international oil companies, who then supplied Japan with 80 per cent of her oil needs. At the peak of the crisis in mid-November 1973 MFA was clearly split in pro-US versus pro-Arab factions, while MITI following its oil procurement interests gradually shifted towards a pro-Arab stand.[91]

The media dramatised the oil crisis as a major issue, and business spokesmen became involved, usually taking pro-Arab positions. Those with strong US ties fearing for Japan's image and the Jewish lobby there demanded more neutralist stands.[92] When the panic mounted LDP faction leaders intervened, with Ohira, then foreign minister, supporting a pro-US stance, and Nakasone, then MITI minister, taking pro-Arab positions. While the cabinet argued, Mizune, the president of Arabian Oil Co. returned from the Middle East. Fearing the nationalisation of his company he as the man of the moment possessed information urgently needed in Japan and having top Saudi messages in hand he personally delivered them to all LDP leaders and to Keidanren, the latter subscribing to his pro-Arab views. The media and even the Tokyo police fearing riots due to the oil shortage supported the policy shift. Finally Ohira gave in and in fully accepting OPEC demands Japan as a 'friendly nation' was resupplied with oil.[93]

In retrospect the oil supply to Japan (due to increased Indonesian and Nigerian deliveries) had never been seriously disrupted. By January 1974 the situation normalised and pro-US bureaucrats regained some of their previous policies – e.g. Japanese participation in the planned oil consumers conference. The issue became de-politicised: media coverage and politicians' interventions declined and the bureaucrats influence returned.

As the most evident deficiency in Japanese crisis management, Juster noted the lack of appropriate information available to the Japanese ministries and the political establishment: to assess the mutual extent of the cutbacks they had to rely fully on the data supplied by Mitsui, Mitsubishi and the US State Department.[94]

In the 1977 Japanese—Soviet fisheries talks, Kimura found culturally-conditioned factors on both sides unnecessarily prolonging and complicating the negotiations.[95] The Soviets had extended their maritime borders to 200 miles, thus claiming sovereignity over Japanese fishing grounds in formerly international waters north of Japan. The issue was complicated by Japan's continued claim on the four Southern Kurile islands annexed in 1945 by the Soviet Union. The Soviets more or less took the fisheries issue to offer fishing concessions in exchange for Japan's acceptance of their sovereignty over these islands. The attempt to split Japan's position failed, not even Hokkaido's fishing lobby nor the JCP were ready to trade fish for the islands. Instead, Japan's negotiators, Foreign Minister Sonoda, and Suzuki (MAFF), later Prime Minister, asked for Soviet concessions both on the islands and on the fish. They followed a purely cognitive approach. Since Japan had good reasons to have them both, the Soviets as the larger and stronger country should concede them, provided Japan in open talks created trust and explained her situation properly. Their cultural prejudice against tactics led the Japanese to neglect offers for trade-offs, manoeuvring, and bargaining and manipulative tactics.[96]

The conflict with the Nixon administration on Japanese textile imports (1969—71) was, by contrast, a low politics issue which due to mishandling and hardened positions on both sides spilled over, leading to a serious deterioration in US—Japanese relations. Implementing a campaign pledge to the Southern textile industry, Nixon had pressed the Japanese for a severe voluntary curtailment of their textile exports to the US. The Japanese resisted strongly both the rationale and the extent of the US demands. After long drawn out negotiations two years later, and after bitter mutual recriminations, the Japanese finally gave in. Earlier, Sato in highly personal encounters with Kissinger and Nixon had twice pledged commitments which he later had to retract. In the tension of the situation he had given concessions without having achieved the necessary prior consensus at home in Japan.

The textile wrangle in retrospect appears as a prelude to the 'Nixon shocks' later in 1971, in which US—Japanese relations reached their all-time low. The subsequent decline of Japan's textile production, due to more competitive NIC textile exports, underlined the textile wrangle as an unnecessary and wasteful exercise [97] in which all participants lost, particularly on the Japanese side.

In evaluating their case study Destler et al.[98] concluded that:

1 The predominance of domestic economic interests on both sides led two national textile industries to take irreconcilable stands and thus enabled them to exercise a strong vetoing power over their governments. For more than two years low politics proved stronger than high politics.
2 On the Japanese side bureaucratic interests and frictions led to in-fights frequently of greater intensity than those with the US. Entrenched bureaucratic influence allowed the parochial hawkish positions to assume a national policy role.
3 There were severe deficiencies in the US perception of Japan's domestic political structure: the limited power of the Prime Minister and of Japanese politicians, the greater strength of Japanese minis-

tries compared to US departments. Lengthy Japanese domestic consensus seeking was seen as a delaying tactic. Finally, there was Sato's repeated carelessness during the summits, which could have been avoided if the US had been less pushy and more aware of the noncommittal goodwill function such high level talks usually have in Japan.

Japanese international negotiating style

From an analysis of selected Japanese international negotiations 1895–1941 Blaker concluded: 'Japan had its own peculiar negotiating style that appeared repeatedly over an extended time span under widely varying historical circumstances'.[99] Such negotiating behaviour usually reflects traditional ways of interaction, of doing business, and is governed by culturally defined norms which determine the appropriate bargaining style, behaviour, strategies, evaluations and finally results and implementation.

Japanese negotiators in the tactically important pre-bargaining stages spend their energies on obtaining a unified Japanese position instead of learning the opponent's position or entering into an effective dialogue with him: 'Japanese leaders and negotiators were so preoccupied with their own demands that they hardly comprehended or appreciated opposing positions'.[100]

Japanese negotiators then adopted strictly defensive strategies: avoiding open confrontations, reducing risks, trying to prevent foreign criticism in public, displaying a desire to elicit early commitments from the other side and to limit the range of topics to be discussed.[101] The other side's concessions should come first to allow Japanese counterconcessions without losing face. At international conferences Japanese diplomats yearned for middle of the road stands, allowing a mediator role.[102]

Whenever they felt that Japanese positions were perceived as too hard by their opponents Japanese negotiators resorted to indecision and vagueness in statements.[103] During negotiations clear policies or instructions were usually missing on at least some questions. There were few officially authorised concessions, and seldom was the technique of artificially inflated demands used.

Japanese negotiators were told that if the foreign party would only understand Japan's just demands it simply would have to concede. Consequently these negotiators were advised to use persuasive approaches: to explain fully and have only a few fall-back positions for concessions.[104]

In the last bargaining stages, when most bargaining options are exhausted and external pressures mount for a conclusion, Japan had usually committed herself already at an earlier stage of the negotiations, which precluded the option of threatening to break them off: Japan then took a last ditch stand, resorted to direct personal appeals and to threats and warnings.[105]

Trying to please everybody Japanese diplomats are told to endorse frequently contradictory positions: to take both pro-Arab and pro-Israel stands in the UN, LDP leaders voicing pro-Taiwanese and pro-PRCh sympathies, ministers declaring solidarity with the Third World and a little later with the developed OECD world, and finally embarking upon policies benefiting Japan's economic interests only. The revocation of concessions and commitments given while on visits abroad is not limited to official policies. When a JSP high level delegation during a visit to Peking endorsed an anti-hegemonist stand, upon return to Tokyo after considerable factional strife with the pro-Moscow faction they reinterpreted their statements given in Peking.[106]

In order to explain Japanese difficulties in negotiating encounters Kinhide contrasts two concepts: 'erabu culture' versus 'awase culture'.[107] 'Erabu' is the Japanese verb for to choose and implies analytical, discriminatory and decisionary approaches. 'Awaseru' means to combine and refers to synthesising, dilatory and harmonising approaches. 'Erabu' consequently represents the dispositions to act upon one's environment according to an analytically structured plan which implies the task of selecting the optimal alternative out of a range of dichotomies. 'Awase', by contrast, implies adjustment to an environment which is perceived not in dichotomies, but in gradual changes and shifts to which one should adapt. It reflects vague and inconclusive thinking but also allows flexibility and openness to the social environment. Awase is an expression of 'amae', a key element in Japan's culture, implying the need to be liked by the relevant others and to depend and presume upon another's benevolence and to grant unyielding loyalty in return.[108]

As negotiating strategy *erabu* is characterised by: (a) clear-cut definitions of items, (b) 'down to business' approaches, (c) viewing treaties as 'final choice' and (d) seeking general principles applicable to cases. Thus erabu is clearly the ideal—typical Western way of handling business or conducting international negotiations.

By contrast *awase* means: (a) a vague notion of issues, (b) a preoccupation with establishing good personal relations, (c) 'do ut des' principles, (d) treaties are non-binding: they are just one manifestation, among others, of a relationship, and can be cancelled if disadvantageous to one side, (e) the essence of a treaty may be inexplicit and only informally conferred, and (f) case by case approaches, avoiding all generalisations.

Traditionally Japanese diplomacy had employed 'awase' concepts — e.g. a willing submission under US tutelage in the post-war years. In the meantime Japan's economic and political potential has outgrown this concept's international applicability and so Japan ought to turn to 'erabu' ways of thinking to handle her international role properly, Kinhide concludes.[109] Cultural preferences certainly are not the sole explanatory factor in international negotiations; they may however explain variance in negotiating behaviour and increase awareness of possibly differing universes of meaning in such tense intercultural encounters.

Conclusion

In conclusion, there are three major factors to be considered when analysing Japanese foreign policies:

1 Difficulties and antagonisms in *decision making,* due to her complex, consensus-oriented, passive coalitions within and among business, bureaucracy and ruling party. This leads to: low politics predominance, the lack of consistent foreign policy designs and pursuits, and inflexibility and unresponsiveness in international negotiations.

2 *Structural factors,* namely: economic and military vulnerability, inhibiting Japan from performing a more active international role.

3 *Cognitive factors:*
   (a)   In the post-war years Japan learned to perceive the world as 'given conditions' and enjoyed a risk-free 'small power mentality'.[110]
   (b)   Japan has problems perceiving her international environment properly, there often are information deficiencies in her decision-making system (usually at the top), and international crises are seen out of proportion.
   (c)   Japan's partners abroad maintain serious misperceptions of Japan's policies and negotiating behaviour: dilatory policy responses needed to allow for domestic consensus are taken as deliberate delay and create resentment. Then Japan's pragmatic and compromising adaptation to the situation creates the mistaken impression that her capacities for adjustment are limitless. This not only invites further foreign pressure but also ignores the creation of deep-seated resentment in Japan.[111]

Interacting politically with Japan requires special talents: to be able to handle Japan with empathy and at the same time recognising that she does not react to the grand designs which in Western tradition are used in attempts to cut the Gordian knots in bilateral and global relations.

Following most analyses of Japan's international role, wise 'Japan-politik' would have to treat her like an ally without obligations and would require the granting of concessions without reciprocation. That this world of unselfish free-ride offers is an illusion, the Japanese should have realised in their diverse overseas 'problems'.

Still, the subsequent chapters on her relations with Europe provide ample evidence of scope for more learning and on the need for change in the structures for foreign policy decisions at both ends of the Eurasian continent.

References

1 Brzezinski, Zbigniew. *The Fragile Blossom.* New York: Harper & Row. 1972, p. 112.
2 Pickert, Perry L. The Foreign Policy of Japan Inc. *Japan Quarterly 21,* 1974, 79—86, p. 79.
3 Yanaga, Chitoshi. *Big Business in Japanese Politics.* New Haven: Yale University Press. 1968, p. 14.
4 Ibid., p. 27.
5 Kaplan, Eugene J. *Japan : The Government-Business Relationship.* Washington, D.C.: U.S. Department of Commerce. 1972, p. 26.
6 Yanaga, 1968. Op. cit., p. 32.
7 Clark, Gregory. 'Japan Unincorporated' Actually is a Better Name. *Japan Economic Journal,* 6.2.1979.
8 Curtis, Gerald L. Big Business and Political Influence. In: Ezra F. Vogel (ed.). *Modern Japanese Organisation and Decision Making.* Tokyo: Tuttle Co. 1979, 33—70, p. 33.
9 Ibid., p. 39.
10 Patrick, Hugh and Henry Rosovsky. Japan's Economic Performance: An Overview. In: Hugh Patrick and Henry Rosovsky (eds.) *Asia's New Giant.* Washington D.C.: The Brookings Institution. 1976, 1—61, p. 51.
11 Vogel, Ezra F. Introduction: Toward More Accurate Concepts. In: Vogel (ed.). 1977. Op. cit., p. xvi.
12 Watanabe, Akio. Foreign Policy Making, Japanese Style. *International Affairs 54,* 1978, 75—88, p. 80.
13 Ibid., p. 88.
14 Yanaga. 1968. Op cit., p. 95.
15 Craig, Albert M. Functional and Dysfunctional Aspects of Government Bureaucracy. In: Vogel (ed.). 1979, 3—32, p. 13.
16 Yanaga. 1968. Op. cit., p. 74.
17 Trezise, Philip E. and Yukio Suzuki. Politics, Government and Economic Growth in Japan. In: Patrick/Rosovsky (eds.). 1976. Op. cit., 753—811, p. 763.
18 Ibid.
19 Ibid., p. 770.

20 Japan's Top Business Organizations. *Japan Economic Journal*, 15.11.1977.
21 Trezise/Suzuki. 1976. Op. cit., p. 770.
22 *The Economist*, 18.6.1977.
23 Bronte, Stephen. Insights into Japan's 'Elite of the Elite'. *Japan Times*, 29.2.1980.
24 *Japan Economic Journal*, 15.11.1977.
25 Kaplan. 1972. Op. cit., p. 50.
26 Ibid., p. 52.
27 Pempel, T.J. Japan's Foreign Economic Policy: The Domestic Bases for International Behaviour. In: Peter Katzenstein (ed.). *Between Power and Plenty: Foreign Economic Policies of Advanced Industrial States*. 1978, 139–90, p. 183.
28 Eto, Shinichi. Foreign Policy Formation in Japan. *Japan Interpreter 10*, 1976, 251–66, p. 252.
29 Tsuchiyo, Hideo. Ministry of Foreign Affairs. *Japan Economic Journal*, 22.8.1978.
30 *Organization of the Government of Japan*. Administrative Management Agency. Prime Minister's Office. Tokyo. 1978, p. 63.
31 Interview.
32 Fukui, Haruhiro. Policy Making in the Japanese Foreign Ministry. In: Robert A. Scalapino (ed.). *The Foreign Policy of Modern Japan*. Berkeley: University of California Press. 1977, 3–35, p. 4.
33 Ibid., p. 20.
34 Kaplan. 1972. Op. cit., p. 23.
35 Fukui. 1977. Op. cit., p. 27.
36 Ibid.
37 Man in the News: Bonruku Yoshino. *The Oriental Economist,45*, October 1977.
38 Man in the News: Nobuhiko Ushiba. *The Oriental Economist,46*, January 1978.
39 Fukui. 1977. Op. cit., p. 11.
40 Nagai, Yonosuke. Social Attitudes and Foreign Policies During the 1970s. In: Japan Center for International Exchange (ed.). *The Silent Power — Japan's Identity and World Role*. Tokyo: Simul Press. 1976, 99–118, p. 113.
41 Fukui. 1977. Op. cit., p. 14.
42 Nagai. 1976. Op. cit., p. 113.
43 Johnson, Chalmers. MITI and Japanese International Economic Policy. In: Scalapino (ed.). 1977. Op. cit., 227–79, p. 261.
44 Oneda, Nobuo. Ministry of International Trade and Industry. *Japan Economic Journal*, 1.8.1978.
45 Organization of the Government of Japan. 1978. Op. cit., p. 84.

46 *The Economist,* 28.7.1973.
47 Organization of the Government of Japan. 1978. Op. cit., p. 86.
48 Ojimi, Yoshihisa. A Government Ministry: The Case of the Ministry of International Trade and Industry (and: 'Discussion'). In: Vogel (ed.). 1979. Op. cit., 101–12, p. 106.
49 Ibid., p. 102.
50 Ibid., p. 104.
51 Ibid., p. 109.
52 Fukui, Haruhiro. The Japanese Farmer and Politics. In: Isaiah Frank (ed.). *The Japanese Economy in International Perspective.* Baltimore: Johns Hopkins University Press. 1975, 134–67, p. 157.
53 Koike, Hirotsugu. Ministry of Agriculture, Forestry and Fisheries. *Japan Economic Journal* 3.9.1978.
54 *The Economist,* 18.6.1977.
55 Yamada, Yoshio. Ministry of Transport. *Japan Economic Journal,* 10.10.1978.
56 Yamada. 1978. Loc. cit.
57 Ibid.
58 Moroboshi, Ryuzo. Ministry of Finance. *Japan Economic Journal,* 11.7.1978.
59 Bronte. 1980. Loc. cit.
60 Hanabusa, Masamichi. Japanese Foreign Economic Policy Decision Making. Lecture at LSE, 17.5.1979.
61 Kanzaki, Masuo. Prime Minister's Office. *Japan Economic Journal,* 26.9.1978.
62 Hosoya, Chihiro. Characteristics of the Foreign Policy Decision Making System in Japan. *World Politics 26,* 1974, 353–69, p. 369.
63 Tsurutani, Taketsugu. The Causes of Paralysis. *Foreign Policy* No. 14, 1974, 126–41, p. 138.
64 Baerwald, Hans H. The Diet and Foreign Policy. In: Scalapino (ed.). 1977. Op. cit., 37–54, p. 48.
65 Ibid., p. 53.
66 Hellmann, Donald C. *Japanese Foreign Policy and Domestic Politics.* Berkeley: University of California Press. 1969, p. 143.
67 Hanabusa. 1979. Loc. cit.
68 Ibid.
69 Wakaizumi, Kai. Consensus in Japan. *Foreign Policy* No. 27, 1977, 158–77, p. 167.
70 Cooper, Gary M. *Would You care to Comment on That, Sir? A Look at Fifty of Japan's Top Businessmen.* Tokyo: The Japan Economic Journal. 1976.
71 Ogata, Sadako. The Business Community and Japanese Foreign Policy. In: Scalapino (ed.). 1977. Op. cit., 175–203, p. 177.

72 Ibid., p. 203.
73 Bryant, William E. *Japanese Private Economic Diplomacy: An Analysis of Business—Government Linkages.* New York: Praeger Publishers. 1975, p. 21.
74 Ibid., p. 2.
75 *Far Eastern Economic Review,* 1.2.1980.
76 Eli, Max. Die Bedeutung der Generalhandelshäuser für die Wirtschaft Japans. In: Heide und Udo Simonis (eds.). *Japan: Wirtschaftswachstum und soziale Wohlfahrt.* Frankfurt/M.: Herder & Herder. 1974. 123—42, p. 124.
77 Ibid., p. 127.
78 Portrait: Tatsuzo Mizukami. *Markt Deutschland—Japan* (Tokyo), No. 12, 1979, p. 15.
79 Halliday, Jon and Gavan McCormack. *Japanese Imperialism Today.* Harmondsworth, Mddx.: Penguin. 1975.
80 Mendel, Douglas H. Jr. *The Japanese People and Foreign Policy.* Berkeley: University of California Press. 1961, p. 103.
81 Langdon, F.C. *Japan's Foreign Policy.* Vancouver: University of British Columbia Press. 1973, p. 191.
82 Hellmann. 1969. Op. cit.
83 Juster, Kenneth I. Foreign Policy Making During the Oil Crisis. *Japan Interpreter 11,* 1977, 293—312.
84 Duncan, William Ch. *US—Japan Automobile Diplomacy.* Cambridge, MA: Ballinger Pub. 1973.
85 Destler, I.M., Haruhiro Fukui and Hideo Sato. *The Textile Wrangle — Conflict in Japanese—American Relations.* Ithaca: Cornell University Press. 1979.
86 Kimura, Hiroshi. Soviet and Japanese Negotiating Behavior: The Spring 1977 Fisheries Talks. *Orbis 24,* 1980, 43-67.
87 Hellmann. 1969. Op. cit., p. 140.
88 Ibid., p. 150.
89 Ibid., p. 157.
90 Juster. 1977. Op. cit., p. 298.
91 Ibid., p. 300.
92 Ibid., p. 301.
93 Ibid., p. 304.
94 Ibid., p. 300.
95 Kimura. 1980. Op. cit., p. 46.
96 Ibid., p. 52.
97 Destler e.a. 1979. Op. cit., p. 317.
98 Ibid., p. 319.
99 Blaker, Michael. *Japan's International Negotiating Style.* New York: Columbia University Press. 1977. p. x.
100 Ibid., p. 40.

101 Ibid., p. 157.
102 Ibid., p. 165.
103 Ibid., p. 167.
104 Ibid., p. 168.
105 Ibid., p. 198.
106 Yamamoto, Mitsuru. An Erosion of Neutralism. In: Japan Center for International Exchange (ed.). 1976. Op. cit., 141—63, p. 154.
107 Kinhide, Mashakoji. The Cultural Premises of Japanese Diplomacy. In: Japan Center for International Exchange (ed.). 1976. Op. cit., 35—49, p. 35.
108 Ibid., p. 49.
109 Ibid., p. 48.
110 Hanabusa, Masamichi. Japan: Problems of Adjustment. *The World Today 34,* 1978, 210—19, p. 210.
111 Ibid., p. 211.

PART II

The empirical development in bilateral relations
and trade policies

4 Euro–Japanese relations 1950–68: the prelude to the common commercial policy and the gradual emancipation of Japan

The theoretical interest in the 1950–68 period

I attempted to analyse the economic diplomacy of the fifties and sixties for three major reasons:

1 It was then that the legal framework for the present state of EC–Japan relations was laid (i.e. the lack of a common EC–Japan trade agreement, the annual renewal of bilateral national agreements, the continued use of discriminatory European restrictions on Japanese imports – most notably the Italian quota on cars).

2 It was a period which served both as a bureaucratic precedent as well as socialising experience for the senior officials and politicians involved in the later diplomatic intercourse. Ohira, Japan's Prime Minister 1978–80 had already toured Europe in the early sixties as Foreign Minister dealing with bilateral economic relations.[1] In the fifties the later Foreign Economic Affairs Minister, Ushiba, negotiated as the head of MFA's Economic Affairs Bureau on trade agreements (TAs) with Western European nations.[2] Mr Ernst, the EC's first ambassador to Tokyo in 1978 was decorated for 20 years of uninterrupted professional concern with Euro–Japanese relations.[3] On a more abstract level we can expect that significant patterns for communication and decision making were laid down at the time.

3 There are the economic consequences as well: they result from the failure of European diplomacy to speed up the opening of the Japanese market at a time when economic conditions in Japan were

more suitable for penetration. When this liberalisation belatedly took place, European business continued to neglect marketing chances and avoided setting up sales networks in an expanding market with significant prospects for rapid increases in purchasing power.

In any case the EC's response to the early Japanese challenge — and the Japanese strategies for emancipation in the international economic order — serve as the first historical case study on the problems arising from the emergence of a newly industrialised country. It should indicate both the extent of resulting conflicts in bilateral trade and the patterns in the attempts to resolve such conflicts. The wide range of actual policy responses among similarly structured countries (namely the former four EEC customs units and the UK) will prove that all of these responses were affected by a plurality of factors. This would actually indicate that a fairly wide range of, largely unused, rational policy choices had been available to decision makers.

This leads us to the main variables to be examined: first there are *structural variables* that affect Euro—Japanese relations. There was the situation of a new international competitor emerging to which Europe had to formulate a response. Under Cold War conditions the Western world was dominated by superpower-clientele relations. The US, fearing Japan's neutralist trends, occasionally intervened in her favour in Europe. Economic conditions in Europe also have to be considered, by comparing the structural conditions for French and Italian protectionist trade policies with those of Germany and the Benelux which followed a liberal line. It should also be asked which structural factors brought about Japan's diplomatic offensive 1954—64.

On a more operational level *variables of decision making* will have to be examined on both sides: who was able to define the 'national interest' vis à vis Japan? To what extent could limited sectoral interests (producers of ceramics, textiles, toys and sewing machines) dominate national decision making? Why did all attempts at Commission co-ordinated policies towards Japan fail? Finally, we will have to trace the factors leading to the politicisation of EC—Japan relations on the Japanese side, and to their bureaucratisation on the Western side.

This leads us to the more *incidental variables* of the negotiating situation. There the European and the Japanese strategies met. In this context the negotiations themselves, the significance of the issues at stake and the political 'input' will be considered.

These variables will help in assessing the consequences of the first twenty years of post-war Euro—Japanese relations, the European failure to bargain effectively for a timely opening of the Japanese market, and later the Western delayed and inconsistent recognition of the Japanese challenge.

84

The chronology of Euro—Japanese post-war relations

The 1950s prior to the creation of the EEC

In the beginning there were not many Japanese involved: US occupation officers were negotiating on their behalf annual trade and payments agreements with the European countries. These agreements contained balanced narrow contingents allowing for annual trade volumes ranging from $7m (with the Netherlands, 1951) to $40m (with France, 1948, including colonies).[4] After the conclusion of the San Francisco Peace Treaty in September 1951 Japan regained her sovereignty in matters of economic diplomacy. Most European nations then resumed diplomatic relations with Japan. Japan deprived of her pre-war colonies (Korea, Taiwan and Manchuria) after 1945, during the Korean War (June 1950—July 1953) could earn the foreign exchange needed to meet her import requirements for food, raw materials and machinery for economic reconstruction largely through the US military's offshore procurements. With the decline of the Korean War boom Japan soon felt the need, in view of her import dependencies, for unrestricted export opportunities. Her foreign exchange reserves fell from $1,140m (1952) to $790m (April 1954).[5]

The need for enlarged export outlets prompted Japan's GATT membership application. This application from its very submission in 1951 received strong US support for political reasons: increased trade by Japan with the West (substituting for the lost Chinese market) was supposed to strengthen the anti-Communist forces in East Asia and to cure Japan's chronic payments crisis. The US State Department expected that the worsening security situation in Indochina and South East Asia would eventually help overcome Britain's and most Commonwealth countries' opposition to Japan's membership.[6]

The strongest centre of opposition was the European textile industry. Particularly active were the British, the Dutch, French and German textile industry associations.[7] Other industries which also in earlier bilateral trade negotiations had already opposed concessions to Japanese imports joined: the producers of sewing machines, of food conserves and of ceramics. They do not seem to have encountered difficulties in convincing their national governments of their plight: memories of Japan dumping 'watches by kilograms' on depressed world markets in the 1930s were still vivid. The flooding of the US market after its opening to Japanese textile exports and the French cotton textile industries' loss of hitherto captive colonial markets in Indochina and Morocco reinforced this fear. As a result the Dutch government demanded Japanese guarantees not to invade their cotton market.[8] Britain, France, Australia and South Africa refused to enter into tariff negotiations with Japan which were preparatory to her GATT membership.[9] *The Times* finally felt compelled to characterise UK's role as leader of the anti-Japanese faction in Geneva as behaving like 'the nigger in the woodpile': using petty and obsolete trade complaints the British government yielded to pressure from Lancashire.[10]

The US now engaged in frantic horse trading offering tariff concessions to the US market to those countries willing to grant most favoured nation (MFN) treatment to Japan.[11] In April 1955 a UK White Paper on Japan's GATT membership predicted an Anglo—Japanese trade war as the result of MFN relation and proposed the conclusion of a bilateral long term Treaty of Commerce and Navigation (TCN) instead.[12] Although no longer opposing Japan's GATT membership in principle Britain had decided to invoke GATT's Art. 35 withholding MFN treatment from Japan.[13] When an increasing number of other GATT members appeared to follow the British example, those countries willing to open their markets to Japan became afraid of becoming the sole and therefore concentrated outlet of a desperate Japanese export drive. In June 1955, the German Federation of Industries (BDI) called for emergency safeguard instruments against Japanese imports.[14]

In early June 1955 after four-months bargaining the tariff negotiations with Japan finally came to a conclusion. A protocol then was opened: Japan would become a GATT member once two-thirds of the member states had signed it.[15] Two months later in August 1955 this quorum was more than filled: 30 countries had signed, but in doing so Britain, South Africa, Australia, Belgium and the Netherlands had invoked Art. 35 GATT, withholding most favoured nation (MFN) treatment from Japan. France reserved her position, but later invoked Art. 35 as well.[16] Among significant trading nations only the US, Canada, Germany, Italy and the Scandinavian countries granted MFN status to Japan.

The German government declared it was aware that it had taken a risk, but Japan's international integration appeared unavoidable and GATT's anti-dumping procedures sufficiently strict against the possible abuse of its liberal rules.[17] Erhard, Minister of Economics 1949—63 and a strong advocate of free trade, had earlier promised the Japanese that Germany would facilitate Japanese imports.[18] The German ambassador to Japan, Kroll, publicly supported Japan's claim.[19] He had an exceptional influence on Germany's foreign policies. Adenauer had earlier told him to design the outlines of German's hitherto non-existing Japanpolitik.[20] Kroll reasoned that under Cold War conditions Germany had a vital interest in a strong, economically healthy and socially pacified Japan. Though of no immediate use to German's reunification policy Japan would constitute a second front to the Eastern bloc. Therefore 90 million Japanese should be granted the export outlet they needed to substitute for the 'lebensraum' they had lost after the war.[21] Now a period of nearly 10 years of intensive Japanese diplomatic efforts began, not only to persuade those European nations who had invoked Art.35 to drop it but also to convince those countries (including Germany) who had already agreed to grant MFN treatment to actually implement it.

Talks to enlarge Italian quotas on Japanese imports went on after 1954. On 18 October 1955 both sides could agree on a protocol regulating trade for one year.[22] In March 1957 another round of talks failed: hitherto 85 per cent of all Italian exports to Japan had consisted of rice, now the Japanese had switched to US rice which was offered at more competitive prices. In turn Italy refused liberalising concessions and started playing for time when it became evident how afraid the Japanese were of the impeding formation of the EC with its CET as the arithmetical average of the member states' tariffs.[23] But even after the EC's creation, trade talks continued to be posponed sine die. Japan insisted on being given MFN treatment, Italy refused in stating that Japan's wage levels were too low to be granted the desired equal treatment with OEEC countries.[24] In September 1960 Italy was still restricting more than 600 Japanese import items. Bilateral trade continued to stagnate around $40m per annum. A GATT general assembly in 1959 had asked Italy to end its discriminatory treatment of Japanese imports. The Italian Ministry of Foreign Affairs then was reportedly willing to do so, but a veto by its fellow ministries blocked this intention.[25]

After Germany had also granted formal MFN treatment to Japan, German lobbyists started intensifying their efforts to obtain exceptions: the Bavarian ceramics industry claimed that 45,000 jobs in the depressed North Bavarian border area were endangered. The Federal Textile Association and the toy producers voiced similar concerns against the expected flooding of the German market.[26] When by December 1955 Germany seemed to delay the MFN implementation the Japanese government complained that despite her GATT membership Japan was still excluded from the 'inner circle of world trade'.[27] In May 1956 after the negotiation of a new trade protocol Germany conceded the liberalisation of 80 per cent of Japan's bilateral imports on MFN basis. Such key Japanese export items as textiles, porcelain, ceramics, sewing machines and buttons however remained subjected to quotas.[28] In January 1957 Japan in a surprising move abrogated the 1951 trade agreement (TA) with Germany which she felt was obsolete due to her GATT membership.[29] Soon infights were reported in Bonn's bureaucracy between a hard line advocating the need for residual quotas and a soft line stressing Japan's need to balance her trade deficit.[30] Ambassador Kroll continued to press for a sustained opening of the German market. He later claimed to have matched German and Japanese producers with agreements on 'prices, markets and product divisions'.[31] But BDI continued to oppose any unilateral and isolated opening of the German market to Japanese products.[32] A break of two years followed the TA's abrogation. Then in July 1959 new negotiations finally got under way. The 14th GATT General Meeting in May 1959 had renewed its call on Germany to liberalise textiles, binoculars, pottery, porcelain and toy imports, all products of eminent interest to Japan.[33] Germany in these talks insisted on Japanese self-restraint assurances, on guarantees against the pirating of German designs and on Japanese quota concessions on optics and chemical imports.[34]

In August 1959 Prime Minister Kishi devoted his visit to Bonn exclusively to trade issues, pleading for German import liberalisation. Japan saw Germany as a test case: if a liberal Germany would refuse it against Japan, then all the rest of Europe would block as well.[35] The CDU press service and the Foreign Office in November 1959 put the talks with Japan in a different context: they were to be seen as a model for talks with other low price countries, such as India and Pakistan.[36] In November 1959 the German delegation after four-months negotiations returned from Tokyo without agreement. They were not sure that Japan could keep her self-restraint promises given the great number of Japanese small-scale sundry producers and the unresolved problem of re-exports via third countries.[37] Germany also insisted that the planned TA should have only a transitional character since a final solution on low price country imports could only be found within an EC framework.[38]

A second round of talks was held in Bonn in January and February 1960. Upon returning to Tokyo Japan's negotiator Ushiba announced that Germany was ready to liberalise in spite of sustained opposition of the textile and chinaware industry.[39] France — fearing re-exports via Germany — argued against a German liberalisation.[40] Japan was ready to concede a five year transition period for this liberalisation, and the sole bone of contention remaining concerned Japan's insistence on voluntary export restraints in case of market disturbances, while Germany preferred import control instruments.[41]

Adenauer's visit to Japan in April 1960 settled this issue in Japan's favour. After his return from Tokyo he made a statement supporting the liberalisation of Japanese imports.[42] Publicly however he spoke only on political issues, denouncing the Soviet Union which in turn condemned his visit as the creation of a new Bonn—Tokyo axis. The Japanese leadership listened sympathetically to his anti-communist tirades, but was more interested in textiles.[43] In Adenauer's four-volume memoirs only one line alludes to his trip to Japan: a casual remark on the need to think beyond the smallness of Europe, to consider the territorial masses of America and the human masses of Asia.[44] On 28 May 1960 the negotiations were concluded, and on 1 July 1960 the TA signed. Five years after Japan's accession to GATT Germany was the first European nation to grant full MFN treatment to Japan: it agreed to liberalise all Japanese imports until January 1965 with a gradual enlargement of annual quotas until then. Only a limited number of textile and ceramics' types should remain restricted.[45]

In respect to the Benelux countries in the immediate years following Japan's GATT entry business went on as usual: in annual trade negotiations quotas for restricted Japanese light industry items were gradually enlarged, and with a $105m volume of annual trade (1960) Benelux, after Germany, was Japan's second most important partner in the EC.[46]

Belgium which hitherto had treated Japanese imports in a fairly liberal fashion, in October 1958 decided that more harmonisation with her fellow European countries was desirable prior to the creation of the EC and restricted textiles, porcelain and sewing machines among 24 items which up to then had been free.[47] Due to Belgium's invocation of Art. 35 (GATT) Japan could neither protest nor ask for compensation. One year later, in October 1959, preliminary trade talks began at the Ministry of Economics in Den Haag in order to prepare for a collective Benelux agreement with Japan replacing the bilateral ones. The Gaimusho was not very optimistic at the outset: it feared Benelux would maintain Art. 35 and continue to keep textile and sundry goods under tight quotas.[48] This fear was reinforced when Belgium introduced a licensing system on all Japanese imports as the Dutch already practised it.[49]

When in May 1960 actual talks on a TA started, US pressure to drop Art. 35 increased and Germany's intention to liberalise became evident. Two months later, on 16 July 1960, a three-year Benelux–Japan TA was signed. Benelux had agreed to grant de facto MFN treatment to Japan and to disinvoke Art. 35 on a provisional basis in exchange for a safeguard clause (SC) of equally limited duration. This SC stipulated bilateral consultations in case of market disruptions caused by imports from the other side. If no restraining action would be taken within reasonable time by the exporting country, the importing country would be entitled to restrict the imports deemed harmful – with compensating rights for the country whose exports are being limited. Twenty-eight Japanese items continued to be the object of import quotas (mostly textiles, porcelain, tableware), subject to annual review.[50]

In France industries continued to press for protection, mainly because they were afraid of Japanese competition in their colonial markets. This proved useless since Japanese products, particularly cotton textiles, were smuggled into French Africa anyway.[51] Disagreement also developed on French exports. While Japan was interested in Alsatian potash, in nickel from New Caledonia and in Moroccan phosphates, France wanted to sell perfumes, wines and cars.[52] Trade talks tended to break down rather than come to conclusions. The French Foreign Ministry's promise to grant MFN treatment to Japan by autumn 1959 remained unfulfilled and Japanese imports continued to be restricted by tight quotas.[53] Germany's and the Benelux liberalisation did not impress the French much. In April 1961 renewed TA talks broke down due to France's refusal to ease her restrictions.[54] In a background article *Le Monde* described France as more protectionist towards Japan than vice versa. The result was the neglect of the Japanese market by French industries who in their defensive attitude left it to German and British exporters.[55] French protectionism employed three instruments vis à vis Japan: (a) Art. 35, (b) a maximum tariff — three times the ordinary rates — and (c) applied rigid quotas.

The creation of the European Communities

It was in the context of continued discrimination in Europe — either legally via Art. 35 or in violation of GATT standards by Germany and Italy — that Japan perceived the conclusion of the Treaty of Rome in 1957. The planned CET would amount to more than 20 per cent on Japan's manufactured exports, namely cotton and silk fabrics, canned goods and toys. Japan therefore felt a $180m export market threatened. Unaffected by the effective tariff rise would only be non-processed exports with limited growth prospects, such as raw silk, copper, animal fat and cultured pearls.[56] All harmonisation of this exclusionist trading club would inevitably lead to the least desirable common denominator, namely uniform restrictions against outside competition or at least to a postponement of all hopes for a European liberalisation.[57] Increased European competitiveness as a result of European integration and the development of economies of scale was seen as a threat to Japanese exports to third markets, particularly to her traditional outlets in South East Asia.[58]

The Japanese perception of threats arising from the EC's creation was enhanced by signs that US patience with the flood of Japanese textiles and ceramics was wearing thin and by the intense feeling of vulnerability for her own economy which suffered from chronic capital shortage, from trade and payments' deficits and which had to accommodate a work force expanding at the rate of one million per annum. The Japanese thought that the bicycle theory was valid for their economy: once expansion stopped it would collapse. With respect to the EC the Japanese media fuelled a near hysteria: WW II had started with trading blocs, Japan should appeal to the world.[59] In April 1957 the latter happened, though in less dramatic terms. Supported by India, Japan called for a GATT General Conference to discuss the creation of the EC, because it felt that both the planned CET with its discriminatory effects on Japanese exports as well as the planned colonial preferences were incompatible with GATT rules.[60]

After the Treaty of Rome had become effective on 1 January 1959, the Japanese assessments appear more realist. As a short term effect the CET as the arithmetical average of the high tariffs of France and Italy and of the low tariffs of Germany and Benelux, which took more than 70 per cent of Japan's exports to the EC, would result in a net tariff increase for Japan. Still, for her typically low priced products the effects of an increased ad valorem tariff would be relatively small. In the long run, there was agreement, an integrated and prosperous Europe with increased purchasing power would serve Japan's economic interests. The African possessions of France and Belgium which would be covered by discriminatory preferences, were of marginal importance for Japan's exports and due to their backwardness were likely to remain so. More worrisome was the EC's competition on third markets, with nearly 40 per cent of Japan's exports going to South East Asia, and what was seen as a general proliferation of trade blocs with the Outer Seven (EFTA) and the Latin American Free Trade Area (LAFTA) coming into being. Still, the EC's transition period would give Japan the chance to adjust, to work harder and to produce more efficiently, to intensify her economic diplomacy and to revise her protectionist import structure in order to enable Japanese industries to withstand international competition.[61]

The latter point led to considerable discussion in the Japanese government. Under the current five year Plan for Economic Autonomy which had been drafted and started in 1955 explicit policies had been adopted to protect Japan's infant industries and to reduce foreign currency spending.[62] In March 1959 MOF decided in principle to agree to the gradual liberalisation of imports, to remove restrictions on overseas travel and to allow foreign firms to remit their profits to their home offices.[63]

Germany, in April 1959, called on its fellow EC countries to set up common import quotas on Japanese textiles.[64] As a result, in May 1959, the Commission and Coreper decided to establish a 'Working Group Art. 115' to examine trade relations with Japan, the effects of Japanese imports in intra-EC trade and the situation of textile industries in respect to imports from low wage countries.[65] The effectiveness of the policy co-ordination by this working group must be rated as poor. Less than twelve months after its establishment Germany and Benelux on the one hand, and France and Italy on the other, vigorously embarked on opposite import policies. Japan however as usual took things in Europe at their face value and was scared, especially when Germany, during ongoing trade talks, refused liberalising concessions with reference to her EC relations.[66]

At the 15th GATT General Meeting Japan took the EC and Art. 35 issues up again. This meeting was held in Tokyo not without purpose: the Japanese government wanted to convince the delegates that Japan was no longer a low wage country.[67] However persuasive this may have been, the US, in the person of Undersecretary of State Dillon, and Canada actively supported Japan's opposition to the Art. 35 invokers. Both were getting impatient at bearing alone the brunt of Japanese exports.[68] Japan was not spared either: she was criticised for being globally more protectionist than the fourteen Art. 35 nations towards her. This was no longer warranted by the balance of payments situation which had been positive since 1957.[69]

The early 1960s

For Japan the events and news from the diplomatic front in Europe during 1960 continued to appear contradictory and sometimes irritating. Trade however developed splendidly: the labour shortage in booming Western Europe resulted in brisk import demand. Supported by substantial removals of restrictions in Germany, Benelux and Britain, Japanese exports to Europe were up 50 per cent in 1960.[70]

In April 1960 France had tried to initiate a joint defence against low priced textile imports. French lobbyists were quoted as arguing: 'If cheap textile imports are permitted, then the deficit in France's "textile account" will rise to $3.820m in 1975' (sic).[71]

The Japanese were pleased at German plans to accelerate the implementation of the customs union and to reduce the planned CET rates.[72] At the same time the EC considered the introduction of a mixed tariff system which would have allowed it to impose tariffs on the basis of price, weight or quantity or to impose charges to achieve a certain minimum price.[73] It would then be certain that Japanese imports would be hit severely. They hitherto due to their low price levels had been able to escape adverse effects of high ad valorem tariffs.

In May—July 1960 Benelux and Germany granted de facto MFN treatment to Japan, and the UK though still insisting on Art. 35 joined the liberalisation drive after bilateral trade talks were concluded by mid-July 1960.[74] By then the Japanese government had different worries. It was soon overthrown by rivalling factions in the ruling party following the popular uprising against the renewal of the US—Japan Security Treaty in June 1960. The Kishi cabinet was succeeded by the Ikeda cabinet. Many Japanese at the time in searching for potential allies on a neutralist course steering between the two bitterly resented superpowers were looking to Europe, where by political potential and prospects the EC appeared to offer promising features.

During 1961 Japanese efforts focussed on France and Italy to have their restrictions removed. The spring round of Franco—Japanese negotiations turned out to end in failure. The expiring protocol then was simply extended for another six months with only slightly increased quotas.[75] During these negotiations French officials more or less admitted that France's position was in contradiction with her commitments in GATT and IMF. Observers noted that the French position, which still bowed to stiff industry pressure was bound to change in due course of time.[76] France's neighbours had liberalised, and Japan's bilateral trade deficit grew dramatically: Japan actually bought more than twice as much from France than France allowed her to sell in return.[77] After six months talks in the subsequent negotiation round in January 1962 a new annual TA was signed. It allowed 50 Japanese products, among them electronics, whose imports hitherto had been entirely banned, as quotas to the French markets. The TA enlarged the existing quotas, especially those on cotton, and the total of French restrictions was lowered to 125 items. An earlier French offer had been more generous, but was withdrawn after encountering the resistance of the Roubaix—Tourcoing wool industry.[78] France continued to maintain Art. 35. This compelled Japan to postpone the liberalisation of 172 items mainly originating from Europe.[79]

Italy under GATT pressure and in perennial on-and-off talks continued to cut down its 600-odd restriction list. In January 1961 the Italian government announced the liberalisation of 120 items,[80] and in July 1961 of another 90 items when Japan's Foreign Minister Kosoka visited Rome during his European tour.[81] Kosoka in principle agreed to the draft of a bilateral TA proposed by his Italian counterpart Segui, which contained a very gradual reduction of Italian restrictions down to the level of Germany. To everybody's surprise, during the subsequent negotiations in November 1961 the Japanese delegation suddenly demanded a complete Italian liberalisation until 31 March 1962, which predictably led to the collapse of the talks. The Italians suspected that the Japanese change of mind was motivated by the expectation of concluding soon a more favourable commercial treaty with the UK (the TCN), and that, based on this precedent, the Japanese planned to negotiate a more advantageous deal.[82]

Japan herself was under IMF pressure to speed up the liberalisation programme which she had announced in June 1960, namely to achieve a 90 per cent liberalisation (measured as share of total imports in 1959) by mid-1963.[83] In November 1961 Japan agreed to accelerate this programme and to implement the 90 per cent pledge by October 1962.[84] A Federation of British Industries paper however noted that planned Japanese tariff increases and intended new NTBs might cancel out these liberalisations.[85]

As the first EC Commissioner ever, Jean Rey in December 1961 went to Tokyo. The Japanese government considered his visit of utmost importance and identified him as the equivalent of a foreign minister.[86] He was received with an imperial audience and had lengthy talks with

Prime Minister Ikeda and Foreign Minister Kosoka.[87] Ikeda asked Rey for EC support for Japan's ensuing diplomatic campaign to obtain admission to OECD.[88] Kosoka stressed Japan's wish to shift emphasis from trade with the US, with which Japan's exports with a share of 30 per cent of their total had reached saturation point, to trade with Europe. He assured Rey that since Japan had adopted orderly marketing policies European markets would not be disturbed. The Commission should therefore abstain from its plans to introduce mixed tariffs (as they were being put into operation on sewing machines) and use its influence to grant MFN treatment towards Japan.[89] Rey's replies were reported as opposing Art. 35 invocations as well ('not up to date').[90] He promised that since the internal development of the EC went smoothly, from now on the Commission would concentrate on international relations.[91] To Keidanren leaders he predicted the 'United States of Europe' at a date which has passed long since. Still, Rey conceded that in the transition period the Commission had 'no full authority to make independent decisions on foreign trade matters'.[92] In a joint communique Rey and Kosoka both agreed to hold regular information meetings of which the first was to take place in Brussels in spring 1962.[93] These meetings however never materialised since the Six chose not to confirm their self-appointed foreign minister's invitation.

The Treaty of Commerce and Navigation between Britain and Japan

The Japanese interest in M. Rey's visit was heightened by the prospect of UK joining the EC, a prospect which appeared likely after July 1961. Japan was torn between fears and hope. It feared that the United Kingdom might postpone their already five-year old negotiations on the TCN until after the British entry into the EC. This would considerably reduce Japan's hope of ever getting MFN treatment either from the UK, her most important export market in Europe, or from any other of the EC nations.[94] MITI expected international competition to increase with Britain's entry,[95] and Japan's shipbuilders called for government assistance to survive the merger of four of the world's most capable shipbuilding nations.[96]

On the other hand, Japan looked forward to the prospect of Commonwealth countries being left outside and hoped then to substitute for Britain as a customer for Australian—New Zealandian raw material and food supplies and in return to gain access to a lucrative export market.[97] Radio Australia fuelled this hope by threatening if Australia did not get associate EC status it would then intensify trade with Asia and grant preferential treatment to its new prospective partners.[98]

As a tactical consequence the Japanese government declared that they

94

would 'go all out' to conclude the planned TCN — which evidently would imply MFN status — before the UK joined the EC: this fait accompli would then swing the EC's attitudes favourably towards Japan.[99] Kosoka tried to stress the urgency of Japan's TCN request in conversations with UK's Foreign Secretary, Lord Home, when touring Europe in July 1961.[100]

As was already evident in the failure of the Italo–Japanese negotiations in November 1961, Britain became the focal point of Japan's ensuing diplomatic offensive. The UK was seen as a sympathetic, understanding country, with favourable liberal trading interests, with which among European nations, Japan maintained the most significant cultural exchanges and with which positive historical links (the Anglo–Japanese Alliance 1902–23) could be rekindled. British business's views as represented in FBI's paper *A Look at Japan* offered an open-minded assessment of Japan's trading policies and growing market potential.[101] A 40 per cent rise in British exports to Japan in 1961 confirmed the view that the revoking of Art. 35 was appropriate. Sir Norman Kipping, FBI's Director General wrote that Art. 35 'is central to Japan's attitude to trade with countries that invoke it and has acquired a political and symbolic significance far outweighing its actual practical effect'.[102] He therefore supported the British government's intention to allow MFN treatment combined with a system of safeguards. Rather than sticking to a protectionist attitude the government should take care that Japan did not annul her liberalisation programme with increased tariffs.

The respected London papers advocated the opening of the British market, including *The Times* and *The Economist*, whose Norman MacRae in his famous survey 'Consider Japan' in September 1962 wrote hitherto unheard news: 'They could beat us competitively in a much wider field of industry than most people in Britain begin to imagine', and : 'British economy has lessons to learn from Japan, not the other way round',[103] by pointing in particular to superior Japanese education levels, Japanese reinvestment rates and effective industrial restructuring (from light to heavy industries), observations which at the time put him in the position of a prophet in the desert.

For his part the Japanese Prime Minister, Ikeda, placed a high value on closer relations with Europe. Aware that his predecessor, Kishi, had failed in overconcentrating on relations with the US, his guiding image of the international system was that of the 'three-pillar theory' which allotted vital world roles to the US, the EC and, of course, Japan.[104]

To be credible to the Japanese public he had to present visible symbols of Japan's emancipation in the Western club. The joys of being member of GATT were still spoiled by Art.35, which had become a major media and public concern in Japan — reinforced by the experience that any LDC after acquiring independence would invoke Art. 35 as well and drop it only after agreeable Japanese concessions in terms of OAD had been made.[105] MFN by European nations therefore had acquired the symbolic value described by the FBI paper, the other status symbol being membership in the OECD, which on 1 January 1961 had been formed by the former OEEC countries and Canada and the US.

In February 1962 talks on the TCN were resumed. Disagreement was still on the safeguard mechanism and the negative list: Britain had drafted a lengthy list, including textiles, toys and radios on which it wanted import controls to be maintained. Japan insisted on a shorter list and agreed only to a safeguard clause (SC) — limited to five years — substituting Art. 35 with GATT arbitration in case of disputes. UK wanted a renewable SC with bilateral proceedings only.[106] In April 1962 the President of the Board of Trade, Erroll, came to Tokyo to insert some political perspective into the talks. His main concern was Japanese export subsidies on whose abolition he made British liberalisation conditional. The Board of Trade objected to Japan's artifically low rates of interest for export financing and the high remissions of domestic taxes on export profits.[107] His Japanese partners assured Erroll that the tax remission rule would expire in March 1964 and would not be renewed thereafter.

In July—August 1962 another round of negotiations took place, again focussing on the negative list and on the SC. Problems also arose from an 'EEC clause': Britain wanted the TCN to expire by the time it joined the Common Market in order to act unrestricted by bilateral commercial agreements when the CCP would be drafted. But Japan by the very rationale of her diplomatic offensive insisted on guarantees against the abrogation of the treaty in case of UK's EC entry.[108]

On the concession of a safeguard clause (SC) the Japanese bureaucracy remained sharply divided. While MFA favoured it as indispensable for a compromise solution, MITI and MOF were bitterly opposed: once an SC is established, they reasoned, it would never be given up.[109]

Ikeda had planned his trip to Europe for November 1962, touring most capitals to unfreeze stalling bilateral trade talks and to solicit support for Japan's OECD application. Since talks with Britain were most advanced and the Japanese electorate in the forthcoming April 1963 election had to be presented with some foreign policy success in the light of the 'three pillars', Ikeda's desire to sign the TCN overruled MITI's and MOF's objections against an SC compromise.[110]

At the time even the Socialists supported Ikeda's European initiative, and on 14 November 1962 the TCN was signed in London in the presence of Macmillan and Ikeda.[111] The TCN put UK—Japanese relations on MFN basis and contained both a renewable SC and a sensitive list on which the Japanese government would maintain voluntary export restraints according to quotas agreed upon by both governments. An additional list referred to items on which Britain would continue import controls — sewing machines, binoculars, toys and pottery — of which most were to be liberalised before 1968.[112] A UK White Paper argued that the treaty benefited UK exporters by guaranteeing their non-discriminatory treatment on a promising market and by reducing the uncertainty which had inhibited British exports to Japan due to the annually changing quotas.[113] The non-inclusion of woollen and cotton products in the sensitive list gave rise to a debate in the Commons in which members of all parties representing textile constituencies raised objections. Erroll replied, since Japan had not made inroads into their overseas markets there was no case for putting these textiles on the sensitive list.[114] On 5 December 1962 the treaty was approved by Westminster. In Tokyo the Diet on 26 and 29 March 1963 ratified the TCN unanimously — a genuine rarity in Japan's parliamentary history.[115]

Japan's diplomatic offensive

Since the years 1962—63 represented the peak of Japan's post-war diplomatic offensive towards Europe it appears justified to take a closer look at her motives which all appear somehow related to the reasoning of the Japanese political leadership as mentioned above. The emotional ground-swell in Japan when thinking about Europe had been a persistent fear of isolation. A MITI paper in January 1962 argued unless Japan invested in European sales networks and production facilities, she would become isolated.[116] After the US and the EC during the ongoing Dillon Round had agreed to lower their industrial tariffs mutually by 20 per cent, the Japanese government offered wholesale tariff reductions to join the deal for fear of becoming an economic orphan.[117] Mr Kiuchi, the Director of Japan's Institute of World Economy, then proposed Japan should with reference to Art. 238 Treaty of Rome, 'seek entry into the EEC as an associate member . . . Then the people will know that it is not the EEC which isolates Japan'.[118]

In early 1962 consensus emerged in government, in LDP, business associations and in ministers' statements that there were two complementary ways to preserve Japan's economic survival and world integration facing the challenge of the enlarged EEC. There should firstly be an unprecedented diplomatic effort which via TCN conclusion, OECD membership and Japanese import liberalisation, would simply force the Europeans to drop their discrimination.[119] Secondly, there would be economic adjustments required by the expected increase in international competition due to the new EC and by the pressure on Japan to liberalise her imports. The government would have to support the industries' modernisation efforts and to revise the anti-monopoly law in order to facilitate mergers in Japan and to avoid competition between Japanese exporters abroad.[120] On how to achieve the diplomatic objectives, especially on how many Japanese concessions were necessary, less consensus prevailed. In July 1962 MFA published a booklet *Japan's EEC Policy*. It opposed a rash approach to the EC since its members still harboured low wage ideas about Japan and 'have not yet shown much interest in future trade with this nation'. MFA then offered both SCs and negative lists to Britain, France and Benelux for the discontinuation of Art. 35, which had allowed them to ban Japanese imports without compensation whenever they felt too much competition.[121] The next day MITI and MOF violently opposed the MFA paper: in exchange for Art. 35 it had accepted continued discrimination (SCs) against Japanese exports, which both ministries were not ready to accept. MFA violated explicit government standards. How could it publish such a paper?[122]

The Japanese media were similarly displeased. They regretted that government disunity was revealed facing the immediate reopening of Anglo—Japanese trade talks (on 18 July 1962).[123]

Whenever in the discreet world of Japan's central bureaucracy controversial views are actually published one can safely assume that interministry fights in the preceding period must have reached boiling point several times. In view of the forthcoming talks with Britain, France and Benelux the publication was most plausible as the desperate attempt by MFA to overcome the stiff resistance by the more powerful MITI and MOF by creating a fait accompli in terms of concessions in order to rescue the subsequent talks.

In early August 1962 an interministerial meeting by MITI, MOF, MAFF, EPA and MFA, probably attended at bureau chief level — with a MITI official as spokesman — decided on a hard-line threat: Japan would withhold benefits of her liberalisation programme from those countries which continued to discriminate against her.[124]

In late August 1962, then somehow reconciled, senior officials of MFA, MITI and MOF met to map out the most comprehensive diplomatic offensive ever to take place in Euro—Japanese post-war relations.[125] During the earlier July—August 1962 UK—Japanese round of talks, the Japanese in principle had agreed to a permanent SC. In the forthcoming September talks France, restricting 271 items, would become a prime target. At the same time talks with Benelux on the final discontinuation of Art. 35 and with Italy restricting some 150 items would begin. These rounds of talks would be followed up by Foreign Minister Ohira on a trip through European capitals beginning 26 September 1962 with a 'political approach'.

Art. 35 would be a major topic at the IMF General Meeting in mid-November and at GATT's General Meeting in late October 1962.[126] Immediately before these meetings took place, EPA Director Miyazawa in a speech before the American Chamber of Commerce in Tokyo asked for US support in these negotiations with Europe.[127] In early October 1962 Sato, then Minister of MITI, happened to make a 'private' visit to Europe and thereby met De Gaulle and Monnet.[128]

Ishizaka, the head of Keidanren, would tour all EC capitals in late October 1962 and on that occasion meet all heads of corresponding employers' federations and most economic ministers.[129] Ishizaka would still be in Europe when Premier Ikeda, in a supportive move, would land in Bonn on 4 November 1962, and talk there with Chancellor Adenauer, Foreign Minister Schröder, and Economics Minister Erhard. Three days later he would converse with De Gaulle, Premier Pompidou and Foreign Minister Couve de Murville. The encounter with De Gaulle became remarkable insofar as the Japanese visitor obviously did not share his host's grand designs, whereupon it became known that the General called Ikeda a 'transistor salesman'.[130]

From the Seine Ikeda went to London to attend the signing of the TCN. Later in Brussels he met with Belgian government leaders and with Hallstein. In Rome he had conversations with President Segni, Premier Fanfani, Foreign Minister Piccioni and the Pope. His final three-day visit would carry Ikeda to the Netherlands, where he had talks with the Prime Minister as well.[131] From Den Haag, in late November 1962 after three strenuous weeks among the gaijin and with an eye to the forthcoming April 1963 elections, he returned home as the untiring three pillar architect.[132]

The signing of the Franco–Japanese trade protocol in January 1962, liberalising 125 French quota positions, has already been mentioned. But during two Euro–Japanese businessmen's conferences the differences in attitudes to bilateral trade became evident: the French who mainly represented textile and electronics industries described this agreement as an experiment, Japanese imports during the period should be 'well adapted to a market, take a place in it smoothly and with a minimum of inconvenience to local manufacturers'. After the expiration of the agreement in September 1962 it would be best to let it lapse and to return to the status quo ante.[133] The Japanese understandably argued the opposite view.

To ensure the conclusion of the 1962 protocol Japanese producers had to promise to adhere to inter-industry agreements on cotton textiles and electronics imports.[134] On cotton textiles, French and Japanese producers thus jointly decided on the volume, the types, qualities and price range of Japanese cotton imports. The Japanese would agree to trade only with importers designated by the French producers' association.[135] This evidently was a nice framework to prevent major trade disputes. It also benefited nicely big firms which were already well established and at the same time prevented competition representing an effective cartelisation at the expense of consumers. In a more global context this scheme prevented the optimal allocation of factors of production according to comparative advantages.

In 1962 M. Duhamel, Directeur General du Centre National du Commerce Exterieur, observed that France had neglected the Japanese markets: her exports there were below those of Germany, Italy, Britain, the Netherlands and even of Switzerland.[136] French machine tools and mechanical products were exports with good marketing prospects in Japan and would benefit from an improved bilateral TA framework. Since Japanese exports via industry-to-industry agreements on sensitive products were under tight supervision, if following this pattern the French government could be generous in the forthcoming September 1962 negotiations, Duhamel recommended.[137] These negotiations however ended with the extension of the existing trade protocol for another six months until March 1963.[138] From his November 1962 visit to Paris, Ikeda brought home a general French consent to bilateral MFN treatment, but no dates were set for negotiations.[139]

In May 1962 in Belgium, M. Barney, chief aide to the Foreign Trade Minister, hinted Belgium might be ready to drop Art. 35, provided Japan agreed to voluntary self restraint (VSR) on steel and nonferrous metal products. The Belgian textile industry (Febeltex) immediately responded with a protest letter and press campaign against the Foreign Trade Minister.[140]

In September 1962, additional protocols between Japan and the Benelux were signed: expanding existing contingents and liberalising several textile imports items.[141] Both the Dutch and the Belgian governments expressed support for Japan's OECD candidacy,[142] and the Belgians during Ikeda's visit had conveyed their willingness to stop the Benelux tariff discrimination against Japan (doubled duties with a minimum of 10 per cent on items of vital interest).[143] Then in December 1962 talks on the definite disinvocation of Art. 35 – and thus of all related discriminatory practices – in exchange for a safeguard clause began.[144]

With Germany not much was to be negotiated. In May 1962 Japan asked for a full liberalisation of all residual restrictions (especially textiles and chinaware), hoping to obtain a precedent for the EEC.[145] In September 1962 a new protocol was agreed upon providing for a 60 per cent increase of the cotton quota over five years and a 10 per cent annual rise in the quotas for lighters, sewing machines and toys.[146]

How did the Community institutions attempt to co-ordinate this maze of disparate member states' activities? We have already mentioned a Working Group 115 meeting occasionally for some co-ordinative attempt vis à vis low wage countries. On 9 October 1961 the Council decided on a consultative procedure prior to the conclusion of member states' agreements with third countries.[147] Following this decision 'consultations preliminaires' on a Community-wide TA with Japan emerged.[148]

These consultations in 1961 evidently did not go far, and Coreper officials made Rey's December 1961 trip to Japan a non-event.[149]

In September 1962 the Council wrote negotiations on a common TA with Japan into its action programme.[150] On tariff matters Commission negotiators during 1961–62 in the Dillon Round in Geneva frequently met with the Japanese. In February 1962 MITI received an informal Commission hint that it ought to put an export adjustment fee, that is: an export duty, on low priced exports.[151] In July 1962, in the Geneva talks, they could agree on mutual tariff concessions.[152] In the same month the Council of Ministers decided as CCP programme: the EC would gradually liberalise towards all GATT countries with the exception of sensitive products from low wage countries.[153]

In October 1962 on one of the hottest sensitive products, cotton textiles, the first GATT long term agreement (LTA) became effective providing world trade with a set of safeguards, enlarged bilateral quotas and restraint agreements for exporters.[154] On 14 November 1962, the same day that the Anglo–Japanese TCN was signed, the Council decided that an identically worded safeguard clause (SC) should be included in all bilateral trade agreements with Japan.[155] This SC would either replace Art. 35 or in case of Germany and Italy ought to be inserted in existing agreements without anything to replace.

This decision also represented a failure of Japanese diplomacy, which so singlemindedly ran after quotas and Art. 35 that it ignored the possibility of a 'harmonising' backlash in the liberated countries. On the Japanese side, the SC had a more psychological than an economic significance. The SC grew straight out of Art. 35 and thus represented discrimination. To the more national minded Japanese ministries (the internationalist MFA, as we saw, tended more towards compromises), to the parties and the media anything smelling of discrimination was as unacceptable and worthy of relentless revision efforts as were the Unequal Treaties to their Meiji ancestors. There was no doubt of the discriminatory character of the SC: originally it was only Japan from whom the EC demanded this clause. Later Japan was put in the company of India and Pakistan, the Comecon countries or the NICs on this or similar demands (which was multilateralised during the Tokyo Round as the 'modernisation' of GATT's Art. 19).

It is not clear whether Ishizaka's reception by Hallstein and Rey on 7 November 1962 went beyond courtesy calls. It was described as an exchange of information on the US trade expansion act and on the British membership aspirations. Japanese 'anxiety over future Common Market policies was clearly explained'.[156] Premier Ikeda was received one week later by Hallstein, one or two days after the Council's SC decision in an hour-long talk, which reportedly centred around the existing restrictions and on the Commission's intention to harmonise import policies towards Japan during 1963.[157]

During January–February 1963 reviewing the outcome of their 1962 policy towards Europe, the Japanese could not avoid the impression that it had been an utter failure. Not only was the EC-wide SC demand considered an exorbitant price to pay for the normalisation of trade relations with Europe,[158] but the sudden breakdown of Britain's entry talks to the EC posed a rude shock to the Japanese. Their concessions, especially the SC, were granted to the UK based on the firm expectation of thereby gaining a valuable ally inside the EC. This the government untiringly sold as its diplomatic achievement to the Japanese public. Now the concessions appeared too dear. With the vision of an enlarged EC — the third pillar of the free world — destroyed, the remaining two pillars in Ikeda's pet phrase looked far less convincing.[159] The Socialists jumped on the government's embarrassment and criticised its European venture as the necessary failure of its pro-Western policies. Within Ikeda's own LDP hostile factions became active: Miki, the head of the 'pro-China' faction, argued that the diplomatic move to Europe had been unnecessary, and ex-Premier Kishi accused the government's handling of the EC as having not been 'sufficiently conscious of their duty and obligation to the free world'.[160] One could certainly wonder why both the visiting Japanese politicians to Paris and the diplomats stationed there had been able to overlook so entirely De Gaulle's attitude towards the British entry.

Senior officials from MFA, MITI, MOF and EPA met in February 1963 to assess the consequences of the situation.[161] The Soviet Union seemed to be pleased: though Ikeda would now try to reduce Japanese exports to the EC, Sovietskaya Rossia wrote, this could only be a temporary respite until new economic wars would break out between the monopolists.[162]

In the meantime bilateral talks with Benelux had started. In March 1963 a protocol amending the trade agreement of 1963 was initialled: Benelux granted definite MFN to Japan in exchange for a similar SC which Japan had already conceded to Britain. Belgium's Premier Lefevre during Ikeda's visit had in principle agreed to the withdrawal of Art. 35.[163] The Japanese government took the agreement as a valuable stepping stone for the forthcoming talks with France and Italy. On 30 April 1963 the protocol with Benelux was signed.[164] But when in June 1963 a second protocol aiming at mutual reductions of restricted products was negotiated, the Japanese refusal to liberalise agricultural imports to reciprocate for Benelux concessions led to the failure of these negotiations.[165] The old list of 38 sensitive items continued to be applied to Japanese imports.

In March 1963 Italy's Foreign Trade Minister Preti, faithful to the Council's November 1962 decision, asked for an SC as precondition for further Italian liberalisations.[166] But since the lack of an SC had not prevented Italy from restricting unwanted Japanese imports, talks started nevertheless. In May 1963 Italy agreed to reduce her negative list from 117 items to 90.[167]

In late March 1963 Lord Home, the British Foreign Secretary, came to Japan and conferred with Ohira and Ikeda. Since the TCN had just been ratified by the Diet, and Britain being the only European power with some political Far Eastern interests left, high politics could dominate the talks. British policies in Malaysia, Chinese incursions into neighbouring countries, and Europe after the failure of the entry negotiations were reported as topics. Both governments agreed to oppose US policies which urged their allies to reduce their trade with communist countries to a minimum.[168] Reciprocating Ikeda's November 1962 visit as well, Couve de Murville, the French Foreign Minister, followed in Lord Home's footsteps, possibly also with the motive of counterbalancing 'le rapprochement anglo—japonais'.[169] After the war in Indochina, political France had started neglecting the Far East due to yet another war, this time in Algeria, and to the ensuing EC business. Le Monde observed: 'Lord Home et M. Couve de Murville ont découvert le Japon en y allant. La Grand Bretagne et la France ont désormais une politique Japonais: cela est nouveau'.[170] For Britain, as we have seen, a Japanese policy was already well under way, while the French one still had to be unveiled. Hitherto the French government had allowed marginal sectoral industrial interests to govern her policies: 'imposant à l'égard du commerce nippon une politique souvent négative et avare'.[171]

During Couve's visit the ongoing bilateral TA did not come to a conclusion, although the French agreed in principle to a treaty modelled on the TCN and to drop Art. 35 for a permanent SC. On quotas and on the possible expiration of the SC, on which Japan insisted, the negotiations continued.[172] After Couve's visit The Times observed that in visible contrast to Lord Home's visit the French and the Japanese had had nothing to talk about — apart from cultural exchange, initiated in 1958—60 when Malraux had been Minister of Culture —[173] while Britain and Japan shared substantial Far Eastern political and economic interests.[174]

On 14 May 1963 in Paris the new Franco—Japanese TA was signed for a duration of six years. On the contentious issues the Japanese had given in on the SC: it was made permanent, or rather, to be renewed automatically unless both agreed on its expiration. France in turn was a bit more generous on quota reductions: their total was reduced from 140 to 84 (still under restriction: radios, TVs, porcelain, cameras, toys, cotton and silk products), and enlarged the remaining ones. Japan tripled her global quotas (since she did not have bilateral, i.e. discriminatory quotas) on cognac, glassware, perfumes, wine, and hinted she might buy 20 Caravelles.[175] The agreement was also intended to enable greater 'inter-industrial and inter-professional collaboration'.[176] Eight years after Japan's accession to GATT France as the last European nation had put commercial relations with Japan on an MFN basis.

Japan joins the OECD

The progress in bilateral negotiations by March 1963 gave rise to an optimistic mood in the Japanese administration.[177] After the conclusion of the TA with France the substantial success of Japan's autumn 1962 offensive seemed assured: France, Britain and Benelux had put bilateral relations on MFN basis. Italy, Britain and France had further reduced their negative lists, a further reduction would only be a question of time; for Japan the European market was now effectively opened. This was the more important as the US appeared to dislike increasingly their role as the sole major outlet for Japanese consumer product exports. The shortage of labour in Europe indicated a significant and — at least in theory — a mutually welcome alternative export outlet. If Japan could employ an effective sectoral export restraint system, so went Gaimusho's reasoning, then nothing could spoil the development of ever-expanding trade. Membership in OECD, the exclusive Western club, would crown Japan's emancipation. To concede SCs were a regrettable, but nevertheless necessary price Japan had to pay for this positive development.[178]

With similar impatience the Commission had waited for the conclusion of the Franco—Japanese TA on 14 May 1963. The ink of its signatures was not yet dry, when the Commission, the very next day, declared that now no obstacles were left to negotiate for the conclusion of a common EC—Japan agreement with a common SC inserted and to scrap all bilateral accords with Japan.[179]

European policy co-operation vis à vis Japan, in spite of Council decisions, had remained insufficient. The national negative lists all had been shortened. But reflecting different protective national interests they had not necessarily become more identical. In February 1963 Coreper's sub-committee on tariffs failed to agree to the French—Italian demand to increase substantially tariffs on Japanese sewing machines, which was opposed by both Germany and Benelux. The Japanese embassy in Brussels reported that it was unlikely that there would be a decision for high tariffs, since in 1962 already a session had ended in disagreement and no action was taken as a consequence.[180] In February 1963 the Commission asked all member governments to inform the Japanese officially of the Council's common SC demand decided three months earlier, as so far none of them had done so.[181]

One month after its initial announcement following the Franco—Japanese TA in June 1963 a Commission session chaired by Hallstein submitted proposals for a common trade policy towards Japan to the Council and asked for a mandate for preliminary negotiations.[182] The Commission note defined four goals for its initiative:

1 To further the mutual liberalisation on MFN basis.
2 To urge equal Japanese treatment to all European imports, regardless of country of origin.
3 To establish a common SC along the French—Benelux lines and a common list of sensitive products (to be subjected to quotas, self control, special tariffs etc.).
4 To set up measures against unfair competition from either side.

In co-operation with a committee (Art. 111) to be designated by the member governments the Commission would hold three months of preliminary talks with Japan, then report back to the member states. During the preliminary negotiations the bilateral talks with Japan should come to a standstill. The Commission noted that earlier Council recommendations for the co-ordination of policies were not observed. The divergence of national policies towards Japan was now greater than towards any other non-communist country. The possibility and the need for community action was given by the facts that in the Commission's opinion:

— all member states (except Italy) had stabilised their commercial relations with Japan,
— the Council decision (of November 1962) on a common SC had to be implemented,
— the forthcoming Kennedy Round required harmonised EC foreign economic policies,
— the free circulation of goods within the EC (Art. 115) was threatened due to different import regimes,
— it was desirable to have Japan enact export controls, and to co-ordinate EC views on these controls,
— Japan's feelings of regional isolation had to be alleviated and Japan ought to be treated as a significant trading partner.[183]

The proposals were supposed to be discussed at the Council session in July 1963,[184] however since Coreper could not make up its mind about them until October, it did not forward them to its ministers and so far they remained undebated.

In February 1963 Ikeda announced Japan would soon formally apply for full OECD membership.[185] Japan had prepared this application carefully, and with strong US support she had had already obtained observer status at the Development Assistance Committee (DAC) and as the world's largest shipbuilder was fully taking part in OECD's Working Party 6, which otherwise obviously could not have functioned.[186]

Ikeda in November 1962 had systematically collected pledges from his hosts in the six capitals he had visited in support of Japan's membership bid, which was actively backed by Britain and the US within the OECD.[187] In a survey MFA found none of the OECD's 20 members overtly opposing Japan's membership, which was essential since the admission required unanimous approval.[188] But some of the neutral countries seemed less enthusiastic fearing as a consequence strengthened US influence and a precedent for countries like Israel, Argentine and Brazil who were interested in joining as well. They feared this would render the organisation too big and ineffective.[189] In early April 1963 the OECD Council gave preliminary approval to Japan's application and in May 1963 accession negotiations would start.[190] Until then Japan's leadership supposedly was not aware that full participation in OECD carried obligations beyond membership fees.[191] After learning its unpopular consequences like increased OAD obligations, and the need to liberalise entirely trade and capital imports, the Japanese government tried to downplay their compulsory character: it hoped Japan could get along like France, i.e. to make reservations on capital liberalisations and to pledge these would be implemented later in due course of time.[192] In June 1963 the Japanese started negotiations with OECD's Committee on Invisible Transactions. Later its Payments Committee would negotiate; both would issue reports which were to serve as recommendations for the OECD Council's decision.[193]

The OECD then demanded a deadline for Japan's liberalisation of capital and invisible transactions and on the abolition of restrictions on overseas travel by Japanese nationals, on the import of foreign films etc.[194] It rejected Japan's subsequent twenty reservations concerning invisibles and capital transactions as incompatible with OECD rules.[195] Between Japanese ministries the usual infights broke out. Foreign Minister Ohira stressed the need to end 'useless government interference' in the economy,[196] thereby attacking MITI's position, whose powerful domestic industry bureaus rejected the idea of freed capital imports, for fear the undercapitalisation of Japan's key industries might invite a foreign takeover and thus end MITI's administrative guidance rule over the Japanese economy. The other economic ministries stalled equally. During a cabinet session in June 1963 in spite of Ikeda's pleas none of his ministers was ready to liberalise in *his* area.[197] Ishizaka, Keidanren's president, intervened and criticised the government's negative stand: it should rather stick to low interest policies and reduce corporate taxes in order to allow for the strengthening of Japan's larger companies to enable them to withstand international competition.[198]

In July 1963 Norway, as the leader of the Scandinavian maritime powers' group, threatened it would veto Japan's admission unless Japan changed her restrictive policies on the long term chartering of foreign vessels.[199] Greece, the Netherlands and UK soon supported Norway's objections.[200] Japan originally had asked to reserve her charter control restricting the hiring of foreign vessels by Japanese shipping lines for another five years. After the OECD objected, Japan had to come up with a compromise proposal. The Japanese ministries to agree on it were MFA, because it was in charge of the OECD negotiations, MOF, for the balance of payments' effects of foreign charter, and MOT, which is in charge of the shipbuilding industry and therefore the most hardline against a liberal compromise. When an interministry meeting of the bureau directors concerned did not arrive at a compromise, Ikeda met with his ministers Ohira (MFA), Tanaka (MOF) and Ayabe (MOT). He then personally decided on Japan's compromise offer: two years reservation for restrictions on the charter of foreign oil tankers and one year reservation for iron, steel and coal shipping vessels.[201]

OECD accepted this as well as Japan's pledge to liberalise capital imports — though its implementation was to drag on until nearly ten years later — and on 26 July 1963 the OECD Council unanimously voted to invite Japan to join.[202] The vote of the ministers' session in November 1963 would be a pure affirmative formality. The Japanese media were jubilant and all mass circulation dailies stressed that finally Japan was now accepted as a full first-rate developed nation.[203]

Only the shipbuilders complained of being helplessly delivered to superior foreign competition and painted a picture of European mammoth tankers smashing little Japanese ships. They claimed to be in desperate need of governmental financial support.[204] Such subsidies were soon provided in plenty for the construction of tankers, and for steel and iron ore carriers.[205] The DSP joined their anti-OECD protest: the workers of the major shipyards were organised in Domei, the (moderate) federation of blue-collar unions, which forms the DSP's organisational backbone. The Socialists (JSP) then started opposing the OECD membership as well. They had originally supported Japan's application in the hope OECD with neutrals participating would be less anti-communist than the US.[206] In the Diet they charged OECD with being a US tool for alienating LDCs from socialist countries, membership was a feather in Japan's cap, but useless in substantial terms.[207] Then the Diet ratified the OECD membership against the votes of DSP, JSP and JCP.[208]

The Commission's attempts on a CCP towards Japan

In autumn 1963 Japan faced bilateral negotiations with Germany and with Italy. From Italy Japan demanded a maximum cut in her restriction list as a positive input to the future CCP. But when Italy insisted on an SC in return, the Japanese refused, and again just the existing quotas were raised enabling a possible 15 per cent increase in bilateral trade.[209] Supported by a variety of industries (sewing machines, umbrellas, metal, tableware, fisheries) German negotiators in August 1963 also demanded an SC which Japan was not ready to grant.[210] Japan in turn was asking for a greater liberalisation on textiles and ceramics. Germany was ready for this only on condition of an SC and threatened to reconsider her friendly attitude.[211] The talks stalled and were to be resumed in spring 1964.

In August 1963 the Commission informally sounded out Japan's attitude on the common SC. Japan's reaction was strongly negative: an extension of the SC to Germany and Italy would supply new weapons to be used against Japan. The problems which Japan encountered in negotiations with both countries she interpreted as the consequence of some EC 'harmonisation' attempt. This reinforced her dislike and suspicion of all such communal endeavours. Japan feared all her year-long diplomatic labours culminating in the spring 1963 successes could be reduced to nothing if the Commission succeeded in scrapping the bilateral agreements.[212]

In October 1963 Coreper finally found time and opportunity to agree on four reservations to the Commission's June 1963 proposals. These were:

1 National bilateral negotiations ought to be concluded beforehand.
2 The intended trade policy (management of community controls and safeguards) towards Japan was not developed sufficiently.
3 Future bilateral trade talks with Japan ought not be inhibited.
4 It was unclear how to set up a common negative list.[213]

In spite of these reservations it was expected that in October 1963 the Council would take up the issue for a preliminary debate on the proposals which were intended to become a blueprint for commercial policy towards other low cost manufacturing exporting countries as well.[214] This however did not happen. The Council found no time to take up the issue of trade with Japan, mainly because it is up to its neck in more urgent work. The Kennedy Round, the chicken war with the US and the financing of the CAP had been on the agenda. Hallstein had repeatedly underlined the importance of starting talks with Japan as soon as possible, and Jean Rey told the EP: 'We must not forget Japan',[215] evidently with little success.

In February 1964 the Japanese government received renewed hints from the Commission, it should enter into informal preliminary talks. The Japanese, however, had refused to engage in collective EC talks. Because of the pressure to extend SC provisions to Italy and Germany

Japan feared the common negative list would also be drawn up on the basis of the largest national restriction list, namely the Italian one.[216] On 26 February 1964 the Commission renewed its proposals to the Council to obtain a formal mandate for talks with Japan.[217] The Commission's note attempted to refute Coreper's earlier objections.

Future bilateral national talks with Japan would not be inhibited by the Commission's talks provided that proper prior consultation had taken place. The outcome of the common negative list ought to be left to the negotiations with Japan. The Council should therefore establish criteria for a *minimum* list of products requiring indispensable protection, and for a *maximum* list which was made up of products restricted in three tariff areas and of a percentage of products whose imports were restricted in two EC tariff areas only. With this common negative list national negative lists could coexist until the end of the transition period. The note underlined again the urgent need for a common trade policy towards Japan arising from the Kennedy Round, and asked for the immediate start of preliminary talks with the aim of reporting its results back to the Council before 30 June 1964. The preliminary negotiations should be conducted by a mixed delegation, in which under the Commission's chairmanship officials from both the Commission and the national governments were represented.[218]

These proposals formed part of the Commission's plan to implement the customs union by 1965, four years ahead of the schedule set by the Treaty of Rome. This also required the speeding up of the harmonisation of external tariffs and trade policies.[219]

On 15 April 1964 the Council finally took up the Commission's policy proposals on Japan. After the French and Italian representatives insisted that the Commission's preparation for the talks was insufficient, the Council decided it needed yet another complementary report on the Commission's planned 'Japanpolitik' before it could make a final decision.[220]

In the meantime on the Japanese side MFA appeared ready to negotiate with the Community and argued it was natural that Japan should study the CCP and comment on it. But MITI felt that the Community's likely demands for a safeguard clause and a negative list put Japan in such a disadvantageous position that it was not advisable to enter negotiations.[221]

On 26 June 1964 the Commission sent the required report to the Council. It had been drafted in co-operation with national experts (i.e. a working group of Coreper), but due to Italian reservations it was finally released on solely Commission responsibility.[222] The Italians commented that the Commission's initiative had arrived at an inopportune moment; more likely however, they disliked the prospect of a shortened list of restrictions.[223] On the composition of the negative list the Commission's position remained unchanged, but was more specific now on the management of the community quotas: until the end of the transition period they would exist parallel to the national lists, gradually expanding their share at the expense of the latter. The imports under the Community list would then, under a community quota, be able to circulate freely within the EC. Benelux, however, supposedly objected to the simultaneous existence of the two negative lists.[224] During the transition period also two parallel SCs would be in force: there was to be a Community SC in Community management while the national French and Benelux SCs would remain in national responsibility until December 1969, their eventual application being co-ordinated with the Community.[225] While preparing for the smooth implementation of the future CCP, the Commission thus was at pains to show that the national bureaucracies would remain in charge of their trade policies until the end of the transition period. The Japanese however were horrified at the prospect of not only simple and extended, but now also of apparently doubled and paralleled safeguards and restrictions. MFA now shifted to MITI's position and joined in the rejection of negotiations with the EC. It cited reports that the new EC negative list would contain nearly 200 restricted items. Thus the proposed TA would be of an exceedingly restrictive nature.[226]

Japanese trading companies and big business in the Japan Foreign Trade Council (JFTC) supported their ministries' stand: the EC's negotiating goals of a common SC and negative lists were discriminatory. If Japan allowed more SCs, she would give up basic rights under GATT. After all those successful bilateral negotiations for reduced restrictions, if dealing with the EC collectively there would be no hope for a substantial relaxation of their trade restriction against Japan.[227] The problem, however, of how to negotiate with someone who does not want to negotiate had not to be faced by the Commission. The Council rejected a negotiation mandate in July 1964 probably due to the Italian veto.[228]

Bilateral relations in the mid-1960s

When ex-Premier Kishi visited Hallstein in September 1964 common trade negotiations were no longer on the agenda. Instead they talked about credits for the Soviet Union. Japan had just given her an eight-year credit, and Britain had given one for fifteen years. Hallstein lectur-'ed his guest on the dangers of granting credits to communists.[229]

In July 1964 after seven weeks of 'routine negotiations' a new German—Japanese trade protocol was signed.[230] As expected Japan again refused to grant an SC, and Germany in turn did not liberalise as much as it claimed it would have done otherwise. Japanese sewing machines, lighters, metal toys and some textiles were to be liberalised by January

1965; Japan in turn offered concessions on typewriters, wine and cosmetics.[231]

As part of their twice-yearly consultations at ministerial level, which had been agreed upon at Ikeda's 1962 visit to Britain — France and Germany had agreed to annual ones — in May 1964 Mr Butler, the British Foreign Secretary came to Tokyo. While the Japanese were interested mostly in the few remaining UK import restrictions, the British main concern was to keep Japan from intervening in the Indonesian—Malaysian dispute on behalf of her commercial Indonesian friends. But since Japan evidently never had considered this, the visit remained a courteous non-event.[232]

Franco—Japanese relations took a slightly more dramatic turn in 1964—65. In February—March 1964 the talks for the annual trade protocol took place. After a stormy passage on the French quota on Japanese umbrella frames, France finally liberalised 20 items, including motor cycles, blankets and sports goods, while Japan increased her global quotas on wine, woollen fabrics, perfumes, cosmetics and cars.[233]

In April 1964 Premier Pompidou and Couve de Murville arrived for their annual consultation in Tokyo. The French had just recognised the People's Republic of China and recommended to Japan to do likewise. The Japanese, faithful to their American masters, disliked this as much as the French plan for the neutralisation of Indochina.[234]

One year later, the 'pacemaker' of De Gaulle's policy, Edgar Faure who also stood behind France's PRCh recognition, came on a 'private' visit to Japan. He again suggested Japan should follow the French example in helping to reintegrate China into the international system.[235] Shortly after his visit in April 1965 the French Cabinet Economic Committee offered an agreement on industrial and technological co-operation to Japan whose scope caused a stir in the Japanese government. The offer covered technological co-operation on nuclear energy, aircraft, computers, electronics and steel production technologies. In addition France offered to cut her 68 restrictions to the Benelux level of 38. The Japanese were expected to reciprocate on car and perfume imports. The offer was part of France's diplomatic offensive in Asia reflecting De Gaulle's global strategies. He was particularly dissatisfied with British and US domination in Japan's technological development.[236] To highlight the projected co-operation De Gaulle planned a visit to Japan in early 1966.[237]

After three months reflection the Japanese agreed to negotiations, and in July 1964, Miki, Minister of MITI, went to Paris for political talks.[238] Though Japan had agreed to the outline of the French offer, three weeks later the talks broke down on details of the French conditions for technological co-operation, which Japan found unacceptable. France then withdrew her liberalisation offer as well.[239]

How can we explain the rationale of this initiative which appears to

111

have come at least three years too late? From 1955 to 1962 Japan was in desperate need of 'allies' in Europe. During all this period France behaved as the least responsive, her policies being almost totally dominated by marginal sectoral interests. Now in 1965 after OECD membership, large-scale liberalisations in Europe and with MFN status as a GATT member, Japan had achieved what it wanted. The only threat to her newly won diplomatic complacency was the nightmare of a community-wide SC which Japan, not without reason, perceived as classifying her back to a second-rate international status. Her diplomatic attitude thus turned into a defensive posture. The Commission's apparent inability of gaining its members' mandate reinforced Japan's intention to let sleeping dogs lie. If there was no Japanese interest in change, then what did motivate the French offer in mid-1965? In De Gaulle's memoirs we find quite a few references to Japan. Most of them refer to Japan's post-war economic achievements. But in one he describes France as the hope for the world, the non-aligned and the larger Asian countries: China, India and Japan who look up to France and the French way of handling world affairs.[240]

As an interesting exercise in the rewriting of history De Gaulle characterises Franco—Japanese relations 1958—62 after referring to the Paris visits of Kishi, Ikeda and Sato:

Au nom d'une grande nation, terriblement éprouvée par son désastre, mais intacte dans sa vitalité, tirant parti de sa soumission, mais impatiente du joug américain, bornant jusqu'à nouvel ordre son effort national au domaine économique, mais déployant pour y accéder au rang des principales puissances d'extraordinaires qualités de travail et de discipline, ces dirigeantes très avisés proposent à la France d'échanger plus largement ses produits, ses idées et ses sentiments avec ceux d'un people qui, jusqu'alors, lui est resté presque hermétique. Leur requête est entendue. Les rapports franco—nippons vont prendre une dimension nouvelle.[241]

When Gaullist France in 1965 generously offered to liberate the suffering Japanese from their Anglophone esclavage, the French assumption was — whatever its timing and the bilateral antecedents in earlier years — that the Japanese regardless of their other immediate concerns would jump on the gracious offer of an 'alliance franco—japonaise'. This evidently was not the case. The failure of French diplomacy towards Japan is reflected vice versa: if there was a streak for 'une dimension nouvelle' in bilateral relations to be kindled among French leaders, why did Japanese officials consistently fail to inspire impressions beyond polite 'transistor salesmen'?

During 1965 due to Italian and French opposition to a common negative list it appeared unlikely that the Council would ever authorise a

Commission mandate for negotiations with Japan.[242] The Commission's warning, that the present national consultation procedure was insufficient and that market disruptions would arise as the consequence of unequal Japanese imports, went unheard.[243] The EP's regret on the lack of a common policy towards Japan was similarly ineffective.[244]

In April 1965 it was known that MFA was studying a change in Japan's diplomacy towards Europe. According to these studies Japan should shift away from her anti-discrimination policy towards export promotion. Among the restrictions left (Germany: 20, Benelux: 38, France: 68, Italy: 116) the German and Benelux ones were purely nominal – Japan's actual exports on these restricted products fell well below the conceded quotas; and France and Italy would not reduce further for social reasons. In any case, restrictions were no longer substantially inhibiting Japanese exports. It would be more productive for Japanese diplomacy, MFA concluded, to promote exports and to focus on Japanese capital investments in Europe.[245] The study reflected what since mid-1963 had already become evident: Japan more or less had achieved its diplomatic objectives, namely emancipation in international status and the creation of legal frameworks to secure export outlets in developed and prosperous markets.

Japanese diplomacy in 1963–64 stopped its offensive, never to take it up again during more recent Euro–Japanese relations. The paralysis of Community institutions 1965–66 due to the French boycott of the Council encouraged this change in strategy.

Japanese diplomacy in a concerted action had cleared the way. Now the offensive was left to her exporters. MFA's new diplomatic role developed: to clear up and to cushion whatever irritation the exporters had left. The implications of this new role would not become evident until after 1974 when Japanese exports actually began to bite in Europe.

In those 'eventless' years 1965–68 the later more crucial sectoral topics, ships and steel, began to be taken up in Euro–Japanese consultations. The effects of the first restructuring of the Japanese economy only gradually entered as issues of economic diplomacy. While the old light industry issues: textiles, pottery, sewing machines, toys and umbrellas, disappeared from the headlines, the import penetration of the new heavy industry products (steel, ships, cars, machinery) was still too weak to cause any serious concern in Europe in the late sixties.

From September 1965 semiannual consultations between senior officials of ECSC and of MITI's heavy industries' bureau started. The talks regularly covered the steel markets, forecasts on steel consumption and production, the global raw material situation and technical innovations.[246] Shipbuilding came up as a Community issue during a Keidanren visit to Brussels in June 1965. The Japanese share in world shipbuilding had climbed to 44 per cent in 1964. The Commission contended that Japan's subsidised low interest rates for heavy tonnage ships were distorting world competition.[247]

Japan's list of exemptions from tariff cuts in the ongoing Kennedy Round was brought up by Hallstein and Rey in their talks with Ishizaka in June 1965.[248] During later Kennedy Round sessions Japan asked the Commission's negotiators to talk about the European quota restrictions which were applied against Japan. When in March 1966 the Commission submitted the request for a negotiating mandate to the Council, Germany and Benelux favoured such Community-wide talks. The French and Italians however rejected the proposal.[249] Both stressed the national responsibility for quantitative restrictions during the remaining two and a half transition years. In October 1966 Japan renewed her demand for negotiations and offered to trade the liberalisation of agro- and industrial imports to Japan for the abolition of the European residual restrictions.[250] The French and Italian objections, however, did not change.

The apparent European deficiencies in policy co-ordination made the EC a far less frightening institution. The Japanese media could therefore give a more relaxed and realist assessment of the consequences of UK's second bid for membership in 1967 and of the working of the Common Market in general, compared to their periodical exercises in near hysteria during 1957–62.[251]

On sectoral problems with identical interests co-operation among the Six was easier to achieve. In March 1968 officials of the member states and of the Commission jointly started negotiations with the Japanese to talk about the Japanese cotton import quota under Art. 4 of GATT's respective LTA.[252] Japan demanded higher quotas and simplified quota subdivisions. The EC initially resisted any substantial quota enlargement, which it wished to reserve for LDCs.[253] Finally, in June 1969 an agreement was concluded, the first ever between the EC and Japan. In the context of the ensuing US–Japanese textile wrangle the EC doubled Japan's cotton quota from 6,500 tonnes to 11,450 tonnes for fifteen months; 6,000 tonnes were to go to Germany, 2,650 tonnes to France, 1,600 tonnes to Italy and 1,200 tonnes to Benelux.[254]

During 1968 the co-ordination of the annual talks between the member states and Japan finally became institutionalised. Prior to each of these bilateral routine negotiations on the protocols (attached to the existing TAs) concerning the annual quotas on sensitive products consultation meetings of national trade policy experts took place. Most likely these officials discussed the national negotiation outlines in a Coreper working group. Such meetings took place three times in 1968 on the ongoing Franco– and Italo–Japanese negotiations.[255]

Italy then cut her bilateral restrictions down to 58. But on cars, ball bearings and sewing machines tight quotas continued. In their removal the Japanese had shown the strongest interest.[256]

France in April 1968 reduced her restrictions from 53 to 45 items – among the freed goods the main items were cameras and antibiotics.[257] In July 1966 Benelux freed 5 products out of its total of 38, some types of yarn, pencils and plastic buttons were liberalised.[258]

Germany kept her 19 restrictions, but in December 1967 agreed to enlarge the quotas by 20 to 30 per cent.[259] In the same round of negotiations the German government informed the Japanese that their voluntary self restraints (VSRs) – offered on sewing machines – were undesirable and a violation of Germany's economic autonomy.[260]

In 1967 with Brandt as the new Foreign Minister, German officials undertook an assessment of their 'Japanpolitik'. The German embassy in Tokyo wrote that Germany throughout the post-war years had neglected her assets in popular sympathy with Japan.[261] In May 1967 Brandt flew to Tokyo to attend a conference of German ambassadors in Asia and to resume the long interrupted 'annual' consultations with the Japanese government. These bilateral talks focussed on the Non-Proliferation Treaty (NPT), on which both had identical positions: they equally disliked the likely prospect of having to sign it.[262] Both, as well, were sceptical at the wisdom of US conduct of war in Vietnam.[263]

The Soviets, fearing that Brandt and Japan's Foreign Minister Miki would jointly search for loopholes in the NPT and co-ordinate their efforts to avoid signature, let the 'Iswestija' condemn the conspiratory axis Bonn–Tokyo–Washington.[264]

As the ambassadors' conference revealed, Bonn's actual plans were less grandiose. Brandt summarised its results: conflicts in Asia aggravate the global political situation, Germany thus has a general interest in detente also in Asia. But Germany has no political objectives of her own in Asia and, therefore, does not need to get tangled in 'unreasonable involvements' (which could be a reference to the Vietnam war). The most suitable German strategy with respect to Asia would be to influence early enough the decision making in the US and in influential Asian countries. Germany supported Japan's role in stabilising South East Asia in co-operation with the US. The EC should be and remain open to Asian exports.[265]

In November 1968 the Secretary of State in the Economics Ministry, von Dohnanyi (later Minister of State in the Foreign Office) went to Japan on a study tour. On his return he dictated a 200 page book on his impressions, the only monograph on Japan so far written by a senior European politician.[266] His theme: what should Germany learn from Japan? Japan in Dohnanyi's view was more advanced in her macro-economic planning, her research policies, her management technique of collective decision making and in the trustful business–government co-operation, e.g. via competent expert advisory councils to the ministries. Also, Japan's trade policies were more clever: while Germany protected her lame ducks (sunset industries), Japan protected her future industries. Finally, Dohnanyi concluded, only a truly integrated Europe could face the technological challenge of the US and of Japan.[267]

Japan held interministerial consultations with Britain more frequently and regularly than with any other European nation. After the previously mentioned visit of Foreign Secretary Butler to Japan in May 1964, in October 1966 the Foreign Ministers Shiina and Brown met to confer on the situation in China, on the British Far Eastern policy and on Japanese OAD in Malaysia.[268] In January 1968 Brown went to Japan and had talks with his new colleague Miki. Japan was interested in the consequences of the UK's withdrawal from East of Suez, while Britain was interested in Japan's systematic sanction busting in Rhodesia, massively importing chrome ore from there.[269] Brown later announced that Miki had promised to crack down on Japanese companies importing from Rhodesia.[270] However Miki as the Foreign Minister was not in a position to make such promises since he needed the — unlikely — co-operation from MITI for this.

Soon both countries changed their foreign ministers and, in March 1969, the new incumbents, Aichi and Stewart, met in London. They talked about the EC's situation after De Gaulle, on Britain's entry prospects and on a possible sterling devaluation.[271] Probably against better knowledge Aichi insisted on Japan's faithful adherence to the UN's Rhodesia sanctions.[272] He was also faced with renewed demands to reduce Japan's 100 per cent import tariffs on Scotch whisky and to increase Japan's OAD substantially. On both issues MFA might have liked to be conciliatory, but resistance from the more powerful MOF blocked all concessions.[273]

In a near dramatic move later in autumn 1969 Mr Crosland as the Director of the Board of Trade gave a strong back-up to the British liberalisation requests by offering the abolition of *all* British restrictions on Japanese imports.[274] The next chapter will deal with this initiative in greater detail.

Apart from the more intense political dialogue British interests towards Japan also appear to have been more diverse in economic matters than the continental Europeans', whose prime concern remained Japanese light industry imports. British business also played a leading role in pressure for Japanese capital liberalisation, both in BIAC and in direct CBI–Keidanren talks.[275] The British aerospace industry went to Japan in a search for suitable partners supplying cheap and effective production methods for joint aircraft development.[276] In support of this and other ventures Mr Benn as Minister for Technology went to Japan in 1966 and 1968.[277] On 6 March 1968 an existing ten-year agreement on UK–Japanese co-operation on nuclear energy development was extended for another thirty years. It basically provides for the reprocessing of spent Japanese radioactive fuels at Windscale. The plutonium extracted in the process would then be sold back to Japan.[278]

Euro—Japanese communication and decision making, 1950—68

The ministries for foreign and for economic affairs, their senior officials and their political leadership are the prime domestic actors in the making of a national trade policy. Still, there is a wide variety of other significant influences on decisions on foreign trade policies, particularly those of lobbyists whose expertise is needed, and of general and specialised media reports that shape the decision makers' perception of the issues at stake. The purpose of this section is, therefore, to answer the following questions on Euro—Japanese relations 1950—68:

- What was the decision makers' general 'definition of the situation'?
- Which governmental institutions and bureaucratic positions were involved?
- What evidence is there of private sector influence?
- How strong were the levels of politicisation of bilateral relations?
- Which high-level bilateral communication channels can be discerned?
- How did policy co-ordination work on the European side—on the Japanese side?
- What was the impact of third international actors (i.e. of the US and of international organisations)?

The decision makers' 'definition of the situation'

In the previous section I have quoted at length decision makers' 'definitions of the situation' wherever first-hand or media reports on them were accessible. Though these represent statements for public consumption and do not reveal more personal motives and evaluations, still they give some indication on the general patterns of reasoning on bilateral issues. These were also reflected in their fairly uniform presentation in the media.

Japan's image in the fifties and early sixties was that a low-wage country with strong development needs which would aggressively market her textiles and sundry products on the European markets, thus stepping on the feet of structurally declining but also politically active and influential industries. Japan's economic growth was considered quite sceptically: it was not yet visible since it did not immediately translate into higher standards of living. With Germany having performed far better in her

117

reconstruction efforts in the fifties, there was hardly any applause for Japan's 'miracle' until the late sixties. Politically, Japan's establishment was seen as a faithful ally to the US. However her internal political order, with spectacular assassinations, militant riots, militarist resurrections of the right and orthodox Marxist rhetoric on the left, made her somewhat unpredictable. Hence the frequent fear that Japan might realign herself with China — and thus the repeated insistence that measures supportive of Japan's Western integration were needed.

The threat of Japanese neutralism at the time was suitable to motivate cold-war politicians in Europe to make economic concessions in order to avoid the strategic destabilisation in the Far East. On the Japanese side, the attitudes towards Europe as evident in reactions to the creation of the EC, were dominated by feelings of inferiority and isolation,[279] which were reinforced by the actual special regime (discrimination) for Japanese products in Europe. The persistent efforts to overcome both were in the best tradition of Japanese external policies since the Meiji days. In her tactical moves to end her isolation Japan in search of friends oscillated between UK and Germany, neither of which was consistently responsive. Japan's inferiority feelings were translated into the social consensus of working harder, of becoming more innovative, of restructuring and reinvesting ever more, and of finally aiming at European market shares with respectable products which would elevate the Japanese name in the world.

The European institutions deciding on 'Japanpolitik'

From the previous section we can summarise the major institutions involved and the more significant official encounters.

France. The main issue of bilateral relations, namely trade, was negotiated by both the French Foreign (Quai d'Orsay) and the Economics and Finance Ministry (Quai Branly). French delegations were led either by the head of Quai d'Orsay's Economic and Financial Affairs Bureau or by the head of Quai Branly's External Trade Bureau. When negotiations aimed at more technical levels, then the head of either bureau's Bilateral Agreements Section led the delegation.

The reasons for this shared competence on trade policies towards Japan are not clear, nor are its consequences. Lobbying efforts against French liberalisation, in which the French textile industry was identified regularly, were successful throughout the fifties and sixties. The sole French political initiative, the technological co-operation offer of 1965, was formally decided upon by the Cabinet Economic Committee. It would be more plausible, however, to understand it as the result of

M. Faure's convincing communication of his Far Eastern policy designs to De Gaulle. This initiative remained singular and then soon got stuck in the habitual bureaucratic wrangling between French and Japanese officials.

As a result of Ikeda's visit, regular annual consultation between the foreign ministers and their senior level staffs took place after 1963. The 1967 French delegation was drawn only from the Quai d'Orsay: the minister, accompanied by his chef du cabinet and by the directors of the bureaus of political affairs, of Asian affairs, and of economic affairs.[280] From 1962 industry-to-industry agreements (on electronics and on textiles) were in force. Such contacts between producers were usually described publicly as aiming at 'more understanding'. Actually they were more likely to end up as cartel-like arrangements. After 1966, Keidanren and the Patronat met for annual businessmen's conferences.

Paris throughout the sixties was a natural stop-over for the many Japanese politicians and business missions touring Europe — it may have been for reasons associated with Moulins Rouges or for some actual mission of 'private economic diplomacy' to be carried out. It was only hesitantly that in 1965 significant French missions started reciprocating with visits to Japan.*

Italy. Most Italian delegations negotiating on trade protocols or trade agreements were led by directors of the Foreign Ministry's Economic Affairs Directorate. At times, but less frequently, they were also managed by the directors of the Trade Ministry's Far Eastern Department or its Foreign Trade Development Bureau.

Though negotiations focussed on Italian import restrictions which were the Ministry of Trade's preserve, the distribution of economic policy competence between six economic ministries in Italy has prevented the Trade Ministry's reputedly free trade preference from prevailing. A 1959 Italian negotiating team in Tokyo was composed of two officials from the Trade Ministry and the Ministry of Industry and Commerce each, and of one from the Foreign Ministry.[281] This dispersion of bureaucratic decision making is not conducive to creating consistently managed trade policies, it also facilitates — e.g. via Confidustria's parentela (which is particularly strong on the Ministry of Industry and Commerce) — specific sectoral interests in exercising a veto power on any significant import liberalisation. Bilateral contacts between Japan and Italy were cultivated less intensively than with Britain, Germany or France. There were no regular ministerial consultations, and Keidanren—Confidustria

---

* M. Berard, a French ambassador to Japan (1956—59), in the fourth volume of his memoirs (*Une ambassade au Japon*) gives an extensive and beautifully written account of his and his embassy's work and experiences.

119

meetings happened less frequently (1964, 1966 and 1968) than with the employers' associations of France, Germany and Britain.

The Japanese seemed to have assigned to Italy a similar medium rank to Belgium or to the Netherlands. During the 1962—63 offensive, high level talks in Rome were evidently considered important, and Rome or Milan were likely stop-overs for Japanese missions touring *all* Europe. But during all the fifties and sixties the Italian Ministers of Trade and of Foreign Affairs visited Japan only once each, which indicates the importance they attributed to Japan. The drawn-out trade talks usually lasted for two to three months each year and their failure — postponements sine die — seemed to have been part of the routine.

Benelux. Prior to the Benelux common negotiations the bilateral negotiations were handled by the Belgian Ministry of Trade and the Dutch Ministry of Economics. Luxembourg's economic interests were represented by Belgium. After 1959 all negotiations were led by the Dutch Ministry of Economics bureau 'Buitenlandse Economische Betrekkingen', which by coincidence is also in charge of the co-ordination of Dutch European policies.[282] It is not clear from my data how Dutch—Belgian co-ordination was facilitated. Both countries' external trade position was equally liberal in principle, with Belgium originally having had fewer restrictions towards Japan. Both countries' textile industries equally opposed any liberalisation of textile imports.

The Belgian government with Brussels as the seat of the Commission already in the sixties got a larger share of high level Japanese visits than Den Haag. There were no regular consultations between Benelux and Japanese Foreign Ministers; visits of Japanese trade missions were seldom reciprocated, and among all official contacts the royal ones appear as the most extensive.

Germany. The trade negotiations with Japan were all handled by the Economics Ministry's Far Eastern Department. In 1959 the German delegation for the annual routine trade talks was led by the head of this department. He was accompanied by two officials from his ministry, and by one official each from the Foreign Office and the Bundesbank.[283] During later ministerial consultations (after 1962) only senior officials from the Foreign Office participated. Kroll's memoirs reveal a curious fact of policy making: after his appointment as ambassador to Japan, Adenauer put him in charge of designing the German Japanpolitik.[284] This goes against the diplomatic rule that ambassadors are the addressees and not the authors of instructions. In any case, in spite of Kroll's efforts, the Ministry of Economics did not implement MFN treatment towards Japan until 1960, two years after he had left his Tokyo post.

Lobbyists in Germany were fairly active, particularly during the late fifties when items under import restriction were more significant: textiles, ceramics, toys and tableware. The Bavarian ceramics industry alarmed the Bavarian industrialists' association, whose protest was so effective that Japanese ceramics are under tight quotas until today.[285] The Federal Industrialists' Federation (BDI) consistently appeared quite unenthusiastic about liberalising Japanese imports. As the sole lobby pushing for liberalisation the German Retailers' Association was active.

Though Japanese ministers and elder statesmen evidently liked their trips to Germany, where they did not have to apologise for Japan's misbehaviour during the war, the 'annual' foreign ministers' consultation between Germany and Japan was taken up less frequently than with France or Britain. Britain, at the time, still had substantial Far Eastern interests, France continued to claim to have some, while Brandt in 1967 admitted that Germany had none. In her post-war foreign policy Germany was eager to keep a low profile in political terms, this even more so in the case of Japan, where Moscow would regularly blow into an embarrassing 'axis' propaganda trumpet. In Japanese eyes in the sixties Germany remained secondary in importance to Britain. To Britain in consequence also more high level industry delegations were sent than to Germany, where after 1960 everything significant that could be liberalised was liberalised and was thus less interesting in terms of economic diplomacy.

European co-operation. The Commission, in 1958, had already set up its DG I to take care of future external relations. Commissioner Rey presided over a group of three Commission members in charge of this directorate general. It was subdivided into four directorates: the first for general affairs and relations with international organisations, the second for associations, the third for bilateral relations, and the fourth was in charge of commercial policies and the negotiations.[286] This latter directorate soon had to become active in the ensuing Dillon Round (1960–61) and Kennedy Round (1964–67). French and Italian opposition however prevented the Commission from negotiating with Japan beyond tariffs in Geneva. They also prevented the Commission's 1963–64 initiative for a mandate on a common TA. In view of Japan's *global* quotas only the aggregate bargaining power of the Six would have been effective in opening Japan's market at an earlier time. In the early sixties when Europe maintained substantial restrictions vis à vis Japan and thus significant bargaining chips, the national bureaucrats assembled at Coreper, however, enjoyed themselves sabotaging whatever prospect of common action there arose. When in November 1962 the Council decided to have identical SCs inserted in TAs with Japan, it came at least two years too late: Germany had already concluded a TA with Japan without an SC in 1960. During the later bilateral negotiations it was impossible to discern any EC co-ordination. Whenever differences in import regimes threatened to 'disrupt' a market (i.e. the protected market got a dose of competitive third country imports via a low tariff—non-quota EC country), then Art. 115 was applied, but not an attempt for a common import policy.

From an institutional point of view the co-ordination of EC policies towards Japan would not have been difficult to achieve: the Belgian, Italian and French ministries in charge of EC affairs were also in charge of or substantially involved in foreign trade policies (and thus dealing with Japan). In Germany and in the Netherlands, where national EC competences are more dispersed, the bureaus in the Economics Ministries which were in charge of foreign trade relations were also the ones which issued directives to their Coreper delegation on the EC's external policies.[287] But it was not until 1968, when German and Benelux restrictions had melted into insignificance, that 'national experts' met to co-ordinate bilateral trade negotiations with Japan. On urgent sectoral issues national officials were less dogmatic in defending their competences.

From 1965, twice-yearly ECSC—MITI consultations were taking place, and in 1968 joint Commission—member states negotiations were conducted with Japan on quotas for Japanese cotton textile imports.

Organised industrial interests were more successful in European co-operation. Keidanren—UNICE conferred regularly from the early sixties, and in 1963 an UNICE delegation visited Japan. In 1962 EC special steel producers tried to negotiate with their Japanese counterparts collectively. German, Italian and French porcelain producers in a joint effort let the Council of Ministers impose a mixed tariff (of value and weight) on Japanese porcelain imports, thus increasing the effective tariffs by up to 100 per cent. Later in November 1964 they successfully persuaded the Council to put porcelain on the exemption list from a linear tariff reduction.[288]

Japanese premiers and foreign ministers on European tours regularly stopped at the Commission at least for courtesy visits, though during the sixties, after Rey's 1961 visit to Japan, Commissioners no longer reciprocated.

Britain. The Board of Trade was in charge of commercial relations, and negotiating teams from the BOT were usually led at under-secretary of state level. In 1962 twice-yearly foreign ministers' consultations were agreed upon.

Though this was twice the intensity of Franco— and German—Japanese consultations, the schedule was kept more regularly. As a result of alternating meetings in Tokyo and London, British Foreign Secretaries had more Far Eastern exposure than all their continental colleagues taken together. The president of the BOT also travelled more frequently to Japan.

With a stronger tradition of ministerial responsibility sectoral lobbyists — that is, mainly textile producers — were less successful in Britain than elsewhere after 1962 (once a Japanpolitik had been decided). FBI–CBI–Keidanren conferences started regularly in 1956, and the Japanese Chamber of Commerce (Nissho) held annual conferences with the London Chamber of Commerce from 1962.

British business eager to invest into an expanding economy bilaterally and within OECD and BIAC urged the case for Japanese capital liberalisation after 1964, when Japan acceded to the OECD.

The role of the US and of international organisations

When one examines bilateral relations the role of third actors and of multilateral exchanges tends to become neglected. Under post-war conditions one could even argue that the script for Euro–Japanese relations could largely have been written in Washington D.C. Was it pure coincidence that Germany and the Netherlands (and later Britain) were at the time the US's most faithful European allies and treated Japan — which in the fifties was slowly recuperating under intense US tutelage — in relative terms the most liberally? But Germany, Benelux and the UK were free trade nations anyway and the state of their economies allowed for a liberal foreign trade regime. The inconsistency of European policies towards Japan and the low level of politicisation of Euro–Japanese relations on the European side would also argue against the notion of massive US political pressure.

The US had a political and an economic interest in European liberalisation towards Japan, and they made no secret of this. Politically they felt their client nation's Western integration could benefit from some European supportive input, that is, Japan ought to be admitted to GATT and OECD as an equal. Moreover Japan with her structural import dependency desperately needed export outlets in order to develop and to prosper. The US were ready to offer their markets, but thought it fair that Europeans helped in burden sharing and alleviated part of the pressure on US markets by opening theirs.

Japan's GATT membership served as legal vehicle to obtain MFN treatment from Europe. The MTN rounds of the sixties ended successfully in mutual tariff reductions. Once admitted to OECD more effective pressure could be put on Japan to liberalise capital transactions and imports. The Japanese dependency on obtaining IBRD–World Bank loans would serve the same ends.

Whatever may have been the actual variables and incidents of European policy decisions, in the late 1960s the US had achieved its objectives: Japan in legal and status terms was treated as an equal by Western Europe, most European markets were entirely open for the more sophisticated, the more promising and higher value added Japanese export products. By this time, however, the Nixon administration would start a trade war against Japan of its very own, upstaging in terms of arrogance and arm-twisting everything hitherto performed in the Euro—Japanese sideshow.[289]

Japanese policy decisions towards Europe

For Japan her economic and political emancipation in relation towards Western Europe (1954—64) was a high politics affair, in which MFA in full national consensus could relentlessly send out the top Japanese political and economic establishment for month-long and at times quite humiliating tours of European capitals.

Hanabusa offered an accurate, but fairly brief and low key account of the Japanese efforts during this period.[290] Based evidently on Hanabusa's monograph, Hosoya concluded that Euro—Japanese relations were politicised only in 1977—78.[291] This evidently is not correct as far as Japanese policies were concerned.

Officially and for most practical operations Japanese policies towards Europe were conducted by MFA. Trade relations were negotiated by its Economic Affairs Bureau and political relations administered by its European and Oceanic Affairs Bureau. The respective bureau chiefs and the administrative vice-minister and their deputies were the operational key figures. Japanese ministers and premiers, all emanating from a purely domestic political scene and untrained for foreign experiences and bargaining styles, had largely to rely on MFA's advice and expertise when deciding on Japan's policies towards Europe, or rather, when approving MFA's policy proposals. MFA in this period of her diplomatic offensive appears to have been stronger than ever later. Its policy recommendations were allowed to overrule both MITI's and MOF's objections against the SC in 1962—63 and MITI's and MOT's dislike of the terms for Japan's OECD entry 1963.

Since the necessary Japanese concessions did not yet require an actual full-scale liberalisation of imports or the implementation of capital liberalisation, evidently both the big business community (zaikai) organised in Keidanren, Nissho, JFTC and Doyukai Keizai were in agreement with MFA's line as was the LDP's powerful Foreign Policy Research Council. Still, the latter appeared more interested in the pretexts this policy would provide to revise Japan's SCAP-inherited anti-monopoly law and for more government subsidies for Japanese businesses exposed to the expected European onslaught.

After the political costs of the renewal of the defence treaty with the US the LDP's mainstream establishment was happy until 1963 with its Three Pillar theory in which the less conspicuous Europeans would play their part.

Since travel restrictions for individual citizens were abolished only in 1965 the Japanese public had no updated idea on what Europe was like. At the time Europe was viewed with a mixture of cultural admiration and a strong sense of Japan's own shortcomings,[292] resembling a handsome collective inferiority complex.

On the operational level MFA's offensive strongly relied on visitors' diplomacy. There were not only countless Japanese politicians touring Europe, but even more business missions 'surveying' some economic fact in Europe, which had an explicit private economic diplomacy task on which they had to report upon return. Thirty of the major respective missions to Europe (1957–68) are listed by Bryant.[293] Their basic objective was to convince their European business counterparts that Japanese imports would not do them any harm. It is a firm Japanese belief that all problems arising in human and national interactions are basically communication failures and since Japan had no bargaining chips that the Europeans might be interested in, Japan's tactical approach was fairly simple and essentially a cognitive one: all diplomats, politicians and businessmen heading for Europe were instructed to persuade, to convince and to plead for import liberalisation.[294] They did this so thoroughly that in 1966 MFA had to rescind its strategy: Benelux and Germany were exempted from this treatment because 'too severe demands even hamper(ed) normal trade relations with them'.[295]

The economic dimension in bilateral relations

The structure of bilateral trade

The figures in Table 4.1 show bilaterally a chronically imbalanced trade of Japan with the EC. Her coverage ratios (imports as percentage of exports) fluctuated between 82.8 per cent (1964) and 93.9 per cent (1968). The deficit towards the EC resulted, because Japanese surpluses with Italy and Benelux were too small to offset her consistent deficits with Germany and France. The German and Benelux share in EC trade with Japan rose from 70.9 per cent (1956) to 76.6 per cent (1960), and then remained fairly stable at 73.6 per cent (1964) and 73.9 per cent (1968).

As a market Britain appeared most attractive throughout the fifties and sixties for Japanese products in Europe, while Germany after 1960

Table 4.1

Euro–Japanese trade by countries[296]
(in million US $)

	Japanese exports (fob)				Japanese imports (cif)			
	1956	1960	1964	1968	1956	1960	1964	1968
Germany	34.1	66.3	149.0	287.4	56.2	123.0	249.5	400.6
Benelux	38.2	63.5	115.1	233.7	23.7	41.1	82.1	133.9
France	14.2	15.6	41.6	94.1	21.6	32.3	70.4	127.4
Italy	16.7	29.2	59.6	77.1	9.8	12.6	42.1	75.0
EC total	103.2	174.6	365.3	692.3	111.3	209.0	444.1	736.9
Britain	63.2	120.6	197.8	364.6	66.6	99.1	185.3	257.4
Total exports and imports	2501	4055	6674	12973	3230	4492	7938	12988

Table 4.2

Japanese trade with the EC in its relative shares[297]

Japanese exports	to EC as share of J's total exports	to G as share of G imports	to NL as share of NL imports	to BL as share of BL imports	to F as share of F imports	to I as share of I imports	to UK as share of UK imports
1960	4.3%	0.7%	0.5%	0.5%	0.3%	0.7%	0.9%
1968	5.3%	1.4%	0.9%	0.8%	0.9%	0.8%	1.5%
Japanese imports	from EC as share of J's total imports	from G as share of G exports	from NL as share of NL exports	from BL as share of BL exports	from F as share of F exports	from I as share of I exports	from UK as share of UK exports
1960	4.7%	1.1%	0.6%	0.6%	0.4%	0.4%	0.8%
1968	5.7%	1.4%	0.8%	0.7%	0.8%	0.7%	1.5%

overtook Britain as Japan's main European supplier.

The relative importance of bilateral trade

Trade with Japan obviously is fairly marginal for Europe. In relative terms bilateral trade is far more important for Japan than vice versa. The absolute strength of UK— and German—Japanese trade is reflected in their comparatively strong shares also in Britain's and Germany's foreign trade. The lower part of Table 4.2 also indicates strong evidence for the neglect of the Japanese market by Benelux, French and Italian exporters. Nevertheless bilateral Euro—Japanese trade for all countries involved increased in relative significance during the sixties. Japan stood at place 32 in 1958 among the Community's suppliers, ten years later she took place 12. As an export market for EC products Japan rose from place 29 (1958) to 11 (1968).[298]

It should therefore be expected that the increase in Japan's relative importance to the EC should have been translated into strengthened diplomatic—political concern.

The global balances of trade

During 1957—68 all EC nations — except for Germany throughout the period and for France in 1959—61 — had substantial annual deficits in their balances of trade.[299] The average annual deficits amounted to $200m for Belgium—Luxembourg, to $870m for the Netherlands, to $960m for Italy, and to $440m for France (including her 1959—61 surplus years). Britain had $2160m deficits per annum, and Germany's surpluses averaged $1780m during 1957—68.

From these figures it follows that France and Germany, whose bilateral balances with Japan had been consistently positive, also in view of their global trade situation were in a difficult position to refuse Japanese liberalisation demands.

The composition of bilateral trade

From 1960 to 1968, as shown in Table 4.3, Japanese exports to the EC nearly quadrupled (from $174m to $692m). To visualise the structural change in the composition of Japanese exports to the EC, those products whose sales actually declined are followed by two asterisks, those who failed to keep up with the quadrupling speed are followed by one asterisk. Thus the effects of Japan's restructuring efforts during the early

128

sixties become fairly obvious. The shares of agricultural exports (tobacco, silk, conserves, fish, whale oil) to Europe declined from 41 per cent (1960) to 16 per cent (1968), those of labour intensive light industries (textiles, clothing, toys) fell from 24 per cent to 17 per cent. The exports of capital intensive, higher value added industries (machinery, steel, precision instruments, chemicals, transportation) increased from 33 per cent to 66 per cent correspondingly.

Table 4.3

Main Japanese exports to the EC[300]
(in million US $)

	1960	1968
Mechanical and electrical machinery	7	100
Iron and steel products	4	72
Precision instruments	9	55
Textiles*	22	46
Chemical products*	16	47
Oils and animal fats**	10	5
Clothing*	6	20
Transport materials	0.5	48
Fish*	21	51
Conserves of fruits or vegetables*	6	13
Silk**	18	3
Raw tobacco*	3	7
Toys	6	21

Table 4.4

Main EC exports to Japan[301]
(in million US $)

	1960	1967
Machines, tools, transporting materials	75	258
Chemical products	68	177
Food and drugs	11	62
Iron and steel	5	—
Other manufactured products	32	146
Raw materials	11	—
Energy	1	1

Judging from the aggregate figures shown in Table 4.4, such dramatic changes as documented in Table 4.3 did not take place in the composition of EC exports. They remained predominantly heavy industry and capital goods which the Japanese imported for their industrial restructuring and modernisation needs.

Restrictions on trade

EC restrictions and Japanese exports. There were general import restrictions (*erga omnes*) practised by EC countries, most of them on agricultural imports. They figure in the first two columns of Table 4.5. In addition to these, EC countries maintained restrictions aimed exclusively at imports originating from Japan. These were those quotas which Japan felt as discriminatory and contradictory to MFN principles.

Table 4.5
EC import restrictions

	Restricted positions towards the $ area		Additional positions restricted towards Japan
	1962[302]	1965[303]	1965[304]
Germany	105	62	20
Benelux	96	32	33
France	500	98	68
Italy	410	38	123

Restricted in all EC countries were synthetic textile fibres, cotton textiles, velvets, carpets, blankets, bed and table linen, underwear, womens' and childrens' clothing, handkerchiefs and porcelain ceramics. In three of the four EC customs zones wool, woollen textiles, table cloths, shoes, tiles and insulators were restricted.[305]

Kanamori observed that EC restrictions were concentrated on products of Japanese low and middle wage industries (light industries in effect).[306] He concluded that — unlike the case of Japanese exports to the US — Japan had been unable to use her low wage levels as a competitive advantage in her trade with the EC.

Apart from a few and increasingly marginal products, such as Japanese raw silk, canned fish and fruits, and animal and vegetable oils, which were successful due to Japan's natural endowment, all other exports had to withstand competition by domestic producers in the EC. Kern examined the comparative strength of the Japanese industry in the early sixties.[307] He found it was disadvantaged by the high costs for raw material imports, by high capital costs and Japan's small scale industrial structure. Even the most important Japanese industries were medium-sized by world standards. Growth conditions created high demand for scarce capital and resulted in costly low equity-debt ratios for expanding companies.

There were two countervailing factors: the low level of salaries, enabling international competitiveness of Japanese labour intensive products, and the increasing productivity in basic industries. These increases in the chemical and the machinery industries were already higher than in any other Western country in the early sixties.

Japanese restrictions. Japan maintained the following three import licensing systems:[308]

1 *Automatic approval* (AA): unlimited licences for products considered essential for the Japanese economy.

2 *Automatic fund allocation* (AFA): within the limits of the foreign exchange budget (to be tightened in case of foreign exchange shortages). This meant virtually free imports for mainly consumer products (automatic licensing).

3 *Fund allocation system* (FAS): referred to a list of products on which strict import controls were exercised.

'Liberalisation' in the Japanese context means the transfer of products from the FAS to the AFA or AA lists. In 1959 MOF announced a 90 per cent liberalisation of Japanese imports until October 1962. This meant that products which counted for 90 per cent of Japanese imports in 1959 (when fairly restrictive conditions for non-essential imports were in force) would be transferred to AA or to AFA. The formal implementation of the 90 per cent goal with reference to France's and Italy's discrimination was delayed until 1963.[309]

In their actual implementation Japanese authorities (that is, mainly but not exclusively, MITI and MOF) were often very skilful in introducing new barriers either via overt tariff increases or via more discreet NTBs such as the introduction of new red tape or discrete hints (administrative guidance) to the big general trading companies (sogo shosha) which in the sixties handled 80 per cent of Japan's foreign trade.[310]

The Japanese policy thereby followed a very clear and fairly explicit principle allowing the effective penetration of foreign imports only after domestic industries were considered competitive enough to withstand this contest without damage.

The fact that Japanese quotas were global complicated negotiations with Europe: Japan had difficulties in offering corresponding concessions to European liberalisations of restrictions which had applied to Japan only. When Japan extended her global quotas on products of special interest to European producers (such as e.g. the quotas for wine, perfumes, women's clothing and cars which were enlarged at the French request), then these, facing global competition, could not be sure of actually benefiting from this concession.

Evaluation

The historical theme of this chapter is the story of the gradual emancipation of the world's first non-Western industrial country into near-equal economic intercourse with her fellow DCs.

For Japan this endeavour was conceptually fairly simple: economically it followed the tradition of catching up with the West. Politically it moved along similar lines to Japan's decade long struggle to revise the 'Unequal Treaties' in the late nineteenth century. National consensus on the desirability of belonging to the 'club' (symbolised first by GATT, later by OECD) was thus easily achieved. Given the public attention and the traditional values involved the politicisation of bilateral relations became self-evident. One could even have expected the Japanese to offer substantial economic concessions to achieve this end.

Against all stereotypes of her supposedly chronic lack of diplomatic talent, Japan did remarkably well. The only price Japan had to pay was an endurance test in terms of patience and in the repetition of the usual anti-discriminatory rhetoric. The senior MFA officials who masterminded Japan's diplomatic offensive 1954—64 succeeded in co-ordinating bureaucratic, big business (zaikai) and the political leadership's efforts towards Europe effectively. Their massive initiative in autumn 1962 was conceptually simple: to flood Europe with successive waves of polite, modest and well-briefed top politicians and business leaders. European disunity and the intellectual untenability of its discrimination facilitated the Japanese success. In economic terms Japan could achieve a substantial opening of the European market without having to make significant concessions.

In political terms — to achieve equality in symbolic treatment and to maintain high level political consultations — the Japanese success was marred by the concession of safeguard clauses, which in economic terms were meaningless, but continued to serve as a residual discriminatory symbol in Japanese eyes.

On the European side thus the political capital gained by granting economic concessions was wasted for a symbolic precaution, intended to satisfy the sectoral interests of light industry producers.

The Commission's role during the 1959—68 period was one of permanent frustration for the officials involved: they were faced with the formidable task of bringing together two utterly divergent trade policy traditions: the 'Romanic' protectionist one, and the free trade orientation of the more successful German and Benelux exporting nations. At the same time they had to face national bureaucratic jealousies which were allowed to flourish under conditions of largely non-existent political leadership. National officials — mostly those of 'Romanic' administrations — were simply unwilling to give up or to share a slice of their foreign trade competences during the transition period, solely urged by functional needs. This explains that in contemporary perspective, the Commission's 1963–64 proposals — with their antagonising effects on the Japanese side — appear as the typical result of the infamous inward looking EC development. The Commission demanded a common SC and a common negative list in a TA with Japan for reasons utterly unrelated to Japan, to the needs of international trade, or to the state of European economies. Harmonisation of import rules (the avoidance of Art. 115 applications) and the Commission's foreign policy role were seen as goals per se. The Commission's concern on policy competence apparently went at the expense of any reflection on the actual quality of her prospective external relations (a product of Coreper's frustrating role). This attitude is mirrored in the emphasis put forward in its documents to the Council: all stress at length with ever more complicated technical formulae that the conflicting national protectionist interests could be accommodated under a Community hat.

They never mention the more convincing prospect that only unified EC level bargaining would have been able to open effectively Japan's global quotas and to achieve European economic penetration there — also via Japanese capital liberalisation — at an advantageous and earlier time in Japan's booming growth period. References to the political importance of strengthening Japan's ties to the West are fairly passing and appear insignificant compared to the energies spent on the modes for doubled safeguards and quotas. A 'common commercial policy' towards Japan thereby did not emerge.

Decision making evidently refers to power. It is clear from earlier sections of this chapter (pages 85–125) that not only the Commission but also the national parliaments had none on trade policies with the Far East.

In Europe policies on Japan were decided by senior bureaucrats. They seemingly followed some general common sense by which they attempted to reconcile the lobbyists' protective interests with the vague political goodwill towards Japan, an American ally in the Far East. In this process the lobbyists' sectoral interests seemed to have been able to veto all the more significant initiatives until the early 1960s when political benefits would have accrued. The casual and infrequent interventions from the political top were too unsystematic to effect any change.

There was a more general deficiency among European decision makers in the 1950s and 1960s: a lack of perspective and of political imagination. National officials muddled along with their restriction lists — never apparently thinking beyond their annual trade protocols, never considering Japan's growth potential unrolling before their eyes, hardly ever looking at the political chances which this potential was ready to offer.

One has to admit that Japanese officials and politicians (De Gaulle's 'transistor salesmen') who shared the same bureaucratic virtues, quite likely were not the persons to offer great inspirations or responsiveness to grand designs. Still, this is no excuse for Europe never attempting any seriously and carefully designed Japanpolitik and leaving the task and the costs of the Western integration of Japan entirely to the US.

It would have been up to the political leadership to put the political perspective straight. This 'leadership' was either susceptible to the domestic interest groups or Japan was such a marginal issue in the fifties and sixties to most European policy makers that other priorities dominated their minds and busy schedules. In any case, the chance for high politics co-operation between Europe and Japan — or anything resembling 'three pillars' — during that period was missed.

References

1 Hanabusa, Masamichi. *Trade Problems between Japan and Western Europe*. Farnborough, Hants.,: Saxon House. 1979, p. 4.
2 *Nippon Times*, 14.5.1953; *New York Times*, 4.7.1959; *Le Monde*, 12 and 13.5.1959.
3 Japanese Mission to the EC. Press Release, Brussels 6.10.1978.
4 *Neue Zürcher Zeitung*, 12.7.1950 and 17.4.1951.
5 Uchino, Tatsuro. Thirty Years of Postwar Economic Policies. In: Ministry of Foreign Affairs (ed.). *Japan's Postwar Economic Policies*. Tokyo. 1976. 5–22, p. 13.
6 *New York Times* 8.7.1954; *Manchester Guardian* 3.8.1954.
7 *Manchester Guardian* 23.7.1954; *Neue Zürcher Zeitung* 21.12.1954 and 11.11.1954; *Le Monde*, 2.8.1955; *Le Figaro*, 29.7.1955.
8 *Nippon Times*, 11.5.1955.
9 *New York Times*, 22.2.1955.
10 *The Times*, 8.11.1954.
11 *New York Times*, 11.7.1954; *Frankfurter Allgemeine Zeitung*, 4.11.1954.
12 *Nippon Times*, 21.4.1955.
13 *Nippon Times*, 26.5.1955.
14 *Süddeutsche Zeitung*, 15.6.1955.
15 *Financial Times*, 8.6.1955.

16 *New York Times*, 12.8.1955.
17 *Frankfurter Allgemeine Zeitung*, 13.8.1955.
18 *Frankfurter Allgemeine Zeitung*, 5.2.1954.
19 *Nippon Times*, 1.2.1955.
20 Kroll, Hans. *Lebenserinnerungen eines Botschafters*. Köln: Kiepenheuer & Witsch. 1968, p. 294.
21 Ibid., pp. 287—88.
22 *ANSA*, 19.10.1955.
23 *Neue Zürcher Zeitung*, 22.3.1957.
24 *Neue Zürcher Zeitung*, 15.12.1958 and 27.8. 1959.
25 *Neue Zürcher Zeitung*, 27.8.1959.
26 *Süddeutsche Zeitung*, 25.8.1955; *Frankfurter Allgemeine Zeitung*, 28.11.1955.
27 *Nippon Times*, 3.12.1955.
28 *Nippon Times*, 30.5.1956 and 16.6.1956; *Neue Zürcher Zeitung*, 18.6.1956.
29 *Frankfurter Allgemeine Zeitung*, 15.1.1957; *Süddeutsche Zeitung*, 16.1.1957.
30 *Japan Times*, 8.2.1957.
31 Kroll. 1968. Op. cit., p. 345.
32 *Neue Zürcher Zeitung*, 17.6.1959.
33 *Japan Times*, 6.6.1958 and 4.7.1959.
34 *Japan Times*, 4.7.1959 and 5.11.1959.
35 *Financial Times*, 4.8.1959.
36 *Japan Times*, 4.9.1959 and 16.9.1959.
37 *Japan Times*, 4.9.1959; *Neue Zürcher Zeitung*, 21.11.1959.
38 *Frankfurter Allgemeine Zeitung*, 8.1.1960.
39 *Japan Times*, 15.2.1960.
40 *Financial Times*, 24.2.1960.
41 *Frankfurter Allgemeine Zeitung*, 13.2.1960.
42 *Frankfurter Allgemeine Zeitung*, 16.4.1960; *Süddeutsche Zeitung*, 23 and 24.4.1960.
43 *The Economist*, 19.3.1960, 2.4.1960 and 9.4.1960.
44 Adenauer, Konrad. *Erinnerungen, 1959—63*. Stuttgart: DVA. 1968, p. 31.
45 *Japan Times*, 28.5.1960, 29.5.1960 and 2.7.1960. The text of the Trade Agreement is reprinted in: *Festgabe zum zehnten Jubiläum der Deutschen Industrie— und Handelskammer in Japan, 1962—1972*. Tokyo. 1972, p. 63.
46 *Neue Zürcher Zeitung*, 1.10.1955 and 3.6.1957; *Financial Times*, 19.11.1956.
47 *Japan Times*, 22.10.1958 and 31.10.1958.
48 *Japan Times*, 12.10.1959 and 23.10.1959.
49 *Japan Times*, 2.3.1960 and 3.3.1960.

50 *Financial Times*, 6.9.1960; *The Times*, 6.9.1960; *Japan Times*, 22.6.1961.

51 *Nippon Times*, 4.3.1956; *Le Monde*, 26.5.1956.

52 *Japan Times*, 29.12.1956.

53 *New York Herald Tribune*, Paris edition, Economic supplement, May 1959.

54 *Japan Times*, 3.4.1961.

55 *Le Monde*, 19 and 20.6.1960.

56 *Japan Times*, 8.3.1957.

57 *Financial Times*, 29.1.1957.

58 *Japan Times*, 19.2.1957.

59 Kahoku Shimpo (Sendai) as translated in *Japan Times*, 26.2.1957; and Chugoku Shimbun (Hiroshima) as translated in *Japan Times*, 21.3.1957.

60 *Financial Times*, 10.4.1957; *Japan Times*, 23.4.1957.

61 *The Times*, 23.1.1959.

62 'Economic Plans'. In: Ministry of Foreign Affairs (ed.).1976. Op. cit., p. 24.

63 *Far Eastern Economic Review*, 2.4.1959.

64 *Japan Times*, 29.4.1959.

65 Dörsch, Hans J. and Henri Legros. *Les Faits et les Décisions de la C.E.E. 1958—64*. Brussels: Presses Universitaires de Bruxelles. 1969.

66 *Japan Times*, 1.8.1959; *Financial Times*, 16.9.1959.

67 Hanabusa. 1979. Op. cit., p. 3.

68 *Neue Zürcher Zeitung*, 27.5.1959; *Daily Telegraph*, 28.10.1959; *Japan Times*, 12.5.1960.

69 *The Economist*, 4.2.1961.

70 *Far Eastern Economic Review*, 17.11.1960.

71 *Japan Times*, 25.4.1960.

72 *Japan Times*, 26.4.1960.

73 *Far Eastern Economic Review*, 5.5.1960.

74 *Far Eastern Economic Review*, 28.7.1960.

75 *Far Eastern Economic Review*, 18.5.1961.

76 *Neue Zürcher Zeitung*, 7.5.1961.

77 *Le Monde*, 24 and 25.12.1961.

78 *Le Monde*, 23.1.1962.

79 *Japan Times*, 12.12.1961.

·80 *Japan Times*, 17.1.1961.

81 *Japan Times*, 26.7.1961.

82 *Neue Zürcher Zeitung*, 26.11.1961.

83 *The Economist*, 4.2.1961.

84 *Far Eastern Economic Review*, 23.11.61.

85 Ibid.

86 *Japan Times*, 1.12.1961.
87 Joint Communique on Visit of Mr Rey, Member of Commission of European Economic Community, 9.12.1961. In: Ministry of Foreign Affairs. *Gaimusho Press Releases.* Tokyo. 1961, pp. 110—11.
88 *Japan Times*, 7.12.1961.
89 *Japan Times*, 6.12.1961.
90 *Japan Times*, 10.12.1961.
91 *Japan Times*, 6.12.1961.
92 *Japan Times*, 7.12.1961.
93 Joint Communique . . . 1961. Op. cit., p. 110.
94 *Japan Times*, 2.8.1961.
95 *The Times*, 18.1.1962.
96 *Japan Times*, 10.3.1962.
97 *Daily Express*, 18.8.1961.
98 *Japan Times*, 18.1.1962.
99 *Japan Times*, 10.12.1961.
100 Japan — United Kingdom Communique. In: *Gaimusho Press Releases.* 1961. Op. cit., pp. 107—8.
101 As quoted in: *Far Eastern Economic Review*, 23.11.1961.
102 Ibid.
103 *The Economist*, 1.9.1962 and 8.9.1962.
104 *Far Eastern Economic Review*, 14.2.1963.
105 *Neue Zürcher Zeitung*, 4.9.1961; *The Economist*, 20.2.1965.
106 *The Economist*, 18.8.1962; *Far Eastern Economic Review*, 24.5.1962.
107 *Far Eastern Economic Review*, 26.4.1962.
108 *Far Eastern Economic Review*, 30.8.1962.
109 Ibid.
110 *The Economist*, 10.11.1962.
111 *Keesing's Contemporary Archives, 24* (1963—64), p. 19171.
112 *The Economist*, 17.11.1962.
113 *Far Eastern Economic Review*, 29.11.1962.
114 Ibid. and *The Economist*, 10.11.1962.
115 *Keesing's Contemporary Archives 24* (1963—64), p. 19397.
116 *Japan Times*, 18.1.1962.
117 *Japan Times*, 21.1.1962.
118 *Japan Times*, 24.1.1962.
119 *Japan Times*, 18.1.1962 and 20.1.1962.
120 *Japan Times*, 17.2.1962 and 1.5.1962; *Far Eastern Economic Review*, 8.2.1962.
121 *Japan Times*, 14.7.1962.
122 *Japan Times*, 16.7.1962.
123 Sankei Shimbun, Chubu Nippon Shimbun, Mainichi Shimbun and Nihon Keizai Shimbun, as translated in: *Japan Times*, 18.7.1962,

20.7.1962 and 22.7.1962.
124 *The Times*, 7.8.1962.
125 *Japan Times*, 26.8.1962.
126 *Japan Times*, 5.9.1962.
127 *Japan Times*, 13.9.1962; *The Times*, 14.9.1962.
128 *Japan Times*, 7.10.1962.
129 *Neue Zürcher Zeitung*, 30.9.1962; *Frankfurter Allgemeine Zeitung*, 27.10.1962.
130 *Der Spiegel*, 26.5.1969.
131 *Keesing's Contemporary Archives*, 24 (1963–64) pp. 19171–72.
132 *Far Eastern Economic Review*, 29.11.1962.
133 *Far Eastern Economic Review*, 22.3.1962.
134 *Far Eastern Economic Review*, 22.2.1962.
135 Dumont, Andre. Du rôle des relations entre organisations professionelles Européennes et Japonaises dans le developpement des e échanges entre l'industrie Européenne et Japonaise — l'exemple de l'industrie cotonière. In: *EEC Symposium*. Presented by UNICE, Keidanren and Sophia University. 8.10.1963.Tokyo. 1963, pp. 121–28. *Far Eastern Economic Review*, 19.7.1962.
136 *Le Monde*, 27.4.1962.
137 *Le Monde*, 17.6.1962.
138 *Le Monde*, 19.12.1962.
139 *Japan Times*, 19.12.1962.
140 *Japan Times*, 19.5.1962.
141 *Neue Zürcher Zeitung*, 21.9.1962.
142 *Keesing's*. 1963–64. Loc. cit.
143 *Financial Times*, 20.11.1962.
144 *Japan Times*, 11.12.1962.
145 *Japan Times*, 27.5.1962.
146 *Japan Times*, 16.9.1962; *Frankfurter Allgemeine Zeitung*, 26.9.1962.
147 Commission. *Journal Officiel*. No. 71. 1961, p. 1273.
148 Baas, Jan. *Rapport sur les relations commerciales entre les Six et le Japon*. Parlement Européen. Documents de Séance 1969–70. Doc. 212. 2.2.1970, p. 6.
149 *Far Eastern Economic Review*, 11.10.1962.
150 *Journal Officiel*. No. 90. 1962, p. 2353.
151 *The Times*, 15.2.1962.
152 *The Hindu*, 4.7.1962; *Neue Zürcher Zeitung*, 30.9.1962.
153 *Frankfurter Allgemeine Zeitung*, 23.8.1962.
154 Monloup, Madalaine. *Les relations économiques du Marché Commun et du Japon*. Bruges: Collège d'Europe. 1969, p. 27.
155 Dörsch. 1969. Op. cit., p. 427. *Neue Zürcher Zeitung*, 15.11.1962.
156 *Japan Times*, 8.11.1962.

157 *Far Eastern Economic Review,* 6.12.1962.
158 *Japan Times,* 1.1.1963.
159 *Far Eastern Economic Review,* 14.2.1963.
160 *Japan Times,* 8.1.1963.
161 *Far Eastern Economic Review,* 14.2.1963.
162 As translated in: *Japan Times,* 25.2.1963.
163 *Far Eastern Economic Review,* 28.3.1963.
164 *Financial Times,* 1.5.1963.
165 *Japan Times,* 4.6.1963 and 27.6.1963.
166 *Neue Zürcher Zeitung,* 21.3.1963.
167 *Japan Times,* 7.5.1963.
168 *Keesing's,* 1963–64. Op. cit., p. 19397; *Far Eastern Economic Review,* 25.4.1963.
169 *Le Monde,* 16.4.1963.
170 *Le Monde,* 4.6.1963.
171 *Le Monde,* 16.4.1963.
172 *Le Monde,* 23.4.1963 and 26.4.1963; *The Economist,* 27.4.1963.
173 *Le Monde,* 1.3.1960.
174 *The Times,* 24.3.1963.
175 *Le Monde,* 15.5.1963; *Keesing's,* 1963–64. Op. cit., p. 19448.
176 *Far Eastern Economic Review,* 23.6.1963.
177 *Japan Times,* 6.3.1963.
178 *Far Eastern Economic Review,* 16.5.1963.
179 *Le Monde,* 16.5.1963.
180 *Japan Times,* 11.2.1963.
181 Dörsch. 1969. Op. cit., p. 434.
182 Ibid., p. 443.
183 Commission. Note 'EXC' No. 12737 aux bureax nationaux. 5.7.1963; *Frankfurter Allgemeine Zeitung,* 31.7.1963.
184 *Neue Zürcher Zeitung,* 28.6.1963.
185 *Japan Times,* 12.2.1963.
186 *Financial Times,* 20.5.1963.
187 *Japan Times,* 30.11.1962.
188 *Japan Times,* 12.2.1963.
189 *Japan Times,* 28.11.1962.
190 *New York Times,* 5.4.1963.
191 *The Times,* 13.5.1963.
192 *Japan Times,* 15.2.1963 and 10.5.1963.
193 *Japan Times,* 21.5.1963.
194 *Japan Times,* 29.5.1963.
195 *Financial Times,* 7.6.1963.
196 *Japan Times,* 8.6.1963.
197 *The Times,* 11.6.1963.
198 *Japan Times,* 13.6.1963.

199 *Japan Times*, 7.7.1963; *Neue Zürcher Zeitung*, 6.7.1963.
200 *The Times*, 12.7.1963; *Japan Times*, 17.7.1963.
201 *Far Eastern Economic Review*, 5.9.1963; *Japan Times*, 26.7.1963.
202 *Japan Times*, 27.7.1963.
203 As translated in: *Japan Times*, 28.7.1963 and 29.7.1963.
204 *Japan Times*, 27.7.1963.
205 *Far Eastern Economic Review*, 5.9.1963.
206 *Japan Times*, 22.12.1962.
207 *Japan Times*, 12.2.1964.
208 *Japan Times*, 10.4.1964.
209 *Japan Times*, 22.8.1963; *Neue Zürcher Zeitung*, 17.12.1963.
210 *Japan Times*, 26.8.1963 and 20.9.1963.
211 *Japan Times*, 6.10.1963.
212 *Japan Times*, 31.8.1963.
213 Commission. *Relations commerciales de la Communauté avec le Japon — Communication de la Commission au Conseil complétant la proposition de la Commission au Conseil du 26.6.1963.* I—COM (64) 52 final, 26.2.1964.
214 *Financial Times*, 10.10.1963.
215 *Japan Times*, 24.10.1963.
216 *Japan Times*, 9.2.1964.
217 Commission. 1964. Loc. cit.; Dörsch. 1969. Op. cit., p. 461.
218 *Far Eastern Economic Review*, 20.3.1964.
219 *Far Eastern Economic Review*, 20.3.1964; *Bulletin of the EEC.* 7, 1964. No. 4, p. 15.
220 *Bulletin of the EEC.* 7, 1964. No. 6, p. 11; *Far Eastern Economic Review*, 28.5.1964.
221 *Japan Times*, 18.4.1964.
222 Commission. *Rapport de la Commission au Conseil sur les bases d'un éventuel accord commercial avec le Japon.* Note DIS 15851 aux bureaux nationaux. 2.7.1964.
223 *Japan Times*, 4.7.1964.
224 *Far Eastern Economic Review*, 16.7.1964.
225 Commission. Note DIS 15851. Loc. cit.
226 *Japan Times*, 2.7.1964.
227 *Japan Times*, 25.9.1964.
228 *New York Herald Tribune*, European edition, 24.7.1964.
229 *Far Eastern Economic Review*, 1.10.1964.
230 *Far Eastern Economic Review*, 28.5.1964; *Japan Times*, 14.5.1964.
231 *Neue Zürcher Zeitung*, 31.7.1964.
232 *The Economist*, 9.5.1964; *Far Eastern Economic Review*, 21.5.1964; *Keesing's*, 1963—64. Op. cit., p. 20284.
233 *Far Eastern Economic Review*, 4.6.1964; *Financial Times*, 10.3.1964; *New York Herald Tribune*, European edition, 8.4.1964.

234 *Far Eastern Economic Review*, 7.5.1964; *Le Monde*, 7.4.1964.
235 *Neue Zürcher Zeitung*, 16.4.1965.
236 *Japan Times*, 19.4.1965; *Le Monde*, 21.4.1965.
237 *Far Eastern Economic Review*, 13.5.1965.
238 *Le Monde*, 3.7.1965 and 4 and 5.7.1965.
239 *Japan Times*, 23.7.1965 and 18.11.1965.
240 De Gaulle, Charles. *Mémoires d'Espoir — Le Renouveau, 1958–1962*. Sin. loc. Librairie Plon. 1970, p. 175.
241 Ibid., pp. 275–76.
242 *Far Eastern Economic Review*, 14.1.1965.
243 Commission. *Réponse au question écrite no. 125/65 de MM. Kriedemann/Hahn*. 23.2.1965.
244 *Japan Times*, 23.3.1965.
245 *Japan Times*, 5.4.1965.
246 ECSC. Press Release, 24.9.1965.
247 *Japan Times*, 24.6.1965.
248 *Japan Times*, 20.6.1965.
249 *Far Eastern Economic Review*, 21.4.1966.
250 *Frankfurter Allgemeine Zeitung*, 31.10.1966.
251 *Japan Times*, 3.5.1967 and 12.5.1967; Yomiuri Shimbun as translated in *Japan Times*, 13.5.1967.
252 *Bulletin des C.E.* 1968. No. 5 p. 72.
253 *Far Eastern Economic Review*, 25.7.1968.
254 *Japan Times*, 22.6.1969; *Far Eastern Economic Review*, 17.7.1969; *Le Monde*, 28.6.1969.
255 *Bulletin des C.E.* 1968. No. 7, p. 36; 1968. No. 8, p. 59; and 1968. No. 12, p. 57.
256 *Japan Times*, 10.8.1968.
257 *Le Monde*, 2.4.1968; *Far Eastern Economic Review*, 9.5.1968.
258 *Japan Times*, 23.7.1966.
259 *Frankfurter Allgemeine Zeitung*, 11.12.1967.
260 *Frankfurter Allgemeine Zeitung*, 13.10.1967.
261 *Frankfurter Allgemeine Zeitung*, 17.2.1967.
262 *Japan Times*, 28.4.1967 and 12.5.1967.
263 *Neue Zürcher Zeitung*, 14.5.1967.
264 As quoted in: *Frankfurter Allgemeine Zeitung*, 16.5.1967.
265 Brandt, Willy. Thesen einer deutschen Asienpolitik. In: *Der Wille zum Frieden*. Hamburg: Hoffmann & Campe. 1971, p. 315.
266 Dohnanyi, Klaus von. *Japanische Strategien oder Das deutsche Führungsdefizit*. München: Piper & Co. 1969.
267 Ibid., p. 184.
268 *Japan Times*, 12.8.1966.
269 *The Times*, 8.1.1968, 9.1.1968 and 10.1.1968.
270 *Financial Times*, 11.1.1968.

271 *Japan Times*, 28.4.1969.
272 *Japan Times*, 4.5.1969.
273 *Financial Times*, 9.1.1968.
274 *Sunday Times*, 5.10.1969; *The Economist*, 11.10.1969.
275 *Japan Times*, 14.10.1966; *Financial Times*, 12.10.1967.
276 *Japan Times*, 10.11.1967.
277 *Daily Telegraph*, 20.7.1967; *Japan Times*, 8.3.1968.
278 *Keesing's Contemporary Archives*, 26 (1967—68), p. 22979;
     Financial Times, 13.9.1969.
279 Inoki, Masamichi. A New Europe and the Japanese Fear of Isola-
     tion. *Journal of Social and Political Ideas in Japan 1*, 1963, 109—
     112; anonymous. L'inquiétude du Japon devant le Marché Commun.
     Revue du Marché Commun 5, 1962, 181—3.
280 *Japan Times*, 22.11.1967.
281 *Neue Zürcher Zeitung*, 27.8.1959.
282 Sasse, Christoph. *Regierungen, Parlamente, Ministerrat — Entschei-
     dungs — prozesse in der Europäische Gemeinschaft*. Bonn: Europa
     Union Verlag. 1975, p. 48.
283 *Japan Times*, 15.7.1959.
284 Kroll. 1968. Loc. cit.
285 *Der Spiegel*, 27.10.1980.
286 Commission. *Premier rapport général sur l'activité de la Commun-
     auté*. 1958. Annex B; and: *Deuxième rapport général sur l'activité
     de la Communauté, 1958—59*. Annex.
287 Wallace, Helen. *National Governments and the European Commun-
     ities*. London: Chatham House—PEP. 1973. p. 18.
288 *Der Spiegel*, 6.1.1965.
289 Destler, I.M., Haruhiro Sato and Hideo Sato. *The Textile Wrangle —
     Conflict in Japanese American Relations, 1969—1971*. Ithaca, N.Y.:
     Cornell University Press. 1979.
290 Hanabusa. 1979. Op. cit., p. 1.
291 Hosoya, Chihiro. Relations between the European Communities
     and Japan. *Journal of Common Market Studies 18*, 1979, 159—74,
     p. 162.
292 Kojima, Kazuto. Public Opinion Trends in Japan. *Public Opinion
     Quarterly 41*, 1977, 206—16, p. 211.
293 Bryant, William G. *Japanese Private Economic Diplomacy: An
     Analysis of Business—Government Linkages*. New York: Praeger,
     1975, p. 108
294 Blaker, Michael. *Japan's International Negotiating Style*. New York:
     Columbia University Press. 1977, p. 168.
295 *Japan Times*, 4.5.1966.
296 Compiled from: *U.N. Yearbook of International Trade Statistics.
     1960*. New York. 1962, p. 329; and *U.N. Yearbook of International*

Trade Statistics 1968. New York. 1970, p. 459.
297 Calculated from: *U.N. Yearbook of International Trade Statistics 1964;* and: *U.N. Yearbook of International Trade Statistics 1968.*
298 Statistisches Amt der EG. *Statistische Grundzahlen der Gemeinschaft 1968−69.* Luxembourg. 1970, pp. 98−9.
299 Ibid., p. 79; and : *Statistische Grundzahlen der Europäischen Gemeinschaft 1975.* Luxembourg. 1975, pp. 106−7.
300 Adapted from: Baas. 1970. Op. cit., p. 12 (where figures were conflicting, their arithmetical average was taken).
301 Ibid., the same qualification applies.
302 Commission. *Note DIS 15851 aux bureaux nationaux, 2.7.1964.*
303 Henkner, Klaus. Die Handelspolitik der EWG gegenüber Drittländern und die Sonderstellung Japans. *Konjunkturpolitik 11,* 1965, 145−70, p. 149.
304 Ibid., p. 157.
305 Baas. 1970. Op. cit., Annex I, p. 23.
306 Kanamori, Hisao. The European Common Market and Japan's Trade. *The Japan Annual of International Affairs.* No. 2, 1962, 117−27, pp. 122−3.
307 Kern, Pierre. L'Europe à la découverte du dualisme Japonais. *Revue du Marché Commun.* 6, 1963, 206−11, pp. 209.
308 Watanabe, Akihiko. *L'économie Japonaise et la C.E.E.,* Nancy: Université de Nancy. Publications du Center Européen Universitaire. 1964; *The Economist,* 29.9.1962.
309 *The Economist,* 6.4.1963.
310 Baas. 1970. Op. cit., p. 18; *The Economist,* 28.11.1964.

5 EC–Japan relations 1969–75: the beginnings of a common commercial policy and the liberalisation of imports in Japan

As evident in the previous chapter, the late 1960s had been a fairly un-eventful period in Euro–Japanese relations. Japan's diplomatic offensive had stopped during 1963–64 after having achieved its objectives of a large-scale European import liberalisation and of international recognition in symbolic terms (MFN treatment, OECD membership, etc.). During this period bilateral trade grew at regular rates in a balanced fashion. Japanese light industry exports (textiles, cutlery, umbrellas, sewing machines) in the late sixties had lost their salience and competitive threat on the European markets. The ensuing penetration by Japan's heavy industry products (steel, ships, ball-bearings, cars) was still too marginal to cause any serious concern.

As a consequence, EC member states made only spurious efforts to co-ordinate their policies towards Japan. As the only significant common initiative in March 1968 negotiations on an EC–Japan cotton agreement started. They were brought to a successful conclusion in June 1969.

Apart from their cotton negotiations – which again resulted in quite disparate *national* import quotas – and occasional national trade policy expert meetings, a common EC policy towards Japan was not initiated. Still, there were international events that could have shaken up the European bureaucracies' complacency: the US–Japanese textile wrangle in 1969 went into full swing – raising European fears of a diversionary effect of Japanese textile exports from the US to Europe.

In the same year, Mr Crosland, as the Director of the Board of Trade, had offered the complete abolition of British discriminatory import restrictions in exchange for large-scale Japanese liberalisations of items of interest to UK exporters.

The chronology of EC–Japanese relations

Preparing for the Common Commercial Policy (1969)

On 1 January 1970 the Common Commercial Policy (CCP) was to go into effect. Whatever contentious issues had to be resolved bilaterally between Japan and individual member states, had to be settled during 1969.

The first European initiative in that year came from Italy. The Council of Ministers in January 1969 authorised Italy to reintroduce restrictions on 50 items from Japan (textiles, ceramics, bicycles, toys and machinery).[1] To Japanese protests the Italian authorities replied, the earlier liberalisation had been done only on an 'experimental basis' and could thus be revoked any time.[2] In May 1969, Mr Colombo, the Italian Minister for Foreign Trade visited Japan and had talks with Aichi (MFA) and Ohira (MITI) on this matter,[3] but to little avail. On Italian–Japanese trade relations, 1969 passed with new Italian restrictions imposed on Japanese car imports and with none of the old ones removed.[4]

Franco–Japanese relations started in February 1969, after France had hinted it was ready to liberalise 22 items coming from Japan.[5] The delegations were led by the heads of each Foreign Ministry's Economic Bureau.[6] During a second round of negotiations they came to an agreement: in February 1970 France agreed to freeing 21 items from Japan (synthetic textiles, electrical appliances, binoculars, cameras). Japan in turn liberalised 9 items of special interest to France (printing machines and machine tools, for the most part).[7] With the CCP taking over in 1970, France's bilateral restrictions stood at 80, while Japan had 180 global restrictions.

In May 1969 the German Chancellor, Mr Kiesinger, went to Japan. Bilateral relations were seen as remarkably free of problems and of substantial issues, and Kiesinger's visit was seen rather as a courtesy call or an exercise in pre-election public relations.[8] Two high politics issues were to be discussed between Kiesinger and Sato: both agreed not to coordinate their policies on the Non Proliferation Treaty (NPT), which Sato wanted to use as a bargaining chip for Japanese membership in the UN disarmament council in Geneva, while Kiesinger only wanted to postpone its signing.[9] Both then allayed their fears of mutually unwanted recognitions: Japan promised not to recognise the GDR nor to exchange trade missions with her — there was some business pressure for doing just this —

the Germans in turn pledged to recognise neither the PRCh nor North Korea which the Japanese had feared for similar motives.[10] In consequence, the Chinese and North Korean media chose to describe their conversations as a new Hitler—Tojo type plot attempting to stage a postwar comeback.[11] Like Benelux, Germany had liberalised most of Japan's imports. A trade protocol signed in October 1969 enlarged the few existing quotas on both sides: wool and cotton products to Germany, while Japan widened her quotas on a series of capital goods imports.[12]

During 1969, Britain revised her policies towards Japan. A governmental policy paper outlined as the basic British interests in Japan:[13] to consider Japan's strong economic potential and growth, and to support Japan's Western integration, to avoid a possible Japan—PRCh alliance.

This was the context of Foreign Minister Aichi's visit to UK, where he met with Wilson, Crosland (BoT) and Stewart (FCO). On the agenda were UK demands for liberalised Scotch imports to Japan, talks on the EC after De Gaulle, Britain's new entry bid, a possible sterling devaluation, and Rhodesia.[14] During a visit to Japan, later Crosland in a conversation with Ohira (MITI) in a bold move proposed the abolition of *all* restrictions to trade between UK and Japan.[15] In particular, Britain would insist on Japanese reciprocity on whisky, confectionery, light aircraft, radar, and footwear imports to Japan.[16]

Against the opposition of the hitherto protected domestic textile, pottery and cutlery industries, Crosland defended his proposals on *political* grounds and for balance of payments' reasons.[17]

Though publicly a senior MITI official, Mr Miyazawa, the head of its international trade bureau, welcomed the British proposal and announced that Japan was ready to accept, no real Japanese response was forthcoming.[18] Japan found the demand for reciprocal liberalisations too hard — originally Britain had asked for the abolition of all 118 Japanese global quotas and for a significant slash in Japan's 100 per cent whisky tariff — and was now playing for time.[19]

The first genuine common EC policy attempt towards Japan derived from a Japanese initiative: Japan had asked the EC for negotiations on cotton textiles[20] in the LTA framework. After a lengthy examination the Community had acceded to the request. Since March 1969, delegations led by Mr Hirahara (from the Japanese Mission to the EC) and by Mr Ernst (director in DG I) met.[21] Both worked out a standard agreement on trade in cotton textiles. Then delegations from the member states would negotiate with the Japanese to specify the types of textiles to be covered by their national global cotton quota.[22] In June 1969, the global cotton quotas had been agreed upon between the Commission and the Japanese but agreement on the bilateral national quota allocations was not achieved until late October 1969. Then MFA's Economic

Affairs' Bureau chief Tsurumi and the EC ambassadors in Tokyo signed the EC–Japan cotton agreement.[23]

A more comprehensive CCP towards Japan took more time to get underway. The Japanese Foreign Ministry actually anticipated the CCP earlier than European officials thought of a CCP towards Japan themselves. Japan then strengthened her representation in Brussels. Though Japanese diplomats found the CCP's concept lacking clarity, they expected the EC to ask for a trade agreement (TA) including a safeguard clause (SC).[24]

In September 1969, Kiichi Aichi (MFA) toured continental European capitals. During a Japanese ambassadors' conference he underlined the need for Japan to be aware of Europe's growing influence in Asia.[25] After a conversation with M. Rey, the Commission's President, Aichi announced at a press conference the visit of External Relations Commissioner Deniau to Japan in October 1969 to talk about bilateral trade.[26] To the question of whether Japan would be prepared to switch from bilateral to community level talks, Aichi replied this choice would be up to the EC. With Rey he had discussed Britain's EC entry, monetary problems, and the EC's internal development.[27] Deniau's actual visit to Japan was not to take place until February 1970.

As a direct consequence of Aichi's visit, the Commission sent a proposal to the Council, aiming at a mandate for exploratory negotiations. These were to find out whether negotiations on a TA with Japan would enable trade to be normalised by means of a mutual liberalisation on the highest level possible.[28] The proposal stated that as a direct effect of the forthcoming enlargement to Ten, EC trade with Japan would double in absolute terms: from $685m to $1,264m in 1968 figures, underlining the urgency to conclude a TA with Japan.[29] During the same period, late in 1969, a first 'Japan-wave' went through the European media: suddenly an awareness of Japan's miracle growth struck as several magazines published respective cover stories. The first 'Japanese Challenge' book was sold,[30] and US protectionist policies were forecast to divert Japan's exports massively from the US to the EC.[31] Early in November 1969, Coreper, based on the Commission's proposals, worked out a mandate for negotiations with Japan to be confirmed by the Council. The Commission's exploratory talks should aim at a TA containing:[32]

   – liberalisations with progressive and reciprocal character,
   – provisions for the elimination of administrative NTBs,
   – a common safeguard clause (SC), and
   – a bilateral consultation procedure.

On its exploratory results the Commission was to report back to the Council by 1 April 1970. The Council then would decide whether and on which basis common negotiations should be conducted with Japan. This exploratory mandate then was granted by the Council without any modifications.[33]

Throughout 1969 Japan was under political pressure — mainly from the US — and was compelled by her balance of payments' surplus as well to liberalise her imports. Her foreign exchange reserves accumulated even more and resulted in strong and unwanted revaluation pressure on the Yen. In January 1969 Japan thus dropped her quotas on 20 items (colour films, typewriters, sewing machines, computer equipment).[34] In July 1969 Japan announced the cutting of her remaining 120 import quota items by 50 to 60 per cent by the end of 1971.[35]

The conference of Japan's ambassadors in Europe — attended by Aichi — in September 1969 had agreed that Japan ought to liberalise further both imports and capital transactions.[36] In February 1969 Japan had published new regulations allowing for more foreign capital inflows,[37] but on the more interesting sectors, such as cars, cosmetics, distribution networks, petro-chemicals and machine tools, foreign investments still were banned.

At the time Fiat was extremely interested in a renewed capital tie-up with Mitsubishi. An earlier Mitsubishi—Fiat plan had already been turned down by MITI in 1960.[38] Agnelli in Japan stressed the need for a Euro—Japanese car alliance to face US competition. In 1969, he again announced a Fiat—Mitsubishi joint venture to produce automatic transmissions in Japan.[39]

After MITI had dashed this hope,[40] Fiat tried another joint venture, this time with Isuzu providing for mutual productive cross-investments.[41] Again MITI thwarted the project. When Mitsubishi in search for another foreign partner chose Chrysler, the US company was unable to employ more powerful political muscles to prevent MITI's sabotage.[42]

Common negotiations with Japan begin (1970)

Early in 1970 the Japanese government was reported as 'waiting cautiously' for the EC's initiatives for TA negotiations.[43] The Foreign Ministry had been in informal negotiation with France and Benelux, in vain attempting to have the SCs removed from their bilateral TAs. Now Japan was preparing a line of defence. This meant reaching inter-administrative agreement on a common negotiation strategy against the EC's forthcoming SC demand. The EC was also expected to press for an accelerated liberalisation of Japan's restricted imports. Japan at the time justified her delayed liberalisation by pointing to EC's continued discriminatory restrictions towards her.[44]

On 2 February 1970 the European Parliament for the first time debated relations with Japan, and subsequently unanimously adopted a resolution proposed by its External Economic Relations Committee.[45]

This resolution fully backed the Commission's positions.[46] It was mildly critical of the past passivity of the Community and of the national governments failing to co-ordinate their policies towards Japan, and asked both for a common SC and a common list of sensitive products on which in a provisional fashion restrictions on Japanese imports ought to be maintained. The resolution argued for a more comprehensive EC—Japan TA which would accommodate for intensified capital exchange, for joint raw material procument and bilateral co-operation in the Third World.

Two days later, Jean Rey outlined 'The Community's Work Programme for the Seventies' to the EP. Only a passing remark referred to the negotiations and talks going on with Austria, Israel, Spain, Yugoslavia, Japan and the UAR.[47] This indicated a fairly low priority for the EC's Japanpolitik. On the very same day, Roy Mason, the new director of the BoT, in Westminster declared total freedom of bilateral UK—Japanese exchanges as his political aim.[48]

Armed with the Council's mandate from November 1969, late in February 1970 Commissioner Deniau as the head of a nine-man delegation, went to Japan for exploratory negotiations.[49] These talks were the first major international talk for the Commission since the conclusion of the Kennedy Round four years earlier.[50]

The EC's main demands were: (a) mutual liberalisations, (b) a safeguard clause, and (c) Japanese capital decontrols. Japan's objectives aimed at the abolition of the EC's import restrictions and preventing the extension of the SC to Germany and Italy. GATT's Art. 19, the Japanese argument went, was a sufficient mechanism for protection.[51]

During talks with Sato, Deniau demanded the SC as necessary for European psychological security.[52] Later he made it simpler: 'Ces clauses (with France and Benelux, A.R.) sont un fait qu'il faut reconnaître'.[53] An EC trade agreement with Japan without a safeguard mechanism replacing the bilateral accords would evidently have deprived France and Benelux of their bilateral SCs. Both made clear to Deniau that they would prefer not to have a common EC agreement with Japan at all than having to renounce of their SCs.[54]

The Japanese official position was to offer an SC limited in time and to only those items which were to be liberated from EC quota restrictions.[55] Below surface, however, serious disagreements between MITI and MFA persisted, and finally the Japanese media called on their government to come up with a coherent negotiation policy.[56]

Mr Miyazawa, as minister of MITI, reflecting the views of his officials categorically declared the SC's extension as undesirable.[57] The Foreign Ministry however warned, if no compromise on the SC issue was reached, the EC in the absence of a TA might draft its CCP towards Japan unilaterally.[58]

150

Though addressing the SC as a thorny key issue, Deniau, upon return to Brussels, declared himself reasonably optimistic on the envisaged TA's prospects. He was confident that the Council, at its April session, would authorise the continuation of the talks.[59]

Based on Deniau's talks in Tokyo, in March 1970 the Commission made its report to the Council.[60] It stressed the joint Euro–Japanese interest in economic co-operation and in liberalised bilateral and world trade. The known divergent views on the SC were mentioned, as were further EC demands to reduce Japanese NTBs. The Commission proposed to negotiate for the improved publication of the Japanese regulations on quotas, on import licences, and on the calculation of the tariff value. It would ask for reduced barriers to capital inflows and for procedural improvements on import credits. The report finally recommended a mandate for TA negotiations to be given to the Commission, in accordance with Art. 113 (3), Treaty of Rome.

At the same time, a new Commission delegation was touring Japan: the Europe Day at the Expo in Osaka was to be celebrated on 25 March 1970, the anniversary of signing the Treaties of Rome. Among the scores of European national politicians visiting the Expo were also Pierre Harmel, the Belgian Foreign Minister and president-in-office of the Council, President Jean Rey, and the Commissioners Coppe and Martino.[61] Harmel, in talks with Aichi, discussed the Taiwan–China problem, and questions of bilateral trade. But both disagreed on the SC issue.[62] Nonetheless, Harmel publicly confirmed his expectation that the TA negotiations would start.[63] Rey estimated the commencing date would be in May 1970.[64] He further announced the EC soon would assign ambassadors to Washington, Tokyo and to Brasilia, and assured the Japanese of the EC's moral support in their textile dispute with the US.[65]

The European media gave the EC's TA plans a mixed reception. *Corriere della Sera*[66] predicted the havoc liberalised Japanese imports would create on the Italian market: the Italian radio, TV, kitchen appliance, car and electrical equipment industries being ruined. *Le Monde*, however saw Japanese competition as a good incentive for the French and Italian industries to make efforts for adjustment and for a stronger export orientation.[67]

The Council however did not decide on the Commission's mandate until late in July 1970. Prior to the Council's July session, Luns, the Dutch Foreign Minister, came to Japan and had lengthy talks with Aichi on the US–Japanese textile dispute, on Vietnam and the European Security Conference.[68] Luns called the forthcoming EC–Japanese talks a 'test case for the Common Market'.[69]

Finally, on 20 July 1970 the Council issued its mandate to the Commission: the negotiations were to be conducted by the Commission with the assistance of the Committee 113.[70] The Council's conception of the desired TA fell short of the Commission's and the EP's desired comprehensive treaty of commerce and co-operation. The mandate envisaged a classical TA, limited to three to five years, including an SC (a non-classical specifity, applicable to Japan only), and should provide for the annual mutual liberation of a percentage of restricted items and similarly eliminate administrative barriers to bilateral trade.[71]

The Commission now hoped for a functionalist spill-over in relations with Japan: once trade relations were improved and expanded with Japan, other spheres of economic co-operation would follow as joint undertakings.[72]

The Council decision on the TA mandate had actually been taken after less than one minute of deliberations. The session on 20 July 1970 had been dominated by the British entry negotiations.[73] The actual driving force behind the EC's TA project was Wolfgang Ernst, director at DG I, who strongly promoted the concept of strengthened institutional ties with Japan.[74] His ideas then had to survive the scrutiny of Coreper deliberations, which finally formulated the draft to be submitted to the Council.

After the summer break, during the week of 17 to 24 September 1970 the first round of negotiations took place. Ernst led the EC delegation, while the Japanese were led by Hirahara, the head of MFA's Foreign Economic Bureau. This round was concluded with the mutual recognition that the negotiations would be neither easy nor short: Japan had stuck to her earlier position of a three-year limit on the SC and its applicability to liberalised products only.[75]

The Commission now saw the September talks as a 'technical preparation' for the coming negotiation stages which would have to solve 'politically' the SC problem.[76] On the three other main elements of the TA, consensus in principle was easily achieved: both approved a 50 to 75 per cent progressive, reciprocal and balanced reduction of bilateral restrictions. (These were at the time: 61 in France, 65 in Italy, 23 in Germany, 27 in Benelux, and 118 global restrictions in Japan.) Lists with NTBs, compiled by exporters, were to be exchanged, and talks on institutional questions — the planned 'committee mixte' — and on legal problems — the elimination of the existing bilateral TAs — were envisaged.[77]

Even here some differences became evident: while on NTBs the EC had nothing to lose from negotiations, Japan was less enthusiastic at the prospect of having MITI's discretionary powers on import quota allocations regulated, or MOF's ability to refuse credit approval for imports abolished.[78]

On the other hand, the Commission was facing considerable difficulties setting up a common schedule for cut-backs on the nationally divergent restrictions and defining the unliberated hard-core negative

152

list.[79] In spite of these difficulties, both sides agreed to a subsequent negotiation round. The Japanese proposed to reopen talks after an extraordinary LDP convention in November 1970. Thereafter, they would invite the new External Relations Commissioner Dahrendorf for talks with Japan.[80]

The motives of the Japanese were based on the strategy of continued export diversification, and on the desire to preclude protectionist measures in Europe and to avoid being excluded from the European ACP and Mediterranean 'trading bloc'.[81] In strategic terms Japan might have even thought of an orientation towards the EC in order to counterbalance the pervasive US political and commercial power over Japan.[82]

The EC's basic interests were to facilitate its industries' access to Japan's rapidly growing commercial and financial market. A second motive was the Commission's desire to harmonise its CCP towards Japan, the country to which — apart from the Comecon area — the strongest divergence on national trade policies was maintained.[83]

Since the negotiations with Japan were considered as the Commission's most important ones since the conclusion of the Kennedy Round (1967), their failure would have meant a set-back for the Community's international prestige and hence for European integration.[84]

In the meantime, during a visit to Paris, Aichi, in personal talks with Pompidou and Foreign Minister Schuman, attempted to modify France's tough position on the SC question. In spite of very fruitful discussions, the French remained unmoved.[85]

In November 1970 Dahrendorf accepted the Japanese invitation and went to Tokyo. The Japanese were interested in getting his assurance that the EC would not demand Japanese VSRs on textiles, in case Japan had to grant these to the US.[86] Dahrendorf's talks — in particular a lengthy conversation with Miyazawa — centred around the US threat of proliferating protectionist policies and on the joint opposition against the pending Mills Bill. On the SC, neither came to an agreement.[87] Aichi (MFA) showed mild interest in the TA, while the other Japanese politicians (Sato and Fukuda), with whom Dahrendorf had talks, were not interested. Dahrendorf then publicly announced that his visit had not been a renewal of the TA negotiations, but had just been intended to clarify the EC position.[88] Privately, he later considered this first official visit to Japan as quite ineffective and poorly prepared.[89]

The overriding preoccupation with the US Mills Bill later in December 1970 also induced the EP to drop a debate on the EC's relations with the US and Japan, for fear of possibly 'poisoning the atmosphere' if holding the debate.[90]

Bilateral relations between individual member states and Japan stood in the shadow of the more significant Community initiative. In February 1970, with Community approval Italy concluded a new trade protocol with Japan. Italy thereafter continued 49 restrictions (on porcelain, textiles, cameras, batteries etc.).[91] Later Italy, in exchange for Japanese concessions on textile and typewriter imports, enlarged its quota on Japanese cars to 1,000.[92]

In 1970 many senior European politicians joined the global flock to inaugurate their national pavilions at the Osaka Expo. Evidently, this created a considerable strain on their Japanese hosts' time budget to grant little more than invitations to courtesy calls to their numerous visitors.[93]

Between Britain and Japan relations seemed to develop along more substantial lines. The British 1969 offer of slashing all UK import restrictions in exchange for Japanese concessions was again renewed in February 1970.[94] In April 1970 MFA hinted, Japan would abolish her quota on whisky by the end of 1971, and cut her 100 per cent tariff.[95] Keidanren—CBI talks were involved in these negotiations. After such a meeting, the CBI at a press conference in Tokyo announced that a breakthrough was imminent in bilateral talks: Britain was ready to abolish quotas on 48 items (mostly textiles and pottery), while Japan offered whisky concessions.[96] On other Japanese concessions, such as on chocolates, biscuits, and shoes, negotiations continued. The visiting Foreign Secretary, Stewart, was reported to have been unusually involved in the details.[97] After his departure however, the powerful Japanese distillery industry (Suntory et al.) used its influence, and to the British disappointment four weeks later Japan cancelled her whisky concession.

After one year of negotiations, the bilateral trade protocol then concluded provided for only marginal quota and tariff adjustments.[98] To the British proposal of a massive package liberalisation, Japan could not overcome her preference for piecemeal deals.

Within OECD, Japan was criticised for her slow implementation of capital imports: few attractive businesses were open for foreign investments, and even these had to be organised as joint ventures with 50 per cent Japanese participation.[99]

In order to reduce the revaluation pressure on the Yen, MOF had further liberalised Japan's overseas investments (both for portfolio and for direct investments) and foreign travel of her citizens (the issuing of passports was facilitated and the travel allowance doubled).[100] But MOF evidently remained more reluctant to do likewise with capital inflows.

The failure of the trade negotiations

In January 1971, the Commission sent a twelve-page memo to the Council, drafted by Dahrendorf and summarising the results of his November 1970 visit to Japan.[101] It described the negotiations as having reached a deadlock on the SC issue. Given the strength of the Japanese resentment on the safeguard demand — indicating a discrimination which they traced back to the 1955 GATT entry conditions, which in turn had reflected Japan's status as loser of WW II — Dahrendorf felt the present mandate as unrealistic and asked the Council for a revision.

As an alternative the memo suggested a SC limited in time, but covering all products (while the Japanese at the time officially would only accept an SC covering products to be liberalised). Further, the report proposed the Japanese concept of orderly marketing ought to be considered as a substitute for the SC. In a supportive speech before the European Parliament, Dahrendorf underlined the need for a smooth management of EC—Japan relations in the global context of looming US protectionism.[102] In a few years, Dahrendorf predicted, Japan would be fully participating in the international economic system and live up to its rules. The present criticism of Japan's economic behaviour would then become invalid. Evidently this expectation justified an SC of limited duration.

For the near future the EC feared a deflection of Japanese textiles to the European market as a consequence of the likely Japanese VSR to the US.[103] In March 1971 it became known that the EC and the UK had asked the Japanese, via embassy channels in Paris and Geneva, to moderate their likely textile diversion. Japan initially reacted ambiguously and declared the issue another knotty problem after the US talks.[104] Japan was unwilling to negotiate on textiles until the frictions with the US were settled.[105] Only on the cotton agreement — concluded 1969 in the LTA context — Japan and the EC agreed to an extension for yet another six months until June 1971.[106]

In view of the heightening US—Japanese textile wrangle, the CBI issued calls for a united front of US and European business to salvage the free trading system by pressing for Japanese liberalisation.[107] This would be a preventive strategy to counter US protectionism, CBI argued. Should the US persist in blocking Japanese imports, these would then flood the markets of Europe and of other DCs — thus provoking the same protectionist measures there and threatening the survival of a liberal trade order.

The CBI sent its proposals to the US and EC industrial associations, calling for a summit of these associations in London focussing on Japan's liberalisation.[108] Reflecting the failure of the British 'package deal slash', CBI reasoned that bilateral talks had proved not effective enough to alter the Japanese import system: 'Japan is still dragging its feet'.[109] Now, a common European strategy was needed, rallying behind them US pressure to open the access to Japan's financial and consumer market.

In March 1971 the member states — as represented within Coreper — rejected the Commission's plea for a mandate with more flexibility on the SC.[110] The political leadership was evidently not involved in this decision. Dahrendorf during a 'tour des capitals' through the member states, found the foreign ministers which he contacted either indifferent or simply uninterested in the Japan issue and its SC problem.[111]

In June 1971 during an OECD minister conference, Dahrendorf met with Aichi, and after a lengthy conversation, the latter proposed the resumption of talks by mid-July.[112]

During this period, Gaimusho had come up with a study on the consequences of the EC's forthcoming first enlargement. As is usual within Japanese intellectual tradition, the forecasts were gloomy: with UK's entry the EC would become an economic superpower.[113] Its economic strength and the expected disintegration of the Commonwealth would lead to trade and other economic sufferings on the part of Japan.[114] Australian and New Zealandian agroproducts would push on the Japanese markets, the African Commonwealth nations would join the ACP scheme — thus threatening Japanese trade and future investments there — and India and Pakistan might enter into special arrangements with the EC — thus equally threatening Japanese exports.[115]

The official pessimism did not go undisputed. Kajima, a former chairman of the Diet's Foreign Relations Committee (LDP), argued that a weakened Commonwealth would provide a good opportunity for better Japanese relations with Canada, Australia and New Zealand.[116] He recalled the Japanese fear of the EC's formation in the late 1950s, and reasoned the present Angst of a Euro—African bloc being similarly unfounded.[117]

The Japanese Angst of EC protectionism, their troubles with the US, and the threat of CBI's united front, in Brussels fuelled hopes for Japan giving a conditional nod to the EC's (unmodified) SC demand.[118] These hopes however were dashed when the US, informally through their embassy in Tokyo, told MITI they would ask for the same SC, if Japan granted one to the EC. The Japanese clearly saw this as a display of US displeasure at the EC's demand for special safeguards and as a message to Japan not to yield to it.[119] The Americans, not without reason, felt that they had to bear the brunt of Japan's exports while Europe on top of her exclusionist ACP and Mediterranean policies largely barred all unwanted imports from Japan.[120] Still, the US hoped for a nondiscriminatory TA between the EC and Japan which would subsequently ease Japanese pressure on the US market.[121]

When the negotiations started, Gaimusho was known to have not wished either to confirm or deny statements according to which Japan would examine the possibility of accepting the SC as the Community asks for it, in exchange for a faster liberalisation programme.[122] While this would have indicated considerable leeway for compromise, the actual negotiations (6 to 8 July 1971) showed that Japan was ready to extend the SC to Germany and Italy only on those products which were

156

to be liberalised there.

The Commission delegation, led by Mr Ernst, still had to operate on the narrow Council mandate of July 1970, and had thus to ask for a SC of the Franco—Japanese TA type.* Predictably, the negotiations after only two mornings of talks reached a deadlock on the SC issue. After the Japanese had presented a new SC formula — the one outlined above — on the morning of 7 July, in the afternoon Committee 113 at French and Dutch insistence rejected it.[124] The next morning, on 8 July, the Japanese were informed. Then the head of the Japanese delegation, Mr Suzuki, the deputy director of MFA's Economic Affairs Bureau, proposed to postpone dealing with the SC issue and to talk about the less controversial details on the liberalisation programme instead.[125] The Commission wanted to continue the talks as well, but Committee 113 advised against it and ordered a reflection period of six months for the negotiations.[126]

Tentatively it was agreed between the two delegations to resume talks late in autumn 1971. Both admitted the need for better preparation through the usual diplomatic channels before the next round would start.[127]

One month after the failure of the EC—Japan talks, Nixon on 15 August 1971 announced a 10 per cent import surcharge, the floating of the US $ and the end of its convertibility into gold. The US measures immediately fuelled EC fears of a massive Japanese export diversion.[128]

A top level Keidanren mission scheduled to tour Europe by mid-October was expected to attempt to allay European fears: there would be only a short-term rise in Japanese exports to the EC. Then domestic demand in Japan would expand, and the expected 10 to 15 per cent Yen appreciation would forestall a further export increase.[129]

Prior to Keidanren, the Japanese Emperor would visit Europe — as the first overseas journey of a Japanese emperor ever. Keidanren thus could expect to benefit from his public relations work.[130] In fifteen days, beginning 29 September 1971, Hirohito had to visit Denmark, Belgium, France, England, the Netherlands, Switzerland and Germany, meeting royal families wherever available, having marine biology expert talks and doing a comprehensive sight-seeing programme.[131]

---

* The SC between France and Japan contains the following provisions, applicable by either side: in case imports seriously damage or threaten to damage domestic industries, consultations between the importing and the exporting country are to be held. If these consultations do not lead to an agreement within reasonable time, then the importing country may apply quantitative restrictions of the extent and time span suitable to prevent or to remedy the damages. In cases of emergency, however, import restrictions can be imposed unilaterally without prior consultation. If the exporting country considers the restrictions imposed on it to be severely harmful to its interests, it may ask for new consultations and, in case no agreement is reached, would be entitled to enact equivalent retaliatory restrictions on products from the importing country. These restrictions would have to be removed as soon as the importing country removed its original restrictions. (See reference 123.)

Apart from its strenuous schedule, the visit represented a serious underestimation of the strength of anti-Japanese feelings in the host countries. While protests against Hirohito were fairly low key in Belgium and England,[132] in the Netherlands survivors among the former internees from the East Indies staged violent demonstrations against what they considered a war criminal. Japanese flags were burned, the windscreen of the emperor's car and the windows of the Japanese embassy were smashed.[133]

In Nottingham, CBI's director general Campbell Adamson voiced fears of a forthcoming EC—Japan trade war and expressed the hope that an enlarged EC could serve the cause of free trade more effectively by pushing with more energy for Japan's opening.[134]

On 16 October 1971, the Emperor having just returned to Japan, a 40-member Keidanren mission led by its chairman Uemura, started a European tour, covering Düsseldorf, Paris, Brussels, Rome and London in two weeks.[135] During their first stop, Keidanren had meetings with a BDI delegation under its chairman Berg. Their talks focussed on the international trade and currency situation after the Nixon shocks — both delegations favoured a return to fixed exchange rates — and on sectoral problems and on the feared trade deflection.[136] During the talks BDI leaders had obtained the impression that Japan had learned from her experience in the US and would react in a preventive fashion to any further market disruption overseas. The Japanese had given assurances that they would not try to compensate for their estimated $2 US billion export decline to the US on the European market.[137]

Two sectoral issues were taken up: on desk-top calculators Japan had conquered 74 per cent of the EC market.[138] The German office machine producers accused the Japanese of dumping and threatened to call Brussels to impose import controls and anti-dumping tariffs.[139] On steel, Japanese imports during January—July 1971 had increased by 21 per cent (compared to the same period in 1970) to 690,000 tonnes in the EC. To the UK the increase in Japanese steel exports had been more than 40 per cent.

Keidanren now promised a VSR on steel, starting 1972 and supervised by MITI.[140] Once this became known, the Japanese steel federation immediately denied any VSR intentions, and Kobe Steel Company announced, it would never participate in such a scheme.[141]

In Paris, Keidanren had talks with the CNPF and with Giscard, then Minister of Finance, on a similar agenda as in Germany. All participants agreed on the need to return to a fixed exchange rate system as soon as possible, and jointly demanded the 'remise en ordre dans les échanges commerciaux entre les deux'.[142] Only a few days later Giscard gave his version of the desired order. To the French garment industries he announced: competition from Asia would be eliminated.[143]

158

In talks with the Commissioners Barre (monetary affairs), Spinelli (industrial affairs) and with President Malfatti, Uemura repeated assurances of Japanese orderly marketing behaviour.[144] He further indicated Japanese business would not object to an SC if conditions for invoking it were made acceptable to Japan.[145]

The Keidanren—UNICE meeting in Brussels was also attended by the CBI and the industrial associations of the three other applicant countries and of Sweden.[146] All in all, more than 100 delegates attended the conference, thus attempting to realise the CBI's 'united front' strategy.

At the outset, Keidanren presented a seven-point plan, which promised the following Japanese policies:[147]

— fiscal measures to boost domestic demand,
— export control by MITI — via export trade ordinances — in 'excessive' cases,
— VSRs, such as on steel,
— the establishment of an early warning system on foreign markets, to be operated by JETRO,
— support for a multilateral SC or a revised Art. 19 GATT,
— intensified inter-industry contacts, and finally
— Japanese structural change towards technology intensive industries which would alter the Japanese export structure in the long run.

Upon return to Japan, Uemura mentioned European keen interest in Japanese orderly marketing and British worries on Japanese overinvestments in steel, ships and ball bearings. He promised to forward the European criticism to his government and expressed concern on the introduction of a 10 per cent import surcharge in Denmark.[148]

European demands however, were far from being consistent. The hardest pressed sectors had pleaded for Japanese VSRs, such as the British on steel, promising to interpret their anti-trust laws in a flexible fashion.[149] At the same time, Borschette, commissioner in charge of competition, had told the Japanese their VSR policy was 'difficult to reconcile with EC competition rules'.[150]

A later Commission note observed that Keidanren, though powerful, had not been able to persuade the Japanese government to a more flexible attitude on the SC issue.[151]

In the meantime EC plans surfaced to open a representation in Tokyo, which was alternately addressed as either a 'trade mission' or a 'press and information office'.[152]

Late in December 1971 the Yen had to be revalued by 17 per cent to the US $. Still, the Japanese industry was expected to fight for their US market shares. Due to the larger and more profitable nature of the integrated American market, observers felt the Japanese would not consider Europe as an adequate substitute.[153]

Early in 1972 the French–Japanese ministerial consultations took place in Tokyo. Foreign Minister Schuman's talks with Fukuda (MFA) and premier Sato centred on nuclear co-operation – reflecting the strength of US–French competition for participation in Japan's nuclear development.[154] In February 1972, a French–Japanese agreement on nuclear co-operation was signed providing for the French supply of refined uranium and plutonium under IAEA auspices to Japan.[155]

Other topics of Schuman's talks concerned Japanese barriers to foreign investment, the developments in China, US–Japanese relations and the US conduct of the war in Vietnam which the French strongly criticised.[156]

In order to facilitate better communication Fukuda proposed regular annual foreign ministers' meetings of the Group of Ten nations.[157] Schuman rejected this idea out of hand: since the USSR and China were excluded, such meetings would run counter to the spirit of detente.[158]

In February 1972 Malfatti and Noël, the Commission's Secretary General, went to Japan for a week of talks with Sato, Fukuda (MFA) and Tanaka (MITI).[159] Again the media reported contradictory accounts on the purpose of their visit. Some wrote Malfatti did not expect to break the deadlock on the SC.[160] Others mentioned his hope for Japan approving an 'SC with prior consultation'.[161] The truth however, was that there was not much purpose in this visit anyway. As was evident beforehand the position of each on the SC had not changed.[162] During the talks Fukuda as the Foreign Minister again had signalled compromise: Japan might possibly accept a general SC limited to three to five years.[163] But Tanaka, as MITI's minister, delivered a hard-line rejection, the SC being entirely unacceptable to Japan.[164]

In the subsequent interministerial debate MITI once again overruled Gaimusho[165] with the argument that a compromising stand would entice the US to ask for an SC as well.[166]

During their talks, both Sato and Fukuda proposed regular minister level consultations with the Commission.[167] Malfatti replied somewhat evasively, the request would have to be examined at a later date 'due to difficulties posed by our decision making process'.[168] At the time the Commission had received similar requests from the US, Canada, India, and Latin America – but the Council had not yet been able to make up its mind about them.[169]

In his final press conference in Tokyo, Malfatti again stressed the SC as a 'minimum necessity'[170] and announced the opening of an EC office in Tokyo by September 1972.[171] There he unveiled his view of the contemporary global changes: 'Since the passing of the dominance of the superpowers, the voices of Europe and Japan must assume a much greater importance'.[172]

Corresponding to the past year's criticism of Japanese steel exports to Europe, MITI by the end of February 1972 announced a steel VSR as a second gesture of goodwill (after the cotton agreement). Down from their 1.9m tonnes exports to the EC (in 1971), the Japanese would limit themselves to 1.22m tonnes in 1972.[173] At the same time the EC authorised Italian restrictions on imports of Japanese-made cars and motorbikes from EC member countries.[174] Already exempted from free Community exports to Italy were Japanese ball-bearings, motors, typewriters, silk, textiles, shoes, umbrellas, ceramics, electric engines, batteries and cooking appliances.

One month after Malfatti's visit, Commissioner Borschette came to Tokyo in March 1972 to prepare for the opening of the EC office there.[175] He could not achieve much on this — the Japanese welcoming the EC's representation anyway — since the project lay paralysed in Coreper under French and Dutch crossfire. The Dutch with Luns as Foreign Minister strongly favoured the idea. The French were equally strong against a more significant EC representation overseas.[176] As a further scout in SC matters, Borschette's assessment upon return was reportedly pessimistic.[177] Shortly afterwards, Dahrendorf's chef du cabinet, Mr Hammer, in a public lecture made an unspecified reference to 'recently promising developments' on EC—Japanese TA matters.[178] In April 1972, Dahrendorf himself, after new informal contacts with the Japanese in Brussels, was reported optimistic about the resumption of the TA talks.[179]

Late in March 1972, a Benelux electronics industry mission went to Japan to ask for VSRs on her electronics exports to their countries.[180] There a Japanese sales offensive was in full swing. The Commission had uttered dumping allegations, and the Dutch government — at the suggestion of Philips — had actually threatened to apply their bilateral SC. Against this background, during the mission's visit MITI announced VSRs on tape recorder, desk top calculator and TV set exports to Europe and ordered a mix of export quotas and price increases.[181] Similar VSRs were felt as being 'in the air' for cars, synthetic fibres, and ball-bearings.[182]

In England, business pressure mounted on the government to initiate anti-dumping procedures or to invoke the SC. In Westminster questions critical of Japanese imports multiplied. Whitehall however still remained hesitant on any form of import control, for fear of chain reactions in the US and in the EC.[183]

The dislike of yet another revaluation of the Yen put MITI into a conciliatory mood to slow down Japan's export drive.[184] The US Treasury had intensified its anti-dumping procedures against both Japanese and European imports. Therefore, MITI favoured detente with Europe, Japan's minor outlet, and rather thought of Euro—Japanese 'joint protests' or 'common actions' against US policies.[185] A French commentary advocated a more fundamental strategy: 'les Européens alliés aux Japonais pour enrayer la domination Americain . . . '[186]

In May 1972, Dahrendorf went to Japan for the second time in order to break the enduring deadlock on the TA and to secure a date for the formal resumption of talks. To his Japanese counterparts, Dahrendorf submitted a four-point programme as a new starting point for the negotiations. Both sides should agree (a) on the reciprocal abolition of quotas and of (b) NTBs, on (c) a mixed ministerial committee to monitor trade and economic co-operation, and (d) on the adoption of a protocol of contingency measures to prevent the mutual disruption of markets. This 'Dahrendorf formula' was a substitute for the SC and was to be valid only until satisfactory multilateral safeguards had been worked out within GATT.[187] If no TA was concluded, Dahrendorf warned, then the 'Italian system' of unilateral import restrictions against Japanese imports might spread in Europe.[188] In his talks with Tanaka (MITI), Dahrendorf nevertheless did not find much interest for the resumption of the negotiations. Reflecting the views of his ministry, Tanaka declared he could not understand why the EC made so much fuss about less than two per cent of her imports.[189] Yamashita, the director general of MITI's International Trade Bureau, declared one should wait for the outcome of the OECD Trade Committee's deliberations on Art. 19 GATT. If problems did occur in the meantime, EC countries should pass them along and Japan was ready to resolve them on a case-by-case basis with each country individually.[190] This certainly did not coincide with the CCP's rationale.

Fukuda and his MFA were more forthcoming. Dahrendorf and Fukuda agreed on an early resumption of the TA talks before the summer break.[191] Keidanren leaders and Uemura also displayed a positive attitude on the new 'contingency protocol' — through reportedly they all fell asleep when Dahrendorf made a speech to them at a formal reception.[192]

Among Community institutions, Committee 113 endorsed the 'Dahrendorf formula' of an SC downgraded in political status to a contingency protocol attached to the TA.[193] When the Japanese — and MFA in particular — had just been convinced that the contingency protocol would not be as offensive to Japan's international standing as an SC would have been, then the French ambassador in Tokyo in the most unhelpful way publicly announced that the contingency protocol in sibstance was nothing but a 'dressing up' of the SC, a view echoed by the French media.[194]

In order to continue their talks, an MFA delegation under Hirahara (director general of MFA's Economic Affairs Bureau) would visit Brussels later in May 1972. Fukuda himself announced his personal visit by autumn 1972, thus indicating his strong interest in continued talks with the Community.[195] Hirahara met with the Commission coming from an OECD conference, where he had presented yet another Japanese programme to reduce her current account surplus via orderly marketing, plus capital outflows, plus more ODA.[196] In his talks with Dahrendorf, Hijzen (DG I's director general), and Ernst, Hirahara however could not commit the Japanese government to the 'Dahrendorf formula'.[197] Hirahara in the domestic Japanese situation of an unresolved succession to Sato in the premiership, had been unable to obtain any instructions on the TA, except to delay.[198]

After the experience with Fukuda's conciliatory attitude and Tanaka's 'tough line', the Commission's sympathies in the ensuing power struggle between the two were an open secret.[199] Still, it was not clear whether any of Fukuda's or Tanaka's positions, professed during the negotiations with the EC, reflected their personal opinions or rather the attitudes of the ministries they happened to preside over.

The UK—Japanese trade negotiations were postponed until May 1972, waiting for the outcome of the EC—Japanese talks. When results were not forthcoming, the British government endorsed its ball-bearing, polyester fibre and colour TV industries' wish for Japanese VSR, and sent Mr Davies, Secretary for Trade and Industry, to Japan for respective negotiations.[200]

The *Observer* gave him the following advice: 'The only way to convince a Japanese that you mean business is to strike him smartly between the eyes. Restrict first, then negotiate'.[201] During his talks in Japan, Davies played a British 'EC card'. In return for Japanese VSR, he promised a benevolent UK influence inside the EC on issues affecting Japan[202] — after joining the EC on 1 January 1973. It is however doubtful whether his Japanese counterparts, Tanaka (MITI) and Fukuda (MFA), engaged in their competition for Sato's succession, had much time to reflect on Mr Davies' tactical deal. Nevertheless, upon return to England, he announced Japan was ready now for orderly marketing on bearings, fibres and on colour TVs.[203]

Four days after Davies' visit, the Japanese ball-bearing industry announced a 10 per cent increase in export prices to the UK.[204] But when later a Japanese industry delegation met their UK ball-bearing counterparts, they discovered that the British producers — encouraged by their political success — had inflated their demands: now they asked for a pledge of a 50 per cent cut in Japanese ball-bearing exports within four weeks. If such a commitment were not forthcoming, they threatened to persuade Whitehall to apply the safeguard clause.[205]

In the meantime the British media discovered that they had fallen victim to a skilled public relations campaign of their bearing producers: the Japanese were not dumping. Japanese bearings were simply processed more efficiently and of better quality.[206] In the end, the Japanese agreed to a 15 per cent cut in ball-bearing exports to Britain during 1972, a VSR allowing for a 10 per cent increase in 1973.[207]

Later a UK aide-memoire was leaked in Japan. Britain was asking for Japanese VSR on cars, synthetic yarn, desk calculators, radios, TV sets, tape recorders, ball-bearings, fork-lift trucks, cutlery, umbrellas, microscopes, electronic components, some steel products and on woven wire fabric.[208] Rising unemployment in 1972, combined with balance of payments' problems, led to the turnround in British import policy during that year.[209]

After industry to industry talks, in June 1972 the Japanese electronics producers agreed to VSRs on TVs, radios and tape recorders to Benelux. The Benelux industries — or rather Philips — originally had insisted on quantitative limitations, but finally accepted Japanese price controls.[210]

By July 1972 a Euro—Japanese VSR agreement on price controls covering electronics in all EC—EFTA—Europe was close to conclusion. Then the German Cartel Office struck.[211] It declared such inter-industry agreements distorting the German electronics market illegal: since they kept prices up at artificially high levels, these agreements could be legitimate only when concluded under government control. MITI and the Japanese electronics industry were startled: the agreement was to be concluded at the request of the German industry. Within the Commission, the debate raged on the desirability of an increasingly cartelised Community market as well. Favoured by the Industry DG, the VSRs were bitterly opposed by the Competition DG, watching over Arts. 85 and 86, Treaty of Rome.[212] As a compromise, it was decided that each VSR agreement had to be screened in a surveillance procedure. Each industry-to-industry VSR henceforth would be considered illegal unless notified to the Commission which would examine it for exemption from the Treaty of Rome's anti-trust rules on a case by case basis.[213] DG Competition was expected to take a narrow interpretation, and to consider VSRs only as exceptions, but not as an import policy.[214]

In August 1972 the German ministries of finance and of economics called VSRs fundamentally undesirable and incompatible with German and EC anti-trust law.[215] They were legitimate only when concluded in accordance with the public interest and in a procedure which should include the representation of importers', retailers' and consumers' interests. Under no circumstances whatsoever could import restrictions be negotiated in inter-industry talks. At most VSRs could be of temporary nature only. The ministerial paper ended with praise for cheap Japanese imports as supportive to the German government's bid to stabilise prices.[216]

At the same time, the Dutch and Belgian governments felt that the effects of the Japanese price hikes on electronics had been negligible. In a joint note to the Japanese, they threatened a temporary invocation of their SC against these imports.[217] The Commission supported the Dutch initiative, behind which again Philips' pressure was discernible.[218]

164

In September 1972 the Japanese electronics industry announced price controls — a system of minimum prices administered by MITI — to go into effect in the UK, Italy, Sweden, Finland, Ireland, Switzerland and Portugal. Germany was excluded. Controls were already in force with Benelux, while bilateral talks with France continued.[219]

The Commission published yet another statement on the VSR, this time more critical.[220] It stressed the EC's rules on competition, and expressed strong displeasure at the compartmentalisation of the Common Market as the result of nationally divergent VSR agreements. Situations were undesirable in which the EC's policies towards Japan were in effect decided by private companies and decisions outside the EC. Japan's interest in a TA with the Community was reduced as a consequence.

In September 1972 Edward Heath visited Japan, where he had two lengthy and cordial rounds of talks with the new premier Tanaka. Among high politics topics, they discussed the feasibility of trilateral co-operation, East—West detente and Asian affairs.[221] On low politics, Heath as 'spokesman for Europe' pressed for a sustained opening of the Japanese market and asked for the lowering of tariffs on consumer product imports and for the abolition of restrictions on car imports.[222] Tanaka was asked to buy Concordes and US planes with Rolls Royce RB 11 engines. Otherwise Concorde would fly to China, and the only thing left for JAL would be to run a shuttle between Beijing and Tokyo. To his political bad luck Tanaka did not heed his new friend's* advice and later rather chose to pocket Lockheed's bribes.

Next to electronics, shipbuilding was the most sensitive sectoral problem aggravating Euro—Japanese relations. Already early in 1972, the Council of EC Builders of Large Ships (CEBLS) had asked for a Japanese VSR to limit Japan's production to 50 per cent of the world market.[224] Later CEBLS and the Shipbuilders' Association of Japan (SAJ) in Tokyo discussed Japanese investment plans which the Europeans feared as creating over-capacities.[225] Both then apparently agreed that there would be a future slump in demand and to set up a committee to exchange information regularly on future demand and production.[226] This arrangement immediately drew the FTC's suspicion. It started an investigation whether both had formed a cartel to control prices and output of large tankers.[227] The German Economics Ministry was equally opposed. It considered that the desired order-sharing was the false response to the deficiencies in management and in modernisation from which German shipyards suffered.[228]

Nevertheless, the European shipbuilders soon felt it would be necessary to get some government backing in order to impress the Japanese.[229] In July 1972 they achieved this relationship with the Commission. Mr

---

* Tanaka reportedly had three portraits in his office: one of the Emperor, one of the Empress and one of Ted Heath (see reference 223).

Krakow, CEBLS' chairman and the head of Krupps' shipyard subsidiary Weser AG, succeeded in setting up a joint CEBLS—Commission 'EEC Working Group on Shipbuilding'.[230] To no one's surprise, three months later a hardline Commission paper came out, demanding Japanese VSR on ships.[231] If the Japanese were not forthcoming, the draft threatened European flag discrimination — only European built ships would have access to EC harbours — and asked for a programme of price subsidies and EIB and regional fund monies for the EC yards.

Within OECD's Working Party 6, Euro—Japanese disagreement on the future demand on ships persisted. When the Japanese forwarded an optimistic forecast of a 30m tonnes deadweight demand in 1975, the Europeans (rightly) called this utter nonsense.[232] During these talks, the EC hinted at unilateral action if Japan did not limit her capacity expansion.[233]

In preparatory talks between the US and Japan prior to the Tokyo Round, the US agreed to support the Japanese proposal of a multilateral SC, which would only be applied after an international watchdog had been satisfied.[234]

Now with sectoral agreements substituting for a global TA, any incentive for the Japanese to grant an extended SC to the EC in exchange for a comprehensive TA had disappeared. The SC demand — born out of national trade bureaucratic interests — had been brought down by the very policies which had brought about its ineffectual existence. The Commission's continued pleading to the Japanese that only a common TA would prevent national import controls and resolve all bilateral economic problems[235] had turned unconvincing. By the end of 1972, the Commission realised it was waiting for Godot and, for the time being, gave up hope for the common TA.[236]

In order to avoid a further appreciation of the Yen, in October 1972 the Japanese government announced a 20 per cent across-the-board cut on two-thirds of its tariffs. The EC welcomed this offer and announced its own 15 per cent CET cuts as anti-inflationary measures.[237]

In December 1972 the FTC ordered a secret EC—Japanese cartel arrangement of synthetic fibre manufacturers to be scrapped. Since 1959 the three major Japanese producers had kept an international pricing and market sharing arrangement with their EC colleagues: Asia for Japan, the US for free competition, the rest of the world for Europe.[238]

Late in December 1972 the Council of Ministers discussed the Japanese orderly marketing. The Commission called VSRs implying serious dangers for the trade autonomy of the Community.[239] During the Council's general discussion, the French — professing that there was no alternative available to the VSRs — disapproved of the Commission's critical attitude. Because they were particularly annoyed at the Commission's order for prior screening of VSRs* they sent a respective 'note verbale' to

* See reference 213.

the Japanese authorities.[240]

Dealing with the enlarged community (1973)

On 1 January 1973 Britain, Denmark and Ireland joined the Community. Since the early 1960s the consequences of Britain's membership had occupied the fears, hopes and tactical considerations of the Japanese officials designing Japan's policies towards Europe. One of their major hopes had been to gain a benevolent ally in Britain inside the Common Market. Occasionally, British politicians fuelled these hopes. After the entry, in February 1973, Mr Royle, parliamentary under-secretary at the Foreign Office, in a lecture before the Japan Society assured his audience that he understood Japanese fears of a protectionist EC, but felt confident this would not happen: 'We pride ourselves on a special knowledge of Japan which will be of value in our discussions with our European partners'.[241]

In February 1973 the Commission published a leaflet on its policies towards Japan.[242] It still dutifully stressed the desire for a speedy TA conclusion, but had to refer to the differences on the SC, a contingency protocol was no longer mentioned. More emphasis however was given to the removal of Japanese NTBs. The Commission demanded the abolition of MITI's secret allocations of import licences under its global quotas.[243] Again the Commission asked for elimination of barriers to foreign investment, especially of the 50 per cent Japanese participation requirement.

From January 1973 the Netherlands had stopped issuing import licences on Japanese electronics imports,[244] and in February bilateral consultations started as the procedure required prior to invocation of the bilateral SC.

The Benelux delegation was led by the head of the Dutch Economics Ministry's Foreign Economic Relations Bureau and demanded a voluntary Japanese export restraint, cutting down her electronics exports to the 1969—71 levels.[245] The Japanese delegation — led by a counsellor from MITI's International Trade Bureau — found this unacceptable, and demanded to be shown evidence for damage to Benelux industries.[246] Gaimusho hinted that Japan might retaliate if Benelux applied the SC.[247] During the negotiations, conducted on and off throughout 1973, an import licensing system was in operation, until in December a Japanese VSR was agreed upon,[248] which soon drew the criticism of the Belgian consumer associations.[249]

When the German electronics' industrial association, encouraged by the Dutch example, called for similar orderly marketing, their plea fell on deaf ears in Bonn.[250] The French electronics federation obtained an

167

extension of Japanese VSRs on radios, TV sets, tape recorders and record players.[251]

The Italian government on tape recorder imports got Community approval for a 150,000 bi-annual quota under GATT's Art. 19.[252] This quota de facto referred to Japan only, as the only significant exporter of tape recorders. According to Community figures, the market share of Japanese tape recorders in Italy had risen from 16 per cent (1969) to 48 per cent (1972). At the same time, the Italian production had fallen from 380,000 units to 136,000 units, thus constituting a case for a serious injury under Art. 19 terms.[253] MITI did not contest these figures, but criticised that 'against accepted international practice' Italy and the Community had applied Art. 19 without prior consultation. The Japanese Electronics Association declared, since Italy was a minor market, this quota would not affect Japanese production.[254]

Facing this pluralist diversity in national policies, Commission attempts to harmonise the Community's import policy on electronics had to fail, and so they did.[255]

On shipbuilding however, to the surprise of the shipyards' lobbyists in Brussels, the Euro—Japanese dispute ended abruptly, when in spring 1973 demand took an unforeseen upturn and the global depression receded.[256]

The same reasons, a sudden boom in ball-bearings in Britain, defused the UK—Japanese dispute on these products. The Japanese were now quite unhappy about having to observe a VSR to the UK market, and announced they would not renew it for 1974.[257]

The public pronouncements of senior European politicians reflected the contradictory character of European policies towards Japan. In March 1973, Mr Friderichs, the German Minister of Economics, called the Japanese criticism of CAP and ACP policies understandable and stressed the gratifying task for both Japan and the EC to eliminate jointly deficiencies in their liberalisation programme.[258]

Two days later, Mr Ortoli, the Commission's new President in an interview with *Time* underlined the need for protectionist measures to salvage European industries threatened by Japanese competition.[259]

The Danish Foreign Minister Norgaard, on a visit to Japan, advocated massive mutual tariff reductions towards a zero tariff goal on industrial products.[260] To the Japanese delight, he professed Denmark's preference for a multilateral rather than a bilateral solution to the redrafting of the SC (Art. 19 GATT) in the Tokyo Round. On bilateral trade, Norgaard asked for an opening of the Japanese market for Danish agricultural exports — since he did not want to restrict Japanese imports.

Sir Geoffrey Howe, UK minister of trade and consumer affairs, stressed the same theme while in Japan. He in addition urged unspecified changes in the Japanese distribution system to allow for more British imports.[261] It appears that he had read the most recent *Economist* issue, which had argued that *the* European demand ought to be for the liberalisation of foreign investment in the retail sector in Japan. It would allow importers to open the Japanese market effectively by short-cutting its inefficient retail system.[262]

In early May 1973 Foreign Minister Ohira, accompanied by MFA's bureau directors for Western Europe and for Economic Affairs, visited Paris and Brussels.

The conversation with his French counterpart, Jobert, centred on Kissinger's recent 'Atlantic Charter' proposal. Originally Ohira seems to have voiced support for Kissinger's idea, with Jobert remaining sceptical.[263] In a later announcement they both agreed, the Atlantic Charter 'pose plus de questions qu'il ne fournit de réponses'. [264] At his press conference, Ohira again sounded like vaguely supporting it, but then professed he considered co-operation within OECD as quite sufficient.[265]

In Brussels, Ohira met with President Ortoli and for three hours with the new external relations Commissioner Soames. This was the first official EC–Japanese meeting since the enlargement. The main result of these talks was to shelve the TA negotiations until after the conclusion of the beginning MTN round, in which a revised Art. 19 GATT would be agreed upon.[266] For the time being sectoral agreements had to substitute for a comprehensive TA.

On the form of future bilateral consultations, there was disagreement within each side. Opposed by MITI for fear of creating just a body for regular VSR demands, the idea of institutionalised high level consultations (HLC) was favoured by MFA.[267] In addition, MITI felt it could pursue Japanese exporters' interests better on a bilateral national level, while MFA was more ready to deal with the EC as a whole.[268]

The Community was equally divided. Some member states opposed the HLC idea on the grounds that in doing so one would give up the last incentive for Japan to conclude a TA.[269] Finally, Soames formally proposed regular semi-annual HLCs to Ohira, who accepted them.[270]

Disagreement persisted on the status of the EC's planned representation in Tokyo. Japan insisted on an embassy type status — similar to the EC Delegation in Washington D.C.[271] The Commission favoured the same idea, but still had to take French opposition into account, and could yet offer nothing but an 'information office'.

Some English observers criticised the European lack of a coherent policy towards Japan as the result of the EC's internal divisions on low politics, which prevented them from thinking about Japan except as an economic threat.[272]

Soames' personal performance in the talks with the Japanese found praise. Up to then 'his unfamiliarity with Asia was compared unfavourably with what they [the Japanese] thought of as the far-ranging vision of his predecessor at the Commission, Herr Dahrendorf'.[273] But in a speech in April 1973, he spoke on the need for triangular co-operation between the US, the EC and Japan, on energy supply, international investments, ODA and diverse research projects.[274] Soames stressed the importance of integrating Japan in the Western world: an isolated Japan shifting anchorless would constitute a serious threat to international stability.[275]

In spite of Soames' noble intentions, Ohira upon return to Tokyo complained that he had sensed among EC leaders 'an absence of trust in Japan's pledged commitment to international society'.[276] The presentation of European low politics interests had evidently created a stronger impression than its lofty global high politics ideas.

In June 1973, the Italian government was faced with a request from Honda to set up an assembly plant for lightweight motorcycles in Italy, thus circumventing the existing import ban. The Italian producers now employed their political strings to prevent this new competition. Particularly active were Fiat and Moto Guzzi. The latter's owner, Mr Benelli-Guzzi, telegraphed to premier Andreotti that he would pull his production out of Italy if the Japanese were allowed in.[277] Honda's request in consequence was turned down. Moto Guzzi later bluntly told the Commission: 'We are insisting that no facilities be granted to foreign competition in our sector'.[278]

The first EC—Japanese HLC were held in Brussels in mid-June 1973. A small Japanese delegation was led by Mr. Tsurumi, MFA's Deputy Vice-Minister. The EC was represented by Mr Wellenstein, Director General in DG I.[279] Since the Commission had not received any explicit mandate — and could only refer to the very general Council resolution of 21 October 1972 advocating the EC's dialogue with the developed world — the Commission had to insist that no real negotiations were held. Nevertheless, all topics of the forthcoming MTN — agricultural exports, tariffs, NTBs, and the SC — were discussed. The Tokyo Round was to start by September 1973.

During the HLC the Japanese took a particularly tough stand on the 'reform' of Art. 19 GATT. They insisted on its non-discriminatory character and that restrictions ought only be applied *after* market disruption had been evident — and not as a prevention beforehand.[280] Among sectoral problems, the Italian tape recorder issue, EC demands on order sharing in shipbuilding, and energy co-operation figured on the agenda.[281]

In August 1973 details of an internal report, written by Coreper and Council of Ministers' Secretariat officials, were leaked to the press. The report recommended the EC to declare its intention to act unilaterally to protect its markets, including possibly re-introducing quotas on Japanese imports. It saw the Japanese as pursuing a well-planned export strategy, concentrating her exports in the initial stage of expansion on those products and markets in which the domestic production was weak such as cameras to France, cars to Benelux, tape recorders to Italy, in order to secure a foothold for a later EC-wide penetration.[282]

The report recommended that the EC ought to formulate a CCP as a response. Still, the report conceded a margin for regional measures on Japanese imports in the initial stage of an EC-wide policy. The report was to be submitted to the Council of Ministers.[283]

For the opening of the Tokyo Round, in September 1973, Soames went to Japan. In his talks with Tanaka and other Japanese politicians, Soames described both Japan's sectoral export concentration as well as global export surplus to Europe as excessive.[284] The Japanese assured their future moderation, they would not repeat their earlier mistakes in the US.

Shortly after these consultations, Tanaka went to Europe for visits to Bonn, Paris and London. His talks with Brandt, Pompidou and Heath centred around EC–Japan relations, economic co-operation and on the energy question.[285] In France a joint Franco–Japanese project on uranium extraction in Niger was discussed. In London, Japan offered productive investments in depressed UK regions in exchange for Japanese participation in North Sea oil development.[286] During the same conversation, Tanaka assured Heath, Japan would exercise restraints on colour TV exports to UK. Up to then, due to their miscalculation of the domestic demand, UK manufacturers had been unable to satisfy the market for colour TVs. Now with expanded capacities they wished overseas imports to be reduced.[287] On high politics, Heath advised Tanaka against accepting Brezhnev's Asian Security plan and supported the Japanese demand for the return of her four Soviet occupied Kurile islands.[288]

While Heath and Brandt were fairly vague about institutionalised forms of trilateral co-operation – as advocated in the context of the founding of the Trilateral Commission[289] – Pompidou explicitly rejected the idea of Japan operating on equal footing with the EC and the US.[290] Upon return to Tokyo, Tanaka remarked that EC–Japanese relations offered much scope for improvement and strengthening of ties.[291]

In October 1973 the Council of Ministers, among other things, discussed relations with Japan. Soames and the German, British and French ministers gave brief accounts on their talks with Tanaka. In the ensuing debate on the Council of Ministers' officials' report, no agreement on the treatment of Japanese imports was reached. Germany advocated 'laissez faire', while an apparent majority of ministers favoured protectionist steps.[292] The Commission's attempts to mediate were equally disliked by all. As a result of the general disagreement, the report was sent back to the authors with the suggestion it needed more precision and depth.

Alarmed, in November 1973 an MFA delegation under Tsurumi came

171

to Brussels for talks on trade problems with their Community counterparts.[293] The same issues dominated parallel Keidanren–CBI talks in Tokyo.[294]

In October 1973, MITI announced new talks on electronics VSRs.[295] In London the British and Japanese electronics manufacturers would negotiate on a voluntary import limit on Japanese colour TVs. With Benelux, the Japanese talked in order to substitute for the import restrictions on a range of electronics by a VSR. Parleys with Italy on tape recorders were for the same purpose. Japan initially offered a VSR limit of 400,000. Italy insisted on 300,000 tape recorder imports. Finally both agreed on 330,000 for 1974.[296]

While these negotiations were underway, the Commission's Competition DG announced it was suing the French and Japanese ball-bearing manufacturers for having distorted free competition in the Common Market with a VSR agreement, concluded without governmental authorisation.[297]

In October 1973 the EC car makers sent an MTN position paper to the Commission.[298] They strongly advocated EC pressure to abolish Japanese NTBs on car imports, but were divided on the question of mutual tariff reductions on cars. British Leyland and the Italian and French makers were against it. They argued that Japan practised social dumping, thus no proper competition was possible. German, Dutch and the other UK producers, however, favoured tariff cuts.

In its session of 3 and 4 December 1973 the Council of Ministers, on the basis of the revised Secretariat–Coreper report, issued general guidelines on a CCP towards Japan.[299] It threatened unilateral action if Japanese imports were not restricted voluntarily and in spite of German opposition and the Commission's recent action on a French–Japanese ball-bearing VSR, approved of VSRs — particularly on electronics. The Council also blessed 'regional' — i.e. national — trade agreements with Japan, but as a soft line concession also stressed the need for more EC exports to Japan as a strategy in principle to be favoured over restrictions on Japanese imports. The sole genuine CCP element in the Council decision referred to the need for the improved exchange of import statistics among the Nine.[300]

The Council thus succeeded in squaring three circles, by endorsing both hard and soft line positions, by blessing both pro and anti VSR stands, and in finally arguing for nationally separate import policies as an essential ingredient to a CCP.

The actual interactions with Japan were in a similar state of disorder. As an American observer noticed:[301]

> Right now, in fact, confusion reigns because of the total breakdown of negotiations for an EEC–Japan trade treaty. Without such a treaty, each country is free to handle its own trade re-

lations with Japan. The result is that, at one and the same
time, the Japanese may be negotiating with industry groups,
governments, national anti-trust groups and the EEC's external
trade and anti-trust departments — multiplicity of bodies that
do not — it goes without saying — always see eye to eye.

The first oil crisis (1974)

In January 1974 Nakasone, MITI's new minister, came to Britain. Reflecting the public shock in Japan, a sudden awareness of the vulnerability of her oil supply, he pursued Japan's newly developed 'resource diplomacy'.[302]

In Britain, Nakasone referred to the Heath—Tanaka communique, which — before the first oil crisis had become evident — had underlined the desirability of bilateral co-operation on securing energy supplies.[303] Nakasone repeated Tanaka's offer to trade British oil concessions for Japanese investments in Scotland, the Midlands, Northern Ireland and Wales.[304] Mr Chataway, DIT's Minister for Industrial Development, told him, when the next oil licences were up to be distributed, Britain would take the investment records of applicant countries into account.[305]

In closer perspective, Japanese businesses turned quite hesitant at the idea of investing in Britain. Having no experience with long term strikes, they were afraid of this English tradition. In addition they felt UK wage levels were too high for productive investments.[306]

The new Labour government was soon speeding up the British retreat from East of Suez which was already well on its way. For UK's Asian policies, the *Far Eastern Economic Review* held personal preferences and experiences as partly responsible:

> Wilson is generally less interested in East Asia than Heath.
> The Tory leader waxed genuinely enthusiastic about what he
> saw in Japan, and established a good rapport with Japan's
> Prime Minister Kakuei Tanaka. Nobody expects Wilson to
> make quite the same number with his Asian counterparts.[307]

and:

> Callaghan is neither knowledgeable nor much interested in
> the Far East, while Peter Shore's sympathies at the Trade
> Ministry are thought to stop at India.[308]

Nevertheless, Britain within the EC made significant efforts to broaden the EC's external preoccupation with Africa towards Asia. With German and Dutch support, it demanded that the Community's ODA be equally split between ACP and non-ACP countries.[309] The French evidently did not like this.

173

The French policy towards Asia, despite its disappointing results, still focussed on China as pivot. Japan ranked second in French perception, but political relations remained tenuous due to France's preoccupation with Eurafrica and to Japan's low foreign policy posture.

Even economic interest in Japan was lacking in France. French exports to Japan were dominated by non-essentials: apparel, cosmetics, liquor, art works, and sundry goods.[310] Pompidou may have wished to change this. For March 1974 he had planned a state visit to Japan, opening an extremely popular Mona Lisa exhibition there (irrespective of Michelangelo's nationality). His visit had to be postponed for health reasons. Pompidou then died during the period in question.[311]

In November 1974 Sauvagnargues, the French Foreign Minister, and Kimura (MFA) met for their regular minister-level consultations. Their main topic was Giscard's proposal of a consumer—producer dialogue on oil. Kimura agreed to the French concept and publicly declared it compatible with the US's planned consumer conference,[312] though the US evidently intended quite the opposite of what the French wanted.

Le Monde indicated that Japan's wavering was a consequence of Kissinger's repeated hints on Japan's food import dependency — most of her food imports coming from the US — showing Japan she could afford 'pas de trop écarts sur d'autres terrains'.[313]

Kimura had consultations with his German counterpart, Genscher, in October 1974, an occasion which both used to sign an agreement on technological co-operation covering ocean, medical and nuclear research. Basically, bilateral relations were so free of problems that the German ambassador in Tokyo 1971—76, Professor Grewe, hinted in his memoirs that the lack of issues to be talked about with the Japanese government had been his greatest problem.[314] Japan had kept Germany waiting for three years for the 1974 consultations and even then no Japanese initiatives or memorable proposals were forthcoming. 'Stummes Japan' complained a German paper.[315] The agenda of the ministerial meeting covered such general issues as world energy and monetary problems. Genscher would talk on East—West questions, and Kimura on the situation in East Asia.[316]

In Japan's relations with Italy, tape recorders were the most evident theme in early 1974. The Commission had refused to extend the Italian quota restrictions (Art. 19 GATT) on tape recorder imports beyond their expiration date of 31 December 1973 and argued, Italy should accept the 330,000 VSR limit it had negotiated with the Japanese.[317] Italy argued that Japan would circumvent the agreement by sending her exports via third countries, and invoked 'independent emergency measures' to restrict the Japanese tape recorders further. Such measures could be taken for one month by a member state if a respective Council decision was pending.[318] The Council discussed the case in February without coming to a conclusion. Then in March 1974 the Italians accepted the 330,000 Japanese VSR, a deal which they had concluded four months earlier.[319]

In February 1974, President Ortoli went to Japan, and after courtesy calls to premier Tanaka, Fukuda (MOF), Miki (Environment), he had more substantial talks with Nakasone (MITI) and Ohira (MFA). Most of his talks touched upon the MTN, energy questions, OPEC, nuclear co-operation and the international monetary situation.[320]

To Nakasone he again proposed a TA with an SC, but Nakasone declined the offer, stating that Japan was well capable of handling her conflicts with Italy and Benelux by herself without such a treaty. He said the Commission was nevertheless welcome to mediate between Italy and Japan on the tape recorder issue.[321] Ortoli agreed to this, but was evasive when Ohira proposed co-operation on North Sea oil development.[322] Ohira's suggestion on a 'Japanese—European declaration' as a counterpiece to Kissinger's Atlantic Charter similarly ended in nothing.[323]

Meeting with Keidanren leaders, Ortoli found a 'single minded interest in energy questions', issues on which the Commission's President, in absence of a common European energy policy, hardly could make any significant statements or promises. The only result of Ortoli's visit was the signing of an agreement granting diplomatic privileges to the EC's forthcoming Delegation in Tokyo — after Washington, Geneva and Santiago the fourth overseas representation of the Commission.[324]

The Commissioners' inability to have meaningful talks with their Japanese partners was based not only on the lack of a respective Council mandate: the Commission itself continued to be divided on VSR initiatives. While the Competition DG insisted that VSRs without government involvement were illegal, DG I — for the sake of Community involvement — opposed any national government participation in external trade matters.[325] In addition, national policies were on opposite tracks on several dimensions: in principle both Germany and Benelux favoured a strengthened CCP. But Germany pursued a liberal import policy, while Benelux on electronics — the sectoral issue of the day — followed a protectionist line.

France advocated protectionist policies and wanted to maintain checks on the CCP, while Britain held liberal trade beliefs, but at the same time preferred industry-to-industry talks over governmental involvement in VSR matters.

Thus the Commission could not do anything positive. The only thing left for her DGs was to oppose certain specific policies or industrial agreements if they did not like them — such as in the French ball-bearing case. In an official statement the Commission professed, the 'contractual and autonomous [sic!] means of commercial policy' would take care of her relations with Japan.[326]

To these policies the Japanese reacted with a strategy of avoidance, though dutifully they continued to send occasional high-level missions to Europe for energy and trade talks.[327] On sectoral trade problems they preferred unilateral Japanese producer—exporter decisions for eventual restraints without their overseas partners' involvement.[328] In the case of Japanese producers being too diverse and their exports not organised by an effective association, then a unilateral governmental export control measure was preferred. Most disliked were bilateral governmental agreements to limit Japanese exports, which not only were inflexible to changing market conditions, but also smelled of the discrimination of the post-war years.

On colour TVs in June 1974, British and Japanese manufacturers — due to a 30 per cent market contraction — agreed to VSR levels below the 1973 figures.[329] Benelux and Japan also agreed on continued VSRs on electronics.[330]

The association of British car producers (SMMT) in October 1974 again asked for an EC-wide quota on Japanese car imports in retaliation for alleged Japanese protectionism on cars.[331] In the aftermath of the oil crisis due to declining European demand, Japanese car exports to the EC had already fallen by 27 per cent in the first half of 1974.[332]

In November 1974 Mr Tsurumi, MFA's Deputy Vice-Minister, came to Brussels for high-level consultations (HLC). His conversations with Soames and Wellenstein as usual covered bilateral trade, the MTN, and energy, food and raw material policies, and the role of the EC Delegation in Tokyo,[333] which was established the same month, after more than two years of intra-EC controversies had passed. Wolfgang Ernst, the Commission's director in charge of non-European industrialised countries in DG I, became the first Head of Delegation.

The Japanese export drive starts (1975)

Since October 1974 EC exports to Japan had fallen dramatically. The recession in Japan had led to the collapse of demand for both capital goods and consumer products.[334] The domestic recession pushed Japanese companies to intensify their export marketing. Wherever sectoral frictions had existed before — they now increased with a reduced Japanese willingness to concede VSR. In November 1974 the Commission had abrogated a Franco—Japanese ball-bearing inter-industry agreement on pricing and quantity limitations of Japanese bearings in France and declared it illegal.[335]

Typical of Japan's attitude at the time was a Japan Economic Centre forecast which — possibly even correctly — predicted a $17 US billion EC trade deficit towards Japan by 1985. Unmoved, it declared the EC would be perfectly able to absorb this permanent deficit without much difficulty.[336]

With Japan having conquered a 9 per cent share in the UK car market, an increasing number of Labour MPs in the Commons voiced support for the SMMT's demands for import controls on non-EC car imports. Chancellor Healey in responses rejected these suggestions.[337] In May 1975, the Queen and the Duke of Edinburgh were touring Japan on a state visit. A sudden consumer wave for all things British swept Japan and importers had problems keeping up with the sudden demand.[338] Both the British embassy in Tokyo and DoT stressed the need for detente on the trade issue in the wake of the Queen's visit.

A visiting French Secretary for Foreign Trade, Mr Segard, similarly felt that there were no serious trade problems with Japan at present. But since MITI's administrative guidance worked as an obstacle to French investments in Japan, France in retaliation would not authorise a few sogo shosha subsidiaries in return.[339]

Even without formal co-ordination, most of European diplomacy now started to aim at Japanese NTBs — a target on which EC agreement was easily possible and which in most cases constituted an enervating and highly annoying obstacle to European investments and imports.

The British Chamber of Commerce in Tokyo listed as Japanese NTBs in a report, which was to serve as policy input for Whitehall decisions:[340]

- The Japanese refusal to test British cars on Japanese standards in UK. Importers were informed on changes in safety and pollution regulations only with a 'little notice'.
- On food products, Japan has a positive list of permissible food additives, while most countries have a negative list. Thus food with new additives cannot be sold in Japan, unless these are put on the list.
- On trade marks, Japanese companies had registered European names and designs as theirs (e.g. Scottish clan names for textiles) at the Japanese patent office.
- Arbitrary customs valuations, e.g. advertising expenditure is computed as part of the value of a product to be subjected to tariffs.
- The processing of applications for branches of foreign banks, taking three years until approval.
- The limitations on foreign investment in the retail sector: 'automatic approval' is given only for 50 per cent shares on up to 11 retail stores. Anything exceeding these limits would have to go through an exceedingly difficult approval procedure.

The Secretary of State in the German Economics Ministry, Grüner, during a May 1975 visit to Tokyo voiced complaints against similar NTBs:[341]

— Japanese non-acceptance of German tests of pharmaceuticals,
— Japanese pollution standards on cars,
— the non-recognition of German tests of diesel engines for trawlers,
— that German banks in Tokyo were not allowed to refinance at discount rates.

In addition, Grüner asked for the reduction of Japanese VSRs to Germany.

On 16 and 17 June 1975 a new round of HLC took place in Tokyo. The EC delegation was led by Wellenstein, the Japanese by Mr Yoshino, the deputy foreign minister.[342] The talks would be followed immediately by the regular bilateral steel talks on 18 and 19 June. They had started in 1965 as bi-annual consultations between MITI and the ECSC. The steel talks were held against a background of a global slump in demand, leading to cut-throat price competition of 40 to 50 per cent discounts on regular sales. Japan's earlier expansion in production capacities was now blamed for having worsened the depression.[343] MITI officially displayed optimism, domestic Japanese demand for steel would pick up by the summer, thus reducing the pressure to export.[344]

For the earlier HLC talks a five-man delegation under Wellenstein had flown in from Brussels. They were reinforced by officials from the EC Delegation. The list of Japanese participants, besides Yoshino, shows two bureau chiefs (Hashimoto, from MITI's International Trade Policy Bureau, and Miyazaki, of MFA's Economic Affairs Bureau), and 25 other officials — mostly from MITI and MFA — at director level.[345]

The HLC's agenda provided for the following items:[346]
— on the world, the EC's and the Japanese economic situation in general,
— the MTN,
— bilateral trade,
— agricultural questions,
— energy and raw materials, the LDC issue, and
— technological co-operation.

According to the agenda, each item was to be dealt with in a 45 minute general session between the EC delegation and selected Japanese officials.[347] The EC's ambassadors and their commercial counsellors would be briefed by the Commission at both formal meetings and probably at more informal luncheons and dinner receptions.[348]

In a telex sent home to Brussels, Wellenstein described his talks as going extremely well.[349] His memo for a later press conference advised him to underline that the talks had been more useful than in the past.[350]

The discussion on bilateral and global economic issues had focussed on the development of bilateral trade, the EC being unhappy about her worsening deficit. Japan explained the drop in EC exports to Japan as a consequence of Japan's domestic recession. They hoped a recently initiated reflationary package would stimulate the Japanese economy to grow by one per cent more, and thereby also spur demand for imports.[351]

On the ongoing MTN, both sides continued to disagree on the SC issue. On energy, the Japanese advocated a strategy of consumer—producer dialogue and were sceptical of the work of the IEA. They took considerable interest in the Commission's programme for a European energy policy.

In a subsequent press conference[352] Wellenstein stressed the similarity of the EC's and Japan's structural situation as developed countries without raw materials — in comparison to Australia, Canada, and the US. This induced both Japan and the EC to advocate a consumer—producer dialogue, in order to stabilise the export revenue of the raw material exporting LDCs.[353] Later Wellenstein gave an interview to Japan's leading economics daily, *Nihon Keizai Shimbun.*[354] The resulting article focussed on the Lomé Agreement — and on Wellenstein's assurance that its regional enlargement was not planned by the EC, on the EC's Stabex scheme, Greece's membership application and on the Euro—Arab dialogue. Only passing reference was made to the bilateral trade deficit, on which Wellenstein expressed the hope it would be balanced by increased EC exports to Japan, and not by EC import restrictions. The low-key treatment of the trade issue was caused by the need for an alliance between raw material lacking DCs in the North—South dialogue.[355]

Among bilateral issues, steel was potentially the most contentious. World steel production suffered from a drastic decline in orders. For EC producers in early 1975 orders were down 30 per cent compared to the boom year 1974,[356] production was down 10 per cent. A global price competition had ensued: export prices were cut by 40 to 55 per cent. Short time work and temporary closures had started in the steel industry. The Belgian steel producers had asked the Commission for mandatory production quotas (Art. 58 ECSC Treaty),[357] and the French producers had demanded Community intervention in pricing policies (Art. 57).[358] The Commission did not see the situation as being so serious as to justify price or production controls[359] but chose to start monitoring the EC's steel imports.[360]

During their bilateral talks, both the Commission and MITI agreed that a degree of competition ought to be avoided on the European market, in which steel prices were cut below unit costs — in the end, all steel producers then would end up as losers.[361]

A Japanese steel VSR had expired by the end of 1974. Since January 1975 Japanese steel exports to the EC had increased by 120 per cent.[362] Now the Commission's steel men presented a forward programme to MITI. It provided for a 15 per cent cut in EC raw steel production for June—September 1975, in the context of 'adapted' steel imports.[363] MITI had shown understanding, and later in June 1975 held discussions with the six largest Japanese steel producers, who then were supposed to become disposed towards self-discipline on exports to the EC —which would help price levels, apart from their quantitative effect. The Commission now was happy about MITI's ability for administrative guidance.

In Japan, however, the nature of MITI's instructions was disputed. While some companies considered them as strict requests, others interpreted them more as suggestions.[364] With a continued recession on their domestic market, Japan's steel producers who usually were quick in announcing joint price hikes, now showed difficulties at putting export restraints to the EC into effect.[365]

During the next months Japanese steel exports continued to grow. But in the following October 1975 MITI—Commission talks on steel, MITI again gave reassuring noises, that it had already advised its exporters for more orders.[366] In December 1975 Nippon Steel actually succeeded in organising a steel export cartel in order to limit sales to the EC effectively to around 100,000 tonnes per month.[367]

Already in May 1975 DoT had asked the Japanese Ministry of Transport (MOT) to send its inspectors to Britain for tests on UK export cars there — as Britain already did vice versa.[368] This demand, of special interest to German and British car exporters, was taken up by the Commission, which through its Delegation had a 'note verbale' — a demarche requiring a specific reply — presented to MFA.[369]

The note stated that the EC in 1974 had exported only 25,000 cars to Japan, which in turn had shipped 250,000 cars to the Community, and emphasised the need for more balanced exchanges in order to resist protectionist moves among member states.[370] The Commission note demanded the abolition of a series of Japanese NTBs, operating as effective deterrents to European low volume car imports.

Reports that Britain was ready for import controls on cars backed the Commission's note.[371] In November 1975 it became known that MOT had started the training of transport attachés, to be stationed in Geneva for travels through Europe informing about Japanese regulations.[372]

Prior to the December 1975 HLC, MFA announced it had accepted the Commission's demands: besides sending the transport attachés, full translations would be provided. Japan would stop insisting on the duplication of safety tests, where European tests were stricter or equivalent to her own. As reference date for new regulations Japan agreed to the cars' date of manufacture, provided these were certified, rather than the dates of import to Japan.[373]

Similar to steel, ships were suffering from severe over-capacities in the post-oil-crisis period. After intensive Commission—AWES—CEBLS discussions,[374] in early December 1975 the Commission sent a verbal demarche again to MFA, MITI and MOT. The demarche asked for urgent talks on ways to reduce surplus capacities and to discuss price cutting and credit conditions for Japanese shipyards.[375] The Commission hoped this note would be supportive for the two EC shipbuilders' associations' and the Japanese association's talks in San Francisco, where they would negotiate on prices and on modes for possible order sharing.[376] In a confidential paper to his fellow commissioners, Spinelli (DG III) proposed unilateral EC measures to safeguard its shipyards, in case Japan did not restrain herself voluntarily.[377]

On textiles the tide had already turned in the Community's favour. Because of Japanese demand for European quality textiles, the EC since the early 1970s had changed into a bilateral net exporter, exporting $420m to Japan, while in turn importing $200m from there (1974). Against this development, the EC's restrictions against Japanese textile exports had become meaningless. The Commission now offered to liberalise Japanese textile imports in return for certain voluntary ceilings and a consultation procedure.[378] After three rounds of talks, a bilateral textile agreement had been agreed upon in negotiations parallel to the HLC on 11 and 12 December 1975. Under the consultation procedure Japan had acceded to temporary VSRs on synthetic fibres and on cotton cloth to the entire Community, and to VSRs on five more textile types to certain member states.[379] Japan had not asked for EC VSRs in return, and announced she would phase out her restrictions on EC textile imports — notably those on wool — by 1977. Hard quotas were thus abolished in favour of a monitoring of sensitive areas, with a possible intervention in case of disturbances.[380]

The Japanese media celebrated the agreement as ending a 50-year-old struggle for free Japanese textile exports.[381] The consultation clause was mutual and not discriminatory, and the EC had freed more than 200 restricted textile types out of a total of 250.[382] With these export outlets opened, Japan could treat her textile imports from Hong Kong, Korea and Taiwan in a more liberal fashion.

In October 1975, Vice President Scarascia-Mugnozza came to Tokyo again, this time to officially open the EC Delegation there. As one Japanese paper observed, this event occurred 17 months after Japan had granted diplomatic status to the Delegation.[383] Scarascia-Mugnozza made known to the press that Japan was now of greater interest to the EC than the year before and told his audience that he expected bilateral problems to be resolved easily.[384] In talks with Komoto (MITI), he had repeated the EC's requests on Japanese car NTBs and on steel exports, and had received a positive Japanese reaction.[385]

The Japanese press quoted Head of Delegation, Mr Ernst, as defining its tasks:[386] it would take care of the common questions of the EC, while the embassies would continue to handle the touchy bilateral questions. The Delegation's reception by the established eight EC embassies had been less than enthusiastic.[387] Some ambassadors let considerable time lapse until they made their initial courtesy calls. The dislike of some embassies — particularly the French — of the EC being formally in charge of trade relations with Japan, made them discourage their business- men to contact the Delegation in case of import problems. Initially, the Eight's (Luxembourg being represented by Belgium) commercial coun- cillors' meetings admitted the Delegation's first secretary (Mr Wilkinson) only as an observer, without the right for proposals on the agenda etc.

Still, the Japanese perceived some change in dealing with Europe. In October 1975, e.g. a former Japanese ambassador to Bonn complained that Germany, with reference to EC competence, was refusing bilateral trade talks and insisting on joint EC negotiations.[388]

In Brussels on 11 and 12 December 1975 the HLC took place. Again the delegations were led by Wellenstein and Yoshino.[389] At the outset the Commission complained that Japan's reflation policies had not work- ed. As a consequence, the EC's exports to Japan had continued to fall (by 29 per cent, January–October 1975), while Japan's exports to the EC had grown by 12 per cent during the same period. The Japanese again promised 2 per cent GNP growth for the current fiscal year 1975–76.[390]

On bilateral trade, Wellenstein argued that according to all forecasts the bilateral EC deficit would worsen in the near future. The Japanese reply referred to Japan's high transfers of invisibles to the City of Lon- don, whose surplus would in payments' terms balance a great deal of the deficit in commodity trade.[391] On energy, both sides looked at ele- ments of a possible coherent energy policy — which both admittedly did not have.[392] The talks on steel were conducted by the acting director general of DG III, Mr Loeff. He presented the Commission's most recent programme on steel. It included continuing 25 to 30 per cent production cuts for January–March 1976, the possible introduction of minimum prices, and the surveillance of imports. But no unilateral import restric- tions were foreseen. Yoshino promised Japan's co-operation.[393]

On ships, Loeff expressed the EC's concern at continued world over- capacities, at Japan's growing market share and her export credit and discount practices. He stressed the need for the co-ordinated reduction of capacities and proposed talks on price stabilisation. In his reply, Yo- shino agreed to continued talks.[394] Other HLC items covered the MTN, raw material policies and relations with third countries: the US, ASEAN, Comecon, China and the Middle East.

Since possible UK import restrictions were 'in the air' Yoshino recall- ed the joint OECD trade pledge and strongly expressed hope that no restrictive measures would be taken.[395]

Shortly afterwards, because of declining exports on these products, the Japanese cabinet decided to lift all Japanese VSRs to Europe on um- brellas, batteries and on electronics (including Benelux).[396]

The economic dimension in bilateral relations

This section emphasises the economic developments which occupied bilateral diplomacy during the 1969—75 period. Bilateral trade grew from $2 US billion, and a $200m deficit (1969), to $8.7 US billion, with a $3.2 US billion deficit (1975).

According to conventional wisdom, two facts hold major significance for the rapid and unparalleled development of Japanese trade expansion in Europe:

1 The 1971 Nixon shocks, the announcement of the devaluation of the US $, and a 10 per cent import surcharge and pressures for Japanese export restraints to the US market. These policies initiated a diversification drive of Japan's exports, seeking new outlets in Europe, a market which hitherto had been neglected due to its fragmented structure and a variety of discriminatory quotas.

2 The decline of Japan's domestic demand due to the recession following the oil crisis. This increased the urgency to intensify overseas marketing, and at the same time reduced Community exports to Japan. German, French and Benelux sales declined by more than 20 per cent 1974—75. The US appeared as barred for a further substantial expansion of Japanese exports by protectionist devices or the threat of them. Most LDCs had to spend their valuta for energy bills. Apart from the Middle East, only OECD Europe offered a substantial market with significant purchasing power, where until then Japan held a share in imports of not more than 2 per cent (1974).[397]

Sales offensives on the kind of sophisticated consumer products which Japan was selling, however cannot be started without massive prior investments in marketing research, sales networks, and advertising. The earlier trend in the establishment of Japanese sales offices and their employees proves that Japan's export expansion was conceived and prepared prior to any of the mentioned external events. Japan's export drive would have started anyway and was only accelerated by these crises. Already in 1969, impressionistic media accounts[398] and more serious economic analyses [399] predicted this development properly.

Diagram 5.1 also strongly suggests the notion of persistent European neglect of the Japanese market.

The structure of bilateral trade

Analysing trade flows by individual countries (Table 5.1), the concentration of bilateral trade on German—British—Japanese exchanges becomes evident. They consistently count for more than 50 per cent of EC—Japanese trade, and represent a similar share in the Community's

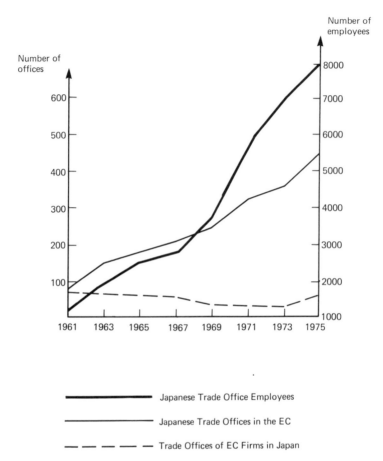

Number of offices

Number of employees

8000
7000
6000
5000
4000
3000
2000
1000

600
500
400
300
200
100

1961 1963 1965 1967 1969 1971 1973 1975

———————— Japanese Trade Office Employees

———————— Japanese Trade Offices in the EC

— — — — — Trade Offices of EC Firms in Japan

Diagram 5.1 Japanese commercial representation in the EC versus EC representation in Japan[400]

Table 5.1

Euro—Japanese trade by countries (1969—75)[401]
(in million US $)

	Imports from Japan (cif)			Exports to Japan (fob)		
	1969	1972	1975	1969	1972	1975
Germany	412	986	1744	397	611	952
Britain	251	777	1480	305	415	674
France	161	368	1000	120	229	378
Italy	118	248	455	81	151	298
Netherlands	101	256	509	31	90	152
Belgium	97	194	420	76	109	153
Denmark	57	104	215	26	37	120
Ireland	15	27	66	6	11	20
EC total	1212	2960	5889	1042	1653	2747
(EC deficit	170	1307	3142)			

bilateral deficit. The Italian— and French—Japanese deficits in absolute terms are particularly small.

This is not without reason, keeping in mind the number of residual import restrictions and VSRs in both countries, reducing the volume of bilateral trade. As evident also from Table 5.2 second part, French exports to Japan were extremely weak. This becomes obvious, when contrasting the French export results with her potential on the rapidly expanding Japanese consumer market, as analysed by a former French Commercial Councillor in Tokyo.[402]

The bilateral cover ratios (imports as covered by exports) in 1975 were as follows (figures for 1972 are in brackets): Germany: 55 per cent (62 per cent), Britain: 43 per cent (55 per cent), France: 37 per cent (62 per cent), Italy: 65 per cent (42 per cent), Belgium—Luxembourg: 36 per cent (55 per cent), the Netherlands: 30 per cent (31 per cent), Denmark: 56 per cent (40 per cent), and Ireland: 30 per cent (42 per cent). With their cover ratios fluctuating between 60 per cent and 30 per cent, in relative terms their bilateral trade deficits were equally bad for all member states. Judging from this aggregate indicator, trade policies should be expected not to vary too much, if they are responsive to such indicators.

The figures in Table 5.2 again suggest that the EC both as a market and a source of supply has a far greater importance to Japan than vice versa. As a temporary trend it appears that while Japan's role as supplier to the EC market rapidly increased, her function as outlet

Table **5.2**

Japan's trade with the EC in its relative shares[403]

Japanese exports	to the EC as share of J's total exports	to G as share of G imports	to UK as share of UK imports	to F as share of F imports	to I as share of I imports	to NL as share of NL imports	to BL as share of BL imports	to DK as share of DK imports	to Irl as share of Irl imports
1969	8.6%	1.6%	1.3%	0.9%	0.9%	0.9%	1.0%	1.5%	1.1%
1975	10.2%	2.4%	2.8%	1.9%	1.2%	1.5%	1.4%	2.1%	1.8%
Japanese imports	from EC as share of J's total imports	from G as share of G exports	from UK as share of UK exports	from F as share of F exports	from I as share of I exports	from NL as share of NL exports	from BL as share of BL exports	from DK as share of DK exports	from Irl as share of Irl exports
1969	7.9%	1.3%	1.7%	0.8%	0.7%	0.3%	0.8%	0.9%	0.7%
1975	5.8%	1.1%	1.5%	0.7%	0.9%	0.4%	0.5%	1.4%	0.6%

for EC products declined. This second trend should later improve, once domestic demand in Japan had recovered from its 1974–75 recession.

The composition of bilateral trade

Table 5.3

Major EC exports to Japan[404]
(in million US $)

	1971	1975
Foodstuffs	74	410
Raw materials	33	87
Chemicals	260	636
Metals	18	89
Textile fibres	47	22
Machinery and equipment	475	934
— of which general machinery	371	709
— of which electrical machinery	43	165
— of which transport equipment	30	51
Consumer products	141	609
— of which textiles	28	306
— of which household equipment	9	53
— of which electrical household appliances	7	21
— of which diverse (optics, musical instruments, books, etc.)	14	202
— of which cars	25	127

Although capital goods and semi-processed products for industrial use continued as the bulk of EC exports to Japan, the export growth 1971–1975 of these products stood at 'only' 112 per cent (Table 5.3). By contrast, the sales of European durable consumer products and of processed foodstuffs had increased by 374 per cent during the same period.

German exporters, whose staple export — in comparison to the Italians, French or Danes — had been industrial equipment, were worried.[405] They feared a long term decline in Japan's demand for machinery and capital goods imports — due to Japan's own technological developments and licence productions. The marketing of capital goods in Japan had been fairly easy: Japanese companies would feel the need and themselves search for suitable suppliers.

The increased demand for European consumer products offered compensatory business: rising Japanese income, more leisure time, and in-

187

creased female employment produced an ever expanding market for household and kitchen appliances, furniture, leisure goods, sports equipment, educational materials, fashion clothing, cosmetics and 'exotic' European foods and drinks. These products, however, were difficult to market: in contrast to capital goods, a costly distribution system had to be set up and expensive advertising to be organised.

Table 5.4

Major Japanese exports to the EC[406]*
(in billion Yen)

	1970	1975
Foodstuffs	44	32
Textiles	41	46
Chemicals	63	90
Non-metal products	14	22
Metal products	99	219
— of which steel	68	167
Machinery and equipment	319	1066
— of which ships	70	120
— of which optics	42	131
— of which cars	17	191
— of which radios	19	83
— of which TV sets	—	34
— of which office equipment	—	60
— of which sewing machines	7	—
Others	83	190
— of which toys	8	7
Total	664	1665

*Figures for Luxembourg and Ireland are not included.

From the figures in Table 5.4, a tendency towards transportation equipment, sophisticated machinery and consumer goods is evident, combined with a relative decline of basic or semiprocessed Japanese exports (steel, textiles, chemicals) to the EC. While the latter's absolute value increased by 76 per cent, the exports of the higher value-added first category more than tripled by 234 per cent.

The structural changes in the Japanese economy, which were already reflected in the changes in the composition of her exports to Europe, 1960—68, continued to be visible in her exports 1970—75. Wilkinson found the export shares of labour intensive industries (shoes, textiles, wood processing) further declining from 15 per cent (1970) to 9 per cent (1975).[407] Energy and raw material intensive products (steel, petrochemicals, synthetic fibres, plastics and non-iron metals) equally fell in relative terms among Japanese exports to Europe, from 25 per cent to 18 per cent. The compensatory increases occurred on mass-production products with above-average knowledge input (cars, ships, consumer electronics), whose share among Japan's exports to the EC went up from 35 per cent (1970) to 45 per cent (1975). High technology exports (pharmaceuticals, telecommunications, energy generating equipment, general machinery) grew from 25 per cent to 28 per cent.

Comparing the commodity structure of Euro—Japanese trade flows, it becomes evident that since the late 1960s the basic complementary character of exchanges — which had existed earlier when Japan exported labour intensive products for European capital goods in return — had disappeared: both produced and traded on more or less the same intermediate technology range. The emergence of numerous sensitive sectors in Europe also indicates that most of Japan's exports were competitive rather than complementary in nature — in strong contrast to most US—Japanese exchanges.

Though emerging from similar factor endowments and technology levels, bilateral trade empirically still followed trading logic. The shares of items were highly distinct in both flows:[408] European chemicals, pharmaceuticals, textiles, machinery, household appliances and processed foodstuffs were exchanged for Japanese steel, consumer electronics, cars and ships.

In 1970 a German study tried to analyse the effects of Japanese exports to third markets.[409] Covering the US, Australia, Thailand, South Africa, Mexico and several other Latin American and African countries, it found at times extremely tough Japanese competition for German cars, trucks, steel and consumer products. Well planned and cost efficient Japanese bids increased competition especially for infrastructural projects at public tenders in LDCs.

Sectoral issues

Japan's exports show a higher degree of concentration than those of any other comparable industrial country. Table 5.5 shows the world market penetration of typical Japanese export items in 1971.[410]

Certainly, the US had to shoulder the lion's share of Japan's sectoral export strategy, but also in OECD Europe a high degree of specialisation in Japanese exports is evident: seventy commodity groups alone counted for 80 per cent of all Japanese exports there.[411] As plain in Table 5.5, on nearly every product Japan pursued a distinct mix of concentrations to certain national markets. Their best known example is, of course, the car sector.

Table 5.5

World market shares of Japanese export products (1971)

	Film cameras–projectors	Cameras	Binoculars and microscopes	Calculators	Ball-bearings	Toys (1970)	Tape recorders
Share in OECD exports (1969)	43.0%	34.0%	41.5%	n.a.	21.0%	40.0%	44.0%
World producer rank	first	first	first	first	second	first	first
Distribution among importing countries:							
France	3.4%	2.2%	2.2%	2.5%	3.6%	0.1%	0.3%
Germany	18.1%	9.1%	10.1%	10.8%	19.2%	5.6%	6.3%
Italy	6.1%	0.6%	2.8%	–	0.4%	3.3%	0.7%
Benelux	12.6%	13.8%	5.6%	11.3%	2.5%	2.2%	2.2%
Britain	2.2%	0.6%	6.3%	5.0%	5.7%	1.7%	2.0%
USA	26.4%	25.9%	39.8%	25.4%	32.7%	38.8%	59.7%

	Radios	TVs	Watches	Steel sheets	Cars	Lorries	Ships
Share in OECD exports (1969)	67.0%	n.a.	11.0%	n.a.	7.0%	11.0%	40.0%
World producer rank	first	first	second	first	sixth	fourth	first
Distribution among importing countries:							
France	0.3%	0.1%	2.4%	0.2%	0.2%	–	–
Germany	4.9%	5.3%	4.6%	0.8%	0.1%	–	–
Italy	0.4%	–	0.9%	2.4%	–	–	–
Benelux	3.2%	0.5%	1.3%	6.2%	3.1%	0.1%	4.1%
Britain	0.7%	2.6%	2.6%	0.5%	1.0%	–	6.0%
USA	59.1%	65.6%	12.3%	20.0%	61.0%	22.0%	–

Cars. In 1955 German businessmen had advised the Japanese to abandon their efforts to produce cars. They would never be able to manufacture cars of international quality, the Japanese were told.[412] Instead they should stick to textiles, the recommendation went.

By 1970 Japanese car exports had only penetrated peripheral European markets without domestic production: Finland, Portugal and Greece. In 1970 fewer than 500 Japanese cars were sold in Italy or Germany.[413] But soon the conquest of sizeable market shares in Norway, Switzerland and Benelux followed. In 1973 it was Britain's turn.[414]

The continued expansion — which particularly hit British production both in its domestic and overseas sales — in 1975 had led to a Japanese share of 5 per cent of the EC's total car market. Japanese cars accounted for 1.7 per cent of those newly registered in Germany, for 1.6 per cent in France, for 0.05 per cent in Italy (there being subject to an annual quota of 1,000 car imports), 10.6 per cent in UK, 14.7 per cent in the Netherlands, and among non-producing countries: 17.4 per cent in Denmark, 19.1 per cent in Belgium and 51.5 per cent in Ireland.[415]

Still, in 1975 no VSRs were in force, the European response aimed rather at opening up the Japanese car market by demanding the removal of NTBs there.

Ships. After an accelerated expansion period in the 1960s and a brief slump in 1972, Japanese shipbuilders reached their peak of production in 1973, when they gained 55 per cent of all world orders, achieved with extremely competitive prices due to efficient production and generous credit conditions.

European shipbuilders were incapable of defending their market shares, even with the help of the most generous subsidies.[416] Massive EC shipbuilders' influence on the Commission, their national governments, and bilateral negotiations with Japanese shipyards until 1974 could not move Japan to enter market sharing arrangements, to abandon her continued expansion plans, or to scrap her already existing over-capacities.[417]

The Japanese readiness to do so, however, rapidly increased when in 1974 her ship production fell by 72 per cent. In 1975 it declined by yet another 10 per cent.[418] Then Japan announced she would reduce her capacities by one third.[419]

Steel. In a similar fashion, Japanese steel producers had been expanding their capacities rapidly during the 1960s, and became aware of their surplus capacities during the 1974—75 crisis. Then, they produced 110m tonnes with facilities well able to produce 150m tonnes.

This created a strong urge to export which ran into protectionist resistance on the part of the recipients. During 1972—74 Japanese key producers had agreed on a voluntary export ceiling of 1.22m tonnes to the EC. The agreement had not been extended during 1974, because Japan's steel exports then had been far below the VSR limits.

Due to the domestic recession Japan's steel exports rapidly increased during 1975. Under Community pressure by the end of 1975 the six largest Japanese producers again announced a VSR for 1976 on 1.22m tonnes for 1976 to the EC.[420]

Electronics. Japanese electronics exports had been subjected to massive VSR pressures since 1972, and agreed to orderly marketing in most of OECD Europe's markets. Because of declining sales, in 1975 most of the VSRs were not renewed, but consultative procedure arranged in case of market disturbances. Due to the Cartel Office intervention the German market had always remained open, France and Italy however, continued to use either quotas or Japanese VSRs to prevent Japanese competition.[421]

Ball-bearings. Japanese ball-bearing imports had reached 'political' limits only in Britain (a 15 per cent market share), where VSRs were enforced in 1972−73.[422] For the rest of the EC the Japanese share of the market remained around 1 per cent.

Textiles. On textiles the bilateral trading situation had reversed already in the early 1970s.[423] In 1973 the EC exported $293m textiles to Japan, while getting $140m Japanese production in return. In a bilateral agreement, concluded in December 1975, the EC therefore dropped most of its residual restrictions on Japanese textile imports.

Barriers to trade

Japanese payments' surpluses (1968−73), international diplomatic pressure and the (unwanted) strength of the Yen induced Japan to speed up her import liberalisation programme. The number of Japanese restrictions was reduced from 118 (1969) to 31 (1973) − out of a total of 1,097 of the Brussels Tariff Nomenclature items. Of the remainder, 23 were agricultural products, 3 mining products (coal), and 5 manufactures. As evident from Table 5.6, of these, intergrated circuits and computers were to be liberalised[424] in 1974−75.

From 1967 to 1973 Japan reduced her tariffs on industrial products from an average of 17 per cent to about 8 per cent and simplified import procedures.[425]

Table 5.6

Japan's import liberalisation[424]

Year	Ratio of liberalised imports* (% at year end)	No. of items liberalised	No. of items under residual quantitative import restrictions (at year end)		
			Total	Non-agricultural products	Agricultural products
1960	42	—	—	—	—
1961	70	—	492[†]	—	—
1962	88	268	224	—	—
1963	92	69	155	—	—
1964	93	32	123	—	—
1965	93	1	122	—	—
1966	93	—[‡]	124[‡]	—	—
1967	93	0	124	—	—
1968	93	3	121	53	68
1969	93	3	118	50	68
1970	94	28	90	35	55
1971	95	50	40	12	28
1972	97	7	33	9	24
1973	97	2	31	8[§]	23[‖]

* Calculated by using as weights the value of Japanese private imports in 1959.
† Number of items as of April 1962 when Japan's system of import restrictions was changed from a positive to a negative list.
‡ The number of items changed as a result of the revision of the Customs Tariff in May 1966.
§ Including integrated circuits and electronic computers (counted as four items) scheduled to be liberalised sometime during 1974 and 1975, respectively.
‖ Including one item (malt) scheduled to be liberalised in October 1974.
Source: Ministry of International Trade and Industry, White Paper on Foreign Trade of Japan.

The six EC countries, which during the TA negotiations 1969–71 were ready to abolish 75 per cent of their 151 restricted items (in one or several member states), by 1972 still restricted 119 product headings from Japan.[426]

To the continued Western accusation of Japan's pursuing protectionist policies, Mr Uemura, then Keidanren's President, remarked mildly (in 1972): 'In the past discussions with Americans and Europeans on the subject of Japanese trade I have observed a rather impressive time-gap between policy development in Japan and general understanding of this policy abroad. . . . The liberalisation process has been rapid . . .'.[427]

European complaints of Japanese NTBs neutralising the liberalisation effects were more justified. Grossmann, the head of the German Chamber of Commerce in Tokyo, considered as the major NTBs the slow and heavy-handed administration of the Japanese import system.[428]

This was evident particularly in:
— the procedures for import licences,
— standard payment procedures (restricting the importer's options to grant generous payment conditions to his clients),
— an overly-strict food control, provided by the Food Sanitation Law,[429]
— the repetition of lengthy tests on pharmaceuticals and technical products.

But also some classical residual barriers to trade remained effective in Japan:
— high tariffs on liquor and wine,
— a disadvantageous regime to newcomers on import quotas, and
— the persisting 50 per cent participation limit for foreign investments.

Mutual investments

Japan's balance on services and transfers vis à vis Europe traditionally was deficient. The deficit on services regularly accounted for 50 per cent of Japan's total, of which the bulk of payments for invisibles went to the City of London (1973: $751), as expenditure for maritime transportation, insurance, overseas travel and investment incomes. Among net transfers again Britain was the net beneficiary.[430]

Still, there is considerable discrepancy between British and Japanese figures concerning the UK invisibles' surplus. For 1975 the Bank of Japan claimed it at £650m, the British government at £250m.[431]

The truth should be expected at some point in between, since the Japanese figures refer to gross payments for services rendered or mediated by the City, while the British figure is a rather conservative estimate of net revenue for UK services from Japanese sources (that is: of the gross payments, subsequent transfers to third countries are deducted (e.g. for shipping) so only the margins for commission remain).

Japanese investment in Europe. In Japan's long term capital account, again most of her transfers to Europe went to the UK, most of it for direct investments then for trade credits, loans, securities and external bonds.[432] Japanese direct investments in all EC countries 1951—77 totalled $3,075m (13.8 per cent of Japan's foreign investment). $1,690m went to the UK (7.6 per cent of the Japanese total), $252m to Germany

(1.1 per cent), $222m to France, $201m to the Netherlands and $142m to Belgium.[433]

Table 5.7

Japanese investments in Europe 1951–73[434]
(in million US $)

Foodstuffs	24	Agriculture	0
Textiles	6	Fishing	1
Wood and paper	0	Mines and extractive	
Chemicals	36	industries	827
Iron and non-ferrous metals	28	Building and construction	1
Mechanical engineering	37	Distribution	143
Electrical industry	7	Banks and insurance	237
Transport equipment	4	Miscellaneous	596
Miscellaneous	13	Total	1,805
Total for manufacturing			
industry	155	Overall total	1,960

Since the data in Table 5.7 are based on Japanese statistics (gross transfers), $780m (mining) has to be deducted for the Japanese acquisition of an oil company, the Abu Dhabi Marine Area Co Ltd, in London, Furthermore at least $530m (miscellaneous) has to be discounted as loans granted to UK based buyers for the purchase of Japanese ships.[435] This reduces the net total to $650m, of which then the bulk consists of investments in banking, insurance and distribution networks.

Until 1969 the Bank of Japan's controls on outward capital flows allowed only such overseas investments which were considered as strictly essential to Japan's national economy. These investments were primarily oriented towards raw material procurement, and were hardly situated in Europe.

In the early 1970s production in Japan became more expensive: costs of land, labour and raw materials increased. Fuel prices, rising costs for shipping and the upward float of the Yen in addition worked against production in Japan. To avoid these costs, and to circumvent tariff or quota barriers, and in order to service and to secure export markets better, Japanese companies hesitantly started productive investment in Europe.[436]

In Western Europe the Japanese invested only where explicitly welcome. That is: where they felt secure in political, psychological or language (English) terms, and where strong regional investment incentives (packages) were available: in Ireland, Belgium, Germany, UK, Spain and in Portugal. In consequence fewer Japanese investments were made in

Table 5.8
Companies with European participation in the top 50
list of companies with foreign equity in Japan   441

Position	Company	Sector	Japanese participants in equity	Foreign participants in equity	Foreign investment (in %)
5	Matsushita Electronics Corporation	Electrical Machinery	Matsushita Electric Industrial Co Ltd	N.V. Philips Gloeilampen-fabrieken (Netherlands)	35
6	Nestlé Japan Ltd	Foodstuffs		Nestlé Alimentana S.A. (Switzerland) Participations industrielles Afib S.A. (Switzerland)	100
9	Fuji Xerox Co Ltd	Engineering	Fuji Photo Film Co Ltd	Rank Xerox Ltd (Great Britain)	50
10	Caterpillar Mitsubishi Ltd	Engineering	Mitsubishi Heavy Industries	Caterpillar Overseas S.A. (Switzerland)	50
13	A.M.F. Japan Ltd	Engineering		A.M.F. Investment (Switzerland)	100
14	Showa Oil Co Ltd	Oil		Anglo-Saxon Petroleum Co. Ltd (Great Britain) Mexican Eagle Oil Co. (Great Britain)	50
21	Asahi-Dow Ltd	Chemical products	Asahi Chemical Industry Co Ltd	Dow Chemical A.G. (Switzerland)	50
23	Sumitomo Rubber Industries Ltd	Rubber	Sumitomo Electric Industries Ltd The Long Term Credit Bank of Japan Ltd	Dunlop Rubber Co Ltd (Great Britain)	43.75
30	Ciba Geigy Japan Ltd	Pharmaceutical products		Ciba Geigy Ltd (Switzerland)	100
35	Nippon Oil Seal Industry Co Ltd	Trade		Freudenberg & Co (Germany, Federal Republic)	25
44	Nippon Tokushu Noyaku Seizo Co Ltd	Chemical products	Tateno Trading Co Ltd	Bayer AG (Germany, Federal Republic)	50

Italy and hardly any in France.[437]

For security reasons, theoretically, Japanese companies prefer joint ventures with some domestic partner. But in actual practice in Europe they created mostly wholly owned subsidiaries, finding it difficult to reconcile European and Japanese management styles, the latter being their main and superior asset when setting up production in Europe.[438]

European investment in Japan. It was only in 1973 that Japan finally fully liberalised the most significant economic sectors for foreign investment. During most of the 1960s MITI would authorise capital imports only if they fulfilled four conditions:

- contribute to the technological development of the Japanese economy,
- contribute to exports or to savings on imports,
- do not significantly compete with domestic industries, and
- have a percentage of less than 50 of foreign equity.[439]

The motive for the restrictions was the Japanese fear of having her under-capitalised industries cheaply (with an undervalued Yen) bought up by foreign capital. US pressure in 1969 — applied to Chrysler's planned tie-up with Mitsubishi — then largely brought about Japan's capital import liberalisation.[440] But foreign investments in agriculture, leather processing, mining and retail trade still remained restricted.

Nevertheless, European investors showed little interest in Japanese stocks, capital link-ups or direct investments. Table 5.8 shows the strong degree of Swiss and UK productive involvement which in many cases originated in the prewar or in the immediate post-war years.

Decision making in bilateral relations

During 1969–75 the structures for national foreign policy decisions on commercial policies towards Japan did not alter significantly from those described in the preceding chapter. The novelty of the early 1970s is the gradual incrementalist emergence of the Commission's foreign policy role, which by the end of 1975 in respect to Japan had achieved a rudementary institutional framework for effective policy initiatives and responses.

The establishment of the Commission's Delegation in Tokyo in November 1974 effected a major breakthrough, enabling a regular direct flow of information and communication between the Commission and the Japanese government.

The 'Community procedure' — as described in Chapter 2 — began first to run parallel to, and then gradually to substitute for bilateral

Euro–Japanese trade diplomacy at the national level. For the Japanese authorities, the media and the interested public alike, this procedure must have been puzzling at times, to say the least.

The decision makers' 'definition of the situation'

On the European side, in high politics terms the old concern of Japan's international and Western integration continued. Under Cold War conditions in the 1960s this issue was put forward in the more fundamental terms of Japan going neutral or aligning herself with China or with the Soviet Union.

Now this question was put in a different version. There was concern of Japan in a 'Gaullist fashion' seeking special deals with OPEC or with the LDCs in order to secure her raw material supplies.[442] Commissioner Soames echoed this perception pointing to the relative lack of historic links of kinships and sentiment between Europe and Japan.[443] He then stressed the need for active trilateral politics in order to reduce Japan's feelings of isolation and to diminish the likelihood of separate global pursuits.

In a more up-to-date analysis, Dahrendorf came to the conclusion that Japan, after the Nixon shocks of August 1971, had changed her policies and drawn closer to the system of her fellow industrialised countries.[444] As a matter of fact, he saw neither Japan's tariffs nor her residual quotas and NTBs as a 'special problem' at the time. This low key view of trade relations with Japan was shared by all of his fellow commissioners during the early 1970s, a time when Dahrendorf was negotiating for the common TA.[445] When he contacted the national foreign ministers, among other things also on the Japan issue, he found them only marginally interested. Council sessions were dominated by the negotiations with the US — with the Mills Bill pending — and with matters concerning the first enlargement. Japan was mentioned only in reference to the US.

According to Dahrendorf's recollection, the Council in its session of 20 July 1970 spent about one minute to approve the TA mandate for the Commission. Reunions of the Commissioners took a similar interest in relations with Japan. No controversial discussion ever came up on Japan while Dahrendorf was on the Commission (1970–74).

He himself felt the TA project a futile exercise since actual trade would remain fairly unaffected by the agreement. Nevertheless, he considered the TA negotiations as a good pretext for bilateral top-level communication.[446]

The response on the TA was mixed in Japan. While MITI and its ministers shared the European indifference on the TA — at the same time strongly opposing to grant an SC — MFA with its professional bias towards contractual relations, in contrast showed strong interest in the TA. In consequence MFA was more willing to compromise on the SC in order not to jeopardise the TA project.

If politicians did not care much about European relations with Japan, then the attitudes of their senior officials counted the more. Among senior Commission officials, Wolfgang Ernst, then director in charge of relations with Japan and Australasia and later the Delegation's first head, was the father and the prime mover of the idea of a TA with Japan. To his personal regret, French and Dutch Coreper officials included the SC demand as an essential condition in the Council's mandate.[447]

Writing on EC—Japanese relations, two other Commission officials stressed the ever growing importance of Japan, and of the need for more co-operative and institutional links between the two: preventing trade conflicts through early warning systems and through a joint reorganisation of the international monetary and trade systems.[448]

Structures for bilateral decision making

Due to structural conditions in bilateral decision making, high politics realities were more sobering. Rockefeller's and Brzezinski's 1973 initiative in trilateralism did not evoke much enthusiasm either in Europe or in Japan.[449]

Brzezinski's concept of close US—EC—Japan co-operation with joint cabinet meetings, and combined staff and planning groups[450] failed to take into account both the degree of non-integration in Europe and the extent of consensus directed decision making in the strongly ethnocentric political environment of Japan. His institutional plans thus never merited serious consideration even after a 'trilateral' administration under Carter took over in the US.

But conventional bilateral relations were similarly unexciting. Professor Grewe characterised his time as German ambassador in Tokyo (1971—1976) with a feeling of redundancy: 'meine Tätigkeit hinterlasse keinerlei markante Spuren: kein Freundschafts — oder Handelsvertrag sei zu unterzeich — nein gewsen, kein Kulturinstitut einzuweihen, keine grosse Ausstellung zu eröffnen, . . . keine Krise zu entschärfen'.[451]

In a way, the establishment of the EC's Delegation since 1975 relieved the embassies partly of low politics trade issues, thus causing a loss of function. The open resentment of some senior embassy staff reflected this development.[452]

On the Japanese side, the development of a dual diplomatic system on trade issues, with distinct national trade policies continued, was viewed with consternation: 'There is no established common EC policy towards

Japan in the absence of a trade agreement between Japan and the EC, and the EC members still maintain individual trade relations with Japan as a transitional measure. This causes lots of inconvenience to Japan.'[453]

This dual structure may have complicated negotiations; in any case however, the lack of a cohesive European position reduced the EC's bargaining leverage, and allowed Japan easily to manoeuvre one country's position against the other, as evident during several VSR negotiations.

The non-existence of a joint European diplomatic initiative after the failure of the TA talks 1970—71 enabled Japan to hide her own internal MFA—MITI disagreements on her policies towards Europe. Japanese policies remained limited to offering occasionally voluntary self restraints, when certain sectors turned overly sensitive in Europe. These VSRs on the Japanese side were organised in a flexible fashion employing administrative guidance techniques between MITI, the respective industrial associations and the major producers. Apart from these self restraints, there were hardly any decisions to be taken in Japan that exceeded the routine administrative level.

On the European side, the difficulties of implementing a CCP were evident. In institutional terms in Tokyo two achievements occurred: the setting up of the Commission's Delegation with embassy functions and the creation of an 'EC Steering Committee' between the existing national European chambers of commerce in Tokyo.

This committee now served as a direct link of communication and information between European exporters in Japan and the Commission's Delegation,[454] similar to the national chamber of commerce supplying their embassies with the necessary details on Japanese NTBs. The shared interests in their removal furthered co-operation between the European chambers, in a fashion showing functionalist theory at work.

The European embassies, as exemplified in their commercial councillors' attitudes, and the national governments' behaviour towards a common 'Japanpolitik' however, evidently followed less functionalist lines. They established a rigid defence against the perceived threat of the loss in functions and competence. Under conditions which lacked political leadership — the British government in the early 1970s being a notable exception — this type of bureaucratic policy making could persevere.

It is not difficult to perceive that the persistence of European internal wrangles enabled the Japanese government to maintain a great deal of NTBs, which facing a more forceful and dynamic European representation, they might have had to abandon far earlier. European economic interests in Japan were the ones to suffer.

Conclusion

The years 1969—75 could be described as a period of normalcy in Euro—Japanese relations. Global economic events — such as the Nixon shocks and the first oil crisis — and relations with third countries (the US, China, the USSR), and the war in Indochina occupied the general public's and the politicians' minds in both Europe and Japan, rather than bilateral relations.

Japan's trade policy towards Europe followed a simple principle: it aimed at a permanent surplus on visibles in order to balance Japan's raw material imports, her capital exports — mostly to South East Asia, to cover Japan's deficits in transfers (ODA) and in services (for shipping, tourism and technology imports).[455] Japanese productive investment had not yet started in Europe to such an extent to eventually be able to offset politically the effects of her trade surplus.

The task of Japan's economic diplomacy was to secure access to her European market. To this end, Japan offered her orderly marketing concept, willing to unilaterally reduce sectoral exports to certain national markets whenever political pressures had built up and import controls were threatened.

At the same time — mainly at US pressure — Japan effectively removed most conventional barriers to imports of industrial products and capital. European pressure had only fairly marginal discernible effects.

Well designed British initiatives, both on government and on CBI level, failed due to the lack of bargaining leverage — a result of lack of European support and co-ordination. The basic European pattern of response to the Japanese export growth thus had to remain negative. 'Whenever I hear the word Japan I reach for my safeguard clause' was the European attitude of the day.[456]

Bark's argument, that the SC demand actually strengthened the EC's bargaining position[457] is hardly plausible. The 'anti-discriminatory' tradition in Japan's foreign policy made it impossible for her to accede to the EC's inflexible insistence on the SC. The SC demand did not strengthen the EC's position, it just wrecked the negotiations. The safeguard clause itself was hardly of any use. Without it, the Italians could 'protect' their domestic market quite effectively. Britain, which had a bilateral SC, never used it, and France and the Benelux employed theirs only once each during a decade and on marginal products (umbrellas and zip fasteners).

The Europeans wanted the SC, and the Japanese resented it, for reasons of pure psychology — wanting security and disliking discrimination. The sentiments of senior bureaucrats had little to do with economic realities. In the end, bilateral trade expanded tremendously even without a TA, declared essential to such an expansion by the very same policy makers.

At most, the TA's negotiations (with restrictions as bargaining chips) and their prolonged pending without chances for a conclusion had a dilatory effect on the bilateral liberalisation of residual import restrictions. While this did not prevent the Japanese export expansion in Europe, it certainly did not help European exporters in Japan.

European machinery exports there were for the most part actively sought after by Japanese producers, not requiring much European effort or marketing investment. To sell European consumer products was considered more expensive and more troublesome, since it ran into more substantial Japanese NTBs, and was therefore — according to all evidence — neglected by exporters. The official EC Japanpolitik was thus adequately reflected in the attitudes of its traders and the marketing policies of their corporate headquarters.

With the lack of an efficient and extensive marketing infrastructure, European exports to Japan fell drastically when Japan's economy in 1975 hit a deep recession. In Europe, Japanese exporters had set up such sales networks, and in 1975 — in spite of a series of sectoral VSRs, and certain setbacks in sales — overall exports continued to grow.

European import policies towards Japan were in a state of disarray. If one Commission directorate would accuse Japan of flooding the EC with indiscriminate waves of imports, the other would attack Japan for practising VSRs and distorting free competition.[458] The national capitals similarly disagreed on the VSRs both in principle and on their scope and details.

The proposal to phase out certain productions in Europe, in order to respond actively with industrial policy measures to Japan's new competitive advantages,[459] was never treated seriously.

On high politics, bilateral Euro—Japanese relations were negligible. Detente conditions had reduced the awareness of joint Western interests towards the Soviet Union. Both Europe and Japan saw with interest the re-entry of China into the international scene, but did not have much means to affect the process. The oil crisis hit both of them, but in spite of 'co-operation' talks they — including the EC countries among each other — immediately scrambled separately for safe supplies. If anything then, both the EC and Japan aligned themselves against the Mills Bill and at times voiced joint opposition to other US protectionist policies.

The real issue of 1969 —75, the US conduct of war against Vietnam and Cambodia — in spite of laudable French attempts — never entered the Euro—Japanese communiqués. Joint high politics did not exist. Trilateralism in official statements was rhetoric and did not describe realities. EC disunity and Japan's inability to solve her international problems through more farsighted designs prevented any such initiative.

Throughout the early 1970s Andrew Shonfield's observations held true: 'European inner compromises tend to be made at the expense of third countries'[460] — as evident in both the Community's treatment of the bilateral TA negotiation and in her import policies. Fortunately only a limited number of compromises could be achieved or implemented.

In Europe, little thought was given to the problem of how to accommodate a phenomenon like Japan in the long run into a civilised world economic order.[461] Japan certainly did not think about Europe in terms of high politics either. Though relations with the US were strained at times and unloved, Japan considered her respective link-ups with the US as sufficient. A silent Japan had little political communication with Europe.

Bureaucratic politics ruled bilateral relations. Negative and positive extremes were avoided. Effective trilateral co-operation did not take place, but predicted trade wars did not happen either. In view of the first oil crisis, this possibly was not a small achievement.

References

1 *Far Eastern Economic Review*, 30.1.1969.
2 *Japan Times*, 11.1.1969.
3 *Neue Zürcher Zeitung*, 5.5.1969.
4 *Le Monde*, 26.12.1969.
5 *Japan Times*, 29.1.1969.
6 *Financial Times*, 5.2.1969.
7 *Japan Times*, 4.2.1969 and 11.2.1970.
8 *Der Spiegel*, 26.5.1969 and *Japan Times*, 3.5.1969.
9 *Frankfurter Allgemeine Zeitung*, 23.5.1969.
10 *Frankfurter Allgemeine Zeitung*, 15 and 16.5.1969.
11 Rondong Shimson, as quoted in *Japan Times*, 25.5.1969, and *Hsinhua News Agency*, 23.5.1969.
12 *Frankfurter Allgemeine Zeitung*, 23.10.1969.
13 As quoted in *Japan Times*, 3.5.1969.
14 *Japan Times*, 28.4.1969.
15 *Sunday Times*, 5.10.1969.
16 *The Times*, 19.2.1969.
17 *Financial Times*, 6.10.1969.
18 *Far Eastern Economic Review*, 15.9.1969.
19 *The Economist*, 11.10.1969.
20 Answer to Written Question No. 250/68 of Pedini, *Bulletin of the European Communities* 1969, No. 3, p. 69.
21 Commission. *Press Release*, IP (69) 109, 24.6.1969.
22 *Bulletin of the European Communities* 1969, No. 8, p. 65, and

Japan Times, 24.8.1969.
23 *Financial Times,* 23.10.1969.
24 *Japan Times,* 2.2.1969.
25 *Japan Times,* 11.9.1969.
26 *Bulletin of the European Communities* 1969, No. 11, p. 64.
27 *The Times,* 12.9.1969.
28 *Bulletin of the European Communities* 1969, No. 12, p. 66.
29 *Japan Times,* 15.10.1969.
30 Hedberg, Hakan. *Die japanische Herausforderung.* Hamburg: Hoffmann & Campe. 1970.
31 *Japan Times,* 15.11.1969.
32 *Agence Europe,* 7.11.1969.
33 Baas, M. *Rapport sur les relations commerciales entre les Six et le Japon.* Parlement Européen. Documents de Séance 1969—1970, Doc. 212, 2.2.1970, p. 20, cif. 44.
34 *Japan Times,* 23.1.1969.
35 *The Economist,* 26.7.1969.
36 *Japan Times,* 12.9.1969.
37 *The Economist,* 22.2.1969.
38 *Le Monde,* 30.10.1969.
39 *Japan Times,* 11.1.1969.
40 *The Economist,* 22.2.1969.
41 *Le Monde,* 24.5.1969.
42 *The Economist,* 7.6.1969.
43 *New York Times,* 24.1.1970.
44 Ibid.
45 *Bulletin of the European Communities* 1970, No. 4, p. 81.
46 Baas, 1970, op. cit., p. 2.
47 *Bulletin of the European Communities,* 1970, No. 3, p. 32.
48 *Japan Times,* 4.2.1970.
49 Commission. *Information à la presse.* IP (70)25, 12.2.1970.
50 *Frankfurter Allgemeine Zeitung,* 14.2.1970.
51 *Japan Times,* 13.2.1970.
52 *Japan Times,* 17.2.1970.
53 *Le Monde,* 19.2.1970.
54 *Le Monde,* 21.2.1970.
55 *Japan Times,* 18.2.1970.
56 *Yomiuri Shimbun,* as translated in *Japan Times,* 24.2.1970.
57 *Japan Times,* 17.2.1970.
58 *Japan Times,* 18.2.1970.
59 *Japan Times,* 19.2.1970.
60 *Frankfurter Allgemeine Zeitung,* 31.3.1970, and *Bulletin of the European Communities* 1970, No. 5, p. 80.
61 *Bulletin of the European Communities* 1970, No. 5, p. 80.

62 *Japan Times*, 24.3.1970.
63 *Le Monde*, 29 and 30.3.1970.
64 *Le Monde*, 26.3.1970.
65 *Japan Times*, 28.3.1970.
66 *Corriere della Sera*, 4.4.1970.
67 *Le Monde*, 7.4.1970.
68 *Japan Times*, 11.7.1970.
69 *Japan Times*, 15.7.1970.
70 *Bulletin of the European Communities* 1970, No. 9/10, p. 81.
71 Commission. Note BIO (70) 75 aux bureaux nationaux. Telex Brussels, 17.9.1970.
72 Ibid.
73 Interview with Professor Dahrendorf, 9.1.1981.
74 Ibid.
75 *Japan Times*, 7.8.1970.
76 Commission. Note BIO (70) 78 aux bureaux nationaux. Telex 33142, Brussels, 25.9.1970.
77 Ibid.
78 *Christian Science Monitor* (London ed.), 16.10.1970.
79 *The Economist*, 26.9.1970.
80 *Japan Times*, 26.9.1970.
81 *Financial Times*, 18.9.1970.
82 Economist Intelligence Unit. Europe and Japan: Rivals or Partners? *European Trends* No. 25, 1970, 22–33, p. 25.
83 *International Herald Tribune*, 17.9.1970.
84 Economist Intelligence Unit. 1970. Op. cit., p. 29.
85 *Le Figaro*, 2.10.1970.
86 *Japan Times*, 6.11.1970.
87 *Japan Times*, 20.11.1970, and interview.
88 *Frankfurter Allgemeine Zeitung*, 19.11.1970.
89 Interview.
90 *Japan Times*, 4.12.1970.
91 *Neue Zürcher Zeitung*, 8.2.1970.
92 *Süddeutsche Zeitung*, 18.8.1970.
93 See also on President Heinemann's visit: *Frankfurter Allgemeine Zeitung*, 11.5.1970 and 16.5.1970, and *Der Spiegel*, 18.5.1970.
94 *Japan Times*, 4.2.1970.
95 *Guardian*, 9.4.1970.
96 *Japan Times*, 22.4.1970.
97 *The Economist*, 25.4.1970.
98 *New York Times*, and *Financial Times*, 30.5.1970.
99 *Japan Times*, 28.4.1970.
100 *The Economist*, 7.3.1970.
101 *Bulletin of the European Communities* 1971, No. 3, p. 73.

Japan Times, 29.1.1971.
102 Dahrendorf, Ralf. Community, United States, Japan: Trade Policy — Problems and Outlook. *Bulletin of the European Communities* 1971, No. 4, 20–30, p. 27.
103 Ibid., p. 28.
104 *Japan Times,* 3.3.1971.
105 *Japan Times,* 16.4.1971.
106 *Agence Europe,* 14.4.1971.
107 *Guardian,* 3.3.1971.
108 *The Times,* 11.3.1971.
109 *Japan Times,* 5.3.1971.
110 *Agence Europe,* 12.2.1971.
111 Interview.
112 *Japan Times,* 13.6.1971.
113 *Japan Times,* 25.6.1971.
114 *International Herald Tribune,* 24.6.1971.
115 *Le Monde,* 25.6.1971.
116 Kajima, Morinosuke, Pan—Europa and Japan. *Japan in Current World Affairs,* Tokyo: Kajima Institute for International Peace. 1972. 193–201, p. 200.
117 Ibid., p. 201.
118 *Japan Times,* 4.7.1971.
119 Ibid.
120 *The Times,* 12.7.1971.
121 *Guardian,* 9.7.1971.
122 *Agence Europe,* 24.6.1971.
123 See the text of the 'Protocole relatif aux relations commerciales entre la Republique Française et le Japon', attached to Franco—Japanese TA of 14.5.1963, in: Bark, Young W. *Le Marché Commun et le Japon.* Université de Paris I. These du doctorat en droit du Marché Commun. 1973, pp. 358.
124 *International Herald Tribune,* 9.7.1971.
125 *New York Times,* 9.7.1971.
126 *Agence Europe,* 8.7.1971.
127 *Financial Times,* 9.7.1971.
128 *The Times,* 9.9.1971.
129 *Frankfurter Allgemeine Zeitung,* 9.9.1971.
130 *The Times,* 11.10.1971.
131 *Keesing's Contemporary Archives 28,* 1971–72, p. 24932.
132 *Daily Telegraph* and *Japan Times,* 1.10.1971.
133 *The Economist,* 16.10.1971.
134 *The Times,* and *Financial Times,* 15.10.1971.
135 *Japan Times,* 28.9.1971.
136 *Japan Times,* 20.10.1971.

137 *Frankfurter Allgemeine Zeitung*, 22.10.1971.
138 Taber, George M. *Patterns and Prospects of Common Market Trade.* London: Peter Owen. 1974, p. 113.
139 *Japan Times*, 20.10.1971.
140 *Financial Times*, 20.10.1971.
141 *Frankfurter Allgemeine Zeitung*, 23.10.1971.
142 *Le Figaro*, 23 and 24.10.1971.
143 *Guardian*, 26.10.1971.
144 *Frankfurter Allgemeine Zeitung*, 28.10.1971.
145 *Japan Times*, 27.10.1971.
146 *The Times*, 14.10.1971.
147 *The Times*, 29.10.1971.
148 *Japan Times*, 2.11.1971.
149 *Financial Times*, 29.10.1971.
150 Commission. London Office. EC Press and Information. *The Trade Negotiations with Japan: Progress to Date*, 30.11.1971.
151 Commission. Note BIO N 166 aux bureaux nationaux. Telex 58930, 15.11.1971.
152 *Le Monde*, 12.11.1971, and *Neue Zürcher Zeitung*, 24.11.1971.
153 *The Economist*, 25.12.1971.
154 *Le Monde*, 18.1.1972.
155 *Le Monde*, 27 and 28.2.1972.
156 *Japan Times*, 18.1.1972.
157 *Japan Times*, 17.1.1972.
158 French Embassy, London, Service de Presse et d'Information. January 1972.
159 *Bulletin des Communautés Européennes* No. 4, 1972, p. 89.
160 See: *Far Eastern Economic Review*, 12.2.1972.
161 See: *Financial Times*, 3.2.1972.
162 Interview.
163 *Le Figaro*, 13.2.1972.
164 *The Times*, 16.2.1972.
165 *Far Eastern Economic Review*, 11.3.1972.
166 *Guardian*, 16.2.1972.
167 *Japan Times*, 15.2.1972.
168 Commission. *Press Release.* IP (72) 30, 16.2.1972.
169 *Neue Zürcher Zeitung*, 18.2.1972.
170 *The Times*, 16.2.1972.
171 *Japan Times*, 19.2.1972.
172 Commission. EC Press and Information. *The EC and Japan: Key Trade Negotiations.* 25.2.1972.
173 *Die Zeit*, 25.2.1972.
174 *Corriere della Sera*, 22.2.1972.
175 *International Herald Tribune*, 31.3.1972.

176 Interview.
177 *International Herald Tribune*, 31.3.1972.
178 Hammer, Dietrich. La Communauté Elargie, les U.S.A. et le Japon. In: *La politique économique exterieur de la Communauté Elargie.* La semaine de Bruges 1972. Bruges: De Temple 1973, 18—39, p. 38.
179 *The Times*, 14.4.1972.
180 *Japan Times*, 18.4.1972.
181 *International Herald Tribune*, 19.4.1972.
182 *Financial Times*, 19.4.1972.
183 *Financial Times*, 24.4.1972.
184 *Der Spiegel*, 1.5.1972.
185 *Financial Times*, 4.5.1972.
186 *Le Monde*, 25.4.1972.
187 *The Times*, 12.5.1972.
188 Ibid.
189 *Japan Times*, 11.5.1972.
190 *Financial Times*, 11.5.1972.
191 *Financial Times*, 16.5.1972.
192 *Der Spiegel*, 27.5.1972.
193 *Japan Times*, 1.6.1972.
194 *Le Monde*, 17.5.1972.
195 *The Times*, 19.5.1972.
196 *The Economist*, 27.5.1972.
197 *Guardian*, 31.5.1972.
198 *Der Spiegel*, 27.5.1972.
199 *Guardian*, 31.5.1972.
200 *Guardian*, 11.5.1972.
201 *Observer*, 14.5.1972.
202 *Sunday Times*, 4.6.1972.
203 *The Times*, 6.6.1972.
204 *The Economist*, 10.6.1972.
205 *The Economist*, 24.6.1972.
206 *Sunday Times*, 18.6.1972.
207 *The Economist*, 23.9.1972.
208 *The Economist*, 2.9.1972.
209 Sked, Alan, and Chris Cook. *Post-war Britain.* Harmondsworth: Penguin, 1979, p. 290.
210 *The Times*, 6.6.1972.
211 *The Times*, 14.7.1972.
212 *Sunday Times*, 9.7.1972.
213 Commission. Avis relatif à l' importation des produits japonais dans la Communauté tombant sous l'application du traité de Rome. *Journal officiel des Communautés Européennes.* No. C111/13, 21.10.1972.

214 *The Times*, 12.7.1972.
215 *The Times*, and *Financial Times*, 17.8.1972.
216 *Neue Zürcher Zeitung*, 19.8.1972.
217 *Japan Times*, 20.8.1972.
218 *Der Spiegel*, 14.8.1972.
219 *International Herald Tribune*, 20.9.1972.
220 *Agence Europe*, 16.10.1972.
221 *Keesing's Contemporary Archives 28*, 1971–72, p. 25515.
222 *The Times*, 19.9.1972.
223 *Guardian*, 16.2.1973.
224 *Der Spiegel*, 3.4.1972.
225 *The Times*, 15.5.1972.
226 *The Times*, 18.5.1972.
227 *The Times*, 9.6.1972.
228 *Die Zeit*, 26.5.1972.
229 *The Times*, 10.6.1972.
230 *The Times*, 11.7.1972 and 17.7.1972.
231 *Financial Times*, 20.10.1972.
232 *Financial Times*, 8 and 9.11.1972.
233 *Financial Times*, 10.11.1972.
234 *The Economist*, 29.7.1972.
235 *Die Zeit*, 6.10.1972 and *Japan Times*, 9.11.1972.
236 Interview.
237 *Japan Times*, 27.10.1972.
238 *Financial Times*, 15.12.1972 and *Japan Times*, 16.2.1972.
239 *Agence Europe*, 15 and 16.12.1972.
240 *Agence Europe*, 22.12.1972.
241 *Japan Times*, 2.2.1973.
242 Commission. Information: *Commercial Policy: Japan and the European Community*, 38–73, February 1973.
243 Ibid.
244 *Financial Times*, 9.3.1973.
245 *The Times*, 15.2.1973.
246 *Japan Times*, 2.2.1973.
247 *Japan Times*, 4.3.1973.
248 *Japan Times*, 14.3.1973 and 15.3.1973.
249 *Neue Zürcher Zeitung*, 11.3.1973.
250 *Financial Times*, 9.3.1973.
251 *Financial Times*, 23.3.1973.
252 *The Times*, 19.4.1973.
253 *Guardian*, 19.4.1973.
254 *The Times*, 21.4.1973.
255 *The Times*, 3.4.1973.
256 *Die Zeit*, 30.3.1973.

257 *The Economist*, 30.6.1973.
258 *Süddeutsche Zeitung*, 10 and 11.3.1973.
259 Quoted in: *Japan Times*, 14.3.1973.
260 *Japan Times*, 18.4.1973.
261 *The Times*, 27.4.1973.
262 *The Economist*, 28.4.1973.
263 *Japan Times*, 3.5.1973.
264 *Le Monde*, 4.5.1973.
265 *Le Monde*, 5.5.1973.
266 *Agence Europe*, 4.5.1973.
267 *The Economist*, 28.4.1973.
268 *Far Eastern Economic Review*, 21.5.1973.
269 *Financial Times*, 2.5.1973.
270 *Japan Times*, 5.6.1973.
271 *Agence Europe*, 7 and 8.5.1973.
272 Miller, J.B.D. The Unassociables: The EEC and Developed Countries Overseas. *The World Today 30*, 1974, 327–34, p. 329; and *Guardian*, 5.5.1973.
273 *Financial Times*, 25.5.1973.
274 Soames, Christopher. The EEC's External Relations. *The World Today 29*, 1973, 190–5, p. 193.
275 Ibid.
276 *Japan Times*, 7.5.1973.
277 *The Economist*, 9.6.1973.
278 *Japan Times*, 21.8.1973.
279 *The Times*, 9.5.1973.
280 *Financial Times*, 22.6.1973.
281 *Agence Europe*, 7.6.1973.
282 *Guardian*, 2.8.1973.
283 *The Times*, and *Financial Times*, 1.8.1973.
284 *Bulletin of the European Communities* No. 9, 1973, p. 50.
285 *Keesing's Contemporary Archives 29*, 1973, p. 26253.
286 *The Times*, 25.10.1973.
287 *The Economist*, 12.7.1973.
288 *The Economist*, 29.9.1973.
289 Novak, Jeremiah. The Trilateral Connection. *Atlantic Monthly*. July 1977, 57–9, p. 58.
290 *The Economist*, 29.9.1973.
291 *Keesing's Contemporary Archives*, 1973, Loc. cit.
292 *Le Figaro*, 2.10.1973.
293 *Bulletin of the European Communities* No. 11, 1973, p. 74.
294 *Japan Times*, 13.11.1973.
295 *The Times*, 24.10.1973.
296 *Japan Times*, 22.11.1973, and *The Times*, 1.12.1973.

297 *Financial Times*, 15.11.197̇3.
298 *The Times*, 31.10.1973.
299 *Bulletin of the European Communities* No. 12, 1973, p. 76.
300 *Le Monde*, 5.12.1973 and *Guardian*, 4.12.1973.
301 Ross-Skinner, Jean. The Japanese Juggernaut — Now it's Europe's Turn. *Dun's 101*, 1973, 54—57 and 122, p. 57.
302 Ozawa, Terutomo. *Multinationalism, Japanese Style*. Princeton, N.J.: Princeton University Press. 1979, pp. 164.
303 *Guardian*, 7.1.1974.
304 *Financial Times*, 7.1.1974.
305 *Financial Times*, 19.1.1974.
306 *The Times*, 31.1.1974.
307 *Far Eastern Economic Review*, 18.3.1974, p. 30.
308 Ibid., p. 31.
309 *Far Eastern Economic Review*, 20.5.1974.
310 *Far Eastern Economic Review*, 29.4.1974.
311 *Japan Times*, 23.3.1974.
312 *Japan Times*, 21.11.1974.
313 *Le Monde*, 26.11.1974.
314 Grewe, Wilhelm G., *Rückblenden 1976—1951*. Frankfurt Propyläen, 1979, p. 20.
315 *Frankfurter Allgemeine Zeitung*, 11.10.1974.
316 *Frankfurter Allgemeine Zeitung*, 5.10.1974.
317 *Japan Times*, 9.2.1974.
318 *Financial Times*, 12.1.1974.
319 *Japan Times*, 3.3.1974.
320 *Bulletin of the European Communities* No. 2, 1974, p. 20.
321 *Japan Times*, 19.2.1974.
322 *Neue Zürcher Zeitung*, 22.2.1974.
323 *Frankfurter Allgemeine Zeitung*, 22.2.1974.
324 *Japan Times*, 23.2.1974.
325 *Financial Times*, 8.2.1974.
326 *Bulletin of the European Communities*, 1974, No. 3, p. 79.
327 *Bulletin of the European Communities*, 1974, No. 5, p. 68; and *Japan Times*, 22.5.1974.
328 *Financial Times*, 8.2.1974.
329 *The Times*, 19.6.1974.
330 *Japan Times*, 27.9.1974.
331 *The Economist*, 2.11.1974.
332 *Financial Times*, 3.9.1974.
333 *Bulletin of the European Communities*, 1974, p. 84; and *Japan Times*, 29.11.1974.
334 *Financial Times*, 28.1.1975.
335 Commission. COM (74) 1958 final, 27.11.1974.

336 *Financial Times,* 14.2.1975.
337 *The Times,* 24.1.1975.
338 *Observer,* 25.5.1975, and *Guardian,* 7.5.1975.
339 *Japan Times,* 28.2.1975.
340 *Financial Times,* 5.3.1975.
341 Commission. Delegation Tokyo. Telex No. 254(EW) to Brussels, 12.6.1975.
342 *Japan Times,* 10.6.1975.
343 *The Economist,* 22.2.1975.
344 *Nihon Keizai Shimbun,* 8.6.1975.
345 Typescript. 'List of participants to Japan—EC consultations, June 1975.'
346 Mission du Japon auprès des C.E. Note, Brussels 26.5.1975.
347 Typescript. Ministry of Foreign Affairs. 'Japan—EC High Level Consultations. Tokyo, 16 and 17. 6.1975.'
348 Typescript. 'EC schedule HLC, June 1975.'
349 EC Delegation. Telex No. 263(EW) to Brussels, Tokyo 18.6.1975.
350 Typescript. EC Delegation. 'Joint Press Conference Wellenstein — Yoshino, 19.6.1975.'
351 EC Delegation, Telex No. 263(EW), op. cit.
352 EC Delegation, Telex No. 264(RV) to Brussels, Tokyo 19.6.1975.
353 *Japan Times, Mainichi Shimbun, Asahi Shimbun,* 18.6.1975; and *Mainichi Daily News,* 19.6.1975.
354 *Nihon Keizai Shimbun,* 20.6.1975.
355 *Agence Europe,* European Report, 18.6.1975.
356 Typescript. Commission. 'The Current Situation of the Iron and Steel Sector of the ECSC'. Agenda Part 2, 20th Meeting of the Contact Group Japan—Commission (ECSC), Tokyo 18 and 19.6.1975.
357 *Economie* (Brussels), 29.4.1975.
358 *Tageblatt/Journal d'Esch,* 24.4.1975.
359 'The Current Situation . . . ', 1975, op. cit.
360 Commission. *Official Journal,* No. C 100/1, 2.5.1975.
361 EC Delegation. Telex No. 264 (RV). Tokyo, 19.6.1975.
362 *Frankfurter Allgemeine Zeitung,* 20.6.1975.
363 *Agence Europe,* 2.7.1975.
364 *The Times,* 2.7.1975.
365 *Japan Times,* 27.7.1975.
366 Commission. Telex No. 82935, Brussels 10.10.1975.
367 *Agence Europe,* 5.12.1975.
368 *The Economist,* 17.5.1975.
369 EC Delegation. Telex No. 448 (EW), Tokyo 24.10.1975.
370 Commission. Telex No. 87315, Brussels 22.10.1975.
371 *The Times,* 19.11.1975.

372 *Agence Europe*, 19.11.1975.
373 *Agence Europe*, 19.12.1975.
374 *The Times*, 3.10.1975 and 3.11.1975.
375 *New York Times*, 2.12.1975.
376 *Financial Times*, 3.12.1975.
377 *Guardian*, 9.12.1975.
378 *Agence Europe*, 27.7.1975.
379 Commission. Note BIO (75) 385 to the National Offices. Brussels 12.12.1975.
380 *Financial Times*, 10.12.1975.
381 *Nihon Keizai Shimbun* and *Yomiuri Shimbun*, 14.12.1975.
382 *Nihon Keizai Shimbun*, 13.12.1975.
383 *Mainichi Daily News*, 22.10.1975.
384 *Agence Europe*, 29.10.1975.
385 *Financial Times*, 30.10.1975.
386 *Japan Times*, 29.10.1975.
387 *Frankfurter Allgemeine Zeitung*, 5.5.1975.
388 Sono, Akira. In: *Nichidoku Geppo*. No. 239, November 1975, p. 3.
389 Commission. Note BIO (75) 371 aux bureaux nationaux, 12.12.1975.
390 Commission. Note BIO (75) 371, Suite 1, aux bureaux nationaux, 12.12.1975.
391 Commission. Telex No. 107520, Brussels 13.12.1975.
392 Ibid.
393 Note BIO (75), Suite 1, op. cit.
394 Telex No. 107520, op. cit.
395 Ibid.
396 *Financial Times*, 17.12.1975.
397 Economist Intelligence Unit. Trade Relations between the EEC and Japan. *European Trends* No. 55, 1978, 24—36, p. 35.
398 *Der Spiegel*, 26.5.1969, p. 118; and: *Business Week*, 15.11.1969, p. 88.
399 Monloup, Madelaine. *Les Relations Economiques du Marché Commun et du Japon*. Bruges. Collège d'Europe. 1969, p. 54; and Economist Intelligence Unit. 1970. Op. cit., p. 26.
400 Bank of Tokyo. *Tokyo Financial Review*, August 1977, p. 7.
401 United Nations. *Yearbook of International Trade Statistics 1972—1973*. New York: U.N. 1974; and U.N. *Yearbook of International Trade Statistics 1975 1*. New York: United Nations. 1976.
402 Pouchard, Jacques. Les exportations francaises au Japon. In: M. Arai et al. *La nouvelle politique commerciale japonaise*. Paris: Dunod. 1973, 45—58, p. 50
403 Computed from: *U.N. Yearbooks 1972/73* and *1975*. Op. cit.
404 Japan External Trade Organisation. *White Paper on International Trade*. Tokyo 1977, p. 176; and: Ministry of Finance, The Sum-

mary Report, Trade of Japan 1971/1972, as quoted in: Deutsche Industrie— und Handelskammer in Japan. *Jahresbericht 1972.* Tokyo 1973, p. 37.

405 Deutsche Industrie— und Handelskammer in Japan. *Jahresbericht 1973.* Tokyo 1974, p. 29; dto. *Jahresbericht 1974.* Tokyo 1975, p. 33; and dto. *Jahresbericht 1975.* Tokyo 1976, p. 32.

406 *Japan Statistical Yearbook 1971.* Tokyo: Bureau of Statistics, Office of the Prime Minister. 1972, p. 304. And: *Japan Statistical Yearbook 1977.* Tokyo. 1977, p. 300.

407 Wilkinson, Endymion. Changement de structure des exportations du Japon 1955—1976 et ses implications pour la C.E. *Chroniques d'actualité de la S.E.D.E.I.S. 18,* 1978, No. 8, 244—65, p. 263.

408 Ceynel, Henry. Economic Relations between Europe and Japan. *Euro—Cooperation,* No. 13, 1975, 28—82, p. 44.

409 Bundesstelle für Aussenhandelsinformation. *Japanische Konkurrenz auf Drittlandsmärkten.* Ausgewählte Berichte der Nachrichten für den Aussenhandel. Köln. 1970.

410 Adapted from: Androuais, Anne. *Croissance du commerce extérieur japonais et ses relations avec la C.E.E.* Mémoire du Diplome d'Etudes Superieur en Sciences Economiques. Universite Paris I. 1972, p. 88.

411 Engels, Benno. Japan's Wirtschaftsbeziehungen zu Westeuropa. In: Alfons Lemper (ed.). *Japan in der Weltwirtschaft.* München: Weltforum Verlag. 1974. 283—378, p. 326.

412 Komatsu. Der Aussenhandel Japans. *Nichidoku Geppo.* No. 233, May 1973, 7—9, p. 8.

413 *Financial Times,* 29.11.1971.

414 *The Economist,* 2.11.1974.

415 Economist Intelligence Unit. 1978. Op. cit., p. 32.

416 *The Economist,* 22.7.1972.

417 *Die Zeit,* 25.5.1972; and: *Der Spiegel,* 3.4.1972.

418 *Agence Europe,* 15.1.1977.

419 Deutsche Industrie— und Handelskammer. *Jahresbericht 1975.* Op. cit., p. 28.

420 Ibid., p. 27.

421 Ibid., p. 27.

422 *The Economist,* 22.1.1972 and 20.10.1974.

423 *The Financial Times,* 11.6.1974.

424 'Japan's Trade Policy'. In: *The OECD Observer,* No. 69, April 1974, 26—32, p. 29.

425 Ibid., p. 30.

426 Commission. Information. *Japan and the European Community* 38—73. February 1973, p. 7.

427 *The Journal of Commerce,* Amersfoort, 1.5.1972, p. 157.

428 Grossmann, Bernhard. Probleme des deutsch—japanischen Aussen-handels im Lichte der künftigen Entwicklung Japans. In: *Festgabe zum zehnten Jubiläum der Deutschen Industrie— und Handelskammer in Japan, 1962—1972.* Tokyo: DIHK. 1972, 15—21, p. 19.

429 Typescript. Verschüer, Charlotte von. Les importations du Japon en matière d'alimentation et les marchés potentiels au Japon pour la C.E.E. Tokyo. 1975.

430 Cheynel, 1975, op. cit., p. 49.

431 Japan Information Centre. *British Trade with Japan.* London. 1977 p. 11.

432 Cheynel. 1975. Op. cit., p. 51.

433 Office France—Japonais d'Etudes Economiques. *Le Japon en chiffres 1979.* Paris. 1980, p. 64.

434 Cheynel, 1975. Op. cit., p. 52.

435 Keck, Jörn and Henry Krägenau. *Japanische und deutsche Direktinvestitionen im Ausland.* Hamburg: Institut für Asienkunde. 1975, p. 31.

436 Beresford, Martin. And now, le défi japonais. *The Atlantic Community Quarterly 13,* 1975, 204—19, p. 205.

437 Gregory, Gene. The Japanese Euro—Strategy. *Management Today,* July 1975, 54—60, p. 59.

438 Takamiya, Makoto. *Japan's Multinationals in Europe: International Operations and their Public Policy Implications.* Discussion Paper. Internationales Institut für Management und Verwaltung. Wissenschaftszentrum Berlin. September 1979, p. 6.

439 *The Economist,* 14.8.1965.

440 Duncan, William Ch. *U.S.—Japan Automobile Diplomacy,* Cambridge, MA: Ballinger Pub. Co. 1973, p. 37.

441 Cheynel. 1975. Op. cit., p. 82.

442 Figgess, John. Une relation naissant: l'Europe face au Japon. In: Curt Gasteyger (ed.). *Le Japon et le Monde Atlantique.* Farnborough, Hants.: Saxon House, Les Cahiers Atlantiques 3, 1973, 68—82, p. 71.

443 Soames, 1973, Op. cit., p. 193.

444 Dahrendorf, Ralf. *Plädoyer für die Europäische Union.* München: Piper & Co. 1973, p. 191.

445 Interview.

446 Ibid.

447 *Japan Times,* 18.12.1974.

448 Terfloth, Klaus. Bruxelles et Tokyo: dialogue entre deux géants de l'économie. In: Gasteyger (ed.). 1973. Op. cit., 83—9.
Beinhardt, Gerd. Japans Stellung in der Weltwirtschaft und zur EWG. *Wirtschaftsdienst* 52, 1972, 138—42.

449 Nickel, Herman. The Rediscovery of Japan. *Foreign Policy,* No. 14,

1974, 157—63, p. 160; and: *The Economist,* 5.5.1973 and 27.10.1973.

450 Brzezinski, Zbigniew. U.S. Foreign Policy: The Search for Focus. *Foreign Affairs* 51, 1973, 708—28, p. 724.

451 Grewe. 1979. Op. cit., p. 20.

452 *Frankfurter Allgemeine Zeitung,* 5.5.1975.

453 Tsurumi, Kiyohiko. A Review of the Economic Situation in Europe. Kajima Institute of International Peace (ed.). *Japan in the World.* Tokyo: The Japan Times, 1976, 143—58, p. 156.

454 Deutsche Industrie— und Handelskammer. *Jahresbericht 1974.* Tokyo 1975, p. 81.

455 Sautter, Christian. *Japon, le prix de la puissance.* Paris: Editions de Seuil. 1973, p. 279.

456 Shonfield, Andrew. Reshaping the Economic World Order — Relations between the E.C., the U.S., and Japan. *Chronique de politique étrangère 26,* 1973a, 48—53, p. 53.

457 Bark. 1973. Op. cit., p. 343.

458 *Far Eastern Economic Review,* 3.1.1975.

459 *Die Zeit,* 21.10.1972.

460 Shonfield, Andrew. *Europe — Journey to an Unknown Destination* London: Allen Lane. 1973b, p. 56.

461 Shonfield. 1973a. Op. cit., p. 53.

6 EC-Japan relations 1976–80: cyclical crises and high politics co-operation

There is a general consensus that EC—Japan relations have been in a prolonged crisis since 1976. Its intensity and rhetorics have followed certain on and off patterns. The issues have remained the same: an ever increasing bilateral Community deficit on trade in visibles towards Japan and the 'disruptive' nature of Japanese sectoral export concentrations.

Hakoshima argued that — in contrast with US—Japanese trade disputes — EC—Japanese conflicts, though milder in tone, were never terminated.[1] They lingered on even after Japan had made concessions. As I will show in the following, while crisis talks, with little variation went on from 1975, more critical stages were reached in 1976—77 and 1980—1981 when several adverse factors coincided and the threshold for possible Community-wide sectoral import controls appeared lowered.

These two crises followed similar patterns: in response to the oil price hikes of 1974 and 1979 Japan started an export drive aiming at OECD markets with exports valued at depreciated Yen rates. The first crisis ended in relative detente 1978—79 when Japanese concessions became visible and a revalued Yen supported EC exports to Japan.

This chapter will further attempt to clarify the influence of the relevant actors in Japan and in the EC, on the varying sectoral, national and Community scenes. In this context I will examine Hosoya's assumption of politicised bilateral relations, which in his perception reached this quality from October 1976 to around March 1978.[2]

The empirical development in EC–Japan relations 1976–80

The 'Doko shock' – the first EC–Japan crisis

There was not much advance warning of the October 1976 EC 'shock' message.[3] The high level consultations (HLC) of June 1976 had largely focussed on a set of sectoral issues, which all required different solutions and differentiated treatment and were largely dealt with by different negotiators.

The Commission's note verbale of December 1975 had asked to have EC car exports to Japan temporarily exempted from Japan's exhaust gas standards. It had also demanded that the testing procedures on these cars should be held in Europe. In March 1976 Commissioner Soames in the European Parliament called the car issue the most salient EC concern in its relations with Japan.[4] The British Foreign Secretary, Mr Crosland's visit to Japan during the same period also focussed on the conditions for EC car exports.[5]

The EC then made a second formal presentation on the issue and had it followed up by the visit of Commission delegation in May 1976. In Tokyo this mission was briefed by the commercial councillors' subgroup on cars and by the Japan Automobile Importers' Association.[6]

The EC's demands were supported by the Japanese manufacturers, who feared a possible retaliation on Japanese exports to the EC,[7] and by MITI and MFA against MOT's opposition.[8] Then, during the negotiations the Japanese in principle accepted tests in Europe, done by European institutions and supervised by Japanese inspectors.[9] They also agreed to earlier advance information for EC exporters on future changes in regulations and invited EC producers to hearings for (tougher) 1978 pollution standards.

Once again ball-bearings figured among the sensitive products in the EC. The European bearings industry had asked the Commission for import quotas on Japanese and Comecon bearings (made in Japanese supplied plants). They argued that Japan – holding a market share of 9 per cent – was about to wipe out a strategic Community industry by selling the standard ('bread and butter') bearings at prices from 25 per cent to 40 per cent below EC producer levels.[10]

On textiles 'technical problems' on the mutual liberalisation programme had to be removed.[11] The original agreement with Japan had been reached in December 1975, and in July 1976 the Council finally accepted the accord.[12]

For the HLC in June 1976 the Commission did not have a specific mandate, except for the July 1972 Council declaration, calling for 'dialogue' with fellow developed countries. The Commission's delegation under DG I's director general Hijzen thus could not enter into a real give and take bargaining situation with the Japanese, who were led by their Deputy Foreign Minister, Mr Yoshino. The talks covered sectoral issues, the confirmation of the understandings on cars and textiles, and the general nature of bilateral trade. Both sides agreed on positive means i.e. an EC export expansion, to rectify bilateral trade.[13] They also continued their earlier discussion on a price stabilisation scheme for primary products for the forthcoming UNCTAD IV talks in Nairobi.[14] The Commission hinted concern at the widening bilateral trade gap — estimated at $4 US billion — but made clear that there was no crisis.[15]

During the subsequent ECSC–MITI talks on steel the Japanese chief delegates, Messrs Yano, the head of MITI's Basic Industries Bureau, and Motono, of MFA's Economic Affairs Bureau, renewed their VSR readiness to the EC market.[16] The EC's representative, DG III's acting Director General Loeff, expressed his satisfaction, but was critical that Japan had also agreed to VSRs on stainless steel to the US market. Japan, the EC and Sweden had earlier agreed to concerted actions against US import restrictions on steel.[17]

One month later, in July 1976, Mr Gundelach, the Commissioner in charge of Internal Markets and the Customs Union, visited Japan in order to back up the Commission's demands for reduced NTBs.[18] After their success on cars, Commission officials were now about to compile a lengthy catalogue on further NTBs obstructing EC imports of pharmaceuticals, processed food, cigarettes, cars, chemicals and capital goods to Japan.[19] Gundelach had a round of 30 minutes' talks with Miyazawa (MFA), Komoto (MITI), Doko (Keidanren) and the Vice Ministers of MOF, MOT, and EPA each, and was assured of Japan's readiness to cooperate on the removal of these NTBs.[20] Gundelach told his hosts of 'considerable concern' in Europe's political circles and labour unions on the extent of the EC's likely $4 US billion deficit in 1976. At the same time he called it a short-lived phenomenon, since the economic upswing in Japan would boost domestic and import demand.[21]

The summit of Rambouillet of December 1975 and the more recent summit in Puerto Rico had come out strongly against protectionist policies.[22] So Japan felt encouraged to continue her export drive to markets in developed countries, which after the oil crisis — and the LDCs, decline in purchasing power — had come into full swing. While cars and electronics were Japan's star exports, chemicals and — for political reasons — steel did not do as well.[23]

In July 1976, French premier Chirac, Sauvagnargues, his foreign minister, and Barre, minister for industry, visited Japan. The visit in substance aimed at the promotion of French sales of helicopters, of the Concorde, the Airbus and of nuclear power stations to Japan. But since the Lockheed scandal had been revealed not too long ago, the Japanese political establishment was in no mood for spectacular purchases from abroad. In 1972, the purchase of 21 Lockheed Tristars had been made in order to straighten out the US—Japan imbalance. Other items on the French agenda concerned co-operation offers on high technology, on electronics, aviation and information processing, and support for the Commission's efforts to get barriers on car and processed food exports to Japan removed.[24]

The Japanese, in turn, were unhappy about the French quotas on TV and radio imports from Japan. Komoto also complained to Barre that France had applied undue political pressure to obtain two plant contracts in Poland and in Brazil, totalling $1.5 US billion, tenders in which the Japanese bids had lost. He expressed his reservations about Giscard and Schmidt recently 'ganging up on Japan' when they jointly criticised Japan's pricing policies.[25]

Schmidt at the time had his first re-election campaign. German business was recovering from the recession — except for the shipbuilding and the ball-bearing industries, which because of their productivity problems suffered under Japanese competition. At a Kiel shipyard, Mr Rohwedder, the Economics Ministry's Secretary of State, announced co-ordinated EC actions against Japanese steel and ship imports and accused Japan of systematically undervaluing the Yen.[26]

In summer 1976, the TUC at a Labour—TUC Liaison Committee meeting called for selective import controls on Japanese imports. These import controls should consist of a mix of anti-dumping measures (additional duties) and of 'import penetration targets' in 35 industries.[27] Callaghan agreed to raise the issue of Japanese imports at the EC summit at The Hague in November 1976. Facing a forthcoming Labour conference in a situation with 1.5 million unemployed, pressure mounted 'to do something' on Japanese imports, especially on monochrome TVs and audio equipment.[28]

Schmidt in an interview, with an eye to his shipyard workers casting crucial Social Democratic votes in the coastal cities of the Baltic and the North Sea, criticised Japan's price cutting on ships and bearings as 'inadmissible' and 'like dumping' and demanded joint EC action on the matter.[29] MITI called his charges completely groundless.[30] It had earlier hinted at an offer to abolish entirely Japan's 6.4 per cent tariff on cars.[31] After DOT had complained about excessive Japanese special steel exports to Britain (stainless steel, high speed steel and tool steel), MITI after an informal visit by an EC mission had been quick to announce VSRs on these products to Britain.[32]

In an EP debate in October 1976, Gundelach refused the request to British MEPs to impose import controls on Japanese products.[33] The EC Delegation in Tokyo gave similar assurances.[34] In Japan large sections of her foreign economic policy establishment felt confirmed in their complacency about trade relations with Western Europe. The stage was set for the Doko mission like 'a summer insect flying into a flame to death',[35] in mid-October 1976 during its visit to the EC.

There had been more signs of European patience wearing thin, apart from Chancellor Schmidt's election speeches: TUC and CBI had issued a joint memorandum calling for selective import restraints.[36] When Sir Peter Thornton, a Permanent Secretary at DOT, in Tokyo asked MITI for Japanese VSRs on TV and audio sales to UK, he had received a negative reply.[37] German, French and British political pressure mounted on the Commission to open an anti-dumping procedure on Japanese ball-bearings.[38]

When during the second quarter of 1976 Japanese steel exports to the EC surged by 45 per cent (to 415,000 tonnes), the Commission sent a note of 'urgent concern' to the Japanese. The 'big six' Japanese steel producers had stuck to their VSRs. But the sixty-odd smaller special steel producers had not done so.[39] The Commission at the time was already toying with the idea of a steel cartel (Eurofer) with set production targets and minimum prices and requiring some control on imports.[40]

In September 1976, a new round of talks between AWES and SAJ on a defensive cartel with order sharing and pricing formulae on ship exports had broken down.[41]

The original purpose of the top level Keidanren mission, led by Mr Doko, its chairman, had been to study 'social problems' in Europe: its transition to 'post-industrialism', the demands for workers' participation and of the rise of the Communist parties in Italy, France and Portugal.[42] Extensive talks with the governments and industrial federations of Denmark, Britain, Germany and France had been planned.

In their talks with the CBI and the British government the exclusive focus on trade may have come less as a surprise. Lord Watkinson, CBI's president, justified his demands for selective import controls with Japan's export strategy, going to the 'brink of dumping' — by settling for minimal profits in order to obtain market shares.[43]

Mr Dell, the Secretary of Trade, also threatened import controls if Japan did not remove her NTBs at a faster pace.[44] In an hour-long discussion with Callaghan and Healey, the Chancellor of the Exchequer, the Japanese were handed a list with 20 NTBs which were considered as obstacles to British exports to Japan. It referred to the testing procedures on cars, on pharmaceuticals, to taxes and tariffs on Scotch and on confectionery and to the purchasing policies of the Japanese monopoly tobacco corporation.

Doko promised to have a study made on these demands. Callaghan then asked to have a copy of this study sent to him — if possible before the 29 November European summit, when trade with Japan would be discussed.[45]

The Times in an editorial recalled a 1971 Keidanren mission, which under the impact of the Nixon shocks had promised Japan would follow orderly marketing policies henceforth. Not much later the on-slaught began . . . Now the Keidanren people 'seemed by all accounts to be at the receiving end of some fairly straight talking about Anglo—Japanese trade'.[46]

Doko however put the blame on British exporters, being too complacent by relying on Britain's past glory as the cradle of industrial progress and not energetic enough when attempting to sell in Japan.[47]

The Japanese were more surprised, when in Bonn they received a fairly stern lecture by Rohwedder ('as if we had returned to Britain'). Japanese ships, steel and bearings exports now had turned into a political issue, they were told. Japanese orderly marketing efforts had remained utterly ineffective. Every day, Rohwedder insisted, German industries petitioned him on Japanese imports.[48]

The French government and the Patronat also took a firm stand. The Patronat's president, Mr Ceyrac, told the Japanese either to reappraise their trade policies or to face European import controls.[49] In August 1976, Renault had succeeded in selling only one single car in Japan (out of an annual French export total of 1,000 there, while Japan in 1975 sold 35,000 cars in France.).[50] The Patronat now demanded that Japan should lower her high tariffs on cognac, ballpoint pens and ski boots, modify her exaggerated sanitary rules on meat and sausage imports and facilitate the testing procedures for cosmetics and pharmaceuticals.[51] Barre called for Japanese VSRs on electronics and car exports to Europe. When the mission refused, the talks ended in mutual disappointment.[52]

Arriving in Brussels the Japanese delegation showed a sudden change of mind. Doko had talks with Gundelach, who also enumerated the pressures he experienced from certain industry circles, trade unions and member states for protectionist measures in a Community suffering from oil import dependency and high unemployment.[53] In his reply Doko now found the trade imbalance a 'very serious issue to which solutions have to be found as quickly as possible' and for the first time admitted that Japan ought to exercise VSRs on (unspecified) sectors threatened by unemployment in the EC.[54] During a later visit in Hamburg, Doko re-iterated his intention to have Keidanren work out a plan for voluntary restraints with Japan's industries and government.[55]

In Japan this announcement was received less than enthusiastically. The Japanese electronics association and key car producers, like Toyota, declared they had no intention of introducing restraints. Japan's car, shipbuilding, bearings and electronics industries later criticised Doko's promise as having been made in ignorance of the real situation and causing unnecessary trouble.[56] Japan had already agreed to VSRs on cars to UK. Japanese market shares on cars in France and Germany were well below 2 per cent. Electronics exports to France and TV exports to Britain were ruled by either industry-to-industry agreements or were under import supervision. The German colour TV market was barred by AEG—Telefunken's patents on PAL. Due to rising production costs the bearing producers were about to raise their export prices.

MITI made public that Doko had only expressed Keidanren's 'wish' and did not represent an official Japanese position.[57] Japanese VSRs would seriously limit Japan's economic growth in fiscal 1977, MITI's Vice-Minister Matsukawa said.[58] Even after personal meetings between Komoto (MITI), Wada, MITI's Vice-Minister for International Affairs, and Doko, after his return to Japan, their agreement did not go beyond vague references to orderly marketing and to organisation of import missions to the EC.[59]

Publicly, Doko warned, unless Japan announced VSRs, the EC summit on 29 November 1976 would announce import controls: in the EC under conditions of severe unemployment economic problems had turned into political and emotional issues.[60] Not being able to muster support for more VSRs Keidanren now had to look for some face-saving device to withdraw Doko's public pledge. He himself declared that VSRs could only be a last resort and that Japan should rather focus on import promotion.[61] To this purpose Keidanren designed a five-point plan which was more likely to achieve consensus among industrial associations. It called for:[62]

- the creation of stronger domestic Japanese demand,
- the review of duties on EC imports,
- the review of NTBs and easier import financing,
- the distribution of more information on the Japanese market, and
- co-operation on third country markets.

This plan was proposed by Doko at a meeting with leaders of Japan's car, ship, bearings and pharmaceuticals' trading firms who found no reasons to object. The meeting was also attended by the respective bureau chiefs from MFA, MOF and MITI.[63] MITI pronounced itself against 'political purchases' of the Lockheed type from the EC.[64] It regretted that the EC did not export bulk agricultural products — such as wheat and soya beans — which would be suitable for stockpiling programmes.

In a separate talk with premier Miki, the latter endorsed the idea of starting the promotion of EC imports. Doko then had a second conversation with Komoto who in principle agreed to the simplification of import procedures and to policies of boosting domestic demand.[65] As a consequence Komoto later made a personal appeal to the presidents of the Japanese general trading companies (sogo shosha) urging them to import more from the EC. In the encounter between Doko and Komoto, VSRs reportedly were not even mentioned. All this fuelled European suspicions that the Japanese strategy was to stave off a tough EC response by vague promises of more EC imports.[66]

On ships a new round of AWES–SAJ and WP6 talks had centred on EC demands for Japanese capacity reductions, 'fair' sharing and 'fair' pricing policies. In Autumn 1976, they all ended in mutual disagreement. Due to the long term nature of shipbuilding orders and manufacturing the argument focussed on an order-sharing formula for 1980. The Japanese insisted on a 50 per cent share of the global market, estimated at 13m gross registered tonnes. Six and a half million tonnes would then be produced in Japan, 4m tonnes by third world producers (Brazil, Taiwan, Korea, Singapore), and the remaining 2.5m tonnes by Western Europe.[67] The EC which earlier had insisted on fifty-fifty order sharing with Japan, now introduced a proposal to base the formula on compensated gross registered tonnes (cgrt) which also considered the labour content of ships produced.

Europe had manufactured more labour intensive ships than Japan which hitherto had relied on tanker production. During the October 1976 WP6 talks the European producers now asked Japan to limit herself to 50 per cent of the OECD's cgrt orders in 1980.[68] Japan refused to change the focus from a global to an OECD level. She also insisted on a quid pro quo: only Sweden and the Netherlands so far were ready to cut their capacities by 35 per cent as Japan was about to do until 1980. Germany and Denmark in principle only announced their readiness to cut. France and Italy remained ambiguous. Britain was fully occupied with its debate on the shipyards' nationalisation.[69]

In addition the European producers were in total disagreement on how to distribute their global order share among themselves. The EC Commissioner for shipbuilding, Mr Guazzaroni, and the Liaison Committee of EC shipbuilders at least could agree on a joint threat against the Japanese: either there would be massively more subsidies and regional and social fund monies for EC yards or measures of commercial maritime policy — i.e. flag discrimination — would be applied if Japan did not comply.[70]

As ball-bearing exporters, the Japanese were unpopular among European producers for their disturbing price policies, quality standards and rationalised production methods. On the German market the Japanese held a market share of 7 per cent. The combined shares of FAG–Kugelfischer and the Swedish SKF were 76 per cent.[71]

The EC ball-bearing association in October 1976 filed an anti-dumping complaint against Japanese imports of ball and conical-roller bearings with a sympathetic EC Commission.[72] The Commission, with the unanimous approval of the member governments initiated an anti-dumping investigation for the purpose of establishing evidence for damage done to EC industries and for illicit pricing. EC producers claimed Japanese imports of ball-bearings 1974–76 had increased by 40 per cent, capturing a market share of 17 per cent (1976) in the EC. Imports of conical rollers doubled and reached a 5 per cent market share (1976). Five thousand jobs were lost in the bearings industry during that period and up to 40 per cent of employees were working on short-time work. Dumping margins of 26 to 52 per cent were alleged on 16 types of ball-bearings.[73] In order to escape a possible anti-dumping duty the Japanese producers soon announced a general 15 per cent price increase.[74]

For overall EC–Japan relations the start of an anti-dumping investigation was considered indicative of the adoption of a tough EC approach, especially in view of the forthcoming HLC talks in mid-November 1976.[75]

The continued global depression on the steel market affected EC–Japan relations as well in 1976. European steel industries worked at 70 per cent capacities. Short-time work was the rule in France, Belgium and the Saar. In Japan, the depressed domestic market forced producers into export efforts.

While the big six producers respected the VSR limit of 1.22m tonnes to the EC, the smaller producers – who had never agreed to any restraint – used South East Asian or EFTA markets to have their semi-finished steels processed and sold to the EC market. Total Japanese steel exports to the EC were estimated at 1.58m tonnes.[76] In November 1976, a boycott action by EC steel producers was made public: steel importers had been urged with special discounts to cancel orders to Japanese suppliers and to switch to EC substitutes instead.[77] For the forthcoming ECSC–Japanese talks MITI's Basic Industries' Bureau announced it would insist on an explanation, since reportedly a 'senior Commission official' had blessed the boycott.[78]

Officially the results of the steel talks in November 1976 were kept secret. The US had already on an earlier occasion expressed their strong displeasure at the deflective effects of Japanese steel VSRs to the Community. Now the Japanese let it be known that they were very sympathetic to the EC's steel problems and were considered likely to discipline their 60 medium and small steel producers.[79] These metaphors were to be read as a VSR of 1.4m. tonnes for 1977. Of these 1.2m tonnes were reserved for the 'Big Six' of the Japan Iron and Steel Federation, the remainder to be shared by the 60 non-organised producers.[80] The EC in turn 'regretted' the boycott action and promised it would not assume serious proportions.[81]

Commission demands for export restraints to 'traditional' EC export markets however were rejected by the Japanese.[82] Tradition here has to be translated as EFTA.

On cars the EC asked for a three-year exemption for EC car imports from the 1978 Japanese exhaust standards. While MITI seemed favourable to this demand, the Japanese Environment Agency, which had the final say on these matters, did not like it.[83]

On 15 November 1976 both a Council of Ministers' session and the HLC would start. The ministers, therefore, informally agreed to leave the Japan issue to be dealt with by the Hague summit on 29 November 1976. The heads of government were expected to make a general declaration on Japan, the draft being prepared by Coreper.[84]

The HLC delegation on the EC side was led by DG I's deputy director generals Caspari and de Kergolay. The Japanese were led by MFA's Vice-Minister Yoshino. The agenda for the HLC was equally divided between a day on multilateral issues ('nothing concrete') and a second day dealing with bilateral problems.[85]

On sectoral issues, steel had been dealt with 'satisfactorily' by the earlier ECSC—Japan talks. On bearings the Japanese informed the Commission that price hikes were on their way. On ships the Japanese felt that negotiations should be held at the next OECD WP6 session three weeks later. The Commission insisted Japan should immediately enter negotiations on the EC's fifty-fifty order sharing demand in order to be able to report to the European Council meeting on 29 November 1976.[86]

The EC's demand for exemption from the Japanese 1978 emission standards was still subject to Japanese interministry fights with MFA and MITI favourable on one side, and MOT and the Environment Agency unfavourable on the other.[87]

On pharmaceuticals Japan in principle had accepted the results of preclinical tests (on animals) in Europe. On shoes Japan for 'social reasons' was not prepared to enlarge her tight quota, allowing for only a 1.7 per cent EC share in the Japanese market. Japan promised to 'study' the EC demands on the import of tobacco — on which a government monopoly controlled the entire distribution chain from imports to retail, including pricing, brand development and advertising policies — and on processed foodstuffs. Among these, EC milk products and pork meat conserves were inhibited by quantitative restrictions. Biscuits and chocolates were handicapped by prohibitive 35 to 40 per cent tariffs. Internal discriminatory taxes blocked whisky and cognac sales. The export of Danish luncheon pork meat to Okinawa posed a special problem: these exports had enjoyed special concessions during Okinawa's reintegration period to Japan which now was about to expire.[88]

While these sectoral negotiations went their usual way, Commissioner Gundelach during a working lunch suddenly put an 'ultimatum' before Yoshino: either Japan would concede on ships, on cars to UK ('well below 10 per cent') and on other substantial issues until 29 November 1976, or it would have to face EC retaliation, e.g. in the form of UK import controls on cars.[89] Later, EC officials had second thoughts about the ultimatum, since the summit was to take place within only ten days. Japan could not be expected to come up with substantial concessions so soon. The ultimatum therefore appeared as rather counterproductive.

The Commission now had to back off from its embarrassing Hague summit deadline.[90] Gundelach's utterances were re-interpreted as having intended only vague warnings to Yoshino, like: 'Time is running out'.[91]

Yoshino, who had initially seen a dangerous crisis on its way,[92] after the official corrections had been made, expected the EC's demands would finally calm down, once the member states' economies had recovered in the forthcoming spring of 1977.[93] Upon return from Brussels he gave a press conference in Tokyo. He described Europe — particularly Italy, France and UK — as facing serious economic problems (unemployment, payments deficits and economic stagnation) and making Japan a scapegoat in this situation. In order to avoid the situation of UK or France resorting unilaterally to import restrictions, Japan would need to show goodwill before 29 November. The most urgent issues were ships, and then food imports — he hinted Japan ought to abolish or enlarge her restrictive quotas — and cars exported to UK. 'The question is whether we should allow them to boycott Japanese goods or make immediate efforts to correct the trade imbalance. Our alternative is clear.' Since EC–Japan frictions had now turned into a political issue, he would seek a 'political judgement' by premier Miki.[94]

Since the 'Doko shock' the major Japanese dailies had given front page treatment to the dispute with the EC, and during the following six days covered in extenso the ensuing inter-ministerial, inter-(LDP-) factional and inter-industrial (domestic versus exporting producers) infights to answer the Commission's non-ultimatum.

The week from 18 November (Yoshino's return) to 25 November 1976 (Yoshino sending the Japanese reply to Gundelach) offers an excellent and fairly transparent case study in Japanese crisis management. The commentaries of the major dailies (*Yomiuri, Asahi, Mainichi, Sankei*) reflected the national consensus. They stressed the need for more imports, for sectoral restraints and for Japan to be considerate towards Europe, which neglected marketing in Japan and — hit by an economic crisis — was ruled by social democratic regimes with full-employment policy goals and inadequate industrial policies.[95]

The desire for more understanding with EC leaders and the proposal for a world economic summit figured prominently in Miki's campaign speeches.[96] Part of the Doko shock's domestic dramatisation had actually derived from zaikai's wish to criticise the (non-big business) Miki faction's foreign policy record — MITI Minister Komoto was Miki's protegé — and to lend support to the more pro-big business factions rallying behind Fukuda, who after the 5 December 1976 election was to oust Miki as the new prime minister.

In the interministerial meetings the more classical and transparent infights took place. At an eight ministry meeting (attended by MFA, MITI, MOF, MOT, MAFF, MHW, EPA and the Environment Agency), MFA

proposed the following measures to accommodate the EC's demands:[97]
- tariff cuts on whisky, cognac, chocolate, biscuits, ballpoint pens,
- procedural simplifications for the imports of pharmaceuticals, marine engines, automobiles and meat,
- an increase in the number of shops selling European tobacco,
- the expansion of import quotas for meat products and others.

The Ministry of Finance opposed unilateral tariff cuts: they should be discussed at the MTN in order to obtain reciprocity. MOF — administering and benefiting from the tobacco monopoly — was opposed to increase the outlets for the less profitable foreign tobaccos. MAFF called the EC's demand for increased processed food imports irrelevant and unreasonable.[98] Larger quotas on cheese and meat would adversely affect Japan's farmers. They as one of Japan's best organised lobbies would make their displeasure felt at the forthcoming elections.

Parallel to the officials' meeting Miki was briefed on the HLC by Kosaka (MFA) and Yoshino. They later met with the ministers of finance (Ohira), of MITI (Komoto), of MAFF (Oishi) and with the director of EPA (Noda).[99] After this cabinet meeting, in which Miki urged urgent action, Oishi hinted that lowered tariffs for foodstuffs were 'under study'. Komoto supported tariff cuts on food and liquor.[100] Then the bureau chiefs of the eight ministries concerned met. Miki warned, if they did not agree on ship and food concessions, he would make a political decision according to Yoshino's recommendation.[101]

In the meantime JAMA had signalled that its members were ready to continue their VSR to Britain at levels below 10 per cent.[102] Knowing well its European counterparts' unwillingness to do so, the SAJ announced it was ready any time to talk on mutual capacity reductions on shipbuilding.[103] Through several channels, the US let it be known that they strongly opposed any further Japanese VSRs to the EC.[104] At their final meeting on 23 November the bureau chiefs appeared to have been little impressed by Miki's political warning. MOT opposed MFA's proposal for bilateral talks on ships with the EC, MAFF rejected its request for enlarged food quotas, and MOF refused to consider unilateral tariff reductions. The meeting only seemed to agree to the non-controversial car VSRs to Britain for 1976 (the year was nearly over anyway).[105]

The actual letter by Yoshino to Gundelach on 25 November 1976 in a version approved by Miki, mentions car restraints to UK for the current 1976 and makes vague references to possible bilateral talks on ships, parallel to the multilateral negotiations within OECD. On agricultural products the letter announced the tripling of the skimmed milk powder quota (for feed use) to 56,000 tonnes, and promised more butter import contracts and simplified tobacco imports. On tariff matters the letter referred to the ongoing MTN hinting at the desirability of reciprocity.[106] The Japanese media commented:[107] 'It is hoped that the EC may duly appreciate this nation's positive stance' (*Asahi*), and: 'But the EC will once again press this nation with unreasonable demands if the world economy is further aggravated' (*Yomiuri*).

Frequently the National Federation of Agricultural Co-operatives (zenno) organised demonstrations against the 'sacrifice of Japan's farmers to Japan's export industries'.[108]

Even before the Yoshino letter was drafted, Coreper debated two versions of a Council statement of concern. These were a Dutch conventional version — the Netherlands were holding the Presidency — and a toughly-worded UK version, calling for an ad hoc institutional body to monitor Japanese imports and to negotiate for an agreement with Japan before the next Council's session. When Coreper discussed the threat of 'unilateral Community measures', Britain hinted at its readiness at least to threaten import controls.[109]

After the Yoshino letter, with its 36,000 tonnes of milk powder as the sole tangible concession, the European Council on 30 November 1976, without any reference to the letter, settled for the Dutch formula;[110]

> The European Council notes with concern the effects of import and export practices followed hitherto in Japan as well as the rapid deterioration in the trade situation between the Community and Japan and the problems which have arisen in certain important industrial sectors. Determined efforts are called for to remedy this situation, paying particular attention to the need for rapid expansion of Japanese imports from the Community . . .

and:

> The European Council accordingly invites the responsible Community institutions to give further urgent consideration to those problems and to pursue vigorously this important aspect of the CCP in discussions with Japan. It expects that substantial progress will have been achieved before its next meeting on the solutions which are urgently needed to realise the Community's objectives.

Joop den Uyl, the Council's president, explained that the Community now expected Japanese VSRs on ships, cars, electronics and steel.[111] MITI was pleased with the Council's resolution. Mr Yoshino announced, for the time being, the EC—Japan feud was over.[112]

During an EP debate in December 1976 most parliamentarians participating did not appear to share this view. Speakers from Gaullist and Socialist ranks took a hard line. Liberals proposed more moderate policies vis à vis Japan.[113] The EP finally settled for a resolution which esentially was supportive of the Commission's known policies and demands towards Japan.[114]

During the OECD (WP6) talks on 6 December 1976 the EC repeated its equitable (fifty-fifty) order-sharing proposal. The Japanese ministries (MITI and MOT) and shipyards, who were about to cut man-hours by one third and to scrap entirely building facilities for supertankers in Japan, insisted that it was now the EC's turn to implement its professed intention to reduce surplus capacity. The EC negotiators replied they would not talk about the reduction of capacities unless Japan agreed to order sharing on an OECD reference basis.[115] Both Commissioner Guazaroni and the French Foreign Minister Guiringaud issued a stern warning: Japan ought to stop her dilatory tactics. Unless the bilateral negotiations on 20 December produced 'concrete, positive and immediately significant results', Japan would face EC retaliation on other sectors.[116]

Other EC governments were less impatient: Japan needed time to settle the political uncertainty following the 6 December elections. Should the bilateral talks on shipbuilding fail, then the EC's discussion would rather centre on credit subsidies, and regional and social fund monies for ailing yards. Maritime policy measures — reserving part of the shipping for EC built vessels — were favoured by Italy and France, but rejected by Germany and Denmark.[117]

During the bilateral pre-Christmas 1976 negotiations Japan again rejected the EC's order-sharing formula (now called 'regional spread of orders'), but agreed to exchange monthly statistics on orders and production figures. This, according to the EC's negotiator, would exercise psychological pressure on Japan to reduce her share.[118]

For the coming year the EC would have to solve the problem on how to induce shipowners to buy higher priced EC made ships. The Japanese were amazed at the conspicious absence of any European sense of urgency for restructuring its shipyards. The national awareness on her dependency on the world market had enabled a consensus in Japan minimising the social tensions accompanying her restructuring efforts.[119]

1977: the crisis continues

With the new Fukuda government in Japan the EC had hoped for new Japanese negotiating instructions and a more flexible Japanese attitude during the OECD WP6 talks in January 1977.[120] These expectations proved mistaken. Japan again refused to accept the EC's order-sharing scheme.[121] In a bid to organise a joint EC stand against Japan, Mr Kaufman, Britain's Minister for Industry, visited Germany, France and Denmark. The EC, in his opinion, should appear ready for sanctions in order to change Japan's stand at a final round in February 1977.[122]

Denmark and Germany were both opposed to a massive subsidy programme and to flag discrimination. Britain preferred direct subsidies to

230

the yards. The Netherlands wanted rather to subsidise the purchase of ships and France professed a preference for cargo preservation measures – yet another euphemism for flag discrimination.[123] The EC shipyards had volunteered a list of thirty possible measures against their Japanese colleagues. These sanctions then ended up figuring on a Commission contingency plan[124] to be considered in case of Japan's continued refusal. It proposed subsidies of $600m needed to 'compensate for Japan's commercial advantages', special dock tariffs for Japanese-built vessels made after a certain date, and suggested penalising Japan on other export sectors as well. A visiting MITI Vice-Minister, Mr Masuda, was told by Haferkamp and Davignon that Japan should soon come up with counter-proposals to the EC's fifty-fifty sharing demand.[125]

At an earlier Council of Ministers' session both the ministers and the Commission had agreed to maintain political pressure on Japan to prevent the deterioration of the sectoral negotiations into technical talks.[126] Britain's Foreign Secretary Crosland, who had taken over the Council's presidency, publicly announced EC-wide talks on all sensitive issues with Japan. Japan up to then had conducted EC-wide talks only on ships and on steel.[127] Bilaterally towards Britain, Japan had agreed to VSRs on cars, special steels, TV sets, potteries and ball-bearings. Japan feared these bilateral VSRs in EC-wide talks would be extended to the Community level.[128]

In order to prepare for the 'final' round on shipbuilding in UK the General Council on British Shipping in early February 1977 met with Callaghan, Dell (the Secretary of Trade) and Varley (the Secretary of Industry). The Netherlands announced a subsidy programme for shipowners and allocated $500m for restructuring.[129] By then Japanese officials had already hinted at a conciliatory approach for the forthcoming OECD talks. On 8 February 1977 the Japanese chief delegate, Mr Shashiki, from MOT, came out against the excessive concentration of orders in Japanese yards and proposed a Japanese programme providing for:[130]
  – (yet unspecified) price increases for all Japanese ships from
    1 January 1977 to 1 January 1978,
  – a reduction of exports to the worst affected European countries,
  – a forthcoming Japanese government order to cut operating hours
    in Japanese yards if Japan's global market share increased conspicuously.
At the time, out of a total of 300,000 Japanese shipyard workers, 30,000 had been made redundant. Another 25,000 were to follow. Britain had 50,000 men employed in its yards, France 40,000 and Germany 60,000. Shashiki now asked the EC countries to make 'complementary efforts' to revitalise their yards.[131] Since the EC had been unable to agree to a joint policy, such a programme was not forthcoming.

Though the Japanese did not specify their intended price increases, both the EC and EFTA delegations to WP6 decided to accept the Japanese offer as a compromise.[132] An explicit order sharing formula had been avoided. Soon the seven largest Japanese shipbuilders decided to cut their exports to the Netherlands and to Germany.[133] Having forced their Japanese competitors at a temporary arm's length distance, the European inclination to implement capacity cuts fully disappeared. In the EC a new subsidy race was on. Each country announced different schemes and none was willing to cut back.[134]

At the same time the EC had its first formal negotiations with Japan on processed food imports to Japan. About 30 EC products were discussed between a DG I delegation and officials from MFA and MAFF: dairy products, canned beef, wines, vermouth, cognac, cheeses, tinned tomatoes, pasta and luncheon meat figured on the agenda.[135] Being a sinner herself, the EC did not call into question Japan's protectionist agricultural policies.[136] This first round of talks did not yield any concrete result.[137]

With no advance warning on 5 February 1977 the Commission announced the imposition of a 20 per cent anti-dumping duty on Japanese bearing imports. The Commission had compared retail prices in Japan and in the EC and had found dumping margins of up to 30 per cent on Japanese bearings sold in Europe. It also claimed evidence for damage done to Community producers with falling profits, sinking production and employment losses.[138] The Japanese were angry at the EC's lack of prior consultations and claimed that bearing prices at wholesale level were the same in the EC and in Japan, and that Japanese business practice usually meant that large discounts were slashed off the formal (inflated) retail prices.[139]

The Japanese government — just having made significant concessions on ships — sent a strongly worded protest to the EC, and announced it would appeal to GATT and to the European Court of Justice.[140] There was speculation on a new Commission switch to strong arm tactics to obtain food and further shipping concessions.[141] But even Community institutions appeared surprised at the measure and afraid of an eventual Japanese retaliation, since Fukuda himself had joined the criticism.[142] Tatsuo Tanaka, the new MITI minister, announced Japan would remain non-compromising on the ball-bearing issue.[143] He felt that Japan was unjustly blamed for, e.g. England's problems which were caused by its 'inclination towards Communist policies'.[144]

As a follow-up to the food talks, which were led at expert level, Gundelach in a conversation with the Japanese ambassador to the EC, Nishibori, underlined the priority the EC put on food exports to Japan. Gundelach asked for Japanese political goodwill before the next European Council meeting on 26 March 1977, which would review relations towards Japan: 'Anything could happen, unless Japan makes a substantial concession', he said.[145] As the Commissioner in charge of agriculture, he felt Japanese concessions on tariffs, quotas and taxes on whisky, brandy, wine, chocolates, biscuits, European cheeses and canned luncheon meat most appropriate.[146] Nishibori replied that it was difficult for Japan to comply at such short notice.

At a new interministerial meeting in Japan, MOF restated its aversion to unilateral tariff cuts and to lowered taxes. MAFF predictably opposed enlarged food quotas. MITI, after the EC's surprise attack on one of its client industries, demanded that the anti-dumping duties on bearings had to be removed first.[147] The Japanese officials wanted to avoid the impression of yielding to an 'ultimatum', again put forward by Gundelach. They were also aware that with the March summit the EC's demands would not end: 'Even if we get through this spring safely, the "autumn battle" is still waiting for us' one foreign trade official was quoted.[148]

MFA was unable to achieve a ministerial consensus on possible concessions and Nishibori had to inform Haferkamp that Japan would prefer to have the food talks after the summit on 24 March.[149]

The European Parliament again held a lengthy debate on Japan and carried a resolution calling for temporary Japanese VSRs to Europe, for a unified EC policy towards Japan and for strong EC efforts to open the Japanese market.[150]

Masuda, MITI's Vice-Minister for International Affairs, commented:

> European leaders just look at trade statistics and claim the Japanese market is closed. . . . People who take life as easy as the Europeans (should not) condemn Japan for working hard. They close up their shops and factories for weeks on end in summer and expect Japan to buy from them while they are on vacation.[151]

Prior to the European Council, Coreper and Commission officials made an assessment of the last four-months' development in relations with Japan. They found Japanese concessions on car imports (testing in Europe and a three-year grace period on emission standards for European cars until 1981) and on steel exports (forecasts for 1977) to be satisfactory. But the question of Japanese processed food and shoe imports remained open. Some national delegations felt this was unsatisfactory and proposed to keep up political pressure. Others insisted that Japan had shown understanding and that there was no need to dramatise the differences, which would only harden the Japanese position. The Commission supported this position. It wanted the Council just to endorse continued negotiations.[152]

The Council did exactly this. It declared[153] that it:

- notes that some progress has been made over the past four months towards resolving certain specific trade problems;
- . . . considers that efforts have to be continued particularly with a view to the sustained expansion of exports from the Community to Japan;
- invites accordingly the responsible Community institutions to continue the intensive discussions with the Japanese authorities with the aim of resolving outstanding difficulties as rapidly as possible.

The *Yomiuri Shimbun* commented, due to Japan's cool and patient response the conflict with the EC would now recede.[154]

The Japanese government announced it would raise its ship prices by 5 per cent retroactive from 1 January 1977. At the next OECD meeting the EC called this increase too low: the price gap to EC made ships would still stand at 25 to 35 per cent, and Japan would continue to take 70 to 90 per cent of all new orders.[155]

Britain in March 1977 had initiated an anti-dumping procedure on Japanese steel sections and flats (used in the construction industry). Their demand in UK had fallen from 400,000 tonnes to 300,000 tonnes per annum.[156]

In April 1977, it became known that a 20,000 tonnes special steel consignment was on its way from Yokohama to the UK. The Secretary of Trade, Mr Dell, personally decided to put a £20 per tonne anti-dumping duty on these steels. Neither he or his department bothered to produce any evidence for the alleged dumping. Then Mr Dell took off for a scheduled visit to Japan.[157] In Japan, according to *The Times,* Dell, usually mild mannered, used the toughest language ever employed by a visiting European politician.[158] He demanded doubled British imports within two years. Later, in May 1977 a UK government delegation, which was to explain both the damage done to Britain's special steel producers and to present evidence for the dumping to the Japanese, postponed its visit to Japan without explanation sine die. Whitehall let it be known that no further action against Japanese steels was planned.[159]

In early May 1977, just ten days before the new HLC in Tokyo, UNICE issued a 'note' on trade relations with Japan. UNICE asked for a reduction in Japanese food tariffs, and a regular EC–Japanese 'consultation formula' – checking on Japan's progress in importing EC manufactures. UNICE also recommended the EC should continue to make swift use of its anti-dumping powers, as in the bearings' case.[160]

The world summit in London in May 1977 rejected the French concept of organised liberalism on trade.[161] Also the Council's March 1977 resolution had put emphasis on improving the EC's access to the Japanese markets, rather than to proliferate Japanese VSRs to Europe.

For the forthcoming HLC the Commission was expected to follow this line. It hoped to receive answers on her various demarches on processed foodstuffs, pharmaceuticals, chemicals, shoes etc.[162] Additional EC interests concerned silk materials, cigarettes, Airbus sales, the inspection procedures for ship diesel engines[163] and recent Japanese restrictions on ski boot imports.[164] The HLC on 20 May 1977 were held at ministerial level between the new Commissioner for external relations (since January 1977), Mr Haferkamp, and the equally recently appointed Japanese Foreign Minister, Mr Hatoyama. In portraying the EC's general economic outlook Haferkamp told his hosts that their exports contributed to Europe's unemployment problem which in turn fuelled the political radicalisation in Europe. Japan should rather import more in order 'to help European governments to cope with rising socialism'.[165] The Social Democrat and former trade union official Haferkamp was correctly informed that conservative Japanese politicians and civil servants would abhor the idea of having contributed to Europe falling into Communist hands.

Haferkamp's hopes for Airbus sales were encouraged,[166] and the Japanese promised the special regime for Danish pork exports to Okinawa would be extended.[167] On food and other sectoral issues talks at technical levels would continue throughout the summer. Both European and Japanese sources agreed that detente again prevailed in EC—Japan relations.[168]

Since January 1977 the Yen had appreciated by 5 per cent. Premier Fukuda at the London summit had promised the Bank of Japan (BOJ) would not interfere in the Yen's upward development. Japan's steel exports to the EC were already affected.[169] Smaller producers were especially hard hit. They did not import their raw materials themselves and did not benefit from cheaper import prices. MITI now agreed to an EC negotiated VSR on Japanese stainless steel (1,200 tonnes in 1977) to Britain.[170]

In June 1977 Italy started blocking the imports of Japanese heavy motorcycles (their import value in 1976 was $24m) and audio equipment components. On these items the Italian Ministry of Foreign Trade had introduced a new procedure requiring import licensing applications which it then refused to process in retaliation for recent Japanese restrictions on ski boot and silk yarn imports.[171]

Already in 1976 the Japanese had asked for EC VSRs on ski boot exports to Japan — most of which ($11m in 1976) were of Italian origin. Both the EC and Italy had refused to comply. In December 1976 Italy got wind of MITI pressure on importers to cut imports by 20 per cent. The EC Delegation then had asked the Japanese government to formally deny that any administrative guidance had been given. It never received a reply.[172] MITI denied any restrictions. Italy in 1976 had flooded the Japanese ski boot market, conquering 60 per cent of it. But after the European VSR refusal MITI claimed to have dropped the matter. Mysteriously then, after MITI had made a 'survey' on ski boot imports, their import levels fell in 1977.[173] MITI in turn accused the Italians that they were only using the ski boots as a pretext to protect their motorcycle and electronics producers. After Italian—Japanese talks under GATT auspices had ended in continued disagreement, the Commission asked the Italians to free the imports of audio parts (sound reproducers—tape heads) and to put a formal quota on motor cycles.[174] It was then fixed at 18,000 items per annum in 1977 — at levels 20 per cent below the 1976 figures. Japan had put the same quota now officially on Italian ski boots.[175]

In June 1977 the Japanese bearing manufacturers gave written pledges to raise their prices by 15 per cent.[176] The Commission favoured acceptance of the offer, since it would bring the Japanese prices up to EC levels.[177] It proposed to the Council to impose formally an anti-dumping duty of 15 per cent, but to suspend its application in consideration of the Japanese price hikes, and to monitor closely the market instead, keeping the duty 'in reserve'.[178] The Council approved of this scheme by majority vote. The French voted against it. They preferred the immediate application of the duty.[179]

The Japanese producers, convinced of their innocence of dumping, appealed against the Council's decision at the European Court of Justice.[180] Two years later the Court decided. It did not decide on the dumping itself, but found the Council's imposition of anti-dumping duties in July 1977 illegal, because this had taken place after the Japanese had increased their prices. The Court of Justice therefore annulled the respective Council regulation and ordered the $1m fines collected from the Japanese to be paid back.[181]

In the meantime, the public statements of European politicians indicated that the bilateral detente stood on fragile ground. Davignon, at a Chatham House conference in July 1977, announced that from 1980 to 1985 the Community would organise a major restructuring of its steel industry, which he did not want to see disturbed by Japanese imports. He also declared Japan as a 'special case outside the framework of GATT', Japan's export drives being organised by a 'Japan Inc.' with co-ordinated government—business linked credit, investment and marketing strategies.[182] This view was echoed by Giscard at the European summit in London, when he doubted the wisdom of continued free trade policies towards Japan.[183] The French government later issued a demand to the Japanese to limit their car sales to below 3 per cent of the French market in 1977.[184]

In July 1977 a second round in the processed food talks took place.

The EC reiterated its familiar demands on lowered tariffs and enlarged quotas on agricultural products with good marketing prospects in Japan.[185] But the Japanese government allowed the equally familiar MOF (tariffs) and MAFF (quotas) opposition to flatly refuse any concession.[186] Japan even rejected having a further round of talks scheduled. An unspecified government source was quoted: 'These talks are a kind of formality, where the EEC likes to dramatise and confront the issues. There won't be much progress'.[187] These attitudes certainly grossly misread the EC's mood and threatened to discredit the strategy of the 'soft liners' favouring export promotion over the hard liners' preference of import controls.

Premier Fukuda, in a French TV interview, criticised the French concept of organised liberalism as likely to lead to international protectionism. He told his audience that protectionism and depression had once pushed Italy and Germany towards fascism and Japan towards militarism, and that he feared the analogous development for the present era.[188]

Though reportedly Fukuda had 'ordered' Japan's import controls on food lowered, his minister for agriculture, Zenko Suzuki (later prime minister) declared Japan could not concede on agricultural imports. This would run counter to her policy goal of improved self-sufficiency on foodstuffs.[189] In tactical terms the Japanese government officially stuck to a passive 'wait and see' policy on foreign trade complaints.[190]

In September 1977, the SMMT on its annual pilgrimage to Tokyo again asked for an extension of Japanese VSRs on cars to UK. The Japanese were also told to stay out of the British truck and van market, which they had not even started to penetrate.[191] JAMA did not commit herself on commercial vehicles but in a joint communique pledged that Japanese cars would not significantly increase on the UK market in 1977.[192]

In Japan, in the meantime, dissident voices made themselves heard. The Industrial Planning Council, headed by Mr Sakurada, the head of Nikkeiren and a textile industry man, who was generally considered a spokesman for small and medium sized businesses in Japan, proposed export controls in Japan's national interest on steel, cars, TV sets, ships — whose industries as the result of excessive exporting, in his opinion, had all grown to undesirable gigantic proportions.[193]

As the result of the export controls, the Yen would fall and enable a more diversified export structure. The share of external trade of Japan's GNP should be reduced from 11—12 per cent to 8 per cent. Predictably, big business reacted in a strongly negative manner to these proposals.[194]

At the invitation of the Japanese government in October 1977, President Jenkins went to Japan 'not to negotiate', but 'to consolidate the political relationship between Japan and the EC'.[195] After a reception by the emperor and courtesy calls to Fukuda and key cabinet ministers, Jenkins pronounced himself against clamping down wholesale on Japanese imports: 'Pulling the plug out of the other end of the boat does not really help anyone in it'.[196] Jenkins nevertheless underlined that he wanted to see a distinct, clear, sharp turnaround in Japan's balance of payments' surplus within the next four months. As a means, with favourable psychological effects, he suggested Japanese purchases of the Airbus. Mr Tanaka (MITI) replied, he could not force Japanese airlines to buy the Airbus.[197]

Most of Jenkins' talks however were dominated by discussing the US' pending protectionist measures on steel.[198] To avoid such frictions in bilateral relations he proposed to Hatoyama (MFA) the setting up of a Joint Study Group. This group should be made up of businessmen and senior officials from both sides to monitor bilateral trade and to discuss sectoral problems prior to each HLC. Hatoyama reacted 'positively' to the proposal.[199]

A new WP6 (OECD) session in November 1977 had to deal with a novel situation on ships. Due to the Yen's appreciation the price of Japanese ships had increased by 17 per cent since January 1977. Japan's global share had fallen to just above 50 per cent, and Greek shipowners — taking usually 30 per cent of Japan's output — demanded a downward price correction, especially the cancellation of the 'political' 5 per cent increase of February 1977.

The Japanese felt that the Koreans and Brazilians had benefited from their restraints rather than the Europeans, though some of them had resorted to 'give away' deals to Third World fleets, as Germany and Norway had done.[200] Rumours circulated that Japan was about to lower the interest rates of Ex—Im Bank loans for ship exports. Now the EC asked Japan not to 'weaken' her February export restraint measures, and to reduce her production forecasts (6.5m grt) for 1980.[201]

Japan promised to continue her restraints. When the Japanese in turn asked about EC shipbuilding policies;

> some member states recalled their explicit involvement in restructuring and also the Commission representative gave indications on Commission thinking on the global strategy for this sector. The UK delegation remarked that this thinking had not yet been formally communicated to member states and that it did not necessarily correspond with member state policies.[202]

The non-existence of an EC shipbuilding policy certainly did not lend much credibility or bargaining power to the Commission.

In spite of MOF's opposition to unilateral tariff cuts, in early November 1977 Japan announced future cuts on cars (from 6.4 per cent to nil), on computers (from 13.5 per cent to 10.5 per cent) and on photographic films (from 16 per cent to 13 per cent). These latter cuts fuelled the EC's suspicion that Japan again gave priority to US interests.[203]

Nonetheless, the feared 'autumn battle' started with harmonious ECSC—MITI steel talks. Messrs Amaya (MITI's Basic Industries Bureau) and Loeff (DG III) again led both delegations and agreed to co-operate in the US's determination of minimum prices for steel imports. They fixed the Japanese steel VSR limit to around 1.4m tonnes to the Community, of which 1.22m tonnes were again reserved for the 'Big Six'.[204] Japan also in principle accepted a minimum price system for the EC.

At this point, Davignon unexpectedly intervened in the talks, which were held at technical level, to secure Amaya's agreement to the proposed steel cartel, which in a new Brussels euphemism would aid 'the maintainance of the customary flow of trade'.[205] The *New York Times* welcomed this tendency towards harmonisation in world steel trade.[206]

A cabinet reshuffle in Japan had made Kiichi Miyazawa head of the EPA, and appointed Mr Ushiba to the newly created post of Minister of External Economic Relations. With these men of profound international experience in key positions, the EC hoped for more Japanese responsiveness on its demands for more access to the Japanese market.[207]

In early December 1977 the European Council in Brussels discussed Japan after Callaghan had put it on the agenda.[208] In view of Japan's global $10 US billion current account surplus Callaghan demanded joint EC action to reduce the bilateral balance on visibles with Japan. Inaction would only encourage protectionism. He was seconded by Giscard who professed that he was not much impressed with Japan's measures to rectify the imbalance (estimated at more than $5 US billion in 1977) and proposed a new trip by Jenkins to Tokyo for renewed negotiations.[209]

The next day Jenkins informed the Japanese mission that the EC wished to urgently hold talks with Ushiba, who at the time was negotiating in Washington. The scope of the talks should be the same as in the US—Japanese talks.[210]

Ushiba in Washington had conceded to the doubling of Japan's beef quota: from 1,000 tonnes to 2,000 tonnes, and to an increase in her orange quota from 22,000 tonnes to 29,500 tonnes. In Sayle's calculation this achievement by Mr Strauss, President Carter's foreign trade negotiator, amounted to one hamburger and 3.2 oranges per Japanese per year.[211]

In Brussels Ushiba explained the Japanese MTN offer of tariff cuts on 318 products by an average of 23 per cent — subject to Diet approval in March 1978. Fifteen per cent of the EC's exports to Japan would benefit from these cuts (such as cars, aeroplane components, whisky, wines and brandy), while only 5 per cent of the US's did.[212] Denman still insisted on deeper cuts, and called the trade imbalance a festering sore which unless reduced would put 'the Western world as a whole, the Tokyo Round, and the future of an open trading system . . . at a risk'.[213] Jenkins proposed Japan should stimulate her domestic demand. Ushiba replied that a forthcoming cabinet session would adopt reflationary policies aiming at 7 per cent growth.[214]

At the same time, Haferkamp attended a meeting of the Socialist International in Tokyo. During a courtesy call to Komoto (MITI) he praised Japan's growth target and welcomed her tariff cuts and quota expansions.[215]

After the Ushiba talks the Council of Ministers told Jenkins the Commission should make a 'comprehensive study' on EC–Japanese relations and submit it to the European Council session of February 1978.[216]

Britain's electronics producers in industry-to-industry talks had asked for Japanese VSRs on audio equipment to UK in 1978.[217] In spite of the mounting protectionist pressure, in December 1977, Hitachi announced it would abandon its plans to set up a TV plant in Britain. British electronics producers and their unions were jubilant. A Philips subsidiary, Mullard, had been the most active opponent to the entry of a new competitor in UK. Though DoI in 1976 had officially welcomed the investment plan, the British government in the final instance had failed to support it.[218]

At the same time, the Irish Minister for Industry and Commerce told a Japanese newspaper that Irish investment incentives were the most generous in Europe. The bilateral trade imbalance should be compensated by Japanese productive investment in Ireland, he told his interviewers.[219]

The year 1978: towards detente

Around the turn of 1977–78 the Commission initiated a flood of new anti-dumping investigations – such as on quartz crystals, wrought titanium heavy forges (a turbine component), hole-punching machines etc., originating from Japan.[220] It also extended the authorisation of Italy's quota of 9,000 Japanese heavy motorcycles, since Japan in the Commission's opinion had not changed her treatment of Italian ski boots.[221]

In the US, Ushiba and Strauss were negotiating on a second 'minipackage' of Japanese concessions. In no uncertain terms the Commission told the Japanese it expected to be granted the same concessions as the US.

Mr Meynell, the Director of DG I's directorate B, informed the Japanese Mission in Brussels that the Commission was doing a 'comprehensive study' on its relations with Japan now. It would therefore be advisable if Japan showed some 'symbolic measure', such as on processed food quotas, before the Council of Ministers' session on 8 February 1978.[222]

The Commission also expected Ushiba to make a second visit to Brussels prior to the Council meeting. MFA however announced Ushiba would visit only Bonn, Paris and London, not to negotiate — any further Japanese concessions should be part of the MTN — but to 'explain' the second mini-package.[223] Japan strongly disliked the notion of being pushed into leapfrogging demands from the US and the EC.

In the US Ushiba had rejected most of Strauss's demands for tariff cuts. Yet he had granted an advance implementation of Japan's earlier MTN offer of tariff cuts on 318 items and a further enlargement of Japan's quotas on oranges (by 15,000 tonnes), on citrus juice (by 3,000 tonnes) and on beef (by 10,000 tonnes).[224]

In an EP debate in January 1978 Davignon expressed the Community's displeasure:[225]

> During the conversations we held with Mr Ushiba in Brussels
> in December (1977), we drew his attention to the fact that
> there was a tariff advantage in favour of three-engined air-
> craft. By a curious coincidence, the Community makes no
> aircraft with three engines. We build four-engined aircraft
> and we would like to sell them, particularly the Airbus. An-
> other curious coincidence is that our American friends do
> make three-engined planes and these planes are wanted on
> the Japanese market. There is a wealth of coincidences, and
> we think it important that they be pointed out and rectified.

The Japanese finally agreed to hold talks with the Commission, and Ushiba had conversations with Haferkamp in Geneva and with Jenkins and Denman in Brussels.

Jenkins hinted that the purchase of 20 Airbuses (at $50m each) would be an appropriate Japanese symbolic gesture.[226] The Commission also urged Japanese action on processed agricultural imports (as opposed to the US's non-processed food exports), on NTBs on chemicals and on import controls on silk.[227]

Ushiba reacted in a 'very reserved' manner to the EC's demands and limited himself to general references to Japan's reflationary programme which would stimulate imports. He basically told the Commission it should not expect any further Japanese concession outside the MTN framework.[228] His bilateral talks with the German and French governments followed the same lines.

Dr Owen, the British Foreign Secretary, in addition asked for massive

Japanese OAD pledges for Zimbabwe after the country would get its independence according to a joint UK—US formula.[229] Chancellor Healey drew attention to the volatile political situation in Europe, and especially to France where Mitterand's challenge to Giscard was still looming. In a déjà vu display of Socialist solidarity he told Ushiba that Japanese concessions could help turn the tide.[230] Talks with the German Foreign Minister Genscher centred on the progress made in Japan's peace treaty negotiations with the PRCh.[231]

Guiringaud, the French Foreign Minister, told Ushiba he would introduce a resolution to the Council demanding comprehensive and cooperative Japanese responses to rectify the trade imbalance.[232] Commission sources threatened, unless Japan came up with a pledge for quick and effective action, the Council would issue a very strong statement in view of Japan having been ready with concessions for the US while having made none to the Community.[233]

Upon return to Japan, Ushiba, apparently unmoved, declared EC—Japan relations would take neither a favourable nor a negative turn.[234] Japan would at most make a few procedural import simplifications before the European summit on 8 April 1978. He agreed to continued JAMA—SMMT arrangements for car restraints to UK, while announcing Japanese opposition to the unilateral 3 per cent French limit on Japanese car imports. He said the EC blamed Japan for its unemployment levels, but he considered their number of immigrant workers as more significant to the problem.

In an interview with *Le Figaro* Ushiba reiterated his conviction that Japan was made the scapegoat for the EC's and the US's unemployment problem.[235] He characterised Fukuda's 7 per cent growth pledge (for 1978) as a goal, not as a commitment — as it had been presented six months earlier at the London summit.

In Brussels, in order to prepare for the negotiations with Japan prior to the April 1978 European summit, there was considerable debate between the Commission and the national authorities as to which demands were to be given priority. Some delegations argued the case for macroeconomic measures, reflationary policies in Japan, by insisting on 7 per cent real growth with a reduced payments' surplus as a result. Others felt microeconomic measures more effective: to open the Japanese market in highly technical talks more thoroughly with product by product concessions. The Commission and Coreper finally settled for both. On microeconomic issues they assembled the following shopping list to be presented to the Japanese to pick some items for 'symbolic measures':[236]

— purchases of aircraft, nuclear power stations, conventional power stations, oil refining equipment;
— liberalisation of shoe imports and free access for ski boots;
— abolition of the new restrictions for silk yarn;

- simplified approval procedures for pharmaceuticals and diesel engines;
- protection for European trade marks in Japan;
- enlarged quotas or reduced tariffs on processed foods; and
- advance implementation of tariff cuts on items of EC interest.

A memorandum by Coreper now asked for full negotiations with Japan on these points and on the familiar macroeconomic measures.[237] The Council of Ministers in February 1978 accepted Coreper's paper as the EC's joint 'strategy'.[238] The Council also decided to let the Presidency of the Council — at the time held by Denmark — participate in the negotiations in order to back up the Commission's demands politically. Jenkins agreed, provided that it would not set a precedent and that the Commission remained the sole effective negotiator.[239] In the Council's discussion Ireland stressed the importance of agricultural exports to Japan. Germany urged more Japanese OAD in multilateral form — given to and distributed by international organisations — and the UK made it known that it did not think much of the macro demands: 'micro measures' ought to be pushed with the Japanese.

The EC's renewed demands for negotiations were regarded by Ushiba as being rather pointless. Japan's concessions to the US were aimed erga omnes — they should settle the EC's demands as well. In a speech before the Harvard Club in Tokyo he complained about the European policies. He said:[240]

> the French parliamentary election in March is casting a long shadow on Europe. We have the Italian situation. Germany, which seems to be the most stable country in Europe, is suffering from terrorism and espionage. And in Great Britain, the government is losing one vote after another in Parliament. It's really a wonder how they can keep on being a government. I think we can not expect much from Europe at this time. Our European friends think that Japan has been neglecting them in comparison with the United States. I asked them whether they had not been neglecting Japan in comparison with (their ties with) the United States. . . .
> What kind of authority they [officials of the Commission] have and what they are up to, I really never could make out in my two visits to the Commission itself. Now we have to negotiate with the Commission because the Commission has the overall competence over economic negotiations. But in fact the Commission cannot move at all without being given a mandate from the member countries, and the Commission has no authority to tell the member countries to do anything. This is the strange position it has and it is with that body I

must negotiate. . . .
Our friends in Europe would like to telescope the whole procedure we had with the United States from September through January into the short time from now [February 1978] until the end of March. That will be a rather difficult enterprise.

It was true that the EC had now started to copy the more successful US negotiating behaviour. But most of the Commission's macro and micro demands were well known to the Japanese since 1976. After reading the above remarks in the *International Herald Tribune,* Denman angrily called for the Minister of the Japanese Mission in Brussels, Mr Tanida, and made remonstrances at Ushiba's lecture.[241] For him as the EC's chief negotiator the references to the Commission's lack of negotiating power had been particularly irritating.[242]

After the Council's session in February 1978 the Presidents of the Commission and of the Council, Jenkins and Jorgensen, wrote a joint letter to Fukuda urging him personally to see that EC efforts to rectify bilateral trade were not stalled at lower levels.[243] Two weeks later they received Fukuda's reply: it alluded to the need for close trilateral cooperation and assured his readiness for a dialogue with the EC in the spirit of friendship.[244]

Ushiba translated this into more lapidary prose: 'We may be able to do a few things that are not very large and outstanding. For example, we could simplify our customs procedures, not just for EC goods, but generally'.[245]

To initiate the EC's negotiation round, in mid-February 1978, Meynell went to Japan to forward EC proposals on 'punctual measures' to the Japanese ministries involved.[246] His explorations would later be followed up by separate visits of Anderson, Denman and Haferkamp.

Meynell's counterparts both at MITI and MFA insisted that Japan had exhausted her ability to concede in the talks with the US.[247] MITI explained the future operations of the planned Manufactured Imports Promotion Organisation (MIPRO), but confessed it was 'too difficult' to set up quantifiable targets for such imports.[248] To MOT, Meynell suggested the Japanese purchase of Airbuses, of BAC 111s, or of Fokker F–28s. MOT replied the decision was up to the airlines.

MOF and MAFF insisted that all tariff reductions ought to be part of the MTN. The Ministry of Health finally rejected the demand for simplified pharmaceutical inspections.[249] The Japanese media applauded the government's hard line. *Yomiuri* and *Asahi* observed that the US successes had provoked the EC to raise demands again.[250] *Yomiuri* remarked the EC had made unreasonable 'emergency import' requests during the negotiations, and found it appropriate that they had been turned down.

244

Fearing European retaliation, however, the paper recommended Japanese symbolic concessions for the March round of talks.[251]

Mr Dell in a TV interview again threatened UK import controls unless Japan redressed its imbalance in 'quite a short period of time'.[252] In February 1978, during the annual talks between JAMA and SMMT, the Japanese agreed to continued restraints (careful export activity) in order not to disturb the British car industry's 'restructuring'.[253] Japan's share of the UK car market in 1977 had reached 10.6 per cent but strikes at British Leyland and Ford plants in early 1978 had created a new flood of imports.[254]

Upon return to Brussels, Meynell reported to Coreper. The talks, according to the media, had reached a virtual 'deadlock' and some delegations urged a tougher negotiating stand for the next round of talks.[255] Ten days after Meynell's talks, which had been held at a senior administrative level (director – deputy bureau chief), in late February 1978, Mr Anderson, the Council's President, went to Tokyo to hold talks at the political level with Fukuda, Ushiba, Sonoda (MFA), and Miyazawa (EPA).[256]

Inside the Japanese administration the habitual infights on which items to concede 'symbolically' had been developing. After a short briefing Fukuda instructed Ushiba to do his best to avoid the rupture of the talks with the EC.[257] The head of the EPA, Miyazawa, however, indicated it was unlikely that Japan would meet the EC's 7 April deadline, when the European Council would meet.[258] In a more general criticism he compared the EC export habits in Japan with 'Kyoto confectioners', small shopkeepers selling candies by sitting quietly in their shops waiting for customers. Japan had sent 'countless' purchasing missions to the EC, where they had found only very few suitable products. He also found the EC's decision making confusing: 'In the background are the demands of all nine countries among which some are important and some are not important to each of the countries'.[259]

Ushiba, after internal negotiations with Japanese ministries, hoped to be able to offer concessions by the end of March.[260] Alternatively he hinted at pharmaceuticals, aeroplanes, luncheon meat, ski boots and silk yarn as the likely candidates for more liberal import regimes.[261] Keidanren strongly supported the purchase of EC aeroplanes.[262]

During Anderson's political talks in Tokyo the known positions were exchanged, but no details discussed.[263] The EC now insisted on a 'joint communique' with Japan. It should be made definite by a visit of Haferkamp in late March, and in its details negotiated by Denman at an earlier visit.[264]

In early March 1978, the Council of Ministers heard Anderson's report, but issued no new instructions, confirming the Commission's mandate for continued negotiations.[265]

In Committee 113 the French criticised a Commission draft on its policies towards Japan for not seeking enough concessions.[266] In typical DG III jargon the document had proposed a 'new industrial relationship' between the EC and Japan: with close consultations and planning of mutual trade flows and production forecasts aiming at the avoidance of industrial competition and of disruptive trade.

After his arrival in Tokyo Denman, at a press conference, stressed the implications his talks would have for the world's system of free trade.[267] He added:[268] 'There is an atmosphere of August 1914 about world trade today. ... Those who insist on believing that nothing serious can be wrong with the existing system may find themselves without their trousers'. With his eight-man delegation from Brussels, reinforced by four officials from the EC Delegation in Tokyo, Denman's schedule, after a thirty-minute call on Ushiba, provided for three hours of talks with his Japanese counterpart Miyazaki, the Deputy Foreign Minister. These talks would cover general topics: macroeconomic policies, the current account situation, the MTN, Japanese ODA and government procurement.[269] For seven hours sectoral problems would be on the agenda: trade marks, shoes, ski boots, silk yarn, chemicals, liquor, wine, tobacco, import credits, foreign exchange control rules, processed foods (chocolates, confectionery, pork meat, dairy products), agricultural chemicals, aircraft, cars, diesel engines and pharmaceuticals. One and a half hours were scheduled for a communique drafting session.

The Japanese government hinted that after extensive studies there was a 'feeling' to buy the Airbus.[270] The Japanese cabinet had also issued an 'order' to its ministries to work out concessions in order to avoid the consequences of a breakdown of the talks and to slow down the upward movement of the Yen. Nonetheless, such concessions were not forthcoming except for lowered Japanese tariffs on biscuits, chewing gum and chocolates, an offer which would be made official only at the MTN.[271] Denman, copying the style of the US negotiators four months earlier, remarked that 'anyone who thinks this is going to solve the basic problem must be a complete fool'.[272]

When the Japanese indicated that this was their last offer, the talks in mid-March 1978 had again reached a deadlock.[273] After Ushiba's disparaging remarks earlier, the Commission felt that their role and image as an effective negotiator was now at stake.[274] The Japanese VSRs on cars to Britain — gained in bilateral talks — so far had been more tangible than any of the effects of the Community-wide talks. After British governmental pressure, MITI had agreed to tighten up its administrative guidance over Japan's car exporters: they would now have to report monthly on their shipments to Britain and would be 'warned' if these grew too rapidly.[275]

When Haferkamp arrived in Tokyo, Denman defined as the EC's main demands:[276] Japanese measures to reduce its surplus visibly from July 1978, to speed up the implementation of the MTN tariff negotiations and the purchase of a 'substantial' number of EC aircraft.

Haferkamp held brief political talks with the heads of the relevant ministries: Sonoda (MFA), Komoto (MITI), Fukunaga (MOT), Murayama (MOF), Miyazawa (EPA) and Nakayawa (MAFF), with Ushiba and with premier Fukuda.[277] Parallel to these political talks Denman continued his negotiations with Miyazaki. Though Fukuda again gave assurances on a reduced global Japanese surplus,[278] Japan's only additional concession concerned a larger share of untied aid in her ODA. When they finally proposed a draft for the planned communique, the Commission negotiators rejected it as too vague.[279] They insisted on explicit commitments on Airbus purchases, on figures for Japan's OAD, for her reflation policies, for her current account reductions and for the enlarged share of industrial imports to Japan. The Commission threatened Haferkamp would give a press conference announcing the EC's dissatisfaction.[280]

Haferkamp prolonged his talks by one day, and on 24 March 1978, the Commission officials decided to accept a reformulated joint statement. It contained references to EC growth targets of 4 to 4.5 per cent real growth, and to a Japanese target of 7 per cent. Ushiba was quoted in the statement as saying the Japanese government would take all appropriate measures to achieve this goal.[281] Japan also promised to have her global balance of payments' surplus in the fiscal year 1978 (April 1978 to March 1979) cut by one third. Their 1977 current account surplus had stood at $13 US billion. To Strauss, in December 1977, Japan had still promised a 50 per cent cut. This intent had already been made public in the Strauss—Ushiba declaration. Also part of both declarations were references to the 'possibility' of advanced tariff cuts after the Tokyo Round's conclusion, to internationally open public tenders in Japan and to the doubling of Japan's ODA over five years. The only EC specific concessions were Japan's promise to take European views into account when reforming the trade mark law and to facilitate the testing of imported marine diesel engines.

It was not difficult for observers to discover the virtual emptiness of the statement for which the Commission's negotiators, in order to save face, had finally settled.[282] Ushiba, after questioning, admitted: 'It would be difficult to say on which demand Japan had made concessions'.[283] This remark evidently destroyed the Commission's 'face'. Haferkamp was quick to assert that though European planes were not mentioned in the statement, they were 'on the runway and ready for the take-off quite soon'.[284]

The Economist wrote that the EC had obtained less than the US — the Community itself in December 1977 had provoked the comparison —

and judged: 'High marks must go to the tough Mr Nobuhiko Ushiba'.[285]
The Japanese observed that the EC's timing — geared exclusively towards
its own Council sessions' schedule — had been at fault:[286]

> Many informants believe that the EC's moves have come at a
> particularly inopportune time. The Japanese government has
> already formulated the budget plan for the new fiscal year
> and the plan is now under study in the National Diet. Under
> the circumstances, it is virtually impossible for Japan to accept
> EC's demands which entail new budgetary appropriations.

Parallel to the Tokyo talks in Brussels in mid-March 1978 the Commission's DG III under Davignon negotiated on steel with MITI's Basic
Industries Bureau, which was represented by its director, Mr Amaya.

An understanding on the quantitative levels (1.3m tonnes) of Japan's
steel exports to the EC had been easy. But a second agreement on the
price levels for Japanese steels had been more contentious.[287] Originally
the EC had demanded Japan should not sell at margins of more than
2.5 per cent below the EC's 'basic price' for ordinary steels, and at no
more than 3 per cent for special steels.[288] The Commission finally agreed
to margins of 4 per cent for special steels and to 6 per cent for ordinary
steels on which the Japanese were allowed to sell below the 'basic price'.

In Coreper however, France and Britain were quick to reject the deal:[289]
In their opinion Japan's margins were too favourable, compared to EFTA
nations which had only been allowed a margin of 3 per cent on ordinary
steels. The atmospherical tensions created by this rejection now urged
the Community to accept the Haferkamp—Ushiba statement. Germany,
Denmark and the Netherlands had indicated that they were not ready
for drastic action. *Le Monde* observed:[290] 'Il reste que les Japonais
savaient que les Européens faisaient beaucoup de bruit sans avoir les
moyens de pression que supposait leur fermeté.'

Denman mentioned as the likely consequences had the communique
not been concluded: negative effects on the promotion of the Airbus,
on the MTN talks and on the recovery of the world economy.[291] The
ambassadors of the Nine in Tokyo agreed. To them the communique
was 'le meilleur resultat qu'il etait possible d'obtenir dans les circon-
stances actuelles'.[292]

MOT in the meantime had informed Haferkamp that it had advised
JAL, All Nippon Airways and TOA to buy European planes. These airlines all depended on Japanese governmental credits for their aircraft
purchases.[293] The sales of the Airbus would accommodate France's maj-
or sectoral demand vis à vis Japan.[294] Denman made known the Japanese would buy 15 to 25 A300s.[295]

In early April 1978, the Council of Ministers discussed the 'joint statement'. Some delegations criticised that with the lack of Japanese short-term commitments it had fallen short of the Council's mandate. But none of the ministers suggested that the communique should not have been signed.[296]

The Commission was told to consider the statement only as a first step, to submit a second report by 27 June, and in the meantime to monitor the fulfilment of Japan's macroeconomic promises on real growth and on the current account surplus (whose reduction would be 'visible' in autumn at the earliest). The Commission's proposals for an extensive industrial co-operation programme did not meet the ministers' approval: most insisted that Japanese trade concessions should come first.

Against French and British opposition in Coreper, the Commission had submitted its draft agreement on steel imports from Japan to the Council.[297] After the two delegations had dropped their reservations, the ministers approved of the agreement.[298]

The European Council, meeting four days later in Copenhagen, repeated the Council of Ministers' decision of considering the joint statement only a first step and called on the Commission and the Council of Ministers to continue their review of Japan's external trade and to report back by July 1978.[299] Ushiba was briefed by the president-in-office, Anderson, on the Councils' decisions and expressed his satisfaction. He hinted, Japan would reduce her list of exemptions from tariff cuts in the forthcoming MTN round.[300]

During a debate in the European Parliament on the EC's policies towards Japan, Labour and Gaullist deputies again displayed a particularly critical attitude towards Japan's export policy and the Commission's 'lack of spine' in the negotiations.

Haferkamp defended himself:[301]

> What would the alternative have been? Break off, impose import restrictions, put an embargo on imports of Japanese goods, start a trade war in an atmosphere in which we are preparing for the Western economic summit in order to take constructive action, do something like this in such an atmosphere and, moreover, at a time when we are in the middle of decisive negotiations in GATT?

The Liberals and a Communist MEP shared his view. Mr Pistillo of the PCI said:[302] 'We have got to equip ourselves not for silly and out-of-date trade wars but for peaceful competititon based on the right methods and with an awareness of the world as a whole'.

A new Keidanren mission, under its chairman Doko, was visiting Europe in mid-April 1978. This time their reception was less of a shock than during their last visit in October 1976. Jenkins told Doko that Japan should with urgency consider going beyond the communique and to implement measures effective in the near future, like setting up more productive investments in Europe.[303] Doko assured his host, he would study the matter favourably and reiterated his active support for Japanese purchases of the Airbus.[304] On macroeconomic policies he referred to the world summit in Bonn, in July 1978, which would do a joint review of the developments.

Upon return to Tokyo, Doko announced EC—Japan relations were now in a far better shape than in 1976.[305] All important issues — like the 'sensitive' exports of cars, TV sets, steel, bearings and ships had been settled or were well on their way to being so. Except for the latter, they were all under MITI's various VSR regimes. For the future, Doko predicted, Japan's long term strategy of restructuring towards high technology industries — abandoning the overseas marketing of mass produced items — would remove all possible frictions.[306]

Mr Rohwedder, one of the key culprits of the October 1976 shock, during a visit to Japan in April 1978 announced that Japan should not curb her exports since Germany did not want to see herself as the next country to be forced into curbs.[307]

The January—April 1978 statistics showed EC exports to Japan growing by 37 per cent. Japan's exports to the EC in $ terms increased by 17 per cent. In Yen terms they even recorded a slight fall.[308]

At a new WP6 session a turning of tables occurred. Japan accused the EC of increasing its ship output, instead of cutting back. The OECD figures for the development of production in cgrt terms showed the EC's production surpassing Japan's. At the end of 1977 the EC's orderbook stood at 14.3m cgrt, double the amount of orders placed in Japan.[309]

Davignon's earlier assurances that the EC would cut her shipyard capacities by 40 per cent (implying the redundancy of 40,000 yard workers) had never been taken seriously by the member governments.[310] Italy and Britain had been particularly opposed. *The Times* judged Britain as the leader in the ensuing subsidy race.[311] The low productivity in its yards forced the British shipbuilding industry to accept orders at almost any price. The Japanese now were 'politely furious'. As *The Economist* put it:[312] 'While Japan has been raising prices and cutting capacity over the past 15 months the Europeans have started subsidising like mad and studiously avoiding any painful cutbacks'. Under these circumstances the Japanese protests in WP6 could not have much effect.

In May 1978, Commissioner Tugendhat went to Japan, opening as the Japanese feared, a 'second front'. He demanded the liberalisation of Japan's financial markets and asked that European banks should be granted the same freedom of operations that Japanese banks enjoyed in the EC.[313]

The European banks in Japan had asked for support in their demands to obtain access to domestic Japanese funding (in buying into smaller Japanese banking institutions, by introducing certificates of deposits in Japan, and issuing Yen bonds in Japan).[314] They also asked for more liberal rules on the opening of new branches and for equal access to the Japanese new import settlement bill scheme. This allowed importers to obtain cheaper Yen procurement by contracting loans with the Bank of Japan.

Up to then foreign banks in Japan had been mainly funded by loans from their parent companies. They were in dispute with MOF requesting the facility to deduct the costs of their respective interest payments from their tax bills.[315] A further demand concerned enlarged allocations for foreign exchange transactions into Yen, which MOF had limited to amounts of $200m to $20m per bank in order to restrict speculatory moves.

Since Japanese banking regulations often give considerable room for discretion to MOF and BOJ for decisions, foreign banks complained about frequent incidents of discrimination which in Tugendhat's words had given rise to 'suspicion and a sense of injustice'.[316]

The Japanese however argued that there was no discrimination against foreign banks, just strict rules applied to all banks.[317] They felt that the European complaints were motivated by the recent fall in profits of foreign banking operations in Japan. Up to then, these had enjoyed the exclusive privilege of being able to grant dollar loans in Japan — given as 'impact loans' (foreign currency denominated loans to corporate borrowers for unspecified uses). The demand for these loans had declined rapidly due to the reduced expansion of the Japanese economy. Since Yen loans now were cheaper in Japan, Japanese companies were paying back their more expensive impact loans at a time when the dollar had dropped vis à vis the Yen. Falling profits for foreign banks were the result. In order to compensate for their losses they now planned to move into currency speculation, Japanese business papers suspected.[318]

Mr Murayama (MOF) and Mr Morinaga, the governor of BOJ, told Tugendhat that Japan was planning a major reorganisation of its banking system in a few years' time aiming at its further liberalisation.

At present a Council for Studying the Financial System (Kinyu Seido Chosakai) was holding deliberations on the future financial system and its recommendations would be ready in two years. Up to then the EC should not expect dramatic changes. Its proposals, however, would be a welcome input into the Council's discussions.[319]

In June 1978 a remnant of the 1950s struck again. The Geneva MTN reached a deadlock on the Euro—Japanese dispute on GATT's safeguard clause (Art. 19).[320] Japan was ready to accept a selective Art. 19, i.e. one that would allow import restrictions against exports originating in a limited number of countries, provided that there was a requirement to obtain the consent either of the exporting nation or of an international surveillance body. The EC insisted on an unconditional Art.19 and threatened to withdraw its tariff concessions. Japan then hinted at a compromise. She might consider the EC's version of an SC if the EC abrogated the bilateral French—, British— and Benelux—Japanese trade agreements and abolished all 70 residual discriminatory restrictions, which on cars, electronics, ceramics etc. continued to exist in individual EC countries.

This exceeded the Commission's negotiating mandate. The SC demand later in July 1978 died effectively, when the Japanese had convinced the LDCs that a selective Art. 19 was also directed against their interests. The LDCs did not hesitate to join the Japanese opposition.[321] This conveniently released the Japanese government from finding a compromise negotiating position between the warring MITI and MFA positions, which since the early 1960s had been unable to agree on a joint stand on the SC.

Late in June 1978 the HLC took place in Tokyo. Denman and Miyazaki again led their delegations. Under the heading of macroeconomic policies they talked about the forthcoming Bonn world summit in July, about Japan's growth and ODA pledge and on the situation at the Tokyo Round.[322]

The EC had enlarged its microeconomic list of demands by including cosmetics, electrical and gas appliances, and sanitary fittings as new items. But no Japanese commitments were forthcoming.[323]

Denman had publicly accused the Japanese of not honouring their pledge to cut their surplus.[324] But the Council of Ministers, who met shortly afterwards and received the Commission's report, considered it premature to make any judgement on Japan's attainment of her macroeconomic promises.[325]

The European Council, meeting in Bremen, was similarly expected not to issue instructions, but only to agree to maintain political pressure on Japan. A respective four-line note had been prepared by Coreper, but Chancellor Schmidt deleted it from the presidency's conclusions.[326] In effect, no stand was taken.

The Commission decided to report again to the Council after the next HLC, planned for October 1978. It hoped the forthcoming visit of Fukuda to Brussels — after attending the summit at Bonn — would inject new political impetus to the ongoing talks on aircraft purchases and on NTBs.

Fukuda was received by Jenkins and Haferkamp and repeated the commitment he had given at the Bonn summit:[327]

— the stimulation of domestic demand and additional budgetary measures, if needed, in autumn 1978, and
— the moderation of exports close to the 1977 levels in volume (due to inflation and to the decline of the dollar, the nominal figures

were inflated).

In order to cut the trade surplus Fukuda promised US $3.5 billion emergency purchases of oil, enriched uranium, food and aircraft. Japan would also buy back ships sold to flags of convenience. Foreign authorities would be allowed to issue bonds on the Japanese capital market. Japan would invest more overseas and double her ODA in three years (in $ terms).[328]

At a press conference in Brussels Fukuda regretted that:[329]

[in contrast to a] very deep and broad relationship between Japan and the US. . . . Europe has not quite treated us as a true friend or a real partner, but rather as something alien to them. The days are past when Japan and Europe could be content with an indirect relationship through the US as an intermediary.

In September 1978 Fukuda at the opening of the 85th session of the Diet gave strong emphasis for strengthened co-operative relations between Japan and Europe in order to revitalise the 'trilateral base of international relations'.[330]

The Japanese government later announced that all foreign companies would be given an equal chance on public tenders on projects involving more than $250,000 per case. Japan now asked for US and EC reciprocity, and warned the actual implementation of the scheme could take time.[331]

In October 1978, a 10-member EP delegation under its Vice President Scott Hopkins visited Japan and held exchanges with the Diet's 112-member strong Japan—EC Parliamentary Friendship League on East Asian politics, and on the global and bilateral economic situation. The resulting EP report, authored by the Dutch Liberal Jan Baas, concluded for EC—Japan relations:[332]

In the short term there will be no fundamental improvement, for the underlying reasons for Japan's success in the EC market continue to apply, despite current problems posed by the world recession and despite the voluntary restraint agreements made between the EC and Japan in certain sectors. While exploring further means of improving the situation, the reasons for Japan's success should be examined so that the EC might learn how to improve its own performances.

Fukuda had told the visiting MEPs that the establishment of close and cordial relations with Europe was one of his fundamental priorities and that he hoped the quality of the relations with Europe would be restored to their pre-war level.[333]

In October 1978 Chancellor Schmidt made an official visit to Japan. In a public lecture he outlined the goals of Germany's Asienpolitik.[334] Its basic interest was to see the stability of the area maintained — based on national independence and political equilibria. Japan held an identical view and pursued this goal in her policies towards ASEAN and China. Schmidt welcomed these policies and underlined that Germany, similarly to Japan, had no interest in a confrontation between the USSR and China. On global economic roles Schmidt stressed Europe's contribution to international monetary stability with his creation of the EMS, which was supposed to slow dysfunctional and speculative exchange rate fluctuations. He defined the US's task as reducing their oil imports and combating inflation while Japan's job was to reduce her current account surplus.

The Japanese media in their usual uniform editorial policies reported only Schmidt's economic utterances. His references to the security situation in the Far East were suppressed, though in Schmidt's entourage Vice Admiral Luther took considerable interest in the build-up of the Soviet Far Eastern fleet.[335] Schmidt on three occasions had had a total of three hours of talks with Fukuda, of which half of the time had to be spent on translations. Of the remainder the exchange of courtesies and formalities took their share. It is not possible, therefore, to judge on how substantial his talks might have been. Then only six weeks later, Fukuda was overthrown by a contender from his own party's ranks, Mr Ohira.

In October 1978, Messrs Meynell and Kunihira, the Deputy Director General of MFA's Economic Affairs Bureau, held a working level meeting in a 'cordial atmosphere'.[336] The Commission appeared satisfied with the improvements in the bilateral trade balance, while the Japanese surplus vis à vis the US had risen sharply. At a later meeting in late October 1978 the Council of Ministers did not bother to discuss the relations with Japan and did not give any instructions to the Commission for its HLC in November.[337] Coreper indicated that the Council would examine the Japan file after these talks.

In the annual Franco—Japanese consultations, Guiringaud demanded from Sonoda (MFA), that Japan should make further efforts to remove their NTBs, to purchase six Airbuses and to buy more enriched uranium from France. She should stick to purchasing her nickel from New Caledonia only and not, as Japan actually intended, diversify her sources to include Indonesia and the Philippines as well.[338] These demands reflected the perception official France had about the working of the Japanese economy. Giscard, at an interview, said:[339]

L'économie japonaise, comme vous le savez, est assez centralisée.

Les Européens doivent reclamer un engagement chiffré de
reduction de l'excédent commercial. Il appartient aux autorités
japonaises d'en definir les modalités.

Seeing Japan as a near centrally-planned economy meant nothing was
impossible for the Japanese government. The non-fulfilment of French
demands, then, could only be due to the bad will of the Japanese system.
    The British—Japanese consultations focussed on industrial co-operation
— such as on the recent link-up between Rank and Toshiba — and on
world politics. Dr Owen and Sonoda reviewed China, Chinese—Soviet
relations, and the conflicts in Southern Africa.

Events in Iran were also discussed by both Ministers, anxious
that the normalisation of the country's affairs be achieved at
an early date and that the country would continue under the
leadership of His Excellency, the Shah.[340]

Within OECD's WP6, shipbuilding was taken up again in November
1978. Japan announced it would not renew its 'political' 5 per cent price
increase when the time limit of this concession expired in December
1978.[341]
    Among all OECD nations Japan had been the only one which had
taken the cut backs in production facilities seriously. With reference to
the UK's $170m and other countries' subsidy programme the Japanese
rejected AWES' criticism against giving up her price controls.[342] With
the EC in 1978 obtaining a larger share in order intake, equitable order-
sharing certainly no longer figured on the agenda.
    In Britain, in October 1978, Ford was on strike again, and as a result
car imports soared. When Japanese car imports appeared to be over-
stepping their 10.6 per cent VSR share, Mr Dell — reflecting the nervousness of politicians in pre-election time — threatened a total ban on Japanese car exports for October.[343] MITI reacted by slashing the normal
monthly flow of cars to Britain from 13,000 to 3,500 in that month.
Davignon lent his support to the British threats by calling for policies
of closer European car cartelisation which should be supported by governmental subsidy programmes. *Die Zeit* commented:[344] 'The outsider,
who for months has considered it as his duty to talk European businesses
out of competition, has found a new object: the car industry'. In November 1978, JAMA assured the SMMT of 'prudent' Japanese car exports
for 1979, given the 'period of continuing reconstruction' in the British
car industry.[345]
    In December 1978, an EC review of the development of bilateral
trade since the Haferkamp—Ushiba statement of March acknowledged
that EC exports to Japan during 1978 had grown strongly, while Japanese

exports to the Community had more or less stagnated.[346] The Commission admitted that this result had not been reached by structural EC achievements. Japanese temporary VSRs had been effective, covering nearly all of her most competitive export products: ships, cars and steel. European exports had benefited from the Yen's appreciation (by 42 per cent against the dollar since September 1977) and by Japan's economic recovery and its subsequent demand for capital goods imports.

During the HLC, in December 1978, the Commission abstained from exercising any public pressure on Japan to concede on the familiar litany of microeconomic demands aiming at a more permanent facilitation of European exports to Japan.[347] The Japanese delegation to the HLC, therefore, did not concede anything.[348] The Ohira government also hinted it might abandon its predecessor's 7 per cent growth pledge, which even after a supplementary budget in autumn 1978 looked illusory anyway.

A little later the European Council in Copenhagen – which was about to launch the EMS scheme – received a report on the HLC's (non-) achievements. The Council then expressed its 'grave concern' that only limited progress had been made and asked the Commission for renewed efforts for both micro and macroeconomic concessions.[349] This declaration was again the result of a stalemate between the French and the British delegation, pressing for a tough EC line, and the Germans expressing confidence in the market mechanism.[350]

In talks on Japan's steel exports to the EC, Japan's producers in December 1978 again agreed to their (now theoretical) VSR of 1.22m tonnes.[351] During the first eleven months of 1978 they had exported only 530,000 tonnes to the EC, far below their restraint limit. Earlier the Japanese had complained that, while their prices were upheld by their accord with the Commission, the European producers were undercutting the EC's 'basic price' by margins of up to $40 per tonne.[352]

The year of the rabbit hutch (1979)

In January 1979 the US, France, Germany and Britain held their summit in Guadeloupe. The summit was fully devoted to security matters – mostly on SALT – but, nevertheless, Japan felt her exclusion humiliating. To the Western powers, Japan's military contributions had appeared as too marginal. They were also disappointed at the continued low profile roles of Japanese prime ministers who were handicapped by their deficient command of English and by their lack of strong personal contacts with Western politicians. Other Japanese sins concerned the abolition of the post of Minister of External Economic Affairs by the new

256

Ohira government – because of poor relations between Ushiba and certain political bigwigs in the LDP.[353] Ohira had also dropped his predecessor's 7 per cent growth promise without prior consultations. As the new EC ambassador to Japan, Mr Fielding, put it, Japan now suffered from a 'credibility gap' in her macroeconomic assurances due to her overoptimistic forecasts and pledges in the past.[354]

Chancellor Schmidt, however, in talks with Sonoda (MFA) – disliking demands for German reflationary policies himself – called Japan's lower growth policies 'politically and theoretically correct'.[355] He and Genscher gave Sonoda an extensive briefing on Guadeloupe. Other items of their ministerial consultations concerned the Iranian revolution and the new round of wars in Indochina.

At their February 1979 meeting, the EC's Foreign Ministers urged more Japanese tariff concessions at the MTN, where an EC–Japanese wrangle had developed into a major stumbling block for the negotiations.

TOA in the meantime announced it would buy three Airbuses in fiscal 1980, and three more in fiscal 1981 – at the cost of $37.5m each.[356]

In early March 1979, the EC trade statistics for 1978 had been compiled. The bilateral deficit towards Japan had reached $6.5 US billion during that year. The Japanese figures, which had come out earlier, had put the deficit at $5 US billion. Throughout the winter 1978–79 US exports to Japan, benefiting from the dollar depreciation, had made a strong comeback, while the EC's exports had been faltering.[357] The European Council in its mid-March 1979 session again called on the Commission to negotiate for a substantial opening of the Japanese market.[358] Shortly afterwards Japan's new chief trade negotiator, Mr Yasukawa, visited the EC in order to explain that the Ohira government's foreign economic policies would continue the policies of the Fukuda administration.

The world economic summit for summer 1979 was scheduled to be held in Tokyo. The Japanese government now started to become nervous at the EC's potential criticism,[359] since four out of the seven participants would be EC member states.

DG III's Deputy Director General Loeff had just completed 'technical talks' on a series of Japanese NTBs – on which negotiations had been dragging on for years – such as duplicate testing required for industrial chemicals, pharmaceuticals, cosmetics and agrochemicals – delaying their exports to Japan by three to four years – and cumbersome and unusual approval systems for electrical and gas appliances, and sanitary fittings. These items accounted for nearly 20 per cent of the EC's exports to Japan. But the progress of Loeff's talks had again been 'rather limited'.[360]

In Brussels Jenkins, Haferkamp and Denman made remonstrances to Yasukawa for Japan's unfulfilled March 1978 promises and the lack of progress during Loeff's talks.[361] They also warned against Japan's 'alarming' export drive on cars and consumer electronics. To Japan's news agency Kyodo, Yasukawa confessed that there were no commodities in Europe whose imports Japan could sensibly increase and that he had no idea on genuinely how to improve the bilateral relations.[362]

Yasukawa's talks with Lambsdorff and van Lennep, the OECD's Secretary General, focussed on their request for a massive increase of Japan's aid to Turkey.[363] In January the Guadeloupe summit had decided that under OECD auspices a $4 billion Western aid package to Turkey should be brought together.

In pursuit of the Council's new mandate, in March 1979, Haferkamp and Denman went to Tokyo in order to press for increased Japanese imports from the EC.[364] Since the Council's mandate did not allow for any EC concessions in reciprocity, Haferkamp in Tokyo argued that Japan's global and bilateral surplus created a special responsibility for her to abolish all remaining quantitative obstacles and NTBs to imports.[365] He mentioned the Japanese quota on shoes, which allowed for only a 2 per cent share of imports on the Japanese market, whereas the EC's quotas allowed for a 26 per cent share of imported shoes. Haferkamp added that he did not like 'the idea of coming here every year with the same list of specific complaints' and that he would rather see bilateral relations cover wider horizons like industrial co-operation. Such a dialogue, however, could not be held unless trade relations improved.[366]

His Japanese counterparts Sonoda (MFA), Kosaka (EPA) and Esaki (MITI) were adamant. They cited the 45 per cent increase in Japanese imports from the EC in 1978 and referred to the change from export-led growth to domestic demand-induced growth during the current fiscal year.[367] The Japanese government's new indebtness in fiscal 1979 stood at $80 US billion, more than the British, German, French and US governmental indebtness combined ($65 US billion). In parallel talks Denman threatened to Miyamoto, the head of MITI's International Trade Policy Bureau that if the bilateral surplus was not cut by summer 1979, then the European Council in June might decide on sanctions.[368]

Upon return to Brussels, Haferkamp admitted his talks had achieved nothing concrete and that the Japanese response was not satisfactory. Nonetheless, he added: 'For the moment we have nothing planned as counteraction', but pressure to do so might mount.[369] The EC would wait for the outcome of the Tokyo summit before deciding on possible actions.[370]

Shortly after Haferkamp's and Denman's return from Tokyo, British papers published excerpts of a 'secret' Commission document, drafted at senior level, which described Japan's foreign economic behaviour in extremely drastic terms. It threatened selective import controls and was interpreted as an alarming sign of the Commission's impatience with

258

Japan.[371] The document was stamped 'Vertraulich/Confidential' and entitled: 'Japan: Consultations in train and envisaged — Working paper of the DG I. — On the Agenda for the 509th meeting of the Commission on 21.3.1979. Item 11'. The paper, dated 19 March 1979, had been completed after the fruitless Loeff mission to Tokyo on the removal of Japanese NTBs and after the equally concession-free Yasukawa talks in Brussels. It was now leaked by Sir Roy Denman after the failure of his and Haferkamp's mission.[372] The text seems to have had at least two authors. The predominant part is a sober, well-structured, academic treatise analysing bilateral trade relations and advocating a fairly tough EC response.[373] The second author, Sir Roy,* had added some 'funnies' to the introduction of the original text:

> [Japan's trade expansion was due to] hard work, discipline,
> corporate loyalties, and management skills of a crowded,
> highly competitive island people only recently emerged from
> a feudal past, a country of workaholics who live in what
> Westerners would regard as little more than rabbit hutches. . . .
> [There is] as much propensity to import as there would be
> carnival spirit on a rainy Sunday morning in Glasgow. . . .
> Competition from a country such as this is not easy to face
> by a Europe where the Protestant work ethic has been sub-
> stantially eroded by egalitarianism, social compassion, en-
> vironmentalism, state interventionism and a wide-spread
> belief that working hard and making money are anti-social. . . .
> [Japanese exporters operate] like soldiers venturing out
> from a fortress, create havoc in concentrated areas of in-
> dustry in the Community with major regional employment
> problems.

Originally the purpose of the 'funnies' may have been to motivate the Commissioners to read through the 17-page memo for agenda point 11, or to make at least Haferkamp read it on his flight to Tokyo as a briefing for his negotiations.[375]

After the failure of these talks the disclosure of the paper — its threat of import controls in combination with the headline-seeking 'work-aholics' and 'rabbit hutches' struck like lightning in Japan and would dominate the Japanese media's discussion of Euro—Japanese relations for months.

These unfavourable references had hit an extremely sensitive spot in Japan's political culture: the concern with how the West perceives Japan and her civilisation. Already enjoying the feeling of having caught up

---

* Several papers, like *Time* (see reference 374) described Sir Roy as the author of the whole draft. This does not make sense either in terms of style or in terms of his time budget.

with the West and GNP-wise having taken over one European country after another, now Japan was again portrayed as the country of neurotic, substandard parvenus. The focus on 'workaholics' and 'rabbit hutches' totally overshadowed the discussion of the more meaningful analytical sections of the draft.

The study set out an analysis of EC–Japanese relations, which were seen as determined by the Japanese economy's competitive strength. The complication for the EC's policies arises from three interrelated problems, which are seen as being not decisive by themselves, but in their combination. These are: (a) Japan's export led growth, (b) the sectoral concentration of Japan's exports, and (c) the difficulties of access to Japan's markets.

The study views a European trade policy towards Japan as affected by four conditions:

1 The US having similar interests towards Japan. Japanese export restraints to the US would flood the European market and Japanese concessions to the US would stimulate the member states' demands.

2 Japan giving higher priority to the US's demands. The US is more important to Japan both as a defence partner and in trade relations, being the destination of 30 per cent of Japan's exports.

3 Protectionist pressures in the EC, which, dangerously easy to stimulate, were always present and undirected.

4 Disunity among member states. The Japanese boasting openly that they are able to play one member state against the other.

The Commission paper then proceeds to list the EC's major policy objectives vis à vis Japan: policies to stimulate domestic demand, the opening of the Japanese market for manufactured imports, an increase in untied ODA and the reduction of Japan's tariffs and NTBs at the MTN.* It then analyses the record of the EC's diplomatic achievements. Japan's macroeconomic promises of March 1978 are unfavourably compared with the actual results. Japan's MTN concessions are described as not very significant. On sectoral issues the EC had succeeded in selling six Airbuses, in loosening Japan's exchange controls and testing procedures, especially on imported cars. It was also able to influence Japan's trade mark laws favourably. Nonetheless, the study described the EC's overall achievements as extremely meagre.

Up to then the EC's policy had followed a line of reasonable persuasion. The study suggests that this policy might have to be reconsidered in the light of this summer's (1979) MTN and Tokyo summit results. If the 'unacceptable' 'surplus balance' (sic) did not improve, then in autumn 1979 the Community should reduce imports from Japan, but without 'running the risk of starting a world trade war'.

* The EC's pressures for Japanese VSRs (on ships, steel, cars, bearings, electronics) are omitted from this list as well as from the following 'balance'.

In order to implement their 'hard line' strategy the author(s) felt it necessary to demand more effective consensus-finding and decision making among member states. They should — as demanded by a Council resolution of 7 February 1978 — form a united front. Eventual import controls should be applied on a Community-wide basis only.

A Commission spokesman later confirmed that import controls on Japanese exports were under study for later in 1979, but that no decision had yet been made.[376]

The Japanese were caught in total surprise. During the recent talks Haferkamp and Denman had only made requests, but not issued any ultimatum, though during the negotiations Denman had taken a markedly harder line than Haferkamp.[377] MITI insisted that the EC saw its deficit with Japan out of proportion: imports from Japan made up only 2.3 per cent of the EC's total (1978).

Most Japanese reacted to the cultural description of Japan with self-mockery — like the trade unions demonstrating in rabbit costumes against the governmental housing policies. Others felt hurt, as this comment shows:[378]

> When Europeans call the Japanese 'workaholic', as the EC document did, they are denying the Japanese spiritual and aesthetic life. . . .
> The heart of the question here is the European racial prejudice as manifest in the way they referred to the Japanese as something subhuman.

The author then recalled the experiences of a MITI official in Europe in the 1960s who felt the European negotiators 'treat us Japanese as if a creature closer to ape'.

Premier Ohira then had a rare meeting with Western journalists. He told them that Japan's surplus was not a healthy development,[379] but the EC should have confidence in the outcome of Japan's reflationary policies.* He regarded the EC's charges of Japanese favouritism towards the US as unjustified, and asked them to consider that the US in 1978 had an overall trade deficit, while the EC had enjoyed a $16 US billion surplus. On cultural NTBs, Ohira admitted that Japan was difficult to understand for foreigners but this would apply even for Japanese and for himself.

A vivid display of the European difficulties in understanding Japan was given at a *Financial Times* symposium by Mr Guiringaud, the former

---

* As the result of these policies — as demanded by the EC — and through the oil price increase later in 1979, Japan's global surplus started falling, accompanied by the fall of the Yen (see reference 380), a side effect which the EC's 'macroeconomists' obviously had overlooked when formulating their demands.

French foreign minister and ambassador to Japan.[381] He called the Japanese market one of the most effectively closed in the world because of the total control the 12 major conglomerates had over it. Japan's rapid transition from feudalism to industrialisation had helped the country to retain a medieval attitude with old ideals of fidelity and devotion to the clan being transferred towards the heads of the big concerns who behaved like the ancient samurais and shoguns.

At the same symposium Haferkamp declared the bilateral deficit had reached political-psychological limits and hinted the EC could introduce discriminatory testing and other NTBs on Japanese imports if Japan did not remove hers.[382] He also mentioned the possibility of EC countries' abolishing their discriminatory import restrictions in exchange for an unspecified Japanese market opening. Among the Japanese participants, Mr Mizukami, the JFTC's chairman, strongly advocated such a liberal policy. Mr Komoto, a former minister of MITI and the chairman of the LDP's powerful Policy Research Council, urged Japanese policies of orderly marketing.

Haferkamp and Komoto, at a later meeting, mainly discussed industrial co-operation, mostly on areoplane development. In this field the cost risks now were considered too high and the markets too small to afford separate developments in Europe and in Japan.[383] Talks with Jenkins also focussed on the co-operation motive and on Japanese investments in Europe.

In May 1979, the Danish Foreign Minister Christopherson put 'Japan' on the Council's agenda — a session which was not attended by Britain. Counting on Dutch and German support, he hoped to direct the Commission's bargaining attitude into a more conciliatory direction for the forthcoming HLC.[384] Christopherson, supported by other foreign ministers, said the rabbit hutch paper should have been more modest and sophisticated.[385]

Earlier in a reply to a parliamentary question the German government called the paper's expressions 'not proper' and 'not helpful to the trade relations'. This comment had been formally communicated to the Japanese ambassador in Germany.[386]

The HLC in mid-May 1979 were again held between delegations under Miyazaki and Denman in Tokyo. Denman, when faced with a volley of questions at a press conference, defended the Commission's right to write what it pleases in its confidential memoranda.[387]

The HLC then took a very harmonious turn and Denman announced that after two years of negotiations significant progress had been achieved on the testing procedures on some imports. The Japanese had agreed to accept European testing data on pharmaceuticals, to simplify import inspection procedures and to shorten the testing period on imported tractors from 18 to 6 months.[388]

MITI announced that European companies co-operating with Japanese in joint ventures on third markets were eligible for ExIm-Bank loans and voiced strong support for other co-operative schemes like the tie-up between Honda and BL, and the IHI—Rolls Royce agreement on a joint jet engine development.[389]

MITI's co-operation programme was dear to the heart of Commissioner Davignon who in a follow-up to the HLC had planned to ask for Japanese concessions on shoes and processed food — on which no agreement had been reached at the HLC.[390] But Davignon appeared not to have pressed these issues.[391] He told Esaki (MITI) he would personally submit ideas on industrial co-operation to the Council and voiced opposition to Giscard's ideas of administered trade.[392]

In June 1979, an abbreviated and strongly-revised version of the rabbit hutch paper was submitted by the Commission to the European Council.[393] It had earlier been approved by the Council of Ministers. The new paper[394] summarised the academic analysis of the February 1979 draft, stressing the problems related to Japan's competitiveness and external trade characteristics. It now called the results of the EC's past diplomatic efforts 'mixed' rather than 'meagre' as the original draft had done. The study acknowledged that Japan's current account surplus was now falling to levels below the Community's own surplus. It described food and shoes as the only remaining sectoral problems, apart from the bilateral imbalance 'problem'.

The paper insisted that priority should be given to co-operation in industrial policies (via two-way investment, on major technical projects etc.), on economic and monetary policies, on energy and research development, and on policies towards the Third World.

The conclusions of the Presidency then were as follows:[395]

> The European Council noted that the imbalance in trade relations between the Community and Japan was continuing and deepening. Wishing to expand and strengthen co-operation with Japan in all fields, it expressed the wish that the Japanese government . . . would help by means of appropriate measures to redress the situation which gave particular cause for concern.

The 1979 Tokyo summit in July, after increased US oil imports and massive price hikes following the Iranian revolution, was fully devoted to energy as the overriding issue. Trade, to the Japanese officials' relief remained only a marginal concern.

In autumn 1979 the Commission inaugurated its own export promotion scheme in Japan. It consisted of 22 annual scholarships for young, aspiring European executives to learn the Japanese language and business ways in Tokyo — a programme which attracted a considerable amount of media attention in Japan— and of more conventional means of export promotion, like the opening of an exhibition centre and the organisation of export missions.[396] This more conventional feature was resented in some member countries as overlapping with their own export promotion programmes. Here Britain was most active: 6—7 per cent of the British Overseas Trading Board's budget was spent on promotion in Japan.

In November 1979, the EC reiterated its policy of detente towards Japan. Fielding, the Commission's ambassador to Japan, announced in Nagasaki:[397] 'On the European side, the dangers of protectionism have for the present at least receded, and are not likely to return while Japanese policies remain as they are . . .'.

Davignon, in the meantime, had sounded out the member governments' responses to his co-operation plans. He felt that joint technological developments, joint bids at tenders in the Third World and joint ventures on the production of cars, chemicals, aeronautics and data processing were necessary. The national responses, however, were reportedly sceptical, telling him, in fact, to leave such matters to the industries concerned.[398] Both the Airbus Industries and the Netherlands' Fokker VFW had proposed to the Japanese aviation industry (Ishikawajima Harima Heavy Industries, Kawasaki Heavy Industries, Mitsubishi Heavy Industries) competing project participations in the development of a future 120—160 seat aeroplane for the mid-1980s.[399] Later Dassault made a similar proposal to the Japanese.[400]

Rolls Royce offered to the Japanese the joint development of a new jet engine for medium-sized passenger planes in order to share the development costs and the subcontracting work.[401] This project soon found MITI's and her aircraft industry's advisory council's blessing.[402] But the Japanese media criticised the amount of Japanese governmental subsidies (52 billion Yen) for the engines' 140 billion Yen development costs as too high.[403] Nonetheless, in April 1980, this deal was finalised.[404]

In a 'tranquil' atmosphere in late November—early December 1979, the HLC under Denman and Miyazaki took place in Tokyo.[405] Japan's current account had turned from a $25 billion surplus (1978) into a $4 billion deficit (January—September 1979), a result of the second oil crisis following the Iranian revolution. The Japanese were now asked by the Commission not to resume their export drive as they had done after 1973.[406] So far in 1979 the EC's exports to Japan had increased by 45 per cent, while Japanese exports to the EC had grown by 'only' 22 per cent. Japan now demanded the abolition of the EC's residual quota restrictions on Japanese imports and hinted she would implement advance tariff cuts on items of interest to the Community in exchange. Since he did not have a respective negotiation mandate Denman rejected this proposal.[407]

On sectoral issues the most contentious concerned Danish pork ex-

264

ports to Japan. According to Danish investigations MAFF had given 'advice' to importers to stop the import of pork until April 1980 in order to stabilise the domestic Japanese pork prices. The 'advice' had made it clear that refusal to respond would be held against them at a later date. Though MAFF strongly denied the story, the evidence was overwhelming: there was a sudden and conspicious decline and massive cancellations on Danish pork export orders to Japan.[408] Denman now asked for a public declaration that the government had no intention of introducing import restrictions on pork imports. The Japanese argued that the discontinuation of imports had been a private agreement between producers and importers, and underlined the political sensitivity of the issue.[409]

While Japan, during the preceding working level talks, had hinted it might consider concessions on taxes for imported whisky, now during the HLC MOF officials again insisted these taxes were internal matters and not subject to international negotiations. For European tobaccos and cigarettes Japan promised improved access to its market. But they refused to extend the exemption of imported heavy cars — that is, Rolls Royces — from her emission standards beyond 1981. On agricultural products talks would be continued at working levels.

The Japanese criticised the EC's anti-dumping regulations as incompatible with GATT's anti-dumping code. The new Commission rules allowed anti-dumping duties notwithstanding the introduction of price corrections.

The Japanese were also critical of the Commission's renewed anti-dumping investigation on Japanese ball-bearings.[410] Immediately after the European Court of Justice had declared the EC's ADD imposition illegal in March 1979, the Federation of European Bearings Manufacturers (FEBMA) had called for a new dumping investigation, charging that the Japanese were under-selling their domestic prices by 15–65 per cent dumping margins in Europe. With a market share of 13 per cent in the EC, the Japanese had contributed to a price depression in the EC, inflicting a loss of profitability on European producers, FEBMA charged — in order to present evidence for 'damages' incurred.[411] In September 1979, the Commission had compiled and opened an anti-dumping investigation.[412]

In spite of these persistent unresolved sectoral problems, Denman, at a press conference after the HLC, welcomed the overall improvement of EC–Japan relations. At a lecture at Sophia University he called for closer trilateral co-operation in the 1980s, when the shortage of key raw materials would coincide with the NICs catching up with the OECD nations.[413]

At a later meeting between officials of DG III and of MITI's Basic Industries Bureau, Japan promised to continue her steel export restraints to the EC during 1980 at the levels of 1979 (at around 700,000 tons) and at the EC's 'guidance prices'. Though promising continued 'co-operation' the Japanese were critical of the European producers' practice of hidden rebates on some steels on the EC market.[414]

The second crisis begins

In January 1980, the new British Secretary of Trade, John Nott, visited Japan. Though the government of Mrs Thatcher, to the Japanese delight, had strongly advocated free trade policies Mr Nott continued the British tradition of calling for Japanese restraints on car, TV and radio exports to Britain. But he emphasised that he considered Japanese productive investment in UK as means to redress the imbalance on trade and welcomed the British Leyland–Honda tie up, through which 80,000 Japanese cars would be built and marketed by British Leyland in Britain.[415] Nott also called on the Japanese to reduce their tariffs and taxes on liquor* and confectionery and to abolish barriers to the operations of foreign banks and insurance companies – fields in which Britain enjoyed strong international competitiveness.

Most of Nott's talks with Sazaki (MITI) centred on the US request for sanctions against the Soviet Union (on their recent invasion of Afghanistan) and against Iran (for taking US hostages). Both publicly professed to favour joint Western approaches, but agreed that more studies of the matter needed to be done.[417]

The same themes, Iran, Afghanistan and the situation in Indochina, also dominated the talks between a Diet delegation, led by Mr Kuranari, a senior LDP politician, and EP members, led by Sir Fred Warner, a Tory and former ambassador to Japan, in Strasbourg in February 1980.[418]

Hardly noticed in Europe, in Japan – her trade balance worsening and the Yen falling – a major turnaround in her trade policies was prepared. Already in January 1980 Japan's car producers announced that they planned to increase their car output by 10 per cent in 1980. Most of this expansion was aimed at increased overseas sales,[419] regardless of mounting frictions with the US on cars.

In February 1980 Mr Sasaki, the Minister of MITI, made the renewed Japanese export drive official. He called on JFTC leaders to ensure that their trading companies (sogo shosha) stepped up their exports in order to strengthen the Yen and to reduce Japan's oil bill.[420] While this move in economic terms was certainly legitimate, in political terms it was bound to lead to increased friction with the US and the EC, both suf-

---

* MOF put a tax of 150 per cent on imported whisky priced at 1,100 Yen at the port of entry. For whisky above this price a tax of 220 per cent applied. Given the pound's appreciation and the fall of the Yen, Britain wanted this threshold to be raised accordingly (see reference 416).

fering from growing oil prices and ever increasing unemployment. The Japanese leadership and the ministerial officials were certainly fully aware of these political consequences.

In order to alleviate the future criticism MITI started sending overseas investment missions to Europe to study possibilities of increased productive investment there.[421]

The prime target of the Japanese car and electronics exports in Europe was the German market. A Mazda spokesman displayed confidence:[422] 'German industry will avoid protectionist moves because it itself depends on foreign trade'.

At a meeting in Acapulco, JAMA and the SMMT had again agreed on prudent levels of Japanese car exports to the UK. But the Japanese warned that not all of their eleven members might comply.[423] Datsun dealers in Britain in full-page advertisements made their displeasure known at restraints which obstructed their business and served only continental importers.[424]

The French government in March 1980 informally restated its 3 per cent import limit on Japanese cars.[425]

Following the US car industry's plans to start massive investments for the production of a world car and with the proliferation of pressures for export restraints in the EC, Japanese car manufacturers started intensifying their search for joint ventures in Europe. Nissan, with a view to Spain's future EC membership, bought a 36 per cent share in Motor Iberica S.A. and developed joint production plans for trucks and cars with the government owned Empresa Nacional de Autocamiones S.A.[426] The French government then warned the Spanish of the adverse consequences this might have on its accession talks with the EC.[427]

Nissan also proposed a joint production scheme to Alfa Romeo, Italy's ailing state-owned car manufacturer: to produce 60,000 cars in the Mezzogiorno with Alfa motors in a Japanese chassis. Fiat was bitterly opposed to this deal, fearing the loss of its control over the semi-closed Italian car market (a quota of 2,000 cars per annum continued to keep the Japanese out) would be caused by this 'Trojan horse',[428] and started to muster all the political support it could to thwart the arrangement. The Italian Industrial Federation soon obediently condemned the deal.[429] The Communists and their engineering and metal workers union — fearing for their jobs at stake at Alfa — supported the venture.[430] The Italian cabinet found itself unable to decide and postponed the decision until an interministerial committee for industrial policy matters (CIPI) made its recommendations. Since this would take months, Iri-Finnmeccanica managers (controlling Alfa) feared Nissan could turn to someone else for its venture.[431]

In March 1980, the German electronics producers called for two to three years of Japanese restraints to Germany, the only remaining major unrestricted electronics market in the EC, on colour TVs, hifi equipment, video sets and car radios.[432] At the time Philips held 30 per cent of the EC market of colour TVs. Thomson, the French electronics producer, held 10 per cent. On tubes they had shares of 40 per cent and 25 per cent respectively. On the German market they and their partially or fully owned subsidiaries held similar shares.[433]

While in most EC countries oligopolistic structures dominated, the German electronics market suffered from overcompetition due to the domestic producers' miscalculation: they had overestimated the demand of a contracting market.[434] By the end of 1980, AEG—Telefunken's PAL patents would expire, allowing Japanese imports to Germany of large-screen TVs as well.

Davignon now endorsed an EC-wide freeze on Japanese TV exports replacing the present patchwork of nationally applicable VSRs. After five to seven years of restructuring the EC market would be opened entirely to Japanese electronics imports.[435] This scheme found the 'enthusiastic support' of Philips and Thompson—Brandt.[436] The latter with French governmental backing — following a new French fascination with 'telematics' (telecommunications cum electronics cum computers) — tried to consolidate its EC market share.

Italy however voiced strong opposition to Davignon's plan. Its restrictions on Japanese electronics were so tight that it feared too much of a competitive inflow with an EC-wide quota regulation.[437]

Other objections stemmed from the fact that Japan had already set up TV manufacturing facilities in UK and that most European TVs contained an increasing share of components made in South East Asia anyway.[438]

Parallel to these 'sensitive' sectoral designs, high politics was negotiated between Western Europe and Japan. Matthöfer, the German Minister of Finance, during a visit to Tokyo in late February 1980, discussed with Takeshita, his Japanese counterpart the credit conditions for the supply of steel pipes to the USSR in the light of the US's call for sanctions. Takeshita announced Japan would follow the French and German solutions (i.e. if possible salvaging the pipe deals without irritating the Americans).[439] Since Germany, in general, and Matthöfer, in particular were in charge of putting together the OECD's $1.2 US billion aid package to Turkey (the 1979 Western aid to Turkey had amounted to $900m), the German request that Japan should double her $70m (1979) aid to Turkey figured prominently on the agenda. Takeshita however stressed Japan's budgetary difficulties and said, if anything, then Japan would prefer to raise her aid to Pakistan and Thailand.[440] The next OECD meeting on aid to Turkey then failed to reach a conclusion on the aid package due to Japan's indecision and due to the Canadian change of government.[441] After having resolved the Rhodesia—Zimbabwe problem the British government also asked Japan to pledge economic assistance to Zimbabwe after its independence.[442] Later, in April 1980, Japan announced it would give 500m Yen (about $2m) in aid to Zimbabwe – about enough to pave five village squares – and $100m in aid to Turkey.[443]

Among the less costly things, Ohira told the assembled Commission, British, German, Italian and French ambassadors, that Japan would support the EC's call for an international arrangement for a neutral Afghanistan after a Soviet military withdrawal.[444]

In March 1980, the German Minister of Defence, Apel, visited Japan. The presence of the Defence Ministry's division heads for armament questions and for military policy in his entourage made it clear that Apel was not merely making courtesy calls.[445] The Japanese media, however, were eager to present his talks as such. With Ohira he supposedly spoke about energy co-operation at the forthcoming Venice summit.[446] With Hosoda, the head of Japan's Defence Agency he discussed the difficulties of increasing defence spending.[447]

Apel supported the Japanese stand against the US for a summary 3 per cent real increase in Japan's defence spending: first planning and strategic decisions had to be made. Only afterwards could budgetary decisions follow.[448] The real German interest however lay in the Japanese perception of the USSR's Far Eastern military build-up. The Japanese had – against their usual habit of only importing technological knowhow – expressed interest in purchasing German armoured aeroplane shelters, anti-aircraft missiles (Roland) and anti-aircraft tanks (Gepard).[449]

When the Dutch premier, van Agt, made a state visit again the sanctions on Iran and the participation in the Moscow Olympics figured high on the agenda.[450] Van Agt nonetheless found enough time to ask the Japanese to co-operate with Fokker on its aeroplane development and to ease quarantine restrictions on Dutch flower bulbs.[451]

In April 1980, Japan had followed the EC nations in temporarily recalling her ambassador from Tehran, after the US had been strongly critical of Japan for not being co-operative enough on the sanctions they had decided upon.[452]

In April Japan's Foreign Minister Okita attended a European foreign ministers meeting in Luxembourg. He was the first non-EC minister ever to attend a Council of Ministers session. Britain at the time professed her eagerness to back the US demand to break off diplomatic and trade relations with Iran, while France was more hesitant to do so. The Council then decided to postpone its decision.[453] Okita then announced Japan would follow the EC's decisions on the second stage of sanctions to be taken in mid-May 1980 if the hostages were not released by then.[454] This second stage was likely to imply a total trade embargo against Iran, except for supplies of food and medicine.

The US's abortive 'rescue' mission in late April 1980 came as a shock both to Europe and to Japan with their confidence in the Carter administration reaching a new low.[455]

Coming from Tito's funeral, in early May 1980, premier Ohira visited Genscher and Schmidt in Bonn. Their talks again centred on Iran and on the Olympics — both agreeing to stay away from the latter.[456] The same topics also dominated Okita's discussions with the German, British and French foreign ministers attending an IEA meeting in Paris on 17 May.[457]

Reflecting the intensity of political co-operation, Mr Diehl, the German ambassador to Tokyo, observed:[458] 'Outside the European Community, Japan today has become our most important partner next to the United States, and Germany has risen to the same position vis à vis the Japanese foreign policy structure.'

In May 1980 a new HLC took place, the Japanese being led by Mr Kikuchi, the new Deputy Foreign Minister, and the Commission delegation by Denman, who had just leaked a new paper — this time denouncing his officials' working style ('drunk all day under the table' and following 'any kind of immorality that takes their fancy').[459]

The Yen in the meantime had fallen by 30 per cent in relation to the dollar, and the Japanese sales drive in full swing made the EC's bilateral deficit grow by 57 per cent in Yen figures and by 30 per cent in dollars. During the talks Denman insisted that he did not want to see Japan paying her oil bill with increased exports to the EC[460] and, supported by Davignon, asked for Japanese restraints on cars and electronics.[461]

During the negotiations the EC again repeated their demands to remove barriers from the importation of cigarettes, liquor, ham, shoes, chemicals and cars, and to enlarged European banking, and insurance activities in Japan.[462] Kikuchi in turn asked the EC to abolish its fifty-odd residual restrictions against Japan — all remnants of the 1950s.[463]

In the conclusion of the talks a Commission spokesman summarised the Community's wisdom:[464] 'We want them to increase their imports from us, but it is not for us to say in what precise sectors or by what policy means.'

In order to develop a more precise policy, the Commission — DG's I and III — worked out a new bargaining strategy towards Japan which also for the first time in a long time attempted to create a coherent CCP towards Japanese imports. A draft to the European Council started out by stating that the EC had, on significant industrial sectors, lost her competitive edge to Japan.[465]

Unmistakably reflecting Davignon's views, but reportedly drafted by Denman, the paper asked for Community-wide Japanese VSRs on electronics and cars in order to enable the Community's industries to restructure. After about five years all these restraints should be abolished. As the EC's concession the Commission proposed to have all her inherited national 'patchwork' of restrictions phased out.[466]

Prior to the Venice European Council meeting, the German Coreper delegation voiced opposition to the plan. It feared the Japanese VSRs on cars and electronics — demanded by Britain in particular — would result in US curbs on a variety of unwanted EC exports (steel and textiles being likely candidates).[467] Following the German opposition, the draft on Japan was dropped from the Council's agenda.

The European summit mainly discussed the EC's planned initiative on the Middle East, calling the PLO's participation necessary to any lasting peace there in order to break the deadlock over Camp David. Okita prior to and after the summit voiced Japan's support for the EC's declaration.[468]

During his election campaign in mid-June 1980 premier Ohira died from a heart attack. The Japanese delegation to the Venice world summit was now composed of the ministers of a caretaker government (Okita, Takeshita, Sasaki) and was severely handicapped from entering any commitments or making any active proposals on the issues at stake (sanctions against the USSR, oil, inflation, etc.).[469] The Japanese media called their low profile a contribution to stability.[470]

In early July 1980 Ohira was buried. Japanese newspapers did not fail to observe that while the Chinese premier Huo and President Carter attended the funeral, the European representatives were only second in line.[471] In addition, they (Haferkamp, Lambsdorff, Sir Ian Gilmour, etc.) did little to conceal their 'mourning dress diplomacy' using their talks in Tokyo mainly to voice their concern at the rising tide of Japanese imports to the EC.[472]

Lambsdorff gave them 'friendly advice' for restraints — especially on cars: the Japanese market share was about to double in Germany.[473] Haferkamp referred to the political 'difficulties' arising from Japan's export boom.[474] Gilmour threatened protectionist steps if Japan's car exports did not stick to their old 10.6 per cent market share.[475] They had been temporarily up at 13.6 per cent. The Japanese producers promised to comply.

In Britain, major union leaders like Moss Evans (Transport and General Workers Union) and Terence Duffy (Amalgamated Union of Engineering Workers) had called for a 50 per cent cut in Japan's exports to UK in 1980.[476]

The CCMC (Committee of Common Market Automobile Constructors) had initiated a campaign on cars and asked Davignon to push for measures restricting Japanese car imports.[477]

While putting his case for Japanese car restraints, Lambsdorff, however, had assured Okita that the German government would resist all further moves for protectionism in Germany and in the EC.[478] Upon return from Tokyo, Lambsdorff unfavourably compared the German rates of absenteeism and productivity gains with the Japanese figures, and to the displeasure of the German trade union federation (DGB) exhorted his countrymen to work harder and to innovate more in order to cope with the Japanese challenge.[479]

Late in July 1980 the Council of Ministers debated the Commission's revised version of her 'new strategy' towards Japan, a paper 'largely the work of Sir Roy Denman'.[480] In the Council, France and Italy showed the strongest opposition against giving up their traditional quota restriction in exchange for what they perceived as insufficient demands for Japanese concessions. Britain's Minister of Trade, Parkinson, was less opposed and called the proposals interesting, but not a plan of campaign.[481] The Commission paper was now sent back to Coreper, to be discussed after the summer break in September 1980.[482]

In June 1980 Nissan gave the Italian government — which had not yet come up with a decision on the Nissan–Alfa link up — two months to decide.[483] An Italian parliamentary commission had approved of the deal, citing that 80 per cent of the components of the jointly produced car would be Italian made and that 50 per cent of the output was planned to be exported. Another argument was Alfa's $66m annual losses, which they hoped to turn into profits by 1985 due to the link-up.[484]

In the ongoing wrangle Italian politicians sided according to their affiliation with either Alfa or Fiat, or with the South (Napoli, where the deal, near the ailing Alfasud plant, would create 3,500 new jobs) or North (Torino) and according to the changing alliances in the power play in Italian coalitions. The Socialist Minister for State Holdings, de Michaelis — like the Socialist and the Communist Party — favoured the deal. De Michaelis even announced he would resign and let premier Cossiga's coalition go bust, if the link-up was not approved. La Malfa, the head of the Republican Party and the Minister of Budget and Planning, and Bisaglia, a Christian Democratic minister, opposed it, as did their parties.[485] Davignon reportedly shared their opposition, fearing like Agnelli, who called the final agreement masochistic, that Nissan in the long run would expand its role and gain a foothold in Italy.[486] Cossiga had postponed his decision for a fourth time until September 1980. Also the interministerial CIPI was blocked between the warring parties and was unable to issue a recommendation.[487] Then, in September, thousands of Alfa workers took to the streets of Napoli in favour of the project and soon afterwards Cossiga approved of the joint venture.[488] A little later his government collapsed.

As usual during the summer months Japan's market shares in Europe — where most plants and distribution centres had been closed during the vacations — had increased conspiciously.[489] Again national and Community authorities feared these figures would be of a lasting nature.

In September 1980 Haferkamp and Davignon met with Mr Kagawa, the Japanese ambassador to the EC, and told him that the rise of Japan-

272

ese colour TV and car exports to the Community was in effect too high.[490] These increases had largely taken place on the German market.

In January–August 1980, Japan's colour TV exports to Germany had increased by 113 per cent, those of cars by 46 per cent. In order not to antagonise the German government, which had to survive a general election in October, MITI announced that Japan, in a 'spontaneous response' would exercise restraints to the German market for the rest of the year on these products.[491] Japan's car exporters would have to present their shipment plans for October–December 1980 to MITI in order to keep their market share below 10 per cent in Germany.[492] MITI's Vice-Minister Amaya at a visit in Bonn underlined the 'unilateral' nature of these restraints. Japan had developed a strong dislike of the institutionalised UK–Japanese (JAMA–SMMT) VSR talks, which since 1975 had restricted Japan's market share to 10 per cent.[493]

The French also decided in favour of unilateralism. Giscard publicly fixed the Japanese market share on cars at 3 per cent:[494] 'The Japanese share has never been and will never be exceeded so long as reciprocal conditions of access to the Japanese market aren't significantly changed.'

From various quarters in the Community protectionist calls were issued. The largest German union, IG Metall, demanded import controls on Japanese cars if the VSR levels were exceeded.[495] Complaints of EC ship and steel producers against Japan's competitiveness were renewed.[496]

Haferkamp, in a public speech, told the Japanese they should in their own interest moderate their exports and complained that the EC was increasingly lagging behind Japan in productivity, sales efforts, technological innovation and production costs.[497] Mr Thorn, the chairman of the Council of Ministers and the Commission's designated next president, after a visit to Japan, called for a gentleman's agreement requiring Japan to freeze her exports to the EC at 1980 levels for two or three years in order to allow the EC to restructure.[498]

Fearing the proliferation of unilateral member state measures the Commission, in October 1980, again attempted to revitalise its July plans to obtain a common mandate for comprehensive negotiations with Japan. The Commission even tried to solicit Japanese support for the scheme in order to convince the European Council.[499]

For the remainder of 1980 Amaya had already promised 'restraints' to Haferkamp and Davignon,[500] but the new bilateral surplus on trade was estimated to reach $10 US billion anyway. Japan's chief trade negotiator, Okita, admitted bad timing for Japan's export drive: the EC's economies were in stagnation (1 per cent growth) and unemployment levels, then at seven million, were rising rapidly.[501] Amaya advocated as the Japanese tactical response:[502]

The basic posture Japan should take in this situation is to observe the Japanese dictum 'the strong walk on tip toe'. In poker, there is nothing wrong in one player winning every game. But he does that at the risk of being excluded from the game next time. If you want to remain in the game, you have to lose once in a while. Let me repeat: wise, strong man walks on tip toe and considers others' positions, and only the wise and strong can become truly powerful.

In early November 1980, the Commission decided on a six-point programme to the Council for a mandate to negotiate with Japan. It asked for:[503]

- Japanese VSRs on cars and electronics, uniform throughout the EC,
- a stronger Yen, which should reflect the strength of the Japanese economy,
- a further opening of the Japanese market, and
- equal treatment of US and EC demands by Japan.

The Commission, after lengthy consultations with the Committee 113, had dropped the abolition of the EC's restrictions as a possible concession to Japan.[504] Since the beginnings of the CCP in fact no EC concessions had ever been offered outside the MTN.

Due to separate Franco–German discussions of the Japan issue, the acceptance of the programme by the Council was still in doubt. Schmidt and Giscard had met in July, and agreed that officials from their economic ministries should make a separate joint assessment on the EC dealing with Japan.

A Germany Ministry of Economics (BMW) study, in November 1980, urged a European export offensive to the Japanese market, which in joint efforts should be opened more effectively.[505] Other recommended policies to respond to the Japanese challenge concerned the promotion of energy savings; aid for the research efforts by smaller and medium sized companies; and pressure for the harmonisation of technical standards in the EC. The study strongly rejected any protectionist step. It was clear that no separate Franco–German agreement on the Japan issue had been reached.

As announced by Okita and Amaya during their earlier visits to Europe, responding to the EC's demands, Foreign Minister Ito made an official statement on Japan's relations with the EC.[506] He underlined the need for broader economic and political relations with Europe and expressed Japan's readiness to accept the EC's 'new initiative' to liberalise bilateral trade. Ito gave assurances on administrative guidance against unspecified 'torrential' Japanese export expansions. The statement conspicuously failed to name cars and electronics in this context. Though the Japanese ambassadors to the EC countries collectively had urged Ito to be explicit on greater Japanese efforts to help European exporters on Japanese markets,[507] Ito's reply had been tougher than expected. There was not a hint of quantifiable Japanese concessions,[508] for which the Commission had asked Amaya in October 1980.[509]

Prior to the European summit, Haferkamp announced in an interview that he was confident that in 1981 Japanese exports to the EC would slow down.[510] Lambsdorff publicly upheld a strong free trade stand in respect to Japanese imports:[511]

> We have told our automobile industry that it has to find the answers, that we are not going to look for protectionist measures. I know that is a tough answer for these people. But 26 per cent of our GNP is exported. If we start protectionist defensive measures in one sector, the responses to us (by other countries) will be much more damaging than what foreign importers could do here.

After a lengthy debate, the Council in late November 1980 approved a resolution along the lines of the Commission's earlier programme. It deleted the references to a uniform EC treatment of Japanese imports and added a point stressing the need for restructuring efforts in the EC.[512] The European Council expressed its serious concern on the deterioration of the Community's position in bilateral trade and asked the Commission — with a vague reference to possible EC liberalisations in return — to negotiate with the Japanese on the basis of this new mandate and to report back to the Council by February 1981. During the Council's debate the French advocated the toughest line, while Germany, the Netherlands and Denmark again formed a (minority) free trade coalition.[513]

In November 1980, the CCMC, under Fiat's chairman Agnelli, and JAMA, led by Ishihara, Nissan's president, met for talks about the present state and future outlook of EC and Japan's car markets,[514] talks which the Japanese had earlier had tried to avoid.[515]

The US International Trade Commission had just rejected the allegation of Japanese car dumping. It ruled the problems of the US car industry were of domestic origin: the US industries' management, labour and productivity problems.[516]

The EC's major fears concerned Japanese expansion plans which were believed to be based on overly optimistic demand forecasts — as on ships and on steel before. The Japanese replied that their new investments were not aimed at capacity expansion, but at the development of new models. They would also go into energy saving, into overseas investment and emission control.[517] The CCMC's subtle demands for additional Japanese VSRs on cars fell on deaf ears.[518]

In early December 1980 it became known that VW's and Nissan's chairman Schmücker and Ishihara had held separate talks on a different topic. It concerned the production of 100,000 to 200,000 VW—designed cars under licence in Japan.[519] Speculation on the future prospects of VW—Nissan co-operation was ripe. It referred to the possibilities of jointly developing a compact car, of producing spare parts fitting into both concerns' models and to Nissan using VW's plants in the US, in Mexico, South Africa, Brazil, Argentina and Australia.[520] While the talks stagnated in the subsequent weeks, one consequence emerged: the prospect of low priced foreign cars for sale in Japan eroded whatever marketing chances there had been for imported cars (including VWs) sold at double and triple the price of equivalent Japanese cars.[521]

In December 1980, Foreign Minister Ito visited France, Belgium, the Netherlands, Germany and Britain. Prior to his trip he announced that he would not wish to talk about trade, but about high politics: the Middle East, detente and the incoming Reagan administration.[522]

Nonetheless Davignon, Haferkamp and Thorn pressed him to have Japan's exports to the EC moderated, to revalue the Yen, to spend more on ODA and not to negotiate separately with the member states on trade issues.[523]

Chancellor Schmidt and the Dutch premier van Agt, unmoved, assured Ito of their commitment to free trade policies.[524] Ito upon return briefed premier Suzuki on his visit. He observed that the Europeans did not complain much about Japanese exports, probably because they were preoccupied with the Poland problem.[525]

To the Japanese, Poland was certainly more distant than the events in the Middle East had been earlier in 1980. Nonetheless, military co-operation between Western Europe and Japan was developing during the latter part of 1980. In September the Royal Navy and the Japanese Navy held joint exercises in the Far East.[526] In November, Mr Mihara, the head of the LDP's Security Affairs Research Council, attended the North Atlantic Assembly, the parliamentary component of NATO.[527] The Carter administration, in September 1980, proposed a six-nation consultation mode — in which Japan would be part — to protect the sea lanes during a possible spill over of the ongoing Gulf war between Iran and Iraq.[528] Both the Germans and the British continued to promote their ground-to-air missile systems ('Roland' and 'Rapier') in Japan, but not surprisingly the less advanced and more expensive domestically-produced Tansam missile appeared to enjoy more political backing in Japan's political system and in her Defence Agency.[529]

In 1980, the French political establishment seemed to have suddenly have become aware of Japan's potential for the 1980s and set up their equivalents to the Trilateral Commission of eight years earlier. Poniatowski, a special advisor on foreign affairs to Giscard, together with Kosoka (a former director of EPA) founded a Japan Paris Club, which should discuss both France's and Japan's joint contribution to the Third World's development and to global technological issues (such as nuclear energy and aerospace).[530]

Servan-Schreiber announced his Club de Paris which was composed of representatives of Europe, Japan and the Arab world, to deal with the 1980s technological, Japanese and Third World challenges (and to lend support to his new bestseller's promotion campaign).[531]

The economic dimension in bilateral relations

Economic diplomacy between the EC and Japan in 1976—80 appears to have been determined by the cyclical consequences of the Japanese economy's reactions to the oil price increases of 1974 and 1979. Each time the doubling of the oil price led to deficits in the Japanese balance of trade and in her current account and to a severe depreciation of the Yen. Then the Yen's undervalued exchange rate vis à vis the US dollar and the EMS currencies greatly helped to support the Japanese government's policies of boasting exports as a trade policy response.

The major outlets of Japan's exports — being concentrated on sophisticated consumer products for the most part — were the markets of the developed countries. Japan's export drive receded under political pressure there — leading to a proliferation of VSRs — and due to the revaluation of the Yen, as the current account turned into a new surplus.

The crises in bilateral relations 1976—77 and 1980—81 usually occurred when the peaks of Japan's export boom were already nearly over. Soon improving trade statistics would help to contain the bilateral frictions.

The structure of bilateral trade

The EC import figures (Table 6.1) clearly suggest that the French and Italian restrictions have distorting effects on Japanese exports to the Community. The bulk of EC—Japan trade (56 per cent) is handled by Britain and Germany.

The discrepancy between European and Japanese figures (Table 6.1) can be explained by the effects of third country trade (re-exports) and by the inclusion of insurance and freight costs into Japanese import figures and their exclusion from exports (the reverse of the EC's statistical practice). The fact however that the Japanese import figures for

1978 e.g. included $345m for ship 'imports' from Denmark,[534] which actually had been freighters coming for repair only to Japanese yards (an 'error' admitted by MITI) would suggest more confidence in European figures.

Table 6.1

European—Japanese trade by countries (1976—79)[532]
(in million US $)

	EC imports from Japan (cif)		EC exports to Japan (fob)	
	1976	1979	1976	1979
Germany	2124	4298	1092	2314
Britain	1506	3406	636	1310
France	1211	2101	416	949
Italy	580	904	315	799
Netherlands	620	1331	188	354
Belgium	547	1037	175	353
Denmark	351	395	126	344
Ireland	91	237	42	60
(Greece	719	923	22	42)
(Spain	555	608	115	375)
(Portugal	130	171	21	41)
Total EC	7030	13709	2990	6483

Deficit, EC figures (1976) 4042 (1979) 7224
Japanese figures[533] (1976) 3610 (1979) 5104

The relative importance of bilateral trade

The figures in Table e.g. 6.2 confirm earlier findings of the EC having a far greater importance for Japan both as a market and as a source of supply than vice versa.

The continuing low shares of Japan-bound exports among European total exports should support the notion of a persistent European neglect of the Japanese market. Had all countries made the relative efforts exemplified by Denmark in 1979 — a country with sophisticated, but only medium sized industries and businesses — then bilateral trade with Japan would have been balanced.

Table 6.2

Japan's trade with the EC in its relative shares (1976–79)[535]

Japanese exports	to the EC as share of J's total exports	to G as share of G imports	to UK as share of UK imports	to F as share of F imports	to I as share of I imports
1976	10.6%	2.4%	2.7%	1.9%	1.4%
1979	12.3%	2.6%	3.3%	1.9%	1.1%

Japanese exports	to NL as share of NL imports	to BL as share of BL imports	to DK as share of DK imports	to Irl as share of Irl imports	to EC as share of EC imports
1976	1.6%	1.6%	2.9%	2.2%	2.1%
1979	1.9%	1.7%	2.1%	2.4%	2.2%

Japanese imports	from the EC as share of J imports	from G as share of G exports	from UK as share of UK exports	from F as share of F exports	from I as share of I exports
1976	5.6%	1.1%	1.4%	0.8%	0.9%
1979	6.9%	1.3%	1.4%	1.0%	1.1%

Japanese imports	from NL as share of NL exports	from BL as share of BL exports	from DK as share of DK exports	from Irl as share of Irl exports	from EC as share of EC exports
1976	0.5%	0.5%	1.4%	1.3%	0.9%
1979	0.5%	0.6%	2.3%	0.8%	1.1%

The composition of bilateral trade

As shown in Table 6.3, during 1976–79 the trend towards consumer products (including foodstuffs and pharmaceuticals) accelerated among EC exports to Japan. In 1976 their share stood at 42 per cent, in 1979 they made up 55 per cent of the EC's total. The share of products for industrial demand declined accordingly.

As Table 6.4 shows, a wide diversity exists between the export structure of individual EC countries.

These exports mostly cater for industrial demand. On the whole they represent a declining share in EC exports to Japan. The opposite is true with the items in Table 6.5 which we summarised as luxury goods (liquor, wines, cosmetics, perfumes, fashion clothing, furs, handbags, sports goods and art work).

While these exports evidently represent a strong growth potential in a prosperous Japan with significant female purchasing power, as non-essentials they are at the same time very vulnerable to possible economic downswings.

Table 6.3

Major EC exports to Japan (1976—79)[536]
(in million US $)

	1976	1979
Foodstuffs	400	904
— of which meat	78	191
— of which alcoholic beverages	109	274
Raw materials	176	318
Metals	104	256
Chemicals	785	1451
— of which pharmaceuticals	232	404
Machinery and equipment	1048	1581
— of which general machinery	578	1059
— of which electrical machinery	213	383
— of which transportation equipment	130	137
Consumer products	744	2593
— of which textiles	306	749
— of which cars	126	385
— of which precision instruments	128	279

Table 6.4

Share of chemicals and machinery and equipment
in EC exports to Japan (1979)[537]

Germany	75%
Netherlands	57%
France	41%
Britain	40%
Ireland	37%
Italy	28%
Belgium	27%
Denmark	26%

Table 6.5

Share of luxury items in EC exports to Japan (1979)[538]

Italy   47%
France   41%
Belgium 36% (diamonds for jewellery)
Britain   18% (mostly whisky)

German, Dutch and Irish exports of this kind were neglegible.

Danish exports altogether represent a different picture. They consist of 64 per cent foodstuffs, of which 82 per cent was meat. Most of it is the pork luncheon meat which during the US occupation had become the staple diet of the people of Okinawa.

Table 6.6

Major Japanese exports to the EC (1976—79)[539]
(in million US $)

	1976	1979
Foodstuffs	129	95
Raw materials	104	185
Light industry products	817	1521
— of which textiles	191	318
Chemicals	355	604
Metals	690	763
— of which iron and steel	500	435
Machinery and equipment	5063	9317
— of which office machinery	264	485
— of which sewing machines	65	72
— of which bearings	102	91
— of which TV sets	156	190
— of which radio sets	422	566
— of which tape recorders	248	700
— of which cars	935	1976
— of which motorcycles	280	448
— of which ships	604	436
— of which precision instruments	673	1466

The share of sensitive products (iron and steel, ships, bearings, tape recorders, radio and TV sets, cars) in Japanese exports to the EC stood at 35 per cent in 1979, up from a share of 33 per cent in 1976 (Table

6.6). This increase was mainly due to the growth of car exports. The sensitive products of the 1960s (textiles, toys, cutlery, pottery and sewing machines) in the late 1970s had fallen to a share of merely 4 per cent.

Compared to 1975* the technology content in Japan's exports to the EC increased further until 1979. The share of mass produced sophisticated goods remained stable at 45 per cent. High technology exports grew to a share of 32 per cent. Labour and raw material intensive exports declined to shares of 7 and 12 per cent accordingly.

Sectoral issues

Trade in cars exceeded the scope of bilateral relations. With 1.5m Japanese cars being sold in the US (1979) and 630,000 marketed in the EC,[541] a trilateral relationship clearly existed.

Any protectionist measure in the US, where Japan held a market share of above 20 per cent, would inevitably produce diversionary effects to Europe. With the US car industries in the late 1970s starting their restructuring programme aimed at the production of fuel-efficient compact cars, the world witnessed novel developments in the alignments of major car producers.

A maze of joint ventures was set up to develop new models, to produce shared components or to merge foreign operations. Such ventures were e.g. set up between Honda and BL, between Nissan and Alfa Romeo, between Nissan and two Spanish auto makers. Relative talks between Nissan and Volkswagen were underway.[542]

The increased competition among producers of medium sized cars was expected to threaten the less viable European makers: Fiat, Alfa, Peugeot and BL. Link-ups with more successful overseas producers and protective governmental interventions against Japanese car imports were the responses chosen.

There was a 10 per cent limit in UK, a 3 per cent limit in France (with severe French pressure on Belgium to impose a ceiling as well) and a quota of 2,000 in Italy.

In 1979 600,000 Japanese cars were sold in the Community and 42,000 European made cars exported to Japan. Eighty per cent of the latter were of German origin, mostly Volkswagens.[543] These European cars were sold at prices 200 to 300 per cent above the levels of comparable Japanese models.[544]

On ball-bearings and electronics Japanese imports — in spite of low market shares — felt governmental objections due to effective lobbying efforts of oligopolistic European based MNCs (SKF for bearings, and Philips and Thompson—Brandt for electronics) which dominated the EC

* Compare with Chapter 5, p. 188–9, and Wilkinson (1977). (See reference 540.)

market.[545] This opposition was also partially successful preventing Japanese attempts to set up productive investments in these sectors in the EC, such as in the case of Hitachi in Britain.

The steel and shipping problems, evident since the early 1970s, were both 'resolved' due to massive governmental interventions. European yards received huge state subsidies, while the Japanese producers of ships, because of administrative guidance and mass bankruptcies, were forced to cut their capacities drastically.[546] On steel, the EC and the US introduced basic price systems. The EC in addition forced the Japanese to accept quantitative self-restraints of 1.2m tonnes to 0.7m tonnes.

Barriers to trade

Formal European quota restrictions were maintained on the following products originating from Japan:[547]

Meat, honey and spirits (France), pharmaceuticals and woven silk (Italy), jute fabrics and carpets (France), sacks (France and Ireland), footwear (Italy and Benelux), umbrellas (Italy and France), pig iron (F), electric cables (I), insulators (F and D), canned fish (I and F), dyestuff (F), films (I), tyres (I and Ireland), tiles (I, F and BNL), tableware and cutlery (F, I, D and BNL), steel (F), bolts (BNL), sewing machines (I), ball-bearings (I), generators (I), batteries (I), microscopes (F), electrical measurement instruments (F), watches (F), toys (F and I), TVs and radios (F and I), TV tubes (I), cars and parts (I), motorcycles and parts (I).

While these restrictions were all specifically aimed against Japan and discriminatory in nature, Japan's import controls were applicable to all importers. Most restricted products concerned unprocessed foodstuffs of little interest to the EC. In 1980 the following imports to Japan were subject to quantitative restrictions:[548]

Beef, milk and cream, processed cheese, canned beef and pork, shore fish and cod roe, herring roe, scallops and cuttle fish, edible seaweeds, oranges, fruit paste, canned pineapple and roasted peanuts, fruit and tomato juice, ketchup and tomato sauce, starch and insulin, glucose, wheat, rice, flours, beans, peas and peanuts, processed foods containing sugar, milk, wheat, and seaweeds, coal, hides, and leather footwear.

Among these restrictions, those on processed meat, cheese, confectionery and footwear proved to be effective barriers to competitive Community exports.

Olechowski and Sampson weighted the EC's and Japan's 1976 tariffs on manufactures. They found Japan's weighted rates consistently higher than the EC's.[549]

During the subsequent Tokyo Round Japan agreed to proportionally deeper cuts towards net rates on manufactured imports below EC level. The wild fluctuations between EMS currencies, the dollar and the Yen however are likely to continue to cancel out whatever effect had been intended for tariff rates below 10 to 15 per cent.

The extent of real and alleged NTBs barring access to the Japanese market have been discussed in the context of the Commission's efforts for their removal. Successful initiatives concerned exhaust gas standards and type approval procedures for cars, testing regulations for pharmaceuticals and chemicals, type approvals for gas fittings etc. While these barriers with arduous efforts were gradually reduced, a different sort of NTB philosophy gained currency in Europe concerning the Japanese market. While in the mid-seventies an Orwellian type Big Brother 'Japan Inc.' was fashionable, five years later a slightly more sophisticated version was in vogue: the Japanese work ethic was simply seen as not compatible with the 'post-industrial' values of Western Europe.

Nonetheless there is little doubt that in most European economies, particularly in the white-collar sector, the distribution system and in agriculture, productivity was still higher than in Japan. Wage levels however disproportionally exceeded this (narrowing) advantage and annulled the EC's potentially competitive position.[550]

Fewer structural barriers to more successful European sales concerned the retail prices of import products in Japan. On whisky 47 per cent of the retail price was the traders' mark-up and 41 per cent tariffs and taxes, on French wine the relative figures were 33 per cent and 19 per cent, and on cars 45 per cent and 12 per cent.[551]

When selecting their Japanese import agent, it is up to the European exporter (who could also do the marketing in Japan eventually himself) to choose between comfortable luxury-type marketing and bulk sales at competitive prices requiring higher initial efforts and capital outlays. This, however, is the only method which would have visible effects on the bilateral balance of trade.

Mutual investments

In fiscal 1979, lasting until March 1980, Japanese companies invested about $5 US billion overseas. Direct foreign investment in Japan during the same period was only one tenth of this figure, $540m.[552] The bulk of Japan's investment in Europe continued to be put into marketing infrastructure. But in Ireland, in Britain and to a lesser extent in Belgium, Japanese productive investments gained economic significance.

In Britain the major investments were:[553]
Matsushita Electric, producing colour TVs and audio equipment in Cardiff, £3m capital, since 1974.
Nippon Seiko, producing bearings in Middlesex, £4m capital, since 1974.
Toshiba, making colour TVs in Devon, £10m capital, since 1978.
Other investments were made by Sony and Sekisui Chemcial Company.
In Ireland the following plants were set up:[554]
Fujitsu (computers), £50m, since 1981, 1,000 prospective employment.
Mitsui Mining (manganese dioxide), £9m, 160 employed.
Asahi Chemical (synthetic fibres), £4m, 1,100 employed.
Nippon Electric (integrated circuits), £1m, 200 employed.
Noritake (pottery, tableware), £2m, 800 employed.
Sord Computer Systems in 1981 announced a major investment project for Ireland.

In 1960–78 Japan, after the US and Britain, was the third largest foreign investor in Ireland, providing for 14 per cent of all foreign investment there. Due to the Japanese fear of the EC's protectionism and due to the Irish government's generous investment schemes – organised in comprehensive 'packages' by the IDA in Tokyo – this share of Japanese investment in Ireland is bound to increase. They are encouraged by the numerous successful precedents set by the already existing Japanese facilities, and by their experience of being welcome without having to overcome the resentments of competing domestic producers.

After yet another liberalisation step in Japan in 1976, when information processing industries were opened for foreign investments, only agriculture, forestry, fisheries, mining, oil refining and leather processing remained off limits for foreign direct investors.[555]

In 1980, MOF 'liberalised' her rules on foreign equity investments, abolishing a general 25 per cent limit for the participation of foreign shareholders purchasing into Japanese companies.[556] However, in order to prevent a wholesale take-over of medium sized Japanese blue-chip companies by the booming inflow of OPEC monies, these and several other companies and industries were exempted from the liberalisation as being of 'national interest'. Every industry, whose foreign shareholdings above 25 per cent MOF does not like, risks being defined as a strategic industry.

More significant for Euro–Japanese economic relations however were mutual direct foreign investments. They are of more lasting nature and represent a more genuine commitment to maintaining a stake in each other's camp. Up to the early 1970s US direct investment in Japan accounted for two-thirds of all foreign investment there. But their share, though still dominant, continuously shrank on an ever expanding volume of direct capital inflow into Japan. In fiscal 1977 European companies invested $420m (or 22 per cent of all foreign investment) in Japanese subsidiaries and joint ventures. Most active were Swiss, British and German companies, then the Swedes and the French.[557]

High technology co-operation

Euro—Japanese co-operation was most effective in nuclear energy development and promised similar perspectives in tie-ups in aviation. Projects on the joint production of sophisticated armament systems, due to constitutional constraints in Japan (the present interpretation of the Constitution's Art. 8 forbids both the overseas deployment of Japanese troops and arms exports), so far failed to achieve any tangible chance for realisation.

Japanese restructuring schemes for shipyards provided for a large shift of redundant shipyard workers to Japan's hitherto underdeveloped aircraft industry.[558] The Japanese interest in participating in joint production schemes was the wish to acquire the technological know-how that Japan so far lacked. The European offers concerned the development of a medium-range passenger jet engine by Rolls Royce, and for a medium-sized plane, on which the Japanese aeroplane triumvirate (IHI, Mitsubishi HI and Kawasaki HI) could chose between competing offers from Airbus, Fokker and Dassault. High development costs and the need to secure marketing outlets in the development's initial stages and the convenience of obtaining subcontracted components manufactured in Japan motivated the European offers.[559]

In the nuclear field co-operation between Japan and Britain, and between Japan and France dated back to the late 1950s. Throughout the sixties and seventies nuclear co-operation with Europe — based mostly on regularly renewed 10-year agreements — served the Japanese interest of lessening her dependence on the US for the supply of enriched uranium. France and Britain offered both technological know-how and a steady supply of enriched uranium by reprocessing spent Japanese nuclear fuels in La Hague and Windscale.[560] Japan would pay $1 US billion for these services until 1982,[561] which were soon unpopular among environmentalists for their safety risks — as evident in frequent leaks at both plants — and with the US, which did not like the prospect of seeing plutonium produced during the reprocessing process.[562]

Agreements with Germany provided for the exchange of information on the fast breeder reactor. The agreement was later multilateralised with French, Dutch, Belgian and Italian participation.[563] A similar UK—Japanese pact on technological co-operation on FBRs was renewed in 1980.[564]

286

Decision making in Euro—Japanese relations*

Basic policies

Due to the establishment of its Delegation in Tokyo the Commission succeeded, during 1976—80, in consolidating its role in the formulation of trade policies towards Japan. Without this institution the EC's policies after the 1976—77 and the 1980—81 crises certainly would have ended up more fragmented than they actually were.

The previous section outlined both the distinct national export interests towards Japan as well as the different national regimes on Japanese imports to Europe. On sectoral themes the pursuit of distinct national European policies can be expected. This tendency is aggravated by the near open competition between two distinct trade philosophies in the EC.

A coalition of free traders, the Netherlands, Denmark and Germany, is opposed by 'organised traders', Italy and France. The Commission appears somehow torn between the two: DG I leaning more towards the first and DG III more towards the second position. Commission drafts which claimed to be leading to a coherent EC commercial policy towards Japan failed to reach any consensus between the competing parties. Britain, which under Labour should have been expected to follow a more protectionist line, and under a Thatcherite government to practise free trade towards Japan, in fact did not change its policies perceptibly. While avoiding the vocal militancy of the managed traders it continued to profess free trade ideals, however quietly in various bilateral deals it obtained a series of more or less informal Japanese self restraints on an ever expanding list of import goods.

Belgium and Ireland seemed to have opened a 'mini-faction' of their own. With the Community's highest unemployment rates and without an industrial base to suffer harm from Japanese imports, they did their best to attract Japanese productive investments — denounced by the French as 'yellow submarines' — whose output was not to be subjected to possible EC import controls.

All this created a healthy diversity of policies. They neither sacrificed the EC's industries to a Japanese onslaught (which Britain, Italy and France certainly prevented, avoiding adjustment costs for the time being) nor did they fully shield off Japanese competition. On a continuously free German and EC-fringe market European producers could continue to experience world market style competition on industrial products. It is hardly understandable therefore why some observers[565] denounce with contempt alleged protectionist EC policies towards Japan.

* This section is largely based on interviews held in Tokyo, London and Brussels, 1979—81.

Such policies were never pursued in a coherent fashion in the 1970s.

The coexistence of bilateral national and Community policies was usually described as 'two track' policies. But their overall picture appears rather as a maze of multi- and cross-track policies.

Just to complicate matters, with the global crises following the Iranian revolution and the Soviets' war of annexation in Afghanistan, the US administration reacted with unpredictably unilateralist responses. In 1980 high politics for the first time took substantial and effective dimensions between the EC and Japan. But the experience was not altogether untroubled. Japan still felt excluded from the more intimate Western decision making. Europeans were disappointed by Japan's low profile strategy, seemingly just looking for a position most suitable to her current interests between the European and American options.

High politics co-operation in institutional terms — except for the most senior (minister) level — ran on completely different tracks on both sides than the trade issues.

Japan in both the 1976–77 and the 1980–81 crises found herself on the defensive in diplomatic terms. Also in terms of low politics she stuck to a low profile. This appeared as the most suitable strategy to maintain political goodwill in the EC in order to keep open the outlet for 12 per cent of Japan's exports.

Only under Okita's brief foreign ministership (1979–80) did Japan appear to follow a more political line. In general, however, Japan's prime ministers and other key ministers changed at such speed and frequencies that whenever they had slowly grown accustomed to their Western counterparts, they usually fell victim to some palace revolution in the governmental party.

On the Japanese side, the notion of bureaucratic politics therefore continued with greater and unqualified plausibility. With little change — and regardless of the alarm the Japanese media had given to the current 'crisis' — interministerial proceedings restaged their alliances and frictions which one would expect according to the sectoral direction of the demands made by the Community.

Structures for bilateral decisions

On the EC's side institutions were involved to differing degrees — depending on whether decisions concerned problems of gaining access to the Japanese market or whether pressure mounted 'to do something' about Japanese exports to the EC.

In the first case, the following Community procedure was described by a senior European diplomat in Tokyo:

If we have a problem and think it is of more general nature and of interest to the Community, then we would call the Commission's Delegation here. They would say: 'Oh, it's very interesting' and would start to collect information. Then at the commercial councillors' meetings (attended by the embassies' economic councillors) things are discussed. Whichever country is interested, attends. The Delegation then sends the dossier to Brussels and waits for instructions. Four months later they get them. They go to the Japanese and bring it up. Then at the next HLC a huge delegation comes from Brussels and discusses with the Japanese. The Japanese then say 'O.K., we'll study it.' Then after six months the EC asks them: 'What were the results of your study?'.

Until 1975 only three officials in DG I had been occupied full time with Japan (and with East and South East Asia). Things improved with the opening of the Delegation in Tokyo. But with one head at ambassador level and two first secretaries the Delegation is still understaffed compared to most European embassies. A shortage in manpower and the fact that DG I's senior officials necessarily spend a great deal of time away from Brussels appear as one of the foremost constraints for the Commission's Japanpolitik. This notion is also supported by Wallace and Hill's findings.[566]

A Japanese journalist, Mr Hakoshima, investigating the origins of the March 1979 rabbit hutch paper, suspected the Commission tended to make things 'intentionally more complicated in order to impress its member states with its existence'.[567] This led it to 'playing with fire' in relations with Japan. Hakoshima went on: 'And the architect of the design is a British group which may be called the British mafia within the EC bureaucracy'.

At the time Sir Roy Denman was director general in DG I. Mr Meynell was the head of Directorate B (North America, Australia, New Zealand and Japan). Under him, his compatriot Mr Hardy was in charge of Oceania and Japan. Mr Fielding was the head of the EC's Delegation in Tokyo, and another Englishman, Dr Wilkinson, one of his first secretaries. Nonetheless, the Commissioner, Mr Haferkamp, and his Cabinet were German, as were several other key officials in our story (e.g. Messrs Keck and Lohan). Due to the activism of Mr Davignon, DG III departments with a different set of nationalities were involved in Commission policies towards Japan as well.

However, the allegation of an English mafia was too much of an eye-catcher to go unnoticed in Paris. French diplomats in Tokyo had never hidden their resentment against the Delegation and had tended to handle their affairs with the Japanese 'by ourselves'.

In July 1979, Giscard may have found that the Commission was stressing the problem of whisky too exclusively. At the Tokyo summit amongst debates on the global energy shortage he suddenly argued the case for lowered taxes on cognacs. The Japanese were astonished and the Commission angered.

In general, however, in Tokyo a smooth division of labour is practised between embassies and the Delegation. The EC's assembled bargaining power combined with its slow decision-making machinery qualifies for 'big pushes on limited issues'. The embassies in turn, abundantly staffed, operate parallel with a soft approach on an extremely wide range of issues. They have both closer relations to 'their' exporters and due to longer assignments and older embassy traditions better informal contacts with the Japanese elite.

The formal link between the Delegation and the embassies was established by the meetings of the commercial councillors. They meet according to need, sometimes two or three times a month, depending on the chairman and on the issues to be discussed for the HLC.

The most decisive input for these meetings and for the part of the HLC agenda dealing with market access to Japan is forwarded to them by the EC Steering Committee.[568] It was set up by the European Chambers of Commerce in Tokyo and represents the joint interests of EC businessmen for co-ordinating their efforts against the Japanese administrative barriers impeding their sales. In subcommittees (on export promotion, banking, cars, chemicals, pharmaceuticals, cosmetics, electrical and household appliances, food, liquor, and on trademarks) papers are produced on issues of concern which go beyond isolated incidents. These drafts are presented to the Delegation as information input and later show up on the Commission's HLC shopping list.

The Commission conducts the High Level Consultations (HLC) on the basis of a general Council mandate. Member governments are not directly involved. This mode has advantages and disadvantages. Among the positive effects are that negotiations can be more informal and flexible than they would be in the alternative case of a 40-man Commission—Committee 113 delegation negotiating. The Commission can use her opportunities for self-presentation. But member states essentially remain untied. The Commission cannot promise anything. The evaluation of the talks with the Japanese side rarely escapes the administrative drawers. There is little feed-back with real business life for the Commission in Brussels.

In principle, Committee 113, composed of the national Foreign Ministries' trade directors ('or depends on who is available'), accompanies the whole Japan dossier, including exploratory talks. Since DG I is in permanent negotiation with most countries of the world, the Committee 113 is fairly overworked even at adjoint level. (The director generals at titulaire level are too dignified for most details.) Still, Japan is considered essential enough for Committee 113 — eventually in an ad hoc subgroup — to engage in real discussions of the issues involved. It then makes preliminary decisions and reports to Coreper.

Coreper also decides if no agreement is reached in Committee 113. This evidently does not help much if both have to act according to the same instructions. If during negotiations disagreement persists, then the Commission at times may be free to decide itself.

Coreper, the permanent member state delegation in Brussels, had lost its competence on dealing with Tokyo Round issues for the preparation of the Council's sessions. In order to stage a comeback in the EC's external relations, it attempted to make an impact on relations with Japan as well.*

At all these levels, fairly complicated technical problems have to be discussed (e.g. the export of fruit liquor to Japan). At each of these stages (Commission—Committee 113—Coreper) expertise has to be consulted in each capital, then discussed in Brussels and possibly checked back again with the capitals and their various ministries and industrial associations, a necessarily lengthy process.

While the Commission's HLC agenda is largely decided by DG I's officials themselves, Coreper and the national governments so far successfully vetoed all of the Commission's grand designs for a more comprehensive management of relations with Japan.

For the Council of Ministers Japan had evolved from a fairly marginal issue in 1976 to a topic which the ministers discussed seriously and after preparation in 1980. The same applied to the heads of governments in the European Council.

The November 1980 Council declaration of serious concern[569] on the future development of relations with Japan developed along the following lines:

From July 1980 until September the relative Commission memo — calling for a mandate for comprehensive negotiations with Japan (see also pages 270 and 274) — was subjected to an easy going discussion in Committee 113. It went through the text paragraph by paragraph and collected national comments on the way. Two weeks before the Council's session the annotated document went to the Council's Secretariat. They and the Council's chairman prepared the Council's 'conclusions', i.e. summarised the essentials of the Council's discussion of the subject. The likely Council decision was prepared in an 'avant projet', a draft for a final document. In order to prepare such a document, the following method is usually applied: contested points are left open [put in brackets]. For each such bracket ['crochet'] the Presidency has prepared

---

* Another theory says that while Committee 113 deals more with technical issues, Coreper 'takes a wider view'.

compromise formulae. The Council then discusses the issue and makes political comments for the press. During the debate Committee 113 is present at titulaire level and reflecting the Council's discussion then presents new formulae.

At times it happens that everybody agrees to put all formulae — regardless of the consistency of the resulting text — into the final document. However, in urgent cases, when a solution is not reached, the ministers themselves have to decide on the final 'crochets'. The others have been 'done' by the Committee 113's director generals in communication with their deputy ministers—secretaries of state. The Council's members are politically responsible to their national cabinets. The Commission is present during Council sessions. It could oppose a Committee 113 formula with equal rights. But due to their earlier interaction with the national authorities on its policy proposals, Commission drafts usually already reflect these views.

In turn the Council's Secretariat takes care that proposals to the Council are always 'filtered' out of Commission proposals and end up not too wide of the Commission's original intention.

Interest groups usually use their national channels or approach the Commission directly. DG III is the recipient for the Community industries' complaints about Japanese imports. The Council is not accessible directly but national ministers and delegations may be approached, especially when economic interests are affected immediately — e.g. when tariff rates for certain products are decided.

European exporters having problems in Tokyo do not only attempt to resolve these directly with the Japanese authorities or to report to their national chamber of commerce or to their embassy, they usually inform their head office in Europe as well, which then can become active. It can contact both the national industries' federation, which in turn can inform the relevant European industries' association, and—or contact the national ministry of economics—foreign trade directly. The ministry now may attempt a bilateral solution via the Japanese embassy in the European capital. The European industries' federation or the ministry concerned could also mobilise the Commission. At times, several of these avenues are taken simultaneously and then issues start to lead an administrative life of their own.

On certain machinery exports to Japan, after initial disagreement, confidential and informal inter-industry agreements had been found with MITI's blessing, when suddenly months later in Brussels with forceful publicity effects — which Japanese officials strongly dislike — a tough worded EC demand was presented. It took pains to settle matters discreetly and amicably again.

In our chronological account, demands from unions, industrial federations, and the national and European parliaments were frequently quoted asking for policy changes towards Japan.

At the Community level, on general policies as decided by the Council, they faced severe difficulties to make any policy impact. The EP's debates therefore were (deservedly so, considering the poor levels of information evident during the debates) utterly ineffectual.

At the national level, as far as Japanese imports were concerned, the impact of domestic economic interests is a different story.

In the foregoing we have presented ample evidence for the power of Fiat, SKF, Philips, BL, Renault and the shipyards to have their own or neighbouring governments eliminate or reduce unwanted Far Eastern competition. There were even individuals, like Mr Rosenthal, a North Bavarian porcelain producer and long term Social Democratic MP, who for more than 25 years secured one of the few remaining discriminatory German quota restrictions (on Japanese porcelains with 'European designs').[570]

Co-operation on high politics is managed by different departments, ministries and in entirely different procedures. In the Commission only its Secretariat General is involved in EPC matters and other high politics issues. On the national level the economics–foreign trade ministries or departments are excluded from EPC matters. It is the domain of the political directors and the political departments in the foreign ministries. At the national level, on the ministers' desks, the high politics and the low politics files would meet for the first time. At the Community level it takes none less than the European Council to evaluate them both in a joint perspective.

In Japan, the situation is similar. MITI and the domestic economic ministries have no say on political co-operation with Europe. In Gaimusho (MFA) the economic affairs bureau deals with EC matters. Political relations are organised bilaterally by two separate divisions (the first Western European division dealing with the 'old' six EC countries, and the second Western European division being in charge of the rest of Western Europe).[571]

Gaimusho is considered a weak ministry in the domestic Japanese power wrangle and faces severe difficulties in asserting the predominance of high politics over low policy issues in the interministerial contest for consensus.

The Japanese decisions for export offensives in early 1974 and 1980 accepted the likelihood of future frictions with the EC, the US and other developed trading partners in order to satisfy the domestic producers' demands for growth stimuli (and cheaper oil imports as a side effect) which governmental deficit spending would not be able to provide.[572]

The Japanese themselves are aware of the shortcomings of their political system when it has to respond to external demands:[573]

Japan's government decisions are made not under the leadership of the prime minister but rather on the basis of requests made by subordinates to their senior officials. This process often delays decisions. In dealing with the EC, the Foreign Ministry acts as a window through which MITI, MOF, MAFF ... (and) the EPA participate in the negotiations. However, as these government agencies discuss what position to take against the EC, their contentions are often watered down and rendered noncommittal. To European eyes the Japanese process of reaching a consensus may look inefficient and sometimes tricky.

On other issues, e.g. on policies concerning textiles or shipyards — once a consensus on the need to restructure is reached — the Japanese capacity to adjust to external pressures may seem limitless. This might invite renewed external political demands. One should however, then be aware of the considerable public resentment such 'unjust' demands create in Japan.[574]

On the other hand, Japanese economic ministers are used to receiving nearly daily some foreign minister, delegation or ambassador urging them to invest more in their respective countries, to give more development aid, to moderate Japanese exports and to import more of their handicrafts—wine—bananas—footwear. The Japanese ministers habitually then reply in a politely positive, but noncommittal manner, 'We'll study the matter'. After such conversations, as in the case of Giscard's request on cognac, the matter — without any more binding instructions — is handed down to the desk officers of the ministries in charge. In the cognac issue the officials of MITI, MFA and MOF met and agreed once again that taxes on imported liquor were internal matters, not requiring immediate Japanese responses to foreign demands. In tactical terms the officials agreed to keep the matter dormant (under study) for the time being.*

Had one of the officials, e.g. the man from Gaimusho fearing serious problems in relations with France as the consequence of a negative reply, opposed the others' position, then the files would have been forwarded to their bosses at the next administrative level — the division heads. They would then consult at their level with the other ministries involved and attempt to reach a consensus. In case of failure the next levels would

---

* I asked several officials involved in the question of liquor imports whether they had ever experienced any high-level political pressure, since Suntory (Japan's major whisky producer) has strong ties to LDP notables (the late Mr Ohira, e.g. attended the wedding of the daughter of its owner), not to yield to demands for lowered import taxes. They all seemed genuinely unaware of such pressures. It is more likely, however, that Suntory liaison managers occasionally invite MOF people to a nice 'treat'. This should not be too difficult for a whisky producer in Japan.

be the deputy director generals of the bureaus, then their director generals. Then the Deputy Vice-Ministers would talk, after them the Vice Ministers.

Such conflicts persisted e.g. between MFA and MOF on the question of Japan's development aid, between MFA and MITI on the safeguard issue, and frequently between MFA—MITI versus MOF—MAFF—MHW on the various EC liberalisation demands.

Only once, in autumn 1976, did the Japanese cabinet discuss EC matters. Significantly it did not come to an agreement on the contentious question of which ministry should concede on its import restrictions to alleviate the EC's complaints in the aftermath of the Doko shock. The contents of the Yoshino letter were finally decided after a new meeting of the bureau chiefs.

The fact that political 'leadership' (in its Anglo—American sense) does not exist in Japan explains that grand foreign policy designs, like Ohira's Pacific Basin Community are rather slogans for domestic consumption than seriously pursued effective concepts.

As a result of decision making habits on both sides, negotiations on macroeconomic measures usually drag on until the situation has changed by itself. This is not the case with microeconomic demands. The negotiations on e.g. the admissibility of brass fittings in water appliances in Japan have now entered their fifth year.

Mutual images

Japanese officials repeatedly stressed the difficulty of dealing with the EC and its Council not being 'in power'. In 1977 Mr Ushiba made his misgivings public (p. 243).

The 'rabbit hutch' paper and the European media alleged that Japan was playing one member state against the other. This perception appears as quite biased. Japan, which gradually had learned to appreciate the Commission's basic free trade stand was actually forced to deal bilaterally with the member states. Repeatedly European ministers in Tokyo made public statements, if only their national demands were fulfilled, then their country would uphold Japanese import interests in the EC.

The European display of disunity in Tokyo and the continuous complaints about Japanese competitive superiority greatly helped to reduce the prestige the EC still had enjoyed in the early 1970s. In 1979, a mass survey in Japan revealed that the EC to the Japanese general public seems to be a fairly vague economic association involving France, Britain and Germany, to which the correspondents professed largely positive feelings. This could as well be interpreted as polite indifference, since only 6 per cent could name all nine member states correctly.[575]

On the attitudes of Japan's intellectual and administrative elite — one of its pastimes being the discussion of the 'British disease' and how Japan should most suitably avoid contamination — two impressionistic quotes may suffice:

> The Japanese have a nostalgia for European culture; they would like to reknit cultural ties that once were so close. But they are also exasperated by what they regard as Europe's decline into a museum of culture, into 'an old men's home', whose inhabitants are content to live out their remaining days with whatever comfort they can find. They believe that the Europeans are morose, 'dying spiritually and economically', unwilling to work, unwilling to compete or collaborate. Underneath the strictures remains the desire for good relations with Europe, for a better understanding with partners once considered inspiriting models.[576]

> People in Europe feel that, without detestable international competition, they could enjoy more tranquil days, and that without Datsuns and Toyotas landing in England, the paradise built up by British Leyland might not have been destroyed.[577]

A 1978 Gallup sample in five EC countries surveying mass attitudes about Japan — similar to the picture in Japan in reverse — showed Europeans displaying a uniform picture of indifferent benevolence towards Japan. A large majority of respondents professed exclusively positive images of Japan and of the Japanese, which were, however, based on little actual knowledge or personal contacts.[578]

Among the better informed published opinion 'Japan' as a stimulus solicits two different attitudinal reflexes in Europe. These responses largely depend on one's political and economic credo. For the neoclassical side Norman Macrae wrote in a remarkable report:[579]

> In the past three and a half decades, the Japanese have built a country which has achieved the most exciting sudden leap in all the economic and social history of the world, Now there seems to be a threat that Japan might lose its dynamism through becoming infected with the worst creeping Western disease of the 1980s, which is non-output-oriented bureaucracy. . . .
> It is important for mankind that this should not happen. The thirteenfold increase in Japan's real GNP in the past 30 years

has not only been the fastest economic growth by any big country ever, lighting a beacon down the road that the poor two thirds of the world can most sensibly follow. Contrary to what is said by its detractors, it is growth that has gone to the right places, as shown by the main social indicators.

In parliamentary debates and in the media these positions were usually shared by those with liberal and conservative—liberal beliefs. Competition from Japan was seen as helpful to shake up the stagnant business ways in Europe: to force European labour to settle for wage increases reflecting productivity gains and to promote managerial and technological innovation.

On the more critical side, the view prevailed that Japan had achieved her export competitiveness unfairly at the expense of her working classes and of her social infrastructure and had sacrificed the development of a liberal and individualist society to the continued enforcement of mass-conformist and semi-feudal industrial relations and work ethics. As a consequence, competing on equal terms with Japan would be impossible without endangering the very cultural and societal achievements which advanced Western civilisations represent. At varying degrees of sophistication this position is forwarded both by the nationalist right and the Labourite left.

Conclusion

In political science terms, Professor Hosoya so far has offered the only existing theoretical explanation of the 1976—78 crisis.[580] He claims that EC—Japanese relations had been politicised from October 1976 (the Doko shock) until March 1978 (when the Haferkamp—Ushiba statement was concluded).

This politicisation occurred because the bilateral deficit overstepped a certain limit ($3 US billion — an 'objective' criterion) in combination with three initiating factors:

1 The fusion of the international political with the economic system since 1971.

2 A bilateral 'perception gap': the EC e.g. saw Japanese imports as a political problem, while the Japanese continued to ignore it as such.

3 A conscious 'tactical ploy' of the EC to shock Mr Doko in order to obtain Japanese concessions after earlier attempts had failed.

While these factors were all effective to some extent, my data suggest that, if anything, the Doko shock rather resembled an accidental politicisation — but certainly not a conscious tactical ploy.

The Keidanren visit was neither prepared nor followed up in any planned co-ordinated manner by the foreign policy makers in Europe. In spite of the fact that the 'objective' criterion — the worsening of the bilateral trade balance under conditions of a domestic recession in Europe — in the 1976—77 crisis had lowered the threshold for political interventions in Europe, the politicisation of bilateral relations did not take place.

First, however, we have to define what 'politicisation' actually means. This means an intervention by the political establishment (the elected officials) in the decision-making process — possibly overruling administrative recommendations — by insisting on the implementation of its very own concepts on matters of public and international interest. Admittedly we are moving in a grey zone. Ministerial preferences might already have been anticipated in the drafts forwarded to the political heads, or the ministers' and their staffs' political convictions might be identical. Then conscious decisions would be indicative of politicisation which after considerable debate with due consideration of high politics would change the hitherto pursued direction or quality of relations towards a third party. This does not necessarily mean an actual change in policies. It could also imply giving an alternate scenario serious consideration: i.e. to threaten with ultimata, or to embark on negotiations which could lead to the envisaged new option.

'Politicisation' of an issue, however, is not given if politicians have their own ideas about a matter, but are unable to implement it. In the case of the Community a stalemate between conflicting concepts, e.g. on external relations, would prevent these relations from becoming politicised during the stalemate's duration since compromises — inoffensive to both sides — have necessarily to be sought at the bureaucratic level.

The Doko shock in October 1976 appeared as politicised for essentially three reasons:
1 The first EC—Japanese crisis had reached a critical threshold at which a politicisation might have been possible.
2 Germany was in the middle of a tough federal election campaign. Schmidt, addressing shipyard workers — people who were part of the traditional electoral backbone of his party — had made angry remarks on Japanese pricing policies which appeared to be destroying these men's jobs. Mr Rohwedder, Doko's main partner in Bonn, then dutifully felt obliged to document his master's fury by banging the table.
3 Mr Doko was out to criticise the record of premier Miki — who also had to face an election campaign — and of his faction member Komoto, who happened to be MITI minister, whose anti-big business policies Doko did not like. He therefore did his best to dramatise his European experience.

There evidently was a political intervention. But it appeared entirely unplanned, and its follow-up in Europe seemed sporadic at best. Surprised by the outburst of public concern in Japan at Doko's dramatic story, during a luncheon Commissioner Gundelach felt encouraged to put a spontaneous ultimatum before Mr Yoshino, a visiting Deputy Foreign Minister. However, since the deadline was measured too short, Commission officials were soon at pains to cancel the 'ultimatum' and to contain whatever damage might have occurred from this second 'accidental politicisation'.

During the present second EC—Japan crisis (1980—81) following its cyclical pattern again a critical threshold has been reached. 'Accidents' of kind experienced in 1976 have not occurred yet at Community level. The threshold however still appears close enough not to exclude the possibility of a policy shift in the Council of Ministers. This would mean that in a possible trade off — in exchange for Franco—Italian concessions in other fields — the 'free trade faction' (Germany, Denmark and the Netherlands) abandoning their stand against Community-wide import controls on selective Japanese products (cars, electronics and numerically controlled machine tools being likely candidates). This has not happened yet. The 'depoliticising' stalemate on the Japan issue continues in the Councils.

If we define bureaucratic politics as the pursuit of policies conceived, prepared, decided in essence and implemented by senior bureaucrats and conducted in a bureaucratic style — having both Kafkaesque (absurd) and Weberian (rational) elements — then Euro—Japanese relations until 1981 were conducted as bureaucratic politics.

The incidence of high politics co-operation in 1980 should not confuse this picture. These exchanges had been made possible by the coincidence of:

1 Very dramatic crises in which Europe and Japan had identical interests.

2 A politically weak and unilateralist US administration.

3 A more internationally-minded Japanese cabinet under premier Ohira, in which an alert academic, Mr Okita, played an exceptionally active role.

While this high politics co-operation certainly was politicised, it did not have any spill over into the mainstay of low politics bilateral relations:

1 High politics co-operation was ad hoc and singular.

2 The respective bureaucratic machineries operated at different levels and in different institutions.

3 The experiences gained in high politics co-operation were not altogether sweet (Japanese still felt excluded, and the Europeans dissatisfied with the lack of any constructive input from the Japanese side).

4 The fact that economic diplomacy was conducted as bureaucratic politics by this politics' very nature (compartementalisation, orien-

tation at precedents etc.) simply did not allow for policy references that were not materially connected with the ongoing files.

For speech writers and academics the high–low politics nexus is obvious. But for the officials involved these matters are nearly completely unrelated.

Bureaucratic decision making in bilateral relations in the late 1970s on both sides succeeded in improving the conflict management mechanism that had been developed in earlier times. The communication channels established between official Japan and official EC were widened and intensified. Bilateral policies on both sides encouraged structures for mutually vested interests in each other's camp (via joint ventures, technological co-operation, cross investments etc.).

Lacking both the potential brilliance and the likely disasters of politicised bilateral relations, Euro–Japanese bureaucratic politics 1976–1981 *summa summarum* showed a positive balance in mastering two serious crises under adverse conditions and in difficult times.

References

1 Hakoshima, Shinichi. Mutual Ignorance and Misunderstanding – Causes of Japan–EC Economic Disputes. *Japan Quarterly 26*, 1979, 481-88, p. 482.
2 Hosoya, Chihiro. Relations between the European Communities and Japan. *Journal of Common Market Studies 18*, 1979, 157–74, p. 160.
3 Hakoshima. 1979. Loc. cit.
4 *Financial Times*, 11.3.1976.
5 *Japan Times*, 10.5.1976.
6 EC Delegation Tokyo. Typescript. Automobile Mission Program in Tokyo.
7 *The Economist*, 28.2.1976.
8 *The Economist*, 15.5.1976.
9 EC Delegation. *EC News*, 12.5.1976.
10 *The Economist*, 15.5.1976; *Agence Europe*, 18.5.1976 and 20.5.1976.
11 Commission. COM (76) 138 final, 6.4.1976.
12 *Official Journal of the EC*. No. L 219, 12.8.1976.
13 *Japan Times*, 12.6.1976.
14 *Japan Times*, 2.5.1976.
15 *Agence Europe*, 4.6.1976; *Financial Times*, 12.6.1976.
16 *The Times* and *Financial Times*. 17.6.1976.
17 *International Herald Tribune*, 16.6.1976.

18 *Agence Europe*, 12.7.1976.
19 *Frankfurter Allgemeine Zeitung*, 7.8.1976.
20 EC Delegation. Typescript. Visit of Mr Finn-Olav Gundelach to Japan — Schedule; *Agence Europe*, 22.7.1976.
21 *Japan Times* and *The Times*, 15.7.1976.
22 *Le Figaro*, 14 and 15.8.1976.
23 *The Economist*, 7.8.1976.
24 *Le Monde*, 3.8.1976.
25 *Financial Times*, 30.7.1976.
26 *Frankfurter Allgemeine Zeitung*, 2.9.1976.
27 *Financial Times*, 21.9.1976.
28 *The Times*, 22.9.1976.
29 *Japan Times*, 22.9.1976.
30 *Financial Times*, 23.9.1976.
31 *Agence Europe*, 2.9.1976.
32 *Agence Europe*, 20.8.1976 and 8.9.1976.
33 *Official Journal*. Debates of Parliament. 1976—77, pp. 106—8.
34 *Japan Times*, 1.10.1976.
35 Hakoshima. 1979. Op. cit., p. 482.
36 *Guardian*, 14.10.1976.
37 *The Times*, 19.10.1976.
38 *Financial Times*, 1.10.1976.
39 *The Times*, 7.10.1976; *Agence Europe*, 5.10.1976.
40 *The Economist*, 16.10.1976.
41 *The Times*, 26.10.1976.
42 *Financial Times*, 28.9.1976.
43 *The Times*, 11.10.1976.
44 *Daily Telegraph*, 19.10.1976.
45 *Japan Times*, 21.10.1976.
46 *The Times*, 19.10.1976.
47 *Guardian*, 20.10.1976.
48 *Japan Times*, 23.10.1976.
49 *International Herald Tribune*, 22 and 24.10.1976.
50 *Financial Times*, 20.10.1976.
51 *Le Monde*, 27.10.1976.
52 *Financial Times*, 23.10.1976; *The Times*, 27.10.1976.
53 *Agence Europe*, 26.10.1976.
54 *The Times*, 27.10.1976.
55 *Japan Times*, 31.10.1976.
56 *Japan Times*, 3.11.1976.
57 *The Times*, 28.10.1976.
58 *Financial Times*, 29.10.1976.
59 *International Herald Tribune* and *Japan Times*, 5.11.1976.
60 *Japan Times* and *The Times*, 1.11.1976.

61 *Financial Times*, 6.11.1976.
62 *International Herald Tribune*, 6 and 7.11.1976.
63 *Japan Times*, 6.11.1976.
64 *Financial Times*, 9.11.1976.
65 *The Times*, 10.11.1976.
66 *The Times*, 10.11.1976.
67 *The Times*, 26.10.1976.
68 *Financial Times*, 29.10.1976.
69 *The Times*, 26.10.1976.
70 *Agence Europe*, 8 and 9.11.1976.
71 *Frankfurter Allgemeine*, 13.10.1976 and 19.10.1976.
72 *Financial Times*, 18.10.1976; *Official Journal* No. C268/2, 13.11.197
73 *Agence Europe*, 10.11.1976; *Frankfurter Allgemeine Zeitung*,
    12.11.1976.
74 *The Economist*, 13.11.1976.
75 *Financial Times*, 11.11.1976.
76 *The Times*, 25.10.1976.
77 *Japan Times*, 7.11.1976.
78 *Financial Times*, 13.11.1976.
79 *Agence Europe*, 12.11.1976.
80 *Japan Times*, 14.11.1976.
81 *Japan Times*, 13.11.1976.
82 *Japan Times*, 13.11.1976.
83 *The Economist*, 13.11.1976.
84 *Agence Europe*, 15.11.1976.
85 *Agence Europe*, 15.11.1976.
86 Commission. Note BIO (76) 391, 17.11.1976.
87 *Financial Times*, 17.11.1976.
88 Commission. Note BIO (76) 391, 17.11.1976.
89 *International Herald Tribune*, 17.11.1976.
90 *Financial Times*, 18.11.1976.
91 Commission. Note BIO (76) 391, 17.11.1976.
92 *International Herald Tribune*, 17.11.1976.
93 *Japan Times*, 18.11.1976.
94 EC Delegation, Telex No. 516 (RV), 19.11.1976; *Japan Times*,
    19.11.1976.
95 EC Delegation. Telex No. 501 (RV), 15.11.1976; Telex 519 (RV),
    22.11.1976.
96 *The Times*, 22.11.1976.
97 EC Delegation. Telex 515 (RV), 19.11.1976; *Japan Times*,
    19.11.1976.
98 *Japan Times*, 18.11.1976.
99 EC Delegation. Telex 518 (RV), 19.11.1976.
100 *Guardian* and *Financial Times*, 20.11.1976.

101 *Japan Times*, 24.11.1976.
102 *Japan Times*, 19.11.1976.
103 *Guardian*, 23.11.1976.
104 *Guardian*, 24.11.1976.
105 *Daily Telegraph* and *Japan Times*, 24.11.1976.
106 Reprinted in: Japan Information Centre. *British Trade with Japan.* London. January 1977, p. 29.
107 Translated in *Japan Times*, 27.11.1976.
108 *Guardian* 26.11.1976.
109 *Agence Europe*, 24.11.1976; *Guardian*, 26.11.1976.
110 *Bulletin des Communautés Européenes 11*, 1976, p. 11.
111 *Financial Times*, 1.12.1976.
112 *Japan Times*, 1.12.1976.
113 *Agence Europe*, 16.12.1976.
114 *Official Journal*, No C 6/70, 10.1.1977.
115 *Financial Times*, 8.12.1976.
116 *Financial Times*, 14.12.1976; *Le Monde*, 15.12.1976.
117 *Agence Europe*, 16.12.1976.
118 *Japan Times*, 23.12.1976.
119 *The Oriental Economist.* December 1976, p. 27.
120 *Guardian*, 4.1.1977.
121 *Agence Europe*, 12.1.1977.
122 *Financial Times*, 13.1.1977.
123 *The Economist*, 15.1.1977.
124 *Guardian*, 14.1.1977.
125 *The Times*, 25.1.1977.
126 *Agence Europe*, 18.1.1977.
127 *Agence Europe*, 19.1.1977.
128 *Guardian* and *The Times*, 22.1.1977.
129 *The Times*, 7.2.1977.
130 *Agence Europe*, 8.2.1977 and 9.2.1977.
131 *The Times*, 9.2.1977.
132 *The Times*, 10.2.1977.
133 *Agence Europe*, 23.2.1977.
134 *The Economist*, 19.2.1977.
135 *Agence Europe*, 5.2.1977.
136 Commission. *Press Release.* IP(77)38, 9.2.1977.
137 *Agence Europe*, 10.2.1977.
138 *Official Journal* No. L 34/60, 5.2.1977.
139 *Far Eastern Economic Review*, 18.2.1977; *Japan Times*, 12.2.1977.
140 *Japan Times*, 9.2.1977.
141 *Far Eastern Economic Review*, 18.2.1977.
142 *International Herald Tribune*, 9.2.1977; *Guardian*, 10.2.1977.
143 *New York Times*, 9.2.1977.

144 *Guardian*, 8.2.1977.
145 *Japan Times*, 4.3.1977.
146 *Agence Europe* and *International Herald Tribune*, 1.3.1977.
147 *Japan Times*, 4.3.1977.
148 *Asahi Evening News*, 3.3.1977.
149 *Japan Times*, 18.3.1977; *Agence*, 15.3.1977.
150 European Parliament. Working Document 1976–77. *Rapport on Economic and Trade Relations between the EC and Japan.* Rapporteur: Jan Baas. Document 570/76. 2.3.1977, p. 5.
151 *International Herald Tribune*, 16.3.1977.
152 *Agence Europe*, 25.3.1977.
153 Typescript. Statement by the European Council on Relations with Japan. Rome, 26.3.1977.
154 Translated in *Japan Times*, 1.4.1977.
155 *Agence Europe*, 24.3.1977; *Japan Times*, 25.3.1977.
156 *Financial Times*, 15.3.1977.
157 *The Times*, 13.4.1977 and 15.4.1977.
158 *The Times*, 19.4.1977 and 30.4.1977.
159 *The Times*, 20.5.1977.
160 *Agence Europe*, 9.5.1977.
161 *Far Eastern Economic Review*, 20.5.1977.
162 Commission. Note BIO (77) 183, and: Note d'information DG X, No. 146/77.
163 *Agence Europe*, 20.5.1977.
164 *Agence Europe*, 21.4.1977.
165 *Japan Times*, 20.5.1977.
166 *Financial Times*, 20.5.1977.
167 *Japan Times*, 21.5.1977.
168 *Japan Economic Journal*, 31.5.1977; *Le Monde*, 31.5.1977.
169 Banque International de Luxembourg S.A. *Bulletin Financier*, 1.6.1977, p. 3.
170 *Japan Times*, 25.5.1977.
171 *Japan Times*, 3.6.1977.
172 *Financial Times*, 3.6.1977.
173 *Japan Times*, 29.7.1977.
174 *Agence Europe*, 23.6.1977.
175 *Japan Times*, 9.7.1977.
176 *Japan Times*, 10.6.1977.
177 *Agence Europe*, 22.6.1977.
178 Commission. COM (77) 322 final.
179 *Official Journal* No. L 196, 3.8.1977; *Agence Europe*, 26.7.1977.
180 *Financial Times*, 22.9.1977.
181 Court of Justice of the European Communities. *Judgement of the Court, Case 120/77.* (Translation). Luxembourg, 29.4.1979.

182 *Financial Times*, 1.7.1977.
183 *Süddeutsche Zeitung*, 2 and 3.7.1977.
184 *Financial Times*, 28.7.1977.
185 *Japan Times*, 7.7.1977; *Agence Europe*, 19.7.1977.
186 *Japan Times*, 21.7.1977; *Agence Europe*, 22.7.1977.
187 *The Times*, 22.7.1977.
188 *Japan Times*, 7.9.1977; *Guardian*, 13.9.1977.
189 *Agence Europe*, 12.9.1977; *Japan Economic Journal*, 20.9.1977.
190 *Japan Economic Journal*, 20.9.1977.
191 *The Economist*, 3.9.1977.
192 *Financial Times*, 8.9.1977.
193 *Japan Economic Journal*, 16.8.1977.
194 *The Economist*, 17.9.1977.
195 Commission. Press Release IP (77) 239, 11.10.1977.
196 *The Times*, 13.10.1977.
197 *Financial Times* and *Japan Times*, 14.10.1977.
198 *The Economist*, 15.10.1977.
199 *Financial Times*, 13.10.1977.
200 *The Economist*, 12.11.1977.
201 *Financial Times*, 9.11.1977.
202 Typescript. OECD Working Party 6, Meeting in Tokyo, 12.11.1977.
203 *Observer Foreign News Service*, 1.11.1977.
204 *Agence Europe*, 30.11.1977.
205 *Financial Times*, 30.11.1977.
206 *New York Times*, 1.12.1977.
207 *The Economist*, 3.12.1977.
208 *The Times*, 15.12.1977.
209 Generalsekratariat des Rates der EG. *25, Überblick über die Tätigkeit des Rates. 1.1.1977 — 31.12.1977.* Luxembourg, 1978, p. 174.
210 *Agence Europe*, 12 and 13.12.1977.
211 Sayle, Murray. Resisting the Japanese Invasion. *New Statesman 95*, 207–9, 17.2.1978.
212 *Financial Times*, 15.12.1977.
213 *The Times*, 17.12.1977.
214 *Agence Europe*, 16.12.1977.
215 *Japan Times*, 17.12.1977.
216 *Japan Times*, 22.12.1977.
217 *Financial Times*, 1.12.1977.
218 *Financial Times*, 8.12.1977.
219 *Japan Economic Journal*, 29.11.1977.
220 *Agence Europe*, 15.12.1977, 2.1.1978, 10.1.1978.
221 *Japan Times*, 7.1.1978.
222 *Japan Times*, 13.1.1978.

223 *Financial Times*, 13.1.1978.
224 *The Economist*, 21.1.1978.
225 *Official Journal*. Debates of the European Parliament, 20.1.1978, p. 227.
226 *Japan Times*, 30.1.1978.
227 *Agence Europe*, 30 and 31.1.1978; *Japan Times*, 29.1.1978.
228 Ibid.
229 *The Times*, 28.1.1978.
230 *Japan Times*, 28.1.1978.
231 *Japan Times*, 27.1.1978.
232 *Japan Times*, 31.1.1978.
233 *International Herald Tribune*, 28 and 29.1.1978.
234 *Japan Times*, 1.2.1978.
235 *Le Figaro*, 4 and 5.2.1978.
236 *Agence Europe*, 4.2.1978.
237 *Japan Times*, 4.2.1978.
238 Generalsekretariat des Rates der EG. *26, Überblick über die Tätigkeit des Rates, 1978.* Luxembourg, 1979, p. 168.
239 *Agence Europe*, 7.2.1978.
240 *International Herald Tribune*, 10.2.1978.
241 *International Herald Tribune*, 11 and 12.2.1978.
242 *Agence Europe*, 13.2.1978.
243 *International Herald Tribune*, 9.2.1978.
244 *Japan Times*, 22.2.1978.
245 *Look Japan*, 17.2.1978.
246 *Japan Times*, 9.2.1978.
247 *International Herald Tribune*, 14.2.1978.
248 *Japan Times*, 15.2.1978.
249 *Financial Times*, 16.2.1978.
250 Translated in *Japan Times*, 10.2.1978.
251 Translated in *Japan Times*, 19.2.1978.
252 *Japan Times*, 14.2.1978.
253 *Japan Economic Journal*, 14.2.1978.
254 *The Economist*, 11.2.1978.
255 *Japan Times*, 25.2.1978.
256 *Japan Times*, 27.2.1978.
257 *Japan Economic Journal*, 7.3.1978.
258 *International Herald Tribune*, 25 and 26.2.1978.
259 Ibid.
260 *Financial Times*, 28.2.1978.
261 *Agence Europe* and *Japan Times*, 27.2.1978.
262 *Financial Times*, 2.3.1978.
263 *Japan Times*, 1.3.1978.
264 *Financial Times*, 2.3.1978.

265 *Agence Europe*, 8.3.1978.
266 *International Herald Tribune*, 8.3.1978.
267 *The Times*, 15.3.1978.
268 *Financial Times*, 15.3.1978.
269 Typescript. Programme for 14 and 17.3.1978 EC—Japan Consultations.
270 *Japan Economic Journal*, 14.3.1978.
271 *Japan Times*, 18.3.1978.
272 *Financial Times*, 21.3.1978.
273 *Japan Times*, 17.3.1978.
274 *The Times*, 18.3.1978.
275 *The Times*, 1.3.1978.
276 *Financial Times*, 21.3.1978.
277 *Japan Times*, 21.3.1978.
278 *Japan Times*, 23.3.1978.
279 *Agence Europe*, 24.3.1978.
280 *Financial Times*, 23.3.1978.
281 Commission. *Press Release.* IP (78) 70. EEC—Japan Joint Statement 28.3.1978.
282 *Neue Zürcher Zeitung*, 26 and 27.3.1978; *Japan Times*, 24.3.1978.
283 *The Times*, 25.3.1978.
284 *Japan Times*, 25.3.1978.
285 *The Economist*, 1.4.1978.
286 *The Oriental Economist*, 46, March 1978, p. 3.
287 *Japan Times*, 19.3.1978.
288 *Agence Europe*, 20.3.1978.
289 *Japan Times*, 24.3.1978.
290 *Le Monde*, 26 and 27.3.1978.
291 European Community Information Service, Washington D.C. *Background Note*, No. 6, 5.4.1978.
292 Commission. Telex 36.508 HER, Brussels 28.3.1978.
293 *Agence Europe*, 28.3.1978.
294 Wacziarg, Alain. Marché japonais: Quelle ouverture? *L'usine nouvelle*, 30.3.1978, p. 51.
295 *Neue Zürcher Zeitung*, 1.4.1978.
296 *Agence Europe*, 6.4.1978.
297 *Agence Europe*, 28.3.1978.
298 *International Herald Tribune*, 5.4.1978.
299 *Bulletin of the European Communities*, No. 3, 1978, p. 14.
300 *Financial Times*, 13.4.1978.
301 *Official Journal*, Debates of the European Parliament, 11.4.1978, p. 69.
302 Ibid.
303 *Agence Europe*, 20.4.1978; *Japan Times*, 21.4.1978.

304 *Japan Times,* 23.3.1978.
305 *Japan Times,* 29.4.1978.
306 *Agence Europe,* 9.5.1978.
307 *Financial Times,* 19.4.1978.
308 *Financial Times,* 31.5.1978.
309 *Financial Times,* 19.4.1978.
310 *Financial Times,* 21.1.1978.
311 *The Times,* 24.4.1978.
312 *The Economist,* 22.4.1978.
313 *Far Eastern Economic Review,* 19.5.1978.
314 *Japan Economic Journal,* 2.5.1978; *Financial Times,* 21.4.1978.
315 *Agence Europe,* 16.5.1978.
316 *Financial Times,* 10.5.1978.
317 *Far Eastern Economic Review,* 26.5.1978; *Japan Economic Journal,* 20.6.1978.
318 *Japan Economic Journal,* 13.6.1978.
319 Commission. Note BIO (78) aux bureaux nationaux, 16.5.1978; *Agence Europe,* 16.5.1978.
320 *Japan Economic Journal,* 20.6.1978.
321 GATT. *Statement by the Delegations of Developing Countries on Current Status of Tokyo Round Negotiations, 14.7.1978,* MTN/INF/38. 17.7.1978.
322 Commission. Note BIO (78) 222 aux bureaux nationaux, 20.6.1978; *Agence Europe,* 20.6.1978.
323 *Financial Times,* 22.6.1978.
324 Ibid.
325 *Agence Europe,* 28.6.1978.
326 *Agence Europe,* 13.7.1978.
327 *Agence Europe,* 18.7.1978.
328 *Agence Europe,* 20.7.1978
329 *International Herald Tribune,* 20.7.1978.
330 European Parliament. *Report on the Results of the Visit by the Delegation of the EP to Japan in October 1978.* Working Documents 1978–79, No. 666/77. Rapporteur Jan Baas. 1979, p. 17.
331 *Japan Economic Journal,* 26.9.1978.
332 European Parliament. 1979. Op. cit., p. 8.
333 Ibid., p. 17.
334 Schmidt, Helmut. Perspektiven der deutsch–Japanischen Zusammenarbeit. Vortrag am 11.10.1978 vor der Deutsch–Japanischen Gesellschaft. *Nichidoku Geppo* No. 302, Februar 1979.
335 *Frankfurter Allgemeine Zeitung,* 11.10.1978 and 16.10.1978.
336 *Japan Times,* 12.10.1978.
337 *Japan Times,* 19.10.1978 and 23.10.1978.
338 *Le Monde,* 5 and 6.11.1978.

339 *Le Monde,* 13.7.1978.
340 Japanese Embassy London. *Japan Information Bulletin 25,* No. 11, November 1978, p. 78.
341 *Japan Times,* 11.11.1978.
342 *The Times,* 9.11.1978.
343 *The Economist,* 7.10.1978.
344 *Die Zeit,* 27.10.1978.
345 *Japanese Embassy London.* 1978. Op. cit., p. 81.
346 Commission. Note BIO (78) 444 aux bureaux nationaux, 6.12.1978.
347 *Guardian,* 12.12.1978.
348 *Japan Times,* 10.12.1978.
349 Generalsekretariat des Rates der EG. 1979. Op. cit., p. 169.
350 Hubert, Agnes. Dialogue Communauté—Japon: A armes égales. *Revue du Marché Commun* No. 222, December 1978, 547–9, p. 549.
351 *Guardian,* 29.11.1978.
352 *Financial Times,* 8.6.1978.
353 *The Oriental Economist 47,* February 1979.
354 *Financial Times,* 31.1.1979.
355 *Frankfurter Allgemeine Zeitung,* 18.1.1979 and 20.1.1979.
356 *Agence Europe,* 9.2.1978.
357 *Financial Times* and *Agence Europe,* 2.3.1979.
358 Generalsekretariat des Rates der EG. 27, *Überblick über die Tätigkeit des Rates 1979.* Luxembourg 1980, p. 161.
359 *Japan Economic Journal,* 20.3.1979.
360 *Japan Times,* 17.3.1979.
361 *Japan Times Weekly,* 24.3.1979.
362 *Kyodo,* 22.3.1979.
363 *Japan Times Weekly,* 31.3.1979.
364 *Agence Europe,* 26 and 27.3.1979.
365 Typescript. Following Introductory Remarks by Mr Haferkamp, Vice President of the Commission of the EC, at the press conference in Tokyo, 28 March 1979.
366 *Japan Times,* 27.3.1979.
367 Ibid.
368 *Japan Times,* 29.3.1979.
369 *International Herald Tribune,* 30.3.1979.
370 *Financial Times,* 30.3.1979.
371 *Guardian* and *Financial Times,* 30.3.1979; *Economist,* 9.4.1979.
372 Ibid.
373 The paper was published in a clumsy retranslation from a French version in the *Japan Times* in six instalments from 11.4.1979 to 16.4.1979.
374 *Time,* 30.4.1979.

375 *Die Zeit*, 6.4.1979.
376 *Guardian*, 31.3.1979.
377 *Financial Times*, 31.3.1979.
378 *Japan Economic Journal*, 10.7.1979.
379 *Agence Europe*, 23 and 24.4.1979.
380 *Guardian*, 19.4.1979.
381 *Financial Times*, 5.5.1979.
382 *Financial Times*, 4.5.1979; *Agence Europe*, 3.5.1979.
383 *Japan Times* and *Financial Times*, 5.5.1979.
384 *Financial Times*, 8.5.1979.
385 *Japan Times*, 10.5.1979.
386 *Japan Times*, 4.5.1979.
387 *Financial Times*, 12.5.1979.
388 *Japan Times*, 12.5.1979 and 22.5.1979; *Financial Times*, 23.5.1979.
389 *Japan Times*, 19.5.1979.
390 Commission. Note BIO (79) 163 aux bureaux nationaux, 14.5.1979.
391 *Agence Europe*, 28.5.1979.
392 *Japan Times*, 29.5.1979.
393 *Agence Europe*, 12.6.1979.
394 Commission. Communication from the Commission to the European Council: Relations with Japan. Brussels, 14.6.1979.
395 Commission. Telex 28.567, 22.6.1979.
396 Commission. Information P—96. *Promotion of Community Exports to Japan*. October 1979; *Japan Times Weekly*, 27.10.1979.
397 EC Delegation. *EC News*, PR 79/51 (E).
398 *Agence Europe*, 22 and 23.10.1979.
399 *Japan Economic Journal*, 23.10.1979.
400 *Japan Times*, 29.3.1979.
401 *Japan Economic Journal*, 25.9.1979.
402 *Japan Times*, 8.12.1979.
403 *Asahi Evening News*, 21.12.1979.
404 *Japan Times*, 29.4.1979.
405 *Japan Times*, 28.11.1979.
406 EC Delegation. Telex 732, 3.12.1979.
407 *Neue Zürcher Zeitung*, 4.12.1979.
408 EC Delegation. Telex 722, 29.11.1979.
409 EC Delegation. Telex 732, 3.12.1979.
410 EC Delegation. Telex 725, 29.11.1979.
411 *Agence Europe*, 3.4.1979; *Financial Times*, 21.9.1979.
412 *Official Journal* No. 235/2, 18.9.1979; Commission. Note BIO (79) 283 to the National Offices.
413 *Japan Times*, 2.12.1979.
414 *Japan Times*, 9.12.1979.
415 *Japan Times*, 22.1.1980.

416 *The Times*, 4.2.1980.
417 *Japan Times*, 23.1.1980.
418 *Agence Europe*, 15.2.1980.
419 *Japan Times*, 30.1.1980.
420 *Japan Times*, 15.2.1980.
421 *Japan Times*, 22.2.1980.
422 *Japan Times*, 24.3.1980.
423 *Financial Times*, 6.2.1980.
424 e.g. in the *Guardian*, 25.1.1980.
425 *Financial Times*, 12.3.1980.
426 *Japan Economic Journal*, 29.1.1980; *International Herald Tribune*, 22.1.1980.
427 *Financial Times*, 12.3.1980.
428 *The Times*, 16.2.1980.
429 *The Times*, 22.2.1980.
430 *Financial Times*, 11.2.1980.
431 *Neue Zürcher Zeitung*, 20.3.1980.
432 *Süddeutsche Zeitung*, 7.3.1980.
433 *Le Monde*, 5.3.1980.
434 *Die Zeit*, 4.4.1980.
435 *Financial Times*, 8.4.1980.
436 *Sunday Telegraph*, 13.4.1980; *Financial Times*, 10.4.1980.
437 Ibid.
438 *Le Monde*, 9.4.1980.
439 *Japan Times*, 28.2.1980.
440 *Japan Times*, 16.3.1980.
441 *Japan Times*, 28.3.1980.
442 *Japan Times*, 23.3.1980.
443 *Japan Times*, 19.4.1980 and 20.4.1980.
444 *Japan Times*, 19.3.1980.
445 *Frankfurter Allgemeine Zeitung*, 2.4.1980.
446 *Asahi Shimbun*, 23.3.1980.
447 *Asahi Shimbun* (evening edition), 24.3.1980.
448 *Frankfurter Allgemeine Zeitung*, 2.4.1980.
449 *Süddeutsche Zeitung*, 25.3.1980; *Der Spiegel*, 7.4.1980.
450 *Japan Times*, 19.4.1980.
451 *Japan Times*, 24.4.1980.
452 *Japan Times*, 12.4.1980.
453 *Japan Times*, 20.4.1980 and 24.4.1980.
454 *Japan Times*, 17.4.1980.
455 *Japan Times*, 26.4.1980.
456 *Frankfurter Allgemeine Zeitung*, 9.5.1980; *Japan Times*, 13.5.1980.
457 *Japan Times*, 13.5.1980.
458 *Japan Times*, 23.5.1980.

459 *Guardian*, 14.4.1980.
460 *Financial Times*, 22.5.1980.
461 *Japan Times*, 9.5.1980.
462 *Frankfurter Allgemeine Zeitung*, 20.5.1980.
463 *The Times*, 22.5.1980.
464 *Guardian*, 22.5.1980.
465 *The Times*, 13.6.1980.
466 *The Economist*, 12.7.1980.
467 *Financial Times*, 13.6.1980.
468 *Japan Times*, 4.6.1980 and 15.6.1980.
469 *Japan Times*, 22.6.1980, 25.6.1980 and 26.6.1980.
470 *Japan Times*, 22.6.1980.
471 *Tokyo Shimbun* and *Asahi Shimbun*, as translated in: *Japan Times*, 5.7.1980 and 10.7.1980.
472 *Guardian*, 7.7.1980.
473 *Die Zeit*, 4.7.1980.
474 *Financial Times*, 15.7.1980.
475 *Guardian*, 10.7.1980.
476 *The Times*, 15.7.1980.
477 *Japan Times*, 4.7.1980.
478 *Japan Times*, 8.7.1980.
479 *Der Spiegel*, 21.7.1980.
480 *Japan Times*, 12.7.1980.
481 *Financial Times*, 23.7.1980.
482 *The Times*, 23.7.1980; *Japan Times*, 24.7.1980.
483 *Japan Times*, 17.6.1980.
484 *Japan Times*, 19.7.1980.
485 *Neue Zürcher Zeitung*, 20 and 21.7.1980; *International Herald Tribune*, 14.8.1980.
486 *Japan Times*, 22.9.1980.
487 *Asahi Evening News*, 18.9.1980.
488 *Japan Times*, 21.9.1980.
489 *Japan Times*, 10.9.1980.
490 *Japan Times*, 12.9.1980.
491 *Financial Times*, 1.10.1980.
492 *Japan Times*, 9.10.1980.
493 *Financial Times*, 9.10.1980.
494 *Japan Times*, 4.10.1980.
495 *Financial Times*, 14.10.1980.
496 *Japan Times*, 10.10.1980 and 5.10.1980.
497 *Japan Times*, 4.10.1980.
498 *Financial Times*, 14.10.1980.
499 *Financial Times*, 28.10.1980.
500 *Financial Times*, 14.10.1980.

501 *Japan Times*, 29.10.1980.
502 Translated in *Japan Times*, 9.11.1980.
503 *Financial Times*, 5.11.1980.
504 *Japan Times*, 14.11.1980.
505 *Financial Times*, 7.11.1980.
506 Mission of Japan to the European Communities. Statement by the Minister for Foreign Affairs of Japan, Mr M Ito, on the Economic Relations between Japan and the European Community. 17.11.1980.
507 *Japan Times*, 18.11.1980.
508 *Neue Zürcher Zeitung*, 19.11.1980.
509 *Japan Times*, 19.10.1980.
510 *Die Zeit*, 28.11.1980.
511 *Businessweek*, 24.11.1980.
512 *Revue du Marché Commun* No. 243, Janvier 1981, p. 51.
513 *Japan Times*, 28.11.1980.
514 *Financial Times*, 14.11.1980.
515 *Japan Economic Journal*, 29.7.1980.
516 *Die Zeit*, 28.11.1980.
517 *Financial Times*, 15.11.1980.
518 *Financial Times*, 20.11.1980.
519 *Japan Times*, 4.12.1980.
520 *Der Spiegel*, 8.12.1980; *Japan Times*, 31.12.1980.
521 *Japan Times*, 23.12.1980.
522 *Japan Times*, 29.11.1980.
523 *Japan Times*, 13.12.1980 and 12.12.1980.
524 *Japan Times*, 14.12.1980 and 17.12.1980.
525 *Japan Times*, 19.12.1980
526 *Japan Times*, 3.9.1980.
527 *Japan Times*, 19.11.1980.
528 *Asahi Evening News*, 27.9.1980.
529 *Financial Times*, 26.11.1980.
530 *Japan Times*, 2.9.1980 and 10.12.1980.
531 Servan-Schreiber, Jean Jacques. *Le Défi Mondial.* Paris: Fayard. 1980, p. 465.
532 Kommission. *Statistische Grundzahlen der Gemeinschaft. 1978.* Luxembourg, 1978, p. 127; *Statistische Grundzahlen der Gemeinschaft 1980.* Luxembourg 1980, p. 127.
533 Japan External Trade Organisation (JETRO). *White Paper on International Trade, Japan 1977.* Tokyo 1978, p. 176; and: *White Paper on International Trade, Japan 1980.* Tokyo 1981, p. 201.
534 JETRO. *White Paper on International Trade, Japan 1979.* Tokyo 1980, p. 153; *Financial Times*, 5.5.1979.
535 Statistische Grundzahlen. 1978. Loc. cit. (The figures include

intra-Community trade.)
536 Adapted from JETRO. 1981. Op. cit., p. 202; and JETRO. 1978.
Op. cit., p. 176.
537 Ibid.
538 Ibid.
539 Ibid.
540 Wilkinson. 1978. Op. cit., p. 263. The 1979 figures are calculated
according to JETRO. 1981. Loc. cit.
541 Diekhof, Dirk. Der Angriff auf Enropa. In: Werner Meyer-Larsen
(ed.) *Auto-Grossmacht Japan.* Reinbek: Rowohlt. 1980, 11–30,
p. 20.
542 Gabus, André, Otto Hieronimy and Pàl Kukorelly. *Japanese–European Trade Relations. The case of the Automobile Industry.* Geneva: The Top 70 Study Group. 1978, p. 39; *Business Week,*
10.11.1980; *Die Zeit,* 12.12.1980.
543 JETRO. 1981. Loc. cit.
544 Gabus et al. 1978. Op. cit., p. 35; Hardy, Ph. *Dossier van de
Japanse wagen in Belgie en het Groothertoogdom Luxemburg.*
Diegem 1980, p. 9.
545 Takahashi, Johsen et al. Japan's Trade Relations with the US and
Western Europe. *Journal of the Mitsubishi Research Institute*
No. 7, 1978, 12–29, p. 16.
546 European Parliament. *Interim Report on the Community Shipping
Industry.* Rapporteur: J.L. Prescott. Working Documents 1976/77,
23.12.1976. Document 479/76, p. 22; *Japan Economic Journal,*
9.5.1978.
547 Japanese Mission to the EC. Typescript.
548 Japanese Mission to the EC. Typescript.
549 Olechowski, Andrzej and Gary Sampson. Current Trade Restrictions in the EEC, the United States and Japan. *Journal of World
Trade Law 14,* 1980, 220–31, p. 224.
550 Rhein, Eberhard. Europe, Japan und die internationale Arbeitsteilung. *Europe-Archiv 36,* 1981, 109–16, p. 210.
551 *Le Monde,* 18.11.1977.
552 *Japan Times,* 19.2.1981.
553 *The Oriental Economist,* December 1979, pp. 47–54.
554 *Agence Europe,* 3.10.1979; *Japan Times,* 17.3.1981; Irish Development Authority. *Japanese Investments in Ireland.* Tokyo 1979.
555 *Industrial Review of Japan,* 1977, p. 59.
556 *Financial Times,* 19.11.1980.
557 *The Oriental Economist,* February 1979, p. 7; *Economist,*
14.5.1977.
558 *Japan Economic Journal,* 3.7.1979.
559 *Japan Economic Journal,* 13.11.1979.

560 *Far Eastern Economic Review*, 18.3.1972; *Keesing's Contemporary Archives 28*, 1971—72, 9.6.1972.
561 BIS. *Survey of Current Affairs 8*, No. 6, 1978, p. 228; *The Economist*, 25.5.1978.
562 *The Economist*, 10.9.1977.
563 *Japan Economic Journal*, 27.6.1978.
564 *Japan Economic Journal*, 12.2.1980.
565 Corbett, Jenny. *The European Community's Trade with Japan—Issues and Implications.* Australia—Japan Economics Research Project. Research Paper No. 48. Canberra 1978, p. 62.
566 Hill, Christopher and William Wallace. Diplomatic Trends in the European Community. *International Affairs*, 1979, 47—66, p. 50.
567 Hakoshima. 1979. Op. cit., p. 485.
568 *Markt Deutschland—Japan* (Tokyo), No. 2/1978, p. 41; and No. 3/1977, p. 5.
569 Reprinted in *Revue du Marché Commun* No. 243, Janvier 1981, p. 51.
570 *Der Spiegel*, 10.1980.
571 *Japan Times*, 10.5.1977.
572 —. Special Report 2. Trade Relations between the EEC and Japan. *European Trends*, No. 55, 1978, 24—36, p. 29.
573 Hakoshima. 1979. Op. cit., p. 486.
574 Hanabusa, Masamichi. Japan: Problems of Adjustment. *The World Today 34*, 1978, 210—19, p. 211.
575 *Agence Europe*, 2 and 3.5.1979; *Japan Times Weekly*, 28.4.1979.
576 Stern, Fritz. The Giant from Afar — Visions of Europe from Algiers to Tokyo. *Foreign Affairs*, 1977, 111—35, p. 133.
577 Hakoshima. 1979. Op. cit., p. 483.
578 Hakuhodo Inc. *Public Opinion Survey Concerning five EC Countries' Attitudes towards Japan.* Sin. loc., 1978.
579 *The Economist*, Survey: Must Japan Slow?, 23.2.1980.
580 Hosoya. 1979. Op. cit., p. 159.

7 Conclusion: explaining and forecasting EC-Japan relations

In the preceding three chapters I have attempted a longitudinal policy analysis. This has produced a larger picture than decision analysis — which is usually employed to examine hypotheses of bureaucratic politics — would have presented.[1] Due to its focus on changes and developments over time — the historical dimension in bilateral relations — my analysis more strongly emphasises the underlying structural conditions for inter-administrative compromises, bilateral negotiations and policy results. In this perspective, the organisational variables thought decisive by the bureaucratic politics approach appear as only one variable set effective among several others.

I will then interpret my empirical data in the framework of a multi-variable explanation (see also p. 8). The working of several variable sets should also serve as a guide for the likely future developments of EC–Japan relations and for policy recommendations on how to improve them.

The quality of EC–Japan relations

The political quality of Euro–Japanese relations since the 1950s covered a wide and ever expanding area of low politics disputes and co-operation — with highly differentiated and at times complicated sectoral issues.

Only since 1980 has high politics co-operation taken place on a bilateral basis. It remained ad hoc and has not yet in a lasting way affected the 'open angle' of Euro—Japanese relations in trilateral relations.[2]

In institutional and tactical terms bilateral low politics and high politics issues remained separate matters and received separate treatment. A Commission official, the principal administrator in charge of Japan, Mr Hardy, estimated the impact of high politics in 1980:[3]

> Thus, whatever points of discord occur (as of course they will) will take in a different setting from the past. The discussions will be over a wider range of topics and policies, *though trade and economic relations will remain the primary focus.* [my italics]

Most of bilateral trade remained free during — or was actually freed by — the 1970s. Mutual investments, technological joint ventures and productive link-ups proliferated, and the frequently predicted trade wars[4] did not take place. The potential for economic co-operation started to be utilised on both sides.

Nonetheless, this co-operation in the conduct of official relations did not resemble the assumptions of functionalist theory. Bureaucrats, not experts, dealt with the issues at the diplomatic and administrative level. Co-operative spill-over into high politics did not occur, and whenever the enthusiasm for co-operation ran too high on the one side, the other would usually dampen it with frustrating delays or by starting petty quarrels.

When experts, like the European exporters with shared material interests in the EC Steering Committee, actually did co-operate, then transnational perspectives easily dominated. These genuine expert meetings, however, were the exception rather than the rule.

There was not much evidence for trilateral co-operation apart from global summitry, the workings of GATT, of the OECD, the Group of Ten and the meetings of the Trilateral Commission itself. If anything, then relations between the three operated as shifting 2:1 alliances. The US and the EC (unwittingly for the most part) joined forces to open the Japanese market. The EC and Japan both opposed US unilateralism in economic and strategic decisions. The US and Japan worked against the EC's threat to impose import controls.

Trilateralism (or Galtung's 'OECD directorate hypothesis' for that matter, (p. 8)) failed because of shortcomings of all three participants. The US showed an irresistible inclination to make their foreign policy decisions unilaterally and to inform their allies — if at all — *ex post facto.* The deficiencies of political leadership both in Japan (for cultural reasons) and in the EC (for reasons of its lacking political integration) made the two in fact frustrating partners to deal with. This does not imply that trilateralism or functionalism are conceptually false. Our data simply suggest that they did not (yet) apply or show significant effects on EC–Japan relations.

At times elements of power politics seemed to threaten bilateral relations. Such arguments usually showed up when economic nationalism was used to prop up protectionist interests. International trade in a neomercantilist fashion was viewed as a zero sum game: bilateral deficits were seen primarily in terms of losses in employment, in adjustment costs and in net foreign exchange payments. The Japanese central bureaucracy, until the 1960s, and the French and Italian administrations certainly had sympathies for this view.

The discussion in the summaries of the preceding three chapters indicated that some form of bureaucratic politics governed bilateral relations. While the views of the BPA would suggest likely conflict patterns in bilateral relations, our data showed EC–Japan relations since the 1950s as by and large free of serious conflicts.

The quality of bilateral relations can be illustrated graphically as shown in Diagram 7.1. This would reflect that some high politics co-operation took place, though it was not very extensive. On low politics conflicts on some trade issues were balanced by co-operative ventures on other issues and were contained by effective conflict control.[5]

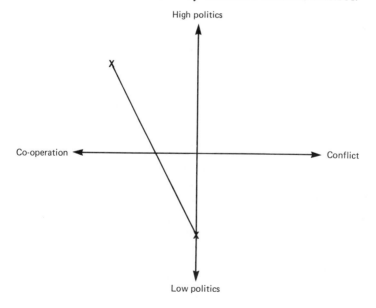

Diagram 7.1 EC–Japan relations, 1980

Bureaucratic politics in EC–Japan relations

Bureaucratic politics, as presented by Allison and Halperin's BPA, presupposes parochial policies which essentially are decided upon by the dysfunctional pulling and hauling of office holders.[6] They, reflecting the intellectual limits of a 'Homo bureaucraticus', are likely to be incapable of taking the larger issues beyond the departmental interests into their proper account. These observations have been made on decisions on US defence and armament questions and may – due to the strength of vested interests there – not have been inaccurate.

But on decisions on foreign economic policies in the EC and in Japan a second side of bureaucratic politics emerged, co-existing with its more parochial tendencies. It concerned more constructive components, namely rationality, predictability, decision making open to information inputs and with broad participation, and largely materially disinterested pursuits on both sides.

Among the more petty frictions in bilateral relations the following were of bureaucratic–symbolic value: the conflicts on the safeguard clause (lasting 20 years); the folly of the EC to demand, and of Japan to grant, a 7 per cent growth pledge in 1978–79; the EC's insistence on a reduced Japanese balance of payments' surplus 1977–79, regardless of its predictable effect on the Yen. Finally both sides showed a strange obsession to retain import restrictions as 'bargaining chips'.

At the same time the bureaucrats managing Euro–Japanese relations succeeded in avoiding serious or harmful bilateral conflicts. On the whole, on a conflict–co-operation continuous bureaucratic politics in EC–Japan relations held official relations at a somewhat neutral intermediate position. Private business and other relations could therefore – relatively undisturbed – develop along co-operative lines.

The second qualification of bureaucratic politics concerns its possibility for politicisation. In our earlier discussion on the conditions for politicisation in bilateral relations in the late 1970s (Chapter 6), it became evident that in certain crisis situations with lowered thresholds a politicisation, that is, policy changes due to the intervention of the political leadership, could occur and did occur.

Such – so far unilateral and unresponded, and therefore ineffectual – initiatives happened during the period 1955–63 on the Japanese side (with the strong personal involvement of premiers Kishi and Ikeda). The French initiative of 1965 (De Gaulle–Faure) and the British of 1969–1970 (Crosland–Mason) followed a similar pattern. All these politically motivated comprehensive offers solicited an uninspiring bureaucratic response.

'Accidental politicisations' triggered the Doko shock of 1976. The high politics co-operation of 1980 was managed by the political bureaus and at times even by the foreign and prime ministers and their immediate staff themselves. They were able to make their own experiences during these ventures and draw their own conclusions.

While Allison and Halperin basically view *all* foreign policy as bureaucratic politics, my empirical data show the limits of this concept's validity.

When thresholds for political interventions were lowered in 1976–77 and 1980–81 a politicisation on both sides could and would have changed the quality of bilateral relations. In the Anglo–American tradition of political leadership (of presidential or ministerial responsibility) this certainly would have happened. The weak structure of the ultimate decision centres[7] – the Councils on the European side and the cabinets in Japan – allowed the bureaucratic game to be played. But if the political leaderships on both sides actually had wanted to intervene, nothing would have prevented them from doing so. This would have been easy on foreign economic policies which intellectually are easier to understand than the more complex strategic and armament questions to which the BPA usually refers. This does not imply of course, that 'creative' trade policies would do any good to the actual flows of trade.

Under conditions of bureaucratic decision making statements of politicians on both sides were non-binding. Commissioners could not threaten with credibility and when national politicians mentioned Japan in public speeches it was for domestic consumption only. The same happened in Japan as well. The agreements which visiting ministers signed had been negotiated by their diplomats beforehand. Ministerial statements at press conferences had been prepared by public relations officials. While bureaucrats certainly tried to fulfil their anticipation of the ministers' preferences, genuine initiatives from the political top – except for the few quoted examples – were not discernible in bilateral relations.

Diagram 7.2 should contrast the nature of bureaucratic versus political decisions as ideal types. It shows bureaucratic decisions as being suitable for managing public issues – such as trade problems – requiring predictability, legality and informed common sense. Political decisions ('politicisations') appear as implying too many risks and possible costs and are an inadequate mode for decisions on such low politics matters.

Heurlin summarised Kissinger's views on the role distribution between bureaucracy and policy[8] as shown in Table 7.1. In the case of EC–Japan relations the bureaucracies on both sides evidently fulfilled functions which in Kissinger's view were policy tasks (the definition of policies and the operationalisation of goals).

A third alternative to politicisation and bureaucratic politics would be the option to minimise both bureaucratic and political interventions in the foreign trade process. German governments, leaving trade to

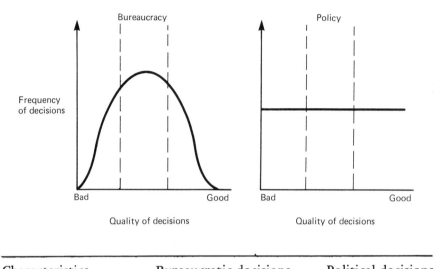

Characteristics	Bureaucratic decisions	Political decisions
Type of decision making	consensus—compromise	autocratic
Speed	slow	high
Information content	high	low
Scope	narrow	large
Functional sphere	low politics	high politics
Ranking	subordination	precedence
Legitimacy	derived	direct
Consistency— predictability	high	low
Legal orientation	strong	weak

Diagram 7.2 Bureaucratic decisions versus political decisions

Table 7.1

Tasks in the foreign policy management

Bureaucracy	Policy
— safety, calculability, routine	— creation
— definition of relationships which can survive mediocrity	— redefinition of goals
	— adjustment of risks
— avoidance of deviation	— conception of the problems

industry — neither engaging in export promotions nor in import restrictions — were until quite recently convinced of the success of their laissez faire (non-) policies.

A multivariable explanation

Our list of variables explaining variance in bilateral relations (see: Chapter 1, p. 8) indicates that organisational factors alone are not sufficient for adequate interpretations. How could they, *ceteris paribus,* be able to explain changes in policies over time? Just by some more effective 'pulling and hauling'?

The latent, basic rivalry between the Commission and the national foreign trade administrations in structural terms had remained the same since 1959. The legal gain in competence for the Commission in 1970 was not the result of contemporary infighting, but followed the regulations provided by the Treaties of Rome of 1957. The actual gains in responsibility evident in relations with Japan only after 1975 certainly had to be achieved by inter-administrative trench warfare — visible e.g. in the efforts to set up an effective Delegation in Tokyo.

The quality of bilateral relations however, — especially the cyclical nature of the 1976—77 and 1980—81 crises — show that organisational variables alone are insufficient for a complete explanation. For bureaucrats there is nothing to be won — neither in terms of budgets nor in administrative expansion — by advocating free trade policies. Nonetheless these policies for the most part have been actively promoted and negotiated by these very same bureaucrats. Still, there are features in bilateral relations in which organisational variables appear decisive.

There is good reason to argue that the European failure to respond to the Japanese drive for export outlets and international emancipation 1955—63 has been due to administrative inertia supported by close ties to protection-seeking domestic industries. A genuine *faux pas* occurred in February 1977 when due to the Commission's lack of policy co-ordination significant Japanese concessions on shipbuilding were answered by the EC slapping massive anti-dumping duties on Japanese bearings exports. The Japanese delay in opening her country to competitive imports — costing dearly in political and economic regards (legitimising the closure of Japan's export markets) — can also be explained by the notion of a coalition of Japanese domestic (protectionist) economic interests and governmental compliance. The bilateral manoeuvres on the planned Japan—EC Trade Agreement, its sensitive list and its safeguard clause, 1969—73 were certainly bureaucratic politics. But, as indicated above, it would be exceedingly difficult to explain the events after 1975 — when matters turned 'serious' exclusively in these terms.

On external variables, challenges and constraints emerging from the international system, OPEC's price increases causing the Western economies' recessions and reinforcing their currencies' rapid fluctuations, had the most profound external effect on EC—Japan relations. The oil shocks of 1974 and 1979 triggered the Japanese decisions for export offensives in the OECD markets. In the 1950s until the mid-1960s the US tutorial policies towards Japan had a strong impact on EC—Japan relations, as had the Cold War climate on the general cohesion of the Western World. Only detente conditions, the US defeat in Vietnam and their resulting economic problems could give birth to the notion of trilateralism as the need for equal co-operation between North America, Europe and Japan.

Trilateral co-operation in diplomatic reality then, however, usually took its characteristic pattern of 2:1 coalitions. Important multilateral conferences, like GATT rounds and UNCTAD negotiations, also affected Euro—Japanese relations. In sum, however, the political situation in the Middle East and the US import policies, among external variables, were most decisive for EC—Japanese low politics relations. Their high politics co-operation was most affected by the unilateralist actions of the superpowers. As middle powers with strong import dependencies their strategic interests were identical on both these external pressures.

The effects of the variables of the domestic economic and social system appear similarly significant. The various restructuring efforts of the Japanese economy — from the light industries of the 1950s to the heavy industries of the 1960s, from mass produced consumer durables of the 1970s towards an increasing share in technology intensive industries in the 1980s — had a decisive impact on the volume, the composition and the direction of Japan's foreign trade. These advanced products find their main outlet in the markets of OECD nations.

> While in the area of high technology products the United States maintain by far the greatest export specialisation (based on their predominance in the aerospace sector), Japan has gained a strong international position in the area of advance applied technology. Here she overtook Germany which was the leading exporter during the 1960s. Advanced applied technology includes various chemicals, gas turbines, metalworking machines, mechanical handling equipment, TV sets, telecommunication equipment, x-ray equipment, as well as motor vehicles.[9]

Japan's export drives were born out of domestic economic considerations: to seek growth stimuli during domestic recessions, but mainly to compensate for Japan's poor natural endowment of raw materials.

Residual economic nationalism in Japan — evident in the ideal of autarchy in key agricultural and industrial productions — worked first (in the 1960s) as a manifest, and later in the 1970s as a more latent barrier to imports. These attitudes and policies created tremendous problems for bilateral economic and diplomatic exchanges.

In Europe, in the growth period of the 1960s, a serious flaw in Europe's socio-economic structure became evident in bilateral relations. The large-scale and discriminatory protection of European light industries from Japanese competition already then indicated the hesitation to restructure radically under favourable conditions and to bear the necessary and inevitable costs in time to adjust to the developments in international competitiveness. The tendency to avoid these costs became notorious during the 1970s when some key EC industries' loss of competitiveness created strong protectionist pressures and a threat to the global free trade system.

EC exports either lost out because of their overpriced levels (on bulk steel, chemicals, cement, ships, textiles), or due to the widening technological gap to the US and to Japan.[10] EC losses in the late 1970s were most evident in those traditional export markets with strong purchasing power: the US, the Middle East and the EFTA countries.

The hesitation of European capital to modernise was aggravated by the high shares of unproductive government spending and by the difficulties of re-allocating labour to growth industries. In the late 1970s the resulting increase in redundancies seriously strained the social fabric of Western European societies. In this situation overseas imports presented themselves as a handy scapegoat for populist appeals looking for simple explanations for the domestic malaise.[11]

More concrete protectionist pressure against Japanese imports in the 1970s emerged from industries either with strong state participation (steel and shipbuilding) or from those with strong oligopolist structures at the national level (cars in Italy, France, Britain) or at the European level (bearings: SKF, and electronics: Philips and Thompson—Brandt). In structural terms the difficulties between the EC and Japan appear as normal frictions, a necessary conflict between the static and the dynamic.

Diagram 7.3 illustrates the development of bilateral trade since 1959. The tremendous expansion of trade after 1970 suggests strong welfare gains brought about to consumers and industries to both sides.

In 1979 Japan had 10,000 businessmen stationed permanently in Europe to achieve this result, while 1,500 EC businessmen were working in Japan. More European export efforts would now be ideal to stimulate entrepraneurial talents and to reward competitive European products on a tough, non-traditional and lucrative export market.[12]

As sociological variables the role of ideologies, sources of information, motivations, experiences and personalities of the decision makers active

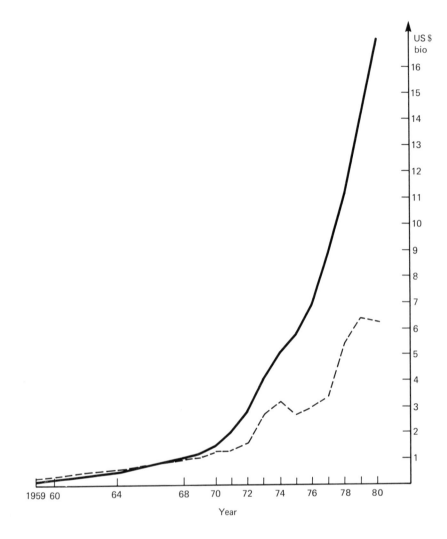

EC (the Nine) imports from Japan

EC (the Nine) exports to Japan

EC (the Nine) imports from Japan

EC (the Nine) exports to Japan

Diagram 7.3 EC–Japan trade 1959–80

326

in bilateral relations were summarised. While it was not possible to investigate the officials' ulterior motives and feelings towards the bilateral partner, on a more general level perceptual patterns can be discerned.

In the 1950s and 1960s Japan in Europe was considered a half-developed country with a closed market and aggressive exporting habits. The perceived Japanese 'free ride' in the liberal trade system was tolerated largely to support Japan's economic growth and her social stability in order to avoid her turning to an alliance with the Soviet Union or with China or becoming neutralist or aggressively nationalist again. Nonetheless, until the mid-1970s, Japan was of little importance to European decision makers and given fairly marginal attention.

After 1976 this picture gradually changed. For the domestic debates on industrial restructuring, on the limits of the welfare state and on desirable import regimes 'Japan' has become a polarising catchword in Europe. For the free trading liberal political centre Japan has turned into a model from whom Europe should learn how to regain its industrial vitality and whose exports would serve as a beneficial stimulus for domestic competition.[13]

The nationalist Right and the Labourite left both advocate protectionist policies fearing damages done by Japanese exports to their political objectives and to the domestic industrial structure.

Usually instrumental in this were allegations of Japan not playing fair, of being socially repressive, of dumping, or being operated as large conspiracy. A European Parliament report discovered the following:[14]

> These giant companies [the sogo shosha] — about ten in all — conceive and organise Japan's international economic strategy and cover all existing products. With their tight network of more than a thousand branches and subsidiaries in almost any country in the world and with the support of the large industrial groups, ... and of the state, which protects them, they represent the most formidable tool in the world.

In Japan, in the broad cultural and social consensus of the tradition established by the Meiji restoration up to the 1970s, Europe was seen as a model to be aspired to and whose positive aspects should be emulated in Japan's political and economic development. In the 1950s and 1960s Japan suffered under her political isolation in the Far East and under the continued European discrimination in economic and in symbolic terms.

After the mid-1970s Japan's mastering of the two oil crises has freed more ambiguous feelings. They range from a realist and sympathetic assessment of Europe's difficulties and achievements to occasional examples of a new 'superiority complex'. In general, however, Japan still views herself as a small power,[15] yet unsure of the lasting nature of her economic achievements. This disbelief in her own economic power and its overseas effects seems to explain part of Japan's insensitivity when invading foreign markets. In addition, the ethnocentric orientation of most Japanese managers, politicians and bureaucrats still is so strong that consensus decisions usually prefer external frictions over domestic problems if they have to choose.

Statements by senior policy makers on both sides about the bilateral partner — as one should expect — range from inaccurate stereotypes to more sophisticated and plausible assessments. The same picture is repeated in the media.

Policy variables concerned the treatment of the respective issues on the agenda of bilateral consultations. The main Japanese policy objectives had been fairly simple. From 1955 to 1964 they actively sought to achieve international recognition in Europe (obtaining MFN treatment, membership in GATT and OECD) and to secure export outlets there. Once these objectives had been achieved, Japan's diplomacy turned to defend these achievements and to attempt to mend whatever irritation their exporters had created in the EC.

On sensitive exports Japan fairly regularly resorted to VSRs to avoid the imposition of quotas.[16] This finally led to cartelised regimes on most key Japanese exports to the Community (on steel, ships, electronics to France and Benelux, cars to Britain). Japan was more hesitant where her imports were concerned. Japan's import liberalisation was effectively delayed until the early 1970s. Obstructive NTBs were removed only hesitantly and after arduous and protracted negotiations. The Japanese pattern in actual policies — though not in public rhetoric and announcements — to prefer export restraints over import liberalisations was not at all helpful either for free world trade or for the position of the defenders of a liberal import regime in the EC.

In Europe in the 1950s and 1960s policies towards Japan concerned the question of which items of Japanese imports to allow and when to grant most favoured nation treatment to Japan. After year-long delays these demands were granted in an unco-ordinated fashion and without achieving any significant Japanese concessions in return. In the early 1970s the Commission's policies focussed on a trade agreement with Japan, which was hoped would facilitate Japan's import liberalisation. Due to the persistent disagreement on a safeguard clause (SC) these negotiations failed. Japan, mainly under US pressure, then finalised the liberalisation of her imports. In the mid— and late 1970s sectoral negotiations and agreements had to substitute for the TA's planned functions. Then a maze of sectoral disputes, compromises and their revisions was handled between the EC and Japan — concerning both EC exports to Japan and Japanese exports to the EC.

While official EC policies also persistently claimed to give preference to Japan's market opening, in fact, due both to strong pressure from the member states and to the Japanese tendency towards export concessions, the Commission and the member states (Britain in particular) were more successful in seeking Japanese export restraints.

In 1981 the Commission demanded Community wide Japanese VSRs on cars, colour TVs and numerically-controlled machine tools. This was a remnant of a once 'comprehensive' Commission approach aiming at liberalising (sic) mutual trade and at unifying the Community's patchwork trade policy vis à vis Japan.

The official interactions between the EC and Japan during negotiations (incidental variables) were largely characterised by delays and by petty issues — unmistakable indicators of mutually pursued bureaucratic politics.

On the Japanese side, frequently, the problem of inadequate 'communication' was stressed. It reflected the Japanese tenet that conflicts are the result of misunderstandings. If the issues were only properly 'understood' by the other side, then these frictions — provided there was mutual goodwill — would cease to exist.

Insensitivity or rudeness (exemplified in the rabbit hutch memo) may at times have adversely affected bilateral relations, but there is not much evidence for a decisive role of cognitive deficiencies and communication failures. Negotiations largely concerned highly technical sectoral issues which both sides could discuss in English without ambiguities. Either one admits brass fittings in imported gas appliances or one does not. Even for a syncretistic thinking Japanese a third option should not really exist.

The Commission's lack of a comprehensive CCP competence never allowed her to offer even symbolic concessions to Japan outside GATT's tariff rounds. Such concessions would have saved the Japanese negotiators' face when conceding in turn.

After the mid-1970s the Japanese were faced with an ever expanding shopping list, presented by EC negotiators during the HLC and other bilateral contacts. Once demands were fulfilled, new ones would be added. The Japanese — who viewed their bilateral surplus in visibles as a legitimate result of their trading efforts (and not as a reason to make unilateral concessions) — concluded that the EC's demands would never end and stuck to a policy of permanent 'studies'.

On the European side, the Japanese delays — which started exceeding the time spans granted for domestic consensus building — discredited those who preferred EC export expansion as the adequate response, and supported the positions of those who had characterised Japan as a special case outside GATT.

At the same time dilatory and piecemeal decision making on both sides enabled tempers to cool down and to occasionally put co-operative perspectives into the strategic and tactical calculations.

In tactical terms one could easily contrast the EC's and the Japanese positions. While Japan was dynamic in actual economic exchanges (trade and overseas investments), the EC — in an economic perspective being in a defensive position — was active at the diplomatic level, at which Japan remained reactive. Theoretically the EC — in relative terms depending less on Japan both as a market and as a source of supplies than vice versa — was in a stronger bargaining position. But the disunity of its member states destroyed this strategic advantage. They quite openly forced Japan to negotiate with them on sectoral export restraints to their national markets and — to a lesser extent — also to have Japanese import restrictions removed on items of their national export interest.

A complicating factor for bilateral negotiations were parallel Japanese negotiations with the US. At times Japanese concessions to US demands — such as in early 1977 on agricultural imports and on tariffs and in early 1981 on car exports — provoked renewed EC demands to obtain the same or similar concessions. A second complicating factor arose from domestic tensions during national election campaigns in Japan and in key European countries with fragile governmental majorities (Britain, France, Germany). These reduced the willingness to concede on the Japanese side (especially on agricultural imports) and doubled European nervousness about Japanese manufactured imports.

Many variables, frequently beyond the control of the bureaucrats in charge, did affect bilateral relations. The next section will attempt to chart options and conditions for the future development of Euro–Japanese relations in the light of our explanations of the past.

Options and forecasts

Organisational variables in themselves do not have much predictive value. The decision on whether (our version of) bureaucratic politics continues or whether bilateral relations might become politicised depends on the economic and social developments on both sides and on the conduct and the results of the bilateral negotiations.

If we assume that the present 1980–81 crisis is of a cyclical nature indeed (as we suspect), then the next one or two years should bring signs of detente. A rising Yen should slow Japanese exports and encourage EC imports to Japan. Supported by symbolic Japanese concessions — in the form of liberalised import regulations and by sectoral export restraints — then bureaucratic politics should continue to manage bilateral relations through the routines of HLCs, technical talks and visitors' diplomacy on

330

a wide variety of sectoral issues with the same rhetoric as in the past. A continued low key and undramatic stalemate between the national EC governments in the Councils would preclude any surprises.

As indicated earlier, certain situations — e.g. a dramatic worsening of economic or social conditions in Europe, political shifts in the US or in key EC countries, like Germany, towards protectionism, accompanied by a worsening development in EC—Japan trade and the lack of alleviating Japanese concessions — could then easily turn the balance towards import controls. With some likelihood this could politicise bilateral relations and trigger a possible Euro—Japanese trade war.

Though EC exports to Japan are mostly non-essentials and therefore suitable candidates for retaliation, judging from the experience since the 1950s it would, however, seem unlikely that Japan — her decision making, in contrast to the EC, even under politicised conditions still needed bureaucratic consensus — would actually retaliate when faced with selective and discriminatory EC import controls. Given the severity of her frustration then a long term reorientation in Japan's foreign and foreign economic trade with serious high politics (i.e. security) implications could be initiated.

Among structural variables likely changes in the Japanese economy will significantly affect relations with Europe. Japan will further restructure its industrial production. The Japanese government's and the major corporations' policies now emphasise the promotion of future industries with high technology content and envisage Japan as a sort of global corporate and service head office.[17] It would focus on data gathering, decision making, banking, insurance, distribution, R & D, studies, art, entertainment and high value-added industries. Such a knowledge-intensive and sophisticated post-industrial structure would only be possible under global free-trade conditions.

In the long run, trade in invisibles is more likely to increase substantially than that in visibles. Already today the international transfer of patents, of know-how, designs, films, records, etc. has better growth prospects.[18]

Yet for the years to come mass-produced consumer durables will remain the staple of Japan's exports. But increasingly Japan will utilise her technological superiority in advanced productions and start to export products — electronically-controlled machinery and telecommunication products, etc. — which Europe has not even started to produce. Japan would then easily avoid frictions with domestic producers in Europe. More Japanese productive investments in Europe will aid both the technology transfer and the employment situation.

In Japan, continued economic growth will enable a streamlining of her inefficient distribution system and lend additional purchasing power to her prospering population. The export prospects of European advanced consumer products should thereby grow conspicuously.

In Europe, in contrast, stagnant growth and declining rates of innovation will lead to reduced international competitiveness in industrial exports. Social antagonisms could be fuelled by increased unemployment and reduced social spending caused by a loss in government revenues. As a result the political willingness and ability to bear the social and economic costs for industrial adjustments would be severely reduced. As crises stimulate demagogic short term cures for long term ills, protectionist policies will loom at the end of the road.

The faster and more effectively Japan modernises and restructures her economic system, the more (via capital exports, technology transfers and increased manufactured imports) she will contribute to preventing these policies from being directed against her exports.

In the long run the changes in the exchange rate situation should correspond to Japan's lessened import dependency on raw materials and to her gain in international competitiveness — i.e. increase the Yen's value — and to Europe's continuing economic stagnation. The EMS currencies should then fall against the dollar and the Yen. This change should help to re-establish more balanced economic exchanges between the EC and Japan.

In terms of policy variables, Japan will remain content if the status quo of a (still) fairly liberal European import policy is maintained.

The EC will certainly expand its list of desired Japanese export restraints. In its dealings with the Japanese and with the national governments the Commission will continue its attempts to rescue its long sought CCP towards Japan, possibly even at the expense of its original liberalising ideals.

It is difficult to perceive to what extent the industrial co-operation schemes of DG III will ever become effective and to whose benefit such Euro—Japanese ventures — likely to end up in global oligopolies — would operate.

One feature of future policies seems certain: the more Japan prospers and gains in international trade, the less tolerable will her residual import restrictions (from shoes to meat and whisky) appear to the Commission and to the national governments in Europe.

Incidental variables by their very nature can only be identified *ex post facto*. Nonetheless two characteristics of the bilateral bargaining situation seem to create increasing signs of strain. One concerns the Japanese tactic of pretending consensus finding ('studies') when in fact they simply intend to delay, especially on questions of import liberalisations.

The second relates to the Community's continued inability to offer the least — not even purely symbolic — face-saving concessions to the Japanese in the ongoing bilateral negotiations. As the structural im-

332

provements initiated by the Japanese will be effective only on a long term basis, the smooth management of bilateral negotiations — with plenty of 'symbolic' niceties to placate the sensitivities of bureaucratic politics — appears essential to prevent the politicisation of Euro—Japanese relations, with all the dysfunctional effects likely to follow.

Sociological variables, the role of images and mutual perceptions by the European and the Japanese population and their policy-making elites — as common in international relations — will remain secondary in comparison to the impact of mutually vested interests. The frequently heard demand for more understanding will in no way resolve trade or other economic conflicts. Nonetheless, as economic, academic and technological exchanges grow between the EC and Japan, mutual levels of information and the density of intercultural communication will increase. On the European side we should expect to see partly resentment of Japan's economic and technological progress, but hopefully more of the willingness to start learning from and to emulate desirable lessons of the Japanese challenge. In Japan the number of uncritical admirers of Europe will certainly be reduced, and some smaller spirits will display signs of a new 'superiority complex' — a reversal of the old equally neurotic inferiority feelings. On the whole, however, even with its economic performance declining, Europe's cultural and scientific achievements will continue to uphold the EC's image in the Far East, providing the basis for exchanges not in hierarchical superiority—inferiority patterns, but on equal terms.

On external variables — among international economic trends we can witness evidence for tendencies both towards increased competition and towards cartelisation on a global scale.

The proliferation of voluntary self-restraints (e.g. on steel, textiles, cars and ships), of national social, industrial and environmental policies introducing new barriers to trade or distorting competitive positions and a wide range of cross-national tie-ups and joint ventures (on cars, electronics, aviation, armament, tenders in the Third World) shows a — fairly chaotic — picture of 'managed trade'. These regulated or cartelised exchanges often are more supported than opposed by the governments concerned.

Nevertheless, in spite of all economic problems, political distortions and domestic pressures trade between members of the developed world is still overwhelmingly free. Subsequent GATT rounds have succeeded in ensuring that tariffs on industrial products will be reduced to insignificance by 1988.

Growth rates of trade above those of industrial output continue to be indicative of an optimal allocation of resources and of the maximisation of welfare for industrial and private customers. Should protectionist distortions be prevented, then the ongoing revolution in intercontinental transportation and information will succeed in creating genuine unitary market conditions between developed countries.

Social policies, policies on regional development, on industrial restructuring, and on consumer and environmental protection then have to be effectively co-ordinated at OECD level in order to avoid serious distortions of trade and grave misallocations of resources. The same reasons evidently require some EMS-type retying of OECD currencies. On a global level oligopolist 'world trust' tendencies would need political checking to ensure proper competitive conditions.

There is no alternative to a free trade world order (with only minimal 'managed trade' shares). A protectionist world order would be an unmitigated disaster. International trade would be stifled by bureaucratic quota allocations and compensatory deals. The patterns of our present international division of labour with transnational modes of production for many goods (from microprocessors to textiles and cameras) would be destroyed. Tremendous welfare losses, the elimination of the development prospects of dozens of NICs and would-be NICs, and the misallocation of productive resources would be the economic consequence. The political result of protectionist regimes — in which geopolitical, natural (raw material suppliers) and military national assets of the trading partner would be decisive for the preferential allocation of import quotas — would be a replay of the discriminatory policies of the 1930s. The weaker countries would be pushed against the wall. 'Lebensraum' concepts and geo-strategic national expansionism would again become convincing strategies for national prosperity and survival.

Hager[19] defined Latin America, South Asia, the NICs and Japan — because they are weak in political terms and in natural resource endowments — as the likely victims of future European protectionism. Cut off from essential oil and raw material supplies by the US and the European colonial powers in East Asia more than 40 years ago Japan had responded with Pearl Harbour . . .

Other external variables affecting Euro—Japanese relations could emerge from unilateral actions by the superpowers. Already in 1980 this had led to bilateral high politics co-operation. A new doubling of oil prices — predicted by Servan-Schreiber to happen by 1985[20] — would certainly again trigger a new bilateral crisis as did the increases of 1974 and 1979.

If not properly managed then the forthcoming global shortages of raw materials and foodstuffs[21] — first noticeable by price increases due to anticipated scarcities — might impede Japan's restructuring efforts and worsen Europe's crisis. Europe would then have to compete with the NICs on products at the same technology range. Whatever productivity advantages Europe then enjoyed the NICs could offset by their lower labour costs.

As an exercise in damage limitation[22] bureaucratic politics (in this version) so far has been (near) perfectly suitable for routine management of EC—Japan relations. For bilateral relations this may suffice in the future.

However, the structural and external challenges of the 1980s in Europe certainly demand political leadership and courage to initiate the policies revitalising and modernising European industries, to popularise the truths of Europe's export dependency, and to provide incentives for innovation, restructuring and for productive work.

The advice to Japan to imitate European ways of striking and vacationing is misguided. The Japanese way of mastering past and future economic challenges does not only light a beacon down the road the developing world should follow, as Macrae put it[23] but also for Western Europe.

References

1 Dormann, Manfred. Faktoren der aussenpolitischen Entscheidung. *Politische Vierteljahresschrift 12*, 1971, 14—28, p. 25; and: Freedman, Lawrence. Logic, Politics and Foreign Policy Processes: A Critique of the Bureaucratic Politics Model. *International Affairs 52*, 1976, 434—49, p. 439.

2 Bressand, Albert. The New European Economies. *Daedalus 108*, 1979, 51—74, p. 58.

3 Hardy, Michael. The EC and Japan: Agenda for Adjustment. *The World Today 36*, 1980, 428—35, p. 431.

4 Stebner, Peter. Japan's Exportoffensive verschärft zwischen imperialistische Gegensätze. *IPW—Berichte 6*, 1977, 56—61, p. 56.

5 Hosoya, Chihiro. Relations between the European Communities and Japan. *Journal of Common Market Studies 18*, 1979, 159—74, p. 173.

6 Allison, Graham T. *Essence of Decision*. Boston: Little, Brown. 1971, p. 166.

7 Heurlin, Bertel. Notes on Bureaucratic Politics in National Security Policy. *Co-operation and Conflict 10*, 1975, 237—59, p. 239.

8 Ibid., p. 242.

9 Laumer, Helmut. Europe and Japan in the 1980s: Co-operation instead of Confrontation. *IFO Digest 3*, 1980, 26—8, p. 26.

10 Hardy. 1980. Op. cit., p. 430.

11 Gabus, André, Otto Hieronymi and Pàl Kukorelly. *Japanese—European Trade Relations. Restrictions or Co-operation*. Geneva: The Top '70 Study Group. 1978, p. 20.

12 Hanabusa, Masamichi. *Trade Problems between Japan and Western Europe.* Farnborough: Saxon House, 1979, p. 80.
13 *Die Zeit,* 12.12.1980.
14 European Parliament. Working Documents 1976—77. *Report on Economic and Trade Relations between the EC and Japan.* Document 570/76. 2.3.1977, p. 20.
15 Hanabusa, Masamichi. Japan: Problems of Adjustment. *The World Today 34,* 1978, 210—19, p. 210.
16 Simonis, Udo E. Problemfelder der japanischen Aussenhandelspolitik. In: Simonis (ed.). *Japan — Wirtschaftswachstum und soziale Wohlfahrt.* Frankfurt: Herder & Herder. 1974, 143—66, p. 158; and: Bindeseil, Reinhart. Zum Problem des japanischen 'orderly marketing'. *Festgabe zum zehnten Jubiläum der DIHK in Japan. 1962—1972.* Tokyo: Deutsche Industrie- und Handelskammer. 1972, 22—33, p. 23.
17 Namiki, Nobuyoshi. Future of the Economic Relations between Japan and the European Community. *Rivista Internazionale di Scienze Economiche e Commerciali 20,* 1973, 758—85, p. 781.
18 Ota, Sadao. Anglo—Japanese Trade — Some Practical Aspects. *Japan Economic Journal.* 11.4.1978, p. 30.
19 Hager, Wolfgang. European Perspectives on World Economic Order. In: Japan Centre for International Exchange (ed.). *Proceedings of the Second Europe Japan Conference.* Tokyo. 1977, 17—31, p. 26.
20 Servan-Schreiber, Jean-Jacques. *Le Défi Mondial.* Paris: Fayard. 1980, p. 89.
21 *North—South: A Programme for Survival.* The Report of the Independent Commission on International Development Issues under the Chairmanship of Willy Brandt. London: Pan Books. 1980, p. 90; and: Organisation for Economic Co-operation and Development. *Interfutures.* Paris: OECD. 1979, p. 10.
22 Shonfield, Andrew. *Europe and Japan: Trade and Structural Change.* Paper prepared for the Fourth Europe—Japan Conference, Hakone, Japan. April 1979.
23 *The Economist,* 23.2.1980.

Bibliography

Books and monographs

Adenauer, Konrad. *Erinnerungen 1959—63.* Stuttgart: DVA. 1968.
Administrative Management Agency. Prime Minister's Office.
Organisation of the Government of Japan. Tokyo 1978.
Albinowski, Stanislaw. *Commercial Policy of the EEC.* Warszawa:
Zachodnia Agenja Prasowa. 1965.
Albonetti, Achille. *Hegemonie oder Partnerschaft in der Europäischen
Aussenpolitik.* Wiesbaden: Nomos. 1972.
Allen, P.A. *Italy — Republic without Government?* London: Weidenfeld
and Nicolson. 1973.
Allison, Graham T. *Essence of Decision.* Boston: Little, Brown,
1971.
Alting von Geusau, F.A.M. *European Organisations and Foreign Rela-
tions of States. A Comparative Analysis of Decision Making.* Leyden:
A.W. Synthoff. 1964.
Alting von Geusau, F.A.M. (ed.). *The External Relations of the Euro-
pean Community: Perspectives, Policies and Responses.* Farnborough,
Hants.: Saxon House. 1974.
Androuais, Anne. *Croissance du commerce extérieur japonais et ses
relations avec la C.E.E.* Mémoire du Diplome d'Etudes Supérieures
en Sciences Economiques. Université de Paris I. 1972.
Ayberk, Ural. *Le mécanisme de la prise de décisions communautaires
en matière de relations internationales.* Bruxelles: Ed. Bruylant. 1977.
Bailey, Richard. *The European Community in the World.* London:

Hutchinson. 1973.

Bark, Young W. *Le Marché Commun et le Japon. Etudes des conditions économiques internationales et les méthodes juridiques de la création des marchés étrangères.* Université de Paris I. Doctorat du 3e cycle. 1973.

Bauer, Robert A. (ed.). *The Interaction of Economics and Foreign Policy.* Charlottesville, VA. 1975.

Bérard, Armand. *Une ambassade au Japon.* Paris: Plon. 1980.

Binder, Heinrich Wilhelm. *Wirtschaftspolitik und Steuerung der Exportwirtschaft in Japan.* Frankfurt: Alfred Metzner Verlag. 1979.

Blake, David H. and Robert S. Walters. *The Politics of Global Economic Relations.* Englewood Cliffs, N.J.: Prentice Hall. 1976.

Blaker, Michael. *Japan's International Negotiating Style.* New York: Columbia University Press. 1977.

Brandt, Willy. *Der Wille zum Frieden.* Hamburg: Hoffmann & Campe. 1971.

Bryant, William E. *Japanese Private Economic Diplomacy: An Analysis of Business—Government Linkages.* New York: Praeger Publishers, 1975.

Brzezinski, Zbigniew. *The Fragile Blossom, Crisis and Change in Japan.* New York: Harper & Row. 1972.

Bundesstelle für Aussenhandelsinformation. *Japanische.Konkurrenz auf Drittlandsmärkten.* Köln. 1970.

Camps, Miriam. *'First World' Relationships – the Role of the OECD.* Paris: Atlantic Institute for International Affairs, and: New York: Council on Foreign Relations. 1975.

Cardozo, Michael. *Diplomats in International Co-operation: Stepchildren of the Foreign Service.* Ithaca, N.Y.: Cornell University Press. 1962.

Coffey, Peter. *The External Economic Relations of the EEC.* London: Macmillan. 1976.

Coombes, David. *Politics and Bureaucracy in the European Communities: A Portrait of the Commission of the EEC.* Beverly Hills: CA: Sage Pub. 1970.

Cooper, Gary M. *Would You Care to Comment on That, Sir? A Look at Fifty of Japan's Top Businessmen.* Tokyo: The Japan Economic Journal. 1976.

Cooper, Richard N., Karl Kaiser and Masataka Kosoka. *Towards a Renovated International System.* New York, Tokyo, Paris: The Trilateral Commission. 1977.

Corbett, Jenny. *The European Community's Trade with Japan – Issues and Implications.* Australia—Japan Economics Research Project. Research Paper No. 48. Canberra: Australian National University. 1978.

Cosgrave, Carol Ann, and K.J. Twitchett (eds.). *The New International Actors: The UN and the EEC.* London: Macmillan 1970.

Crozier, Michael J., Samuel P. Huntington and Joji Watanuki. *The Crisis of Democracy.* New York: The Trilateral Commission. 1975.

Dahrendorf, Ralf. *Plädover für die Europäische Union.* München: Piper & Co. 1974.

De Gaulle, Charles. *Mémoires d'espoir, Le renouvaau. 1958—62.* Paris: Librairie Plon. 1970.

Déstler, I.M., Haruhiro Fukui and Hideo Sato. *The Textile Wrangle — Conflict in Japanese—American Relations.* Ithaca: Cornell University Press. 1979.

Deutsche Industrie- und Handelskammer in Japan. *Jahresbericht.* (editions 1972—1979). Tokyo.

Dohnanyi, Klaus von. *Japanische Strategien oder das deutsche Führungsdefizit.* München: Piper & Co. 1969.

Dörsch, Hans J. and Pierre Legros. *Les faits et les décisions dans la C.E.E., 1958—64.* Brussels: Presses Universitaires de Bruxelles. 1969.

Dougherty, James E. and Robert L. Pfaltzgraff Jr. *Contending Theories of International Relations.* Philadelphia: Lippincott. 1971.

Duchêne, François, Kinhide Mushakoji and David D. Owen. *The Crisis of International Co-operation.* Brussels, New York, Tokyo: The Trilateral Commission. 1974.

Duncan, William Ch. *US—Japan Automobile Diplomacy.* Cambridge, Mass.: Ballinger Pub. 1973.

Europäische Gemeinschaften. Generalsekretariat des Rates. *Leitfaden der Räte der Europäischen Gemeinschaften.* Brussels. 1979.

Europäische Gemeinschaften. Generalsekretariat des Rates. *Überblick über die Tätigkeit der Räte.* (editions of 1977—1979). Luxembourg.

European Parliament. *Rapport sur les relations économiques entre les Six et le Japon.* Rapporteur: Jan Baas. Documents de Seance 1969—1970. Document 212. 2.2.1970.

European Parliament. *Report on Economic and Trade Relations between the European Community and Japan.* Rapporteur: Jan Baas. Working Documents 1976—77. Document 570—76. 2.3.1977.

European Parliament. *Report on the Results of the Visit by the Delegation of the EP to Japan in October 1978.* Working Documents 1978—79. Document 666—79. Rapporteur: Jan Baas. 1979.

European Parliament. *Interim Report on the Community Shipping Industry.* Rapporteur: J.L. Prescott. Working Documents 1976—77. 23.12.1976.

Everts, Philip P. *The European Community in the World.* Rotterdam: Rotterdam University Press. 1972.

Feld, Werner. *The European Common Market in the World.* Englewood Cliffs, N.J.: Prentice Hall. 1967.

Feld, Werner. *The European Community in World Affairs.* New York: Alfred. 1976.

—.*Festgabe zum zehnten Jubiläum der Deutschen Industrie- und Handelskammer in Japan. 1962—1972.* Tokyo: DIHK. 1972.

Fröbel, Volker et al. *Die neue internationale Arbeitsteilung.* Reinbek: Rowohlt. 1977.

Fukuda, Haruko. *Japan and World Trade: The Years Ahead.* Farnborough, Hants.: Saxon House. 1979.

Gabus, André, Otto Hieronymi and Pàl Kukorelly. *Japanese—European Trade Relations. Restrictions or Co-operation.* Geneva: The Top 70 Study Group. 1978.

Galtung, Johan. *The European Community: A Superpower in the Making.* Oslo: Universitetsforlaget. 1973.

Gerbet, Pierre and Daniel Pepy. *Le décision dans les Communautés Européennes.* Brussels: Presses Universitaires de Bruxelles. 1969.

Grewe, Wilhelm G. *Rückblenden 1976—1951.* Frankfurt: Propyläen. 1979.

Groom, A.J.R. and Paul Taylor (eds.). *Functionalism.* London: University of London Press. 1975.

Grosser, Alfred (ed.) *Les politiques extérieures européennes dans la crise.* Paris: Presses de la Fondation Nationale des Sciences Politiques. 1976.

Hakuhodo Inc. *Public Opinion Survey Concerning five European Community Countries towards Japan.* Tokyo. 1978.

Halliday, Jon and Gavan McCormack. *Japanese Imperialism Today.* Harmondsworth, Middx.: Penguin. 1975.

Halperin, Morton H. *Bureaucratic Politics and Foreign Policy.* Washington D.C.: Brookings Institution. 1974.

Hanabusa, Masamichi. *Trade Problems between Japan and Western Europe.* Farnborough, Hants.: Saxon House. 1979.

Hardy, Ph. *Dossier van de Japanse wagen in Belgie en het Groothertogdom Luxemburg.* Diegem. 1980.

Hedberg, Hakan. *Die japanische Herausforderung.* Hamburg: Hoffmann und Campe. 1970.

Hedberg, Hakan. *Japan: Europes Markt von morgen.* Hamburg: Hoffmann und Campe. 1972.

Hellmann, Donald C. *Japanese Foreign Policy and Domestic Politics.* Berkeley: University of California Press. 1969.

Henïg, Stanley. *External Relations of the European Communities: Associations and Trade Agreements.* London: Chatham House. 1971.

Hosoya, Chihiro, Henry Owen and Andrew Shonfield. *Collaboration with Communist Countries in Managing Global Problems: An Examination of the Options.* New York, Tokyo, Paris: The Trilateral Commission. 1977.

Ingram, James C. *International Economic Problems.* Santa Barbara, CA:

John Wiley & Sons. 1978.

Japan External Trade Organisation. *White Paper on International Trade.* (editions 1977—1980). Tokyo.

Japan Information Centre. *British Trade with Japan.* London. 1977.

Japan Information Centre. *Japan's Relations with Britain and Europe.* London. 1977.

Kahn, Herman and Thomas Pepper. *The Japanese Challenge.* London: Harper & Row. 1979.

Kaplan, Eugene J. *Japan: The Government—Business Relationship.* Washington D.C.: US Department of Commerce. 1972.

Keatinge, Patrick. *The Formulation of Irish Foreign Policy.* Dublin: Institute of Public Administration. 1973.

Keck, Jörn and Henry Krägenau. *Japanische und deutsche Direktinvestitionen im Ausland.* Hamburg: Institut für Asienkunde. 1975.

Kinhide, Mushakoji. *The Strategies of Negotiation — An American— Japanese Comparison.* Research Papers, Series A—4. Institute of International Relations. Sophia University. Tokyo. 1970.

Kitamura, Hiroshi. *Choices for the Japanese Economy.* London: Macmillan. 1976.

Kohnstamm, Max and Wolfgang Hager (eds.). *A Nation Writ Large?* London: Macmillan. 1973.

Kojima, Kiyoshi. *Japan and a Pacific Free Trade Area.* London: Macmillan. 1971.

Kroll, Hans. *Lebenserinnerungen eines Botschafters.* Köln: Kiepenheuer & Witsch. 1968.

Langdon, F.C. *Japan's Foreign Policy.* Vancouver: University of British Columbia Press. 1973.

Lemper, Alfons (ed.). *Japan in der Weltwirtschaft.* München: Weltforum Verlag. 1974.

Lenin, V.I. *Der Imperialismus als höchstes Stadium des Kapitalismus.* Ostberlin: Dietz Verlag. 1975 (1917).

Lindberg, Leon N. and Stuart A. Scheingold. *Europe's Would-be Policy.* Englewood Cliffs, N.J.: Prentice Hall. 1970.

Malmgren, Harald B. *International Economic Peacekeeping in Phase II.* New York: Quadrangle Books. 1972—73.

Mandel, Ernest. *Die EWG und die Konkurrenz Europa—Amerika.* Frankfurt: EVA. 1968.

Mende, Tibor. *Soleils levants.* Paris: Editions de Seuil. 1975.

Mendel, Douglas H. Jr. *The Japanese People and Foreign Policy.* Berkeley: University of California Press. 1961.

Mendes France, Pierre. *Dialogues avec l'Asie d'aujourd'hui.* Paris: Gallimard. 1972.

Merritt, Richard L. (ed.). *Foreign Policy Analysis.* Lexington, Mass.: Lexington Books. 1975.

Meyer-Larsen, Werner (ed.). *Auto—Grossmacht Japan.* Reinbek: Rowohlt. 1980.

Mills, C. Wright. *The Sociological Imagination.* London: Oxford University Press. 1977 (1959).

Monloup, Madelaine. *Les relations économiques du Marché Commun et du Japon.* Bruges: Collège d'Europe. 1969.

Monroe, Wilbur F. *International Trade Policy in Transition.* Lexington, Mass.: Lexington Books. 1975.

Morgan, Roger. *High Politics, Low Politics: Toward a Foreign Policy for Western Europe.* London: Sage, Washington Papers. 1975.

Northedge, F.S. *The International Political System.* London: Faber & Faber. 1976.

—. *North—South: A Program for Survival.* The Report of the Independent Commission on International Development Issues under the Chairmanship of Willy Brandt. London: Pan Books. 1980.

Okita, Saburo. *Japan in the World Economy.* Tokyo: The Japan Foundation. 1975.

Organisation for Economic Co-operation and Development. *Economic Survey, Japan.* Paris. 1978.

Organisation for Economic Co-operation and Development. *Interfutures, Facing the Future.* Paris: OECD. 1979.

Ortona, Egidio, J. Robert Schaetzel and Nobuhiko Ushiba. *The Problem of International Consultations.* New York, Tokyo, Paris: The Trilateral Commission. 1976.

Ozaki, Robert S. *The Control of Imports and Foreign Capital in Japan.* New York: Praeger. 1971.

Ozawa, Terutomo. *Multinationalism, Japanese Style.* Princeton, N.J.: Princeton University Press. 1979.

Poullet, Edouard and Gerard Deprez. *Struktur und Macht der EG Kommission.* Bonn: Europa Union Verlag. 1976.

Preeg, Ernest H. *Traders and Diplomats.* Washington D.C.: Brookings Institution. 1970.

Prime Minister's Secretariat. *Public Opinion Survey on Japan's Foreign Policy.* Tokyo: Foreign Press Centre. 1979.

Raux, Jean. *Les relations externes de la CEE.* Paris: Edition Cujas. 1966.

Richardson, Bradley M. *The Political Culture of Japan.* Berkeley: University of California Press. 1975.

Roon, Ger van. *Europa en de Derde Wereld.* Utrecht: Uitgeverij Het Spectrum. 1975.

Rosenthal, Glenda G. *The Men behind the Decisions: Cases in European Decision Making.* Lexington, Mass: Lexington Books. 1975.

Sansom, George. *The Western World and Japan.* Tokyo: Charles & Tuttle Co. 1977 (1950).

Sasse, Christoph. *Regierungen, Parlamente, Ministerrat — Entscheidungs-*

prozesse in der Europäischen Gemeinschaft. Bonn: Europa Union Verlag. 1975.

Sautter, Christian. *Japon, le prix de la puissance.* Paris: Seuil. 1973.

Servan-Schreiber, Jean-Jacques. *Le défi mondial.* Paris: Fayard. 1980.

Shonfield, Andrew. *Europe — Journey to an Unknown Destination.* London: Allen Lane, 1973.

Shonfield, Andrew (ed.). *International Economic Relations of the Western World 1959—71.* 2 Vols. London. 1976.

Sjöstedt, Gunnar. *The External Role of the European Communities.* Farnborough, Hants.: Saxon House. 1977.

Sked, Allen and Chris Cook. *Postwar Britain.* Harmondsworth: Penguin. 1979.

Swann, Dennis. *The Economics of the Common Market.* Harmondsworth: Penguin. 1977.

—. *Sweet & Maxwell's European Community Treaties.* London. 1972.

Taber, G.M. *Patterns and Prospects of Common Market Trade.* London: Peter Owen. 1974.

Takamiya, Makoto. *Japan's Multinationals in Europe: International Operations and their Public Policy Implications.* Discussion Paper. Berlin: Wissenschaftszentrum. 1979.

Taylor, Paul. *International Co-operation Today.* London: Elek. 1971.

Ueda, Naoharu. *Le problème des relations commerciales du Japon et de la C.E.E.* Université de Strasbourg. Centre universitaire des hautes études européennes. 1965.

Vernon, Raymond (ed.). *Big Business and the State: Changing Relations in Western Europe.* Cambridge, MA: Harvard University Press. 1974.

Vizoso, A. *Japon, Tercera Potencia Economica Mundial.* Madrid: Guaiana de Publicaciones. 1970.

Vogel, Ezra F. *Japan as Number One, Lessons for America.* Cambridge, MA: Harvard University Press. 1979.

Wallace, Helen. *National Governments and the European Communities.* London: Chatham House—PEP. 1973.

Wallace, William. *The Foreign Policy Process in Britain.* London: The Royal Institute of International Affairs. 1976.

Wallace, William, Carole Webb and Helen Wallace (eds.). *Policy Making in the European Communities.* London 1977.

Watanabe, Akihiko. *L'économie japonaise et la C.E.E.* Université de Nancy. Publications du Centre Europeen Universitaire. 1964.

Weil, Gordon L. *A Foreign Policy for Europe? The External Relations of the European Community.* Bruges: College of Europe. 1970.

Wilkinson, Endymion. *Misunderstanding, Europe versus Japan.* Tokyo: Chuokoron-sha Inc. 1981.

Yanaga, Chitoshi. *Big Business in Japanese Politics.* New Haven: Yale University Press. 1968.

343

Articles

Abe, Isao. La Communauté Européenne vue par un Japonais. *Chronique de la politique étrangère 26*, 1973, 21—7.

Allen, David. 'Foreign Policy at the European Level: Beyond the Nation—State?' In: William Wallace and W.E. Patterson (eds.). *Foreign Policy Making in Western Europe.* Farnborough, Hants.: Saxon House. 1978. 135—54.

Alting von Geusau, F.A.M. 'Les sessions marathon du Conseil des Ministres'. In: Pierre Gerbet and Daniel Pepy (eds.). *La décision dans les Communautés Européennes.* Brussels: Presses Universitaires de Bruxelles. 1969. 99—107.

Autorenkollektiv. USA, Westeuropa, Japan — imperialistische Zentren der Rivalität. *IPW Forschungshefte 11*, 1976, 5—138.

Baehr, Peter R. 'The Foreign Policy of the Netherlands'. In: J.H. Leurdijk (ed.). *The Foreign Policy of the Netherlands.* Alphen aan den Rijn: Sijthoft & Noordhoff. 1978. 3—27.

Baerwald, Hans H. 'The Diet and Foreign Policy'. In: Robert A. Scalapino (ed.). *The Foreign Policy of Modern Japan.* Berkeley: University of California Press. 1977. 37—54.

Beinhard, Gerd. Japans Stellung in der Weltwirtschaft und zur EWG. *Wirtschaftsdienst 52*, 1972, 138—42.

Beresford, Martin. And now, le défi japonais. *The Atlantic Community Quarterly 13*, 1975, 204—19.

Bergsten, C. Fred et al. International Economics and International Politics: a Framework for Analysis. *International Organisation 29*, 1975, 3—36.

—. Between Power and Plenty: Foreign Economic Policies of Advanced Industrial Societies. *International Organisation 31*, 1977, 587—920.

Bindeseil, Reinhart. 'Zum Problem des "orderly marketing"'. *Festgabe zum zehnten Jubiläum der DIHK in Japan, 1962—72.* Tokyo. 1972. 22—33.

Bourbon—Busset, Jacques de. How Decisions are Made in Foreign Politics. *The Review of Politics 20*, 1958, 591—614.

Bressand, Albert. The New European Economies. *Daedalus 108*, 1979, 51—74.

Bridgford, Jeff. European Political Co-operation and the Institutions of the European Communities. *Studia Diplomatica 30*, 1977, 393—412.

Brugmans, Henri. 'Synthèse des travaux'. *La politique économique extérieur de la Communauté Européenne élargie.* Semaine de Bruges 1972, Bruges: De Temple. 1973. 214—23.

Brzezinski, Zbigniew. U.S. Foreign Policy: The search for Focus. *Foreign Affairs 51*, 1973, 708—23.

Calleo, David P. The European Coalition in a Fragmenting World.

Foreign Affairs 54, 1975, 98—112.

Cartou, Louis. 'Le rôle de la Commission'. In: Pierre Gerbet and Daniel Pepy (eds.). *La décision dans les Communautés Européennes.* Brussels: Presses Universitaires de Bruxelles. 1969. 3—11.

Casadio, Gian Paolo. Industrial Co-operation between Italy and Japan. *Rivista Internazionale di Scienze Economiche e Commerciale 27*, 1980, 433—47.

Cassiers, Juan. Le rôle de l'OECD. *Chronique de la politique étrangère 25*, 1972, 755—68.

Cheynel, Henry. Les relations économiques entre l'Europe et le Japon. *Euro—Co-operation*, No. 13, 1975, 25—78.

—. CEE—Japon: sourires et grimaces. *Le moniteur du commerce international* (Paris), No. 240. 2.5.1977, 12—28.

Corbet, Hugh. Industrial Tariffs and Spheres of Influence. *The Round Table 63*, 1973, 145—59.

Cosgrave, Carol Ann and Kenneth J. Twitchett. 'International Organisations as Actors'. In: C.A. Cosgrave and K.J. Twitchett (eds.). *The New International Actors.* London: Macmillan. 1970. 11—54.

Craig, Albert M. 'Functional and Dysfunctional Aspects of Bureaucracy'. In: Ezra F. Vogel (ed.). *Modern Japanese Organisation and Decision Making.* Tokyo: Tuttle Co. 1979, 3—32.

Cudlipp, Reginald. One Man's Thoughts on Anglo—Japanese Relations. *Pacific Community 1*, 1970, 651—63.

Curtis, Gerald L. 'Big Business and Political Influence'. In: Ezra F. Vogel (ed.). *Modern Japanese Organisation and Decision Making.* Tokyo: Tuttle Co. 1979. 33—70.

Curzon, Gerard and Victoria. 'The Management of Trade Relations in the GATT'. In: Andrew Shonfield (ed.). *International Economic Relations of the Western World 1959—71, 1.* London: Oxford University Press. 1976. 143—283.

Dahrendorf, Ralf. Communauté, Etats Unies, Japon: problèmes et perspectives de politique commerciale. *Bulletin des Communautés Européennes 2*, 1971, 21—34.

Dahrendorf, Ralf. Greatness Creates Responsibility: the New Transatlantic Partnership. *International Journal of Politics 5*, 1975, 28—47.

Dahrendorf, Ralf. International Power: A European Perspective. *Foreign Affairs 56*, 1977, 72—88.

Dahrendorf, Ralf. It is not Easy for a Community to Have a Foreign Policy. *International Journal of Politics 5*, 1975, 11—28.

Dahrendorf, Ralf. Possibilities and Limits of the European Community's Foreign Policy. *The World Today 27*, 1971, 148—61.

Dahrendorf, Ralf. The Foreign Policy of the EEC. *The World Today 29*, 1973, 47—57.

Dolan, Michael B. and James A. Caporaso. The External Relations of the European Communities. *The Annals, AAPSS 440,* 1978, 135–55.

Dormann, Manfred. Faktoren der aussenpolitischen Entscheidung. *Politische Vierteljahresschrift 12,* 1971, 14–28.

Duchêne, François. Aussenpolitik in einer erweiterten Europäischen Gemeinschaft. *Europa Archiv 34,* 1979, 125–36.

Economist Intelligence Unit. Europe and Japan, Rivals or Partners? *European Trends,* No. 25, 1970, 22–33.

Economist Intelligence Unit. Trade Relations between the EEC and Japan. *European Trends,* No. 55, 1978, 24–36.

Eli, Max. 'Die Bedeutung der Generalhandelshäuser für die Wirtschaft Japans'. Heide and Udo Simonis (eds.). *Japan: Wirtschaftswachstum und soziale Wohlfahrt.* Frankfurt–M.: Herder & Herder. 1974. 123–42

Engels, Benno. 'Japans Wirtschaftsbeziehungen zu Westeuropa'. Alfons Lemper (ed.). *Japan in der Weltwirtschaft.* München: Weltforum Verlag. 1974. 283–378.

Ernst, Wolfgang. Japan – Rätsel ohne Lösung? Zur neueren Entwicklung der europäisch–japanischen Beziehungen. *Europa Archiv 32,* 1977, 760–72.

—. Etat actuel des relations commerciales entre la CEE et le Japon. *Bulletin Financier* (Luxembourg), No. 19. 1.6.1977, 1–3.

Eto, Shinkichi. Foreign Policy Formation in Japan. *The Japan Interpreter 10,* 1976, 251–66.

Feld, Werner. Diplomatic Behaviour in the European Community: Milieus and Motivations. *Journal of Common Market Studies 11,* 1972, 18–35.

Feld, Werner and John K. Wildgen, National Administrative Elites and European Integration – Saboteurs at Work? *Journal of Common Market Studies 13,* 1975, 244–65.

Figgess, John. 'Une relation naissant: L'Europe face au Japon'. Curt Gasteyger (ed.). *Le Japon et le Monde Atlantique.* Farnborough, Hants: Saxon House. Les Cahiers Atlantiques 3, 1973, 68–82.

Franck, Christian. La capacité européenne d'une politique extérieur commune. *Bulletin du Centre européen de la Culture 16,* 1976, 39–48.

Freedman, Lawrence. Logic, Politics and Foreign Policy Processes: A Critique of the Bureaucratic Politics Model. *International Affairs 52,* 1976, 434–49.

Frieden, Jeff. The Trilateral Commission: Economics and Politics in the 1970s. *Monthly Review 29,* 1977, 1–18.

Fukui, Haruhiro. 'Policy Making in the Japanese Foreign Ministry'. Robert A. Scalapino (ed.). *The Foreign Policy of Modern Japan.* Berkeley: University of California Press. 1977. 3–35.

Fukui, Haruhiro. 'The Japanese Farmer and Politics'. Isaiah Frank (ed.).

The Japanese Economy in International Perspective. Baltimore: Johns Hopkins University Press, 1975, 134—67.

Fuse, Toyomasa. Japan's Economy in the Seventies. Some Problems and Prospects. *Cultures and Development, No. 1 and 2,* 51—89 and 315—351.

Genscher, Hans-Dietrich. Notwendigkeit und Möglichkeit einer europäischen Aussenpolitik. *Europa Archiv 31,* 1976, 427—34.

Goodwin, G.L. The External Relations of the European Communities — Shadow and Substance. *British Journal of International Studies 3,* 1977, 39—54.

Goodwin, G.L. A European Community Foreign Policy? *Journal of Common Market Studies 12,* 1973, 7—27.

Gregory, Gene. The Japanese Euro-Strategy. *Management Today,* July 1975, 54—60.

Grewe, Wilhelm G. 'Japan und Deutschland — gestern, heute und morgen'. In: A. Barning and M. Sase (eds.). *Zwei zaghafte Riesen? — Deutschland und Japan seit 1945.* Stuttgart: Belser Verlag. 1977, 621—46.

Grossmann, Bernhard. 'Die deutsch—japanischen Beziehungen'. In: H. P. Schwarz (ed.). *Handbuch der deutschen Aussenpolitik.* München: Piper & Co. 1975, 345—48.

Haferkamp, Wilhelm. Zwischen Protektionismus und freiem Welthandel — Die Handelspolitik der EG am Scheideweg. *Neue Gesellschaft 24,* 1977, 736—39.

Hager, Wolfgang. 'European Perspectives on World Economic Order'. Japan Centre for International Exchange (ed.). *Proceedings of the Second Europe Japan Conference.* Tokyo, 1977, 17—31.

Hakoshima, Shinichi. Mutual Ignorance and Misunderstanding — Causes of Japan—EC Economic Disputes. *Japan Quarterly 26,* 1979, 481—88.

Hammer, Dietrich. 'La Communauté élargie, les USA et le Japon'. Collège d'Europe (ed.). *La politique extérieure de la Communauté Européenne élargie.* Bruges: De Temple, 1973. 18—39.

Hanabusa, Masamichi. Japan: Problems of Adjustment. *The World Today 34,* 1978, 210—19.

Handke, Werner. Japan und Deutschland in der Weltwirtschaftspolitik. *OAG aktuell* 1976, 41—62.

Hansen, Niels. Politische Zusammenarbeit in Westeuropa: Der neue Ansatz des Luxemburger Berichts. *Europa Archiv 26,* 1971, 456—65.

Hardy, Michael. The EC and Japan: Agenda for Adjustment. *The World Today 36,* 1980, 428—38.

Henig, Stanley. From External Relations to Foreign Policies. *Journal of Common Market Studies 12,* 1973, 1—6.

Henkner, Klaus. Die Handelspolitik der EWG gegenüber Drittländern und die Sonderstellung Japans. *Konjunkturpolitik 11,* 1965, 145—170.

Heurlin, Bertel. Notes on Bureaucratic Politics in National Security Policy. *Co-operation and Conflict 10*, 1975, 237—59.

Hill, Christopher and William Wallace. Diplomatic Trends in the European Community. *International Affairs 55*, 1979, 47—66.

Hirschmeier, Johannes. Japanese Economy in Western Press. *The Oriental Economist*, November, 1969, 22—29.

Homan, J. Linthorst. The EEC and the World Economy. *Journal of World Trade Law 5*, 1971, 509—22.

Hosoya, Chihiro. Relations between the European Community and Japan. *Journal of Common Market Studies 18*, 1979, 159—74.

Hosoya, Chihiro. The Characteristics of the Foreign Policy Decision Making System in Japan. *World Politics 26*, 1974, 353—69.

Hubert, Agnes. Dialogue Communauté—Japon: A armes égales. *Revue du Marché Commun*, No. 222, 1978, 547—49.

Inoki, Masamichi. A New Europe and the Japanese Fear of Isolation. *Journal of Social and Economic Ideas in Japan 1*, 1963, 109—12.

—. Japan und die Deutschen. *INFAS—Report*, 5.10.1973.

Johnson, Chalmers. 'MITI and Japanese International Economic Policy'. In: Robert A. Scalapino (ed.). *The Foreign Policy of Modern Japan.* Berkeley: University of California Press. 1977. 227—79.

Juster, Kenneth I. Foreign Policy Making during the Oil Crisis. *Japan Interpreter 11*, 1977, 293—312.

Kajima, Morisonuka. 'Pan—Europa and Japan'. *Japan in Current World Affairs.* Tokyo: Kajima Institute for International Peace. 1972. 193—201.

Kanamori, Hisao. The European Common Market and Japan's Trade. *The Japan Annual of International Affairs*, No. 2, 1962, 117—27.

Kern, Pierre. L'Europe à la découverte du doualisme japonais. *Revue du Marché Commun 6*, 1963, 206—11.

Kimura, Hiroshi. Soviet and Japanese Negotiating Behaviour: The Spring 1977 Fisheries Talks. *Orbis 24*, 1980, 43—67.

Kinhide, Mushakoji. 'The Cultural Premises of Japanese Diplomacy'. In: Japan Centre for International Exchange (ed.). *The Silent Power — Japan's Identity and World Role.* Tokyo: Simul Press. 1976, 35—49.

Kojima, Kazuto. Public Opinion Trends in Japan. *Public Opinion Quarterly 41*, 1977, 206—16.

Kosoka, Matasaka. Japan's Major Interests and Policies in Asia and the Pacific. *Orbis 19*, 1975, 793—808.

Krelle, Wilhelm. Entscheidungstheoretische Methoden in der auswärtigen Politik. *Europa Archiv 27*, 1972, 387—98.

Lambert, John. Decision Making in the Community: The Commission — Council Dialogue. *Government and Opposition 2*, 1967, 391—97.

Laumer, Helmut. Europe and Japan in the 1980s: Co-operation instead of Confrontation. *IFO Digest 3*, 1980, 26—28.

348

—.Le Japon dix ans après son adhesion à l'OECD. *L'Observateur de l'OECD,* April 1974, 11—42.

—.Le Japon. *Sondages 32,* No. 3, 1970, 1—58.

Lüdemann, E. Japans Stellung in der kapitalistischen Weltwirtschaft. *IPW Berichte 1,* 1972, 12—22.

Mackintosh, John P. Gemeinsame Europäische Aussenpolitik. *Europa Archiv 27,* 1972, 365—76.

Malmgren, Harald B. 'Managing International Trade'. In: Don Wallace Jr. and Helga Escobar (eds.). *The Future of International Economic Organisations.* New York: Praeger Publishers. 1977, 103—24.

Maneval, Pierre. Le Japon et l'Europe. *CNPF 78, Patronat,* No. 393, 1978, 35—39.

Mayrzedt, Hans. Erfahrungen mit der multilateralen Wirtschafts— diplomatie zwischen westlichen Industriestaaten. *Aussenwirtschaft 33,* 1978, 254—71.

McGeehan, Robert and Steven J. Warnecke. Europe's Foreign Policies: Economics, Politics, or Both? *Orbis 17,* 1974, 1251—79.

Meynaud, Jean and Dusan Sidjanski. 'L'action des groupes de pression'. In: Pierre Gerbet and Daniel Pepy (eds.). *La décision dans les Communautés Européennes.* Brussels: Presses Universitaires de Bruxelles. 1969, 133—48.

Miller, J.D.B. The Unassociables. *The World Today 30,* 1974, 327—34.

Morgan, Roger P. Introduction: European Integration and the European Community's External Relations. *International Journal of Politics 5,* 1975, 3—10.

Mouer, Ross E. and Yoshio Sugimoto. The Future of Japanese Studies. *Centre News* (Japanese Studies Centre, The Japan Foundation) *4,* 1980, 2—6.

Muyser, Guy de. 'La preparation de la décision communautaire au niveau national luxembourgeois'. In: Pierre Gerbet and Daniel Pepy (eds.). *La décision dans les Communauté Européennes.* Brussels: Presses Universitaires de Bruxelles. 1969, 229—35.

Nagai, Yonosuke. Social Attitudes and Foreign Policy during the 1970s. In: Japan Centre for International Exchange (ed.). *The Silent Power — Japan's Identity and World Role.* Tokyo: Simul Press. 1976, 99—118.

Nakagawa, Toru. 'Changing Europe'. In: Kajima Institute for International Peace (ed.). *Japan in the World.* Tokyo: The Japan Times. 1976, 129—42.

Namiki, Nobuyoshi. Future of the Economic Relations between Japan and the EC. *Rivista Internazionale di Scienze Economiche e Commerciali 20,* 1973, 758—85.

Nellas, Pierre. 'La nouvelle politique commerciale japonaise'. In: M. Arai et al. (eds.). *La nouvelle politique commerciale japonaise.* Paris: Dunod. 1973, 13—32.

Nickel, Herman. The Rediscovery of Japan. *Foreign Policy* No. 14, 1974, 157—63.

Nicolaus, Martin. The Universal Contradiction. *New Left Review*, No. 59, 1970, 3—18.

Nish, Ian. Themes in Japan's Foreign Relations. *The World Today 34*, 1978, 157—65.

Nishiyama, Chiaki. The Japan Problem or the EC Problem? *Chronique de politique étrangére 26*, 1973, 649—71.

Noël, Emile. 'Le comité des réprésentents permanents'. In: Institut d'Etudes Européennes, Université Libre de Bruxelles (ed.). *Institutions Communautaires et institutions nationales dans le développement des Communautés*. Brussels: Editions de l'Institut de Sociologie. 1968, 9—49.

Noël, Emile. The External Relations of the EEC and its Internal Affairs. *Government and Opposition 10*, 1975, 159—66.

Noël, Emile and Henri Etienne. 'Quelques aspects des rapports et de la collaboration entre le Conseil et la Commission'. In: Pierre Gerbet and Daniel Pepy (eds.). *La décision dans les Communautés Européennes.* Brussels: Presses Universitaires de Bruxelles. 1969, 33—55.

Novak, Jeremiah. The Trilateral Connection. *Atlantic Monthly*, July 1977, 57—9.

Ogata, Sadako. 'The Business Community and Japanese Foreign Policy'. In: Robert A. Scalapino (ed.). *The Foreign Policy of Modern Japan.* Berkeley: University of California Press. 1977, 175—203.

Ojimi, Yoshihisa. 'A Government Ministry: The Case of the Ministry of International Trade and Industry' (and: 'Discussion'). In: Ezra F. Vogel (ed.). *Modern Japanese Organisation and Decision Making.* Tokyo: Tuttle Co. 1979, 101—12.

Olechowski, Andrzej and Gary Sampson. Current Trade Restrictions in the EEC, the United States and Japan. *Journal of World Trade Law 14*, 1980, 220—31.

Olivetti, Marco M. 'La préparation de la décision communautaire au niveau national italien'. In: Pierre Gerbet and Daniel Pepy (eds.). *La décision dans les Communautés Européennes.* Brussels: Presses Universitaires de Bruxelles. 1969, 209—27.

Overholt, William H. Japan's Emergent World Role. *Orbis 19*, 1975, 412—33.

Paarlberg, Robert L. Domesticating Global Management. *Foreign Affairs 54*, 1976, 563—76.

Passin, H. Sociocultural Factors in the Japanese Perception of International Order. *Japanese Institute of International Affairs Annual Review 5*, 1969—70, 51—75.

Patrick, Hugh and Henry Rosovsky. 'Japan's Economic Performance: An Overview'. In: Hugh Patrick and Henry Rosovsky (eds.). *Asia's*

New Giant. Washington D.C.: The Brookings Institution, 1976, 1—61.

Pempel, T.J. Japan's Foreign Policy: the Domestic Bases for International Behaviour. *International Organisation 31,* 1977, 723—74.

Pempel, T.J. The Bureaucratisation of Policy Making in Post-war Japan. *American Journal of Political Science* 1974, 647—64.

Pentland, Charles. Linkage Politics: Canada's Contract and the Development of the EC's External Relations. *International Journal 32,* 1977, 207—31.

Peters, Theo. 'The Community and the Changing World Economic Order'. In: Max Kohnstamm and Wolfgang Hager (eds.). *A Nation Writ Large?* London: Macmillan. 1973, 22—50.

Pfaltzgraff, R.L. Jr. American — European — Japanese Relationship: Prospect for the late 1970s. *Orbis 19,* 1975, 809—26.

Pickert, Percy. The Foreign Policy of Japan Inc. *Japan Quarterly 21,* 1974, 79—86.

Pickles, William. 'Political Power in the EEC'. In: Carol A. Cosgrave and Kenneth J. Twitchett (eds.). *The New International Actors.* London: Macmillan, 1970, 201—21.

Pittman, John. Le trilateralisme, un nouveau scenario de l'impérialisme US. *La nouvelle revue internationale,* May 1978, 118—31.

Posner, Alan R. 'Italy: Dependence and Fragmentation'. In: Peter J. Katzenstein (ed.). *Between Power and Plenty: Foreign Economic Policies of Advanced Industrial States.* Madison: University of Wisconsin Press. 1978. 225—54.

Pouchard, Jacques. 'Les exportations francaises au Japon'. M. Arai et al. *La nouvelle politique commerciale japonaise.* Paris: Dunod. 1973. 45—58.

Poulantzas, Nicos. Internationalisation of Capitalist Relations and the Nation State. *Economy and Society 3,* 1974, 145—79.

Rhein, Eberhard. Die Europäische Gemeinschaft auf der Suche nach einer gemeinsamen Aussenpolitik. *Europa Archiv 31,* 1976, 171—80.

Rhein, Eberhard. Europa, Japan und die internationale Arbeitsteilung. *Europa Archiv 36,* 1981, 209—14.

Rieber, Roger A. The Future of the European Communities in International Politics. *Canadian Journal of Political Science 32,* 1976, 207—31.

Rolef, S.H. Changing Circumstances of Japan's Foreign Policy. *Asian Survey 16,* 1976, 1034—42.

Ross-Skinner, Jean. The Japanese Juggernaut — Now it's Europe's Turn. *Dun's* (New York) *101,* 1973, 54—57 and 122.

Rothacher, Albrecht. Das Werden des Pazifischen Zeitalters. *Merkur,* No. 302, 1981, 103—7.

Rothacher, Albrecht. Der Trilateralismus als internationales Politikmanagement. *Aus Politik und Zeitgeschichte,* B6/81, 1981, 25—30.

Rothacher, Albrecht. The European Community's Policies towards Japan. *The Journal of Social Sciences* (Tokyo), No. 19 (1), 1980, 27—45.

Rothacher, Albrecht. Ways of Analysing Japanese Society: Proposals for a Comparative Sociology of National Culture. *Centre News* (Japanese Studies Centre, The Japan Foundation) *4*, 1980, 7—9.

Salmon, Jean J.A. 'Le rôle des réprésentants permanents'. In: Pierre Gerbet and Daniel Pepy (eds.). *La décision dans les Communautés Européennes.* Brussels: Presses Universitaires de Bruxelles. 1969, 57—73.

Sautter, Christian. Tensions économiques entre le Japon et l'Europe. *Défense Nationale 33*, 1977, 105—22.

Sayle, Murray. Resisting the Japanese Invasion. *New Statesman 95*, 1978, 207—9.

Schwarz, Hans Peter. 'Die Bundesregierung und die auswärtigen Beziehungen'. *Handbuch der deutschen Aussenpolitik.* München: Piper & Co. 1975, 43—111.

Scotto, Marcel. Vers une guerre commerciale entre la CEE et le Japon? *Revue du Marché Commun 20*, 1977, (No. 203) 1—3.

Shapiro, M.J. and G.M. Bonham, Cognitive Processes and Foreign Policy Decision Making. *International Studies Quarterly* 1973, 147—74.

Shonfield, Andrew. Reshaping the World Economic Order — Relations between the EC, the US and Japan. *Chronique de politique étrangère 26*, 1973, 48—53.

Sidjanski, Dusan. 'Pressure Groups and the European Economic Community'. In: C.A. Cosgrave and K.J. Twitchett (eds.). *The New International Actor.* London: Macmillan. 1970, 222—36.

Simonis, Udo E. 'Problemfelder der japanischen Aussenhandelspolitik'. *Japan: Wirtschaftswachstum und soziale Wohlfahrt.* Frankfurt: Herder & Herder. 1974, 143—66.

Smith, Gerald C. The Vital Triangle. *The World Today 30*, 1974, 142—50.

Soames, Christopher. Europe's Wider Horizons. *The Round Table.* No. 262, 1976, 121—34.

Soames, Christopher. The EEC's External Relations. *The World Today,* 29, 1973, 190—95.

Soldatos, Panayotis. La théorie de la politique étrangère et sa pertenance pour l'étude des relations extérieures des Communautés Européennes. *Etudes Internationales 9*, 1978, 7—42.

Staden, Berndt von. Die politische Zusammenarbeit der EG Staaten. *Aussenpolitik 23*, 1972, 200—9.

Stebner, Peter. Japanische Exportoffensive verschärft zwischen imperialistische Gegensätze. *IPW Berichte 4*, 1977, 56—61.

Steiner, Miriam. The Elusive Essence of Decision. A Critical Comparison of Allison's and Snyder's Decision Making Approaches. *International Studies Quarterly 21*, 1977, 389–422.

Stern, Fritz. The Giant from Afar. Visions of Europe from Algiers to Tokyo. *Foreign Affairs 55*, 1977, 111–35.

Streit, M.E. European External Economic Policy at the Crossroads. *Konjunkturpolitik 19*, 1973, 189–203.

Takahashi, Johsen. et al. Japan's Trade Relations with the US and Western Europe. *Journal of the Mitsubishi Research Institute*, No. 7, 1978, 12–29.

Taylor, Paul. Intergovernmentalism in the European Communities in the 1970s: Patterns and Perspectives. Manuscript. 1981.

Taylor, Paul. The Politics of the European Communities: The Confederal Phase. *World Politics 27*, 1975, 336–60.

Terfloth, Claus. 'Bruxelles et Tokyo: Dialogue entre deux géants de l'économie'. In: Claus Gasteyger (ed.). *Le Japon et le Monde Atlantique.* Farnborough, Hants: Saxon House. Les Cahiers Atlantiques 3, 1973, 83–9.

Thayer, Nathael B. 'Competition and Conformity: An Inquiry into the Structure of the Japanese Newspapers'. In: Ezra F. Vogel (ed.). *Modern Japanese Organisation and Decision Making.* Tokyo: Tuttle Co., 1979, 284–303.

Tomsa, Branko. La CEE et le Tokyo Round. *Studia Diplomatica 31*, 1978, 281–304.

Torrelli, Maurice. L'élaboration des relations extérieures de la CEE. *Revue du Marché Commun*, No. 167, 1973, 328–40.

Trezise, Philip E. and Yukio Suzuki. 'Politics, Government and Economic Growth in Japan'. In: Hugh Patrick and Henry Rosovsky (eds.). *Asia's New Giant.* Washington D.C.: The Brookings Institution. 1976, 753–811.

Tsurumi, Kiyohiko. 'A Review of the Economic Situation in Europe'. In: Kajima Institute of International Peace (ed.). *Japan in the World.* Tokyo: The Japan Times, 1976, 143–58.

Tsurutani, Taketsugu. The Causes of Paralysis. *Foreign Policy* No. 14, 1974, 126–41.

Uchino, Tatsuro. 'Thirty Years of Post-war Economic Policies'. In: Ministry of Foreign Affairs (ed.). *Japan's Post-war Economic Policies.* Tokyo. 1976, 5–22.

Ullman, Richard H. Trilateralism: 'Partnership' for what? *Foreign Affairs 55*, 1976, 1–19.

Vignes, Daniel. 'Le rôle du Secretariat des Conseils'. In: Pierre Gerbet and Daniel Pepy (eds.). *La décision dans les Communautés Européennes.* Brussels: Presses Universitaires de Bruxelles, 1969, 75–81.

Vogel, Ezra F. 'Introduction: Toward More Accurate Concepts'. In: Ezra F. Vogel (ed.). *Modern Japanese Organisation and Decision*

Making. Tokyo: Tuttle Co. 1979, xiii–xxv.

Wacziarg, Alain. Marché japonais: quelle ouverture? *L'usine nouvelle,* No. 13, 30.3.1978, p. 51.

Wakaizumi, Kai. Consensus in Japan. *Foreign Policy.* No. 27, 1977, 158–77.

Wakaizumi, Kai. Japan's Dilemma: To Act or not to Act. *Foreign Policy,* No. 16, 1974, 30–47.

Wallace, William. The Management of Foreign Economic Relations in Britain. *International Affairs 50,* 1974, 251–67.

Watanabe, Akio. Foreign Policy Making, Japanese Style. *International Affairs 54,* 1978, 75–88.

Watanabe, Akio. 'Japanese Public Opinion and Foreign Affairs: 1964–1973.' In: Robert A. Scalapino (ed.). *The Foreign Policy of Modern Japan.* Berkeley: University of California Press. 1977, 105–45.

Wilkinson, Endymion. Changement des structures des exportations du Japon 1953–1976 et ses complications pour la C.E. *Chroniques d' Actualité de la SEDEIS 18,* 1978, 244–65.

Williams, Ikuko. Politiek en handelsstrategie: de EEG en Japan. *Internationale Spectator,* No. 11, 1978, 691–99.

Yamamoto, Mitsuru. 'An Erosion of Neutralism'. In: Japan Centre for International Exchange (ed.). *The Silent Power — Japan's Identity and World Role.* Tokyo: Simul Press. 1976. 141–63.

Zahl, Karl F. The Social Structure of the Political Elite in Postwar Japan. *The Transactions of the Asiatic Society of Japan 11,* 1973, 126–46.

Zysman, John. The French State in the International Economy. *International Organisation 31,* 1977, 255–93.

Newspapers, periodicals and agency dispatches

Agence Europe
ANSA
Asahi Evening News
Asahi Shimbun
Bulletin of the European Communities
Business Week
Christian Science Monitor
Corriere della Sera
Daily Express
Daily Telegraph
Economie (Brussels)
The Economist
Far Eastern Economic Review

Le Figaro
Financial Times
Frankfurter Allgemeine Zeitung
The Guardian — Manchester Guardian
Hsinhua News Agency
International Herald Tribune
Japan Economic Journal
Japan Information Bulletin (London)
Japan Times
Japan Times Weekly
Kyodo

Look Japan
Mainichi Daily News
Mainichi Shimbun
Markt Deutschland—Japan (Tokyo)
Le Monde
Neue Zürcher Zeitung
Newsweek
New York Times
Nichidoku Geppo
Nihon Keizai Shimbun
Nippon Times
Observer
Observer Foreign News Service
OECD Observer

Official Journal of the European Communities
The Oriental Economist
Revue du Marché Commun
Der Spiegel
Süddeutsche Zeitung
Tagblatt—Journal d'Esch
Time
The Times
Tokyo Financial Review
Trialogue (New York)
Die Welt
Yomiuri Shimbun
Die Zeit

Archive and PR materials

Archive and PR materials provided by the following institutions were used:

Anglo—Japanese Economic Institute, London.
British Chamber of Commerce and Industry, Tokyo.
Chambre de Commerce et d'Industrie Français du Japon, Tokyo.
Commission of the European Communities, Brussels.
Commission. Press and Information Office, London.
Delegation of the Commission of the European Communities, Tokyo.
Deutsche Industrie— und Handelskammer in Japan, Tokyo.
Japan External Trade Organisation, Tokyo and London.
Japan Foundation, Tokyo and London.
Japan Information Centre, London.
Japanese Ministry of Foreign Affairs, Tokyo.
Keizai Koho Centre, Tokyo.
Mission of Japan to the European Communities, Brussels.
Office Franco Japonaise d'études économiques, Paris.
Royal Institute of International Affairs, Press Library, London.

Interviews

The following interviews were held:

1 Charlotte von Verschüer, Stagiaire at the EC Delegation 1974–75, 1.10.1979.
2 The Attache, Commercial Section, French Embassy, Tokyo, 6.11.1979.
3 Dr Wolfgang Penzias, Assistant Austrian Trade Delegate, 8.1.1980.
4 Rolf-Dieter Schnelle, Second Secretary, Economic Section, German Embassy, 16.1.1980.
5 Nobuyoki Fujimoto, Assistant to the Commercial Councillor, Royal Danish Embassy, 17.1.1980.
6 Guido Sonck, First Secretary, Embassy of Belgium, 22.1.1980.
7 Hans von Schaper, German Chamber of Industry and Commerce in Japan, 11.1.1980.
8 Paul Murray, First Secretary, Embassy of Ireland, 20.1.1980.
9 Johan Kramer, Commercial Secretary, Royal Netherlands Embassy 1.2.1980.
10 Adrian Thorpe, First Secretary, Economic Department, British Embassy, 3.2.1980.
11 Tassos G. Kourrousis, Commercial Attache, Greek Embassy, 30.1.1980.
12 Hideaki Hoshi, First International Economic Affairs Division, Japanese Ministry of Foreign Affairs, 21.1.1980.
13 H. Tanaka, General Manager of the Europe & Africa Department, Marubeni Corporation, 4.2.1980.
14 Tsumoto Yuno, Deputy General Manager, International Investment Division, Bank of Tokyo, 7.2.1980.
15 Noritake Egawa, Assistant General Manager, Research Department, Mitsubishi Corporation, 14.2.1980.
16 Dr Galway Johnson, Deputy Director Far East, Industrial Development Authority of Ireland, 15.2.1980.
17 Carlo Addis, Trade Analyst, Italian Institute for Foreign Trade, 18.2.1980.
18 Fred M. Walker, British Chamber of Commerce in Japan, 22.2.1980.
19 The Assistant, Commercial Section, Spanish Embassy, 26.2.1980.
20 Teiji Hirao, Deputy General Manager, and Atsuro Mogi, Assistant Manager, Europe & Africa Department, Overseas Planning Division, Mutsui Bussan, 26.2.1980.
21 Stewart Jack, Foreign and Commonwealth Office, Far Eastern Department, London, 27.8.1980.
22 Professor Ralf Dahrendorf, Commissioner for External Relations 1971–1973, London, 6.1.1981.

23 Gerhard Lohan, Commission, DG I, Brussels, 13.1.1981.
24 Dr Bandela, Council of Ministers, General Secretariat, Brussels, 13.1.1981.
25 Mr Miyazaki, Director of the Cultural & Information Service, Japanese Embassy in Belgium, 14.1.1981.

Subject index

Abu Dhabi Marine Area Ltd. 195
ACP 153, 168, 173
AEG Telefunken 223
Aerospace 324
Afghanistan 69, 266, 269, 288
Agricultural exports 168, 170, 178, 223, 232, 237, 243, 265
Agrochemicals 257
Airbus 219, 235, 238, 241, 244, 246—7, 254, 257, 260, 264, 286
Aircraft 111, 116, 147, 241—2, 245, 248, 252—3, 262, 269, 286;
    components 240
    shelters 269
Alfa Romeo 267, 272, 282
Algeria 103
All Nippon Airways 248
American Chamber of Commerce 98
AMF Investment 196
Anti-aircraft missiles 269
Anti-aircraft tanks 269
Antibiotics 115
Anti-dumping duty 158, 220, 225, 232—4, 236, 265, 323;
    procedure 221, 224—5, 240, 265
Anti-trust laws 159, 164
Apparel 174
Arabian Oil Co. 71
Argentina 106, 276

Armament 269, 286, 333
Art works 174, 279
Asahi Chemical Industries 196, 285
ASEAN 182, 254
Atlantic Charter 169, 175
Audio equipment 220–1, 235–6, 240, 285
Australia 69, 85–6, 94, 156, 179, 189, 276, 289
Austria 150
Aviation 220, 264, 286, 333
Awase culture 74
AWES 180, 221, 224

BAC 244
Ball bearings 114, 159, 161, 163, 168, 172, 176, 190, 192, 218, 220–2,
    232, 236, 250, 265, 281–3, 285, 323, 325
Ballpoint pens 222, 228
Banking 177, 195, 250–1, 266, 331
Bank of Japan 235, 251
Batteries 154, 161, 182, 283
Bayer 196
BDI 158, 121
Beef 62, 239, 241, 283
Belgium 86, 120, 157, 179, 182, 191, 195, 282;
    African possessions 91;
    EC policies 39;
    policies towards Japan 89, 100, 102, 287
Benelux 38, 98, 110, 115, 125, 149, 175, 182, 191;
    Japan Trade Agreement 89, 102, 252;
    quotas 115, 283;
    relations with Japan 89, 92, 100, 103, 120;
    trade with Japan 125–9, 167, 183–6, 277–81
BIAC 116, 123
Bicycles 146
Binoculars 97, 146, 190
Biscuits 154, 226, 228, 233, 246
BL 172, 245, 263, 266, 282, 293, 296
Blankets 130
Bolts 283
Books 187
Brandy 233, 240
Brazil 220, 224, 238, 276
Britain 85, 107, 110–1, 118, 120, 123, 157, 177, 182, 191, 194, 224,
    227, 243, 248, 250, 268–70, 285;
    foreign policy making 36–7, 122;

Japanese investments 173, 240, 268, 284–5;
joining the EC 94, 102, 114, 116, 147, 152, 167;
policies towards Japan 86, 92, 94–7, 106, 111, 116, 122, 145, 147,
  150, 154, 168, 171, 173, 177, 201, 220–2, 229, 234, 246, 266,
  271, 287, 329;
trade policies 287;
trade with Japan 125–8, 184–6, 277–81
British mafia 289
British Overseas Trading Board 264
Bureaucratic decisions 320–2
Bureaucratic politics 6–7, 200, 203, 288, 299–300, 317–23, 330, 333,
  335
Butter 228

Calculators 190
Cambodia 202
Cameras 103, 115, 146, 154, 171
Camp David 271
Canada 86, 96, 156, 160, 179, 268
Canned beef 232, 283
Capital goods 130, 147, 187, 219, 256
Caravelles 103
Carpets 283
Car radios 267
Cars 89, 111, 114, 149, 165, 171–2, 176–7, 180, 187–91, 219, 222,
  225–6, 228–9, 231, 236–7, 240, 242, 245–6, 250, 252, 258,
  264–5, 267, 270–6, 280–3, 324, 329;
Italian quota 154, 161, 267, 282;
testing 177–8, 180, 218, 221, 233, 283
Caterpillar 196
CBI 123, 154–5, 158, 172, 221
CCMC 271, 275
CEBLS 165–6, 180
Cement 325
Ceramics 89–90, 108, 146, 252
Ceramics industries 85, 87, 121
Charter control 107
Chatham House 236
Cheese 232, 283
Chemicals 129, 187–8, 195–6, 219, 235, 246, 257, 264, 281, 324–5
Chewing gum 246
China 103, 111–2, 116, 118, 146, 151, 160, 174, 182, 198, 200, 202,
  254, 271;
Soviet relations 254–5

Chocolates 154, 226, 228, 246
Chrysler 149, 197
Ciba Geigy 196
Cigarettes 219, 235, 265
CIPI 267, 272
Citrus juice 241
City of London 182, 194
Club de Paris 277
Coal 283
Cognac 103, 222, 226, 228, 232, 290, 294
Cold War 84, 118
Comecon 153, 182
Commercial councillors 182, 200, 218, 289—90
Commission of the European Communities 243, 323;
    Commissioners 20, 198, 259, 289;
    Delegation in Tokyo 159—61, 169, 175—6, 181—2, 197, 199—200,
        287, 289—90, 323;
    DG I 19—20, 121, 170, 175, 270, 287, 289, 291;
    DG III 246, 270, 287, 332;
    DG VIII 20;
    officials 31—3, 198—9, 270, 291;
    policies towards Japan 93, 104—5, 108—10, 113, 121—2, 132—4,
        148, 153, 160, 175, 179—81, 226—7, 229, 233, 240, 242—3, 246,
        258—61, 274, 287, 328—9;
    President 21, 23, 244, 273;
    Secretariat General 20—1, 29
Committee 113 18, 26—7, 151, 157, 162, 246, 274, 290—2
Commonwealth 85, 94
Communication 329, 333
Communism 221, 232, 235, 267
Computers 111, 239, 268, 285
Concorde 165, 219
Confectionery 147, 221, 266, 283
Confidustria 119
Conserves 129—30
Consumer electronics 189, 258
Consumer products 187, 279—80
Cooking appliances 161
Coreper 18, 24—6, 105, 108—9, 114, 121, 133, 148, 170, 199, 229,
    233, 242—3, 248, 254, 270—2, 291
Cosmetics 110, 149, 174, 188, 222, 252, 257, 279
Cotton textiles 99, 103, 114, 122, 130, 145, 147, 181;
    industries 85
Council of Ministers 18, 22—3, 108, 110, 113, 121—2, 148, 171, 242,

262, 269, 272, 291–2, 299;
policies towards Japan 171–2, 243, 248–9;
presidency 243–5;
Secretariat of the Council 23, 25, 170, 291–2
Cultured pearls 90
Curve of influence 31
Customs union 18, 40
Cutlery 282–3

Dahrendorf formula 162
Dairy products 226, 232, 283
Dassault 264, 286
Data processing 264
Datsun 267, 296
Davignon Report 19
Decision analysis 15–6, 317
Decision making 7, 298, 317, 322, 325
Denmark 157, 191, 224, 243;
    EC policies 39, 167;
    policies towards Japan 262;
    trade policies 168, 230, 275, 287;
    trade with Japan 185–6, 278–81
Desk top calculator 158
Detente 160, 165, 202, 276
Devon 285
Diesel engines 178
Diet 65, 156, 239, 248, 253, 266;
    EC–Japan Parliamentary Friendship League 253
Doko shock 68, 221–3, 227, 250, 297–8, 320
Domei 107
Dow Chemical 196
DSP 65, 107
Dumping 161, 225, 234, 236, 327
Dunlop 196
Dyestuff 283

East Indies 158
EC:
    association agreements 17, 153, 168;
    Commission 19–21, 197;
    common agricultural policies 108, 168;
    common commercial policy 17, 40, 91, 109, 132–3, 146, 148, 162,
        171–2, 175, 200, 270, 332;
    common external tariff 17–8, 90–1, 109, 166, 283–4;

Community cycle 22;
competition policy 164–5, 172, 175–6, 202, 255;
competitiveness 270, 284, 325, 332;
creation 90, 156;
customs union 109, 133;
decision making 33–4, 133, 245, 288–93, 329–30;
Economic and Social Committee 27–8;
elite network 31;
exports 129, 184, 187–8, 234, 239, 279–81, 284, 325;
export promotion 263–4;
external policies 40–2, 202;
first enlargement 148, 167;
foreign policy making 15, 94, 122, 133, 197, 242–3, 287–93, 323–5;
import restrictions 85, 90, 109, 113–4, 122, 130–1, 133, 149, 152,
    183, 193, 252, 268, 274, 283–4, 332;
industrial policy 202, 227, 268;
interest groups 30–1, 222, 292–3;
intergovernmentalism 34–5, 288, 318;
legal foundations 17–9;
national governments 34–5, 171, 175, 274, 287, 292;
policies towards Japan 93–4, 100–10, 147–8, 175, 202, 271, 287–8,
    297–300, 325
EC–Japan relations:
    EC deficit 219, 257, 263, 275, 278, 297;
    high politics relations 70, 134, 171, 175, 202, 269–70, 288, 299–300,
        317–8, 324;
    Joint Study Group 238;
    negotiations 150, 169, 172–3, 199–201, 219, 234, 243–4, 246–7,
        264, 276, 320, 328–30;
    trade 125–30, 148, 178–9, 182–94, 277–84, 326;
    Trade Agreement 148–52, 156, 162, 166, 169, 172–3, 175, 198,
        201, 252–3, 256, 323, 328;
    Trade Agreement – first round of negotiations 152–3, 156, 323, 328;
    Trade Agreement – second round of negotiations 156–7;
    trade composition 128–30, 187–9, 279–82;
    trade cover ratios 185;
    trade relative shares 128, 186, 278–9;
    trade war 158, 249, 318, 331
EC Steering Committee 200, 290, 318
ECSC–MITI consultations 113, 122, 178–9, 219, 225, 239, 248, 265–6
ECSC Treaty 179
Educational materials 188
EFTA 91, 164, 225, 232, 248, 325
Egypt 150

Electric appliances 146, 151, 161, 187, 252, 257, 283
Electric cables 283
Electronics 164, 167, 172, 175—6, 182, 192, 222—3, 229, 240, 252, 267—8, 270—1, 274, 282, 333
Electronics industries 99, 111, 161, 167, 196, 325
Elite socialisation 4, 32
Empresa Nacional de Autocamiones 267
EMS 254, 256, 277, 284, 332
Energy 129, 170, 173, 175, 179, 182, 274, 290
Engineering 196
English 195, 256, 329
Erabu culture 74
Espionage 243
Euro—Arab dialogue 179
Eurofer 221
European Council 18, 23—4, 220—1, 223, 226, 229, 232—4, 236, 239—40, 249, 252, 256—8, 263, 270—1, 275, 293;
    Presidency 263
European investment in Japan 196—7
European Parliament 27, 113, 149—50, 152—3, 155, 220, 229, 233, 249, 253, 266, 293
European Political Co-operation 19, 28—30, 293;
    Political Committee 21, 28
European Security Conference 151
Ex—Im Bank 238, 263
Expo 1970 151, 154
Export control 237

FAG Kugelfischer 224
Fascism 237
Fashion clothing 188, 279
Fast-breeder reactor 286
FEBMA 265
Fiat 149, 170, 267, 275, 282, 293
Films 283
Film cameras 190
Finland 191
Fish 71—2, 108, 129, 283
Flag discrimination 166, 224, 230—1
Flowers 283
Flower bulbs 269
Fokker 244, 264, 269, 286
Food 129, 187—9, 195—6, 232, 253, 279, 281, 283
Food Sanitation Law 194, 222

Ford 245
Forges 240
France 85–6, 88, 98, 106, 111–4, 118–9, 146, 153, 160, 174, 219–20;
  African possessions 91;
  foreign policy making 36, 118–9, 161;
  Japan Trade Agreement 252;
  quotas 115, 220, 272, 277, 283;
  relations with Japan 89–90, 92–3, 99–100, 103–4, 111–3, 118–9,
    146, 153, 160, 174, 219–20, 222, 242, 254–5;
  tariffs 91;
  trade policies 90, 100, 237, 242, 275, 287, 319;
  trade with Japan 125–9, 185–6, 236, 277–81;
Freudenberg 196
Fruit paste 283
Fuji Photo Film Co. 196
Fuji Xerox 196
Fujitsu 285
Furniture 188
Furs 279

Gas turbines 324
Gas appliances 252, 257, 284
GATT 93, 110, 132, 232, 318, 324;
  Art. 19 150, 168, 170, 251–2
  Art. 35 86, 89, 91, 95;
  Dillon Round 121;
  General Meeting 87–8, 91;
  Japanese membership 85–6, 123, 155, 328;
  Kennedy Round 41, 105, 108, 114, 121, 150, 182;
  Tokyo Round 62, 166, 169–70, 179, 239–41, 246–7, 251–2, 260,
    284, 290–1
GDR 146
Gepard 269
Germany 91, 118, 123, 125, 191, 224, 230, 232, 238, 243, 268–70,
  286, 324;
  Cartel Office 164, 192;
  foreign economic policy making 37, 120, 175, 182, 267, 293, 298;
  Japan Trade Agreement 88–9;
  policies towards Japan 86–9, 92, 99–100, 114–5, 120–1, 146–7,
    174, 199, 220, 222, 254, 262, 271;
  quotas 98, 115, 283;
  Retailers' Association 121;
  tariffs 91;
  trade policies 267, 274–5, 287, 321, 323, 331;

trade with Japan 125—9, 183—6, 277—81
Glassware 103
Glucose 283
Greece 107, 191, 238, 278;
   EC membership 179
Group of Ten 318

Hamburgers 239
Handbags 279
Harvard Club 243
Heavy industry 113, 324
Helicopters 219
Hides 283
Hifi equipment 267
High Level Consultations 169—70, 176, 178, 182, 218—9, 225—6, 235,
   238, 252, 256, 262, 264—5, 270, 289—90, 330
High politics 4, 28, 124, 170, 198—9, 276, 288, 293, 298, 318—20, 331
High technology exports 189, 250, 282, 324
Hitachi 240, 283
Homo bureaucraticus 320
Honey 283
Honda 170, 263, 266, 282
Hong Kong 69, 181
Household equipment 187—8

IAEA 160
IDA 285
IEA 179, 270
IHI 264, 286
IMF 93, 98
Immigrant workers 242
Impact loans 251
Imperialism 4—5, 67—8
Import controls 161, 166, 180, 201, 217, 220, 222—3, 226, 229, 245,
   249, 258, 261, 283, 299, 318, 331
India 88, 90, 112, 136, 160, 173
Indochina 85, 103, 200, 257, 266
Indoesia 69, 111, 254
Industrial co-operation 246, 249, 255, 258, 262
Inflation 254, 271
Information processing 285
Insulators 283
Insulin 283
Insurance 194—5, 266, 331

Integrated circuits 285
Interest groups 118, 133
Inter-industry agreements 119, 163—4, 175—6, 292
Investment schemes 195, 285
Invisibles 194, 331
Iran 69, 255, 257;
   revolution 263—4, 288;
   sanctions 269—70
Ireland 191, 195, 243;
   EC policies 39, 167;
   Japanese investments 240, 284—5, 287;
   quotas 283;
   trade policies 287, 319;
   trade with Japan 185—6, 278—81
Iri-Finnmechanica 267
Iron and non-ferrous metals 195, 281
Israel 70, 106, 150
Italy 86, 98, 109, 168, 191, 197, 221, 224, 227, 230, 243;
   foreign economic policy making 37—8, 119, 170, 267, 272;
   quotas 114, 272, 277, 283;
   relations with Japan 87, 93, 99, 102—3, 107—8, 114, 119—20, 146, 174, 235—6;
   trade with Japan 125—9, 185—6, 277—81

JAL 165, 248
JAMA 228, 237, 245, 267, 273, 275
Japan:
   administrative guidance 52, 106, 159, 177, 179, 235, 274, 283;
   advisory councils 54, 115, 237, 251, 264;
   agricultural policies 55, 62, 192—3, 197, 228—9, 232—3, 337, 285, 325;
   banking system 251;
   bargaining style 70, 73—5, 125, 132, 294—5;
   big business 55—7, 65—7, 227, 237, 262, 298;
   budgeting 61—3, 248, 268;
   capital exports 113, 171, 194—5, 201, 283—4, 332;
   capital liberalisation 106—7, 116, 149, 154, 167—8, 177, 197, 201, 285;
   central bureaucracy 51—4, 245, 288, 293—5, 319;
   current account surplus 254, 263;
   customs regulations 131, 177, 194, 228, 244, 262;
   decision making 51—2, 75, 115, 124, 199, 293—5, 327—30;
   Defence Agency 269, 276;
   defence spending 269;

distribution system 149, 168–9, 177, 188, 197, 232, 284, 331;
Emperor 157–8, 165;
entertainment 54, 331;
Environment Agency 225–6, 228;
export economy 92, 94, 118, 123, 130–1, 145, 156, 170–1, 176–7,
    183–4, 188–92, 201, 219, 221, 237, 252, 259–60, 266, 270, 273,
    277, 296–7;
export promotion 113, 266;
Fair Trade Commission 166;
feudalism 262, 297;
food imports 174, 177, 219, 227, 237;
foreign exchange 149, 246, 260;
Foreign Ministry 57–60, 96, 98, 107, 109, 113, 116, 124, 132, 150,
    156, 160, 171, 178, 198, 200, 218, 226–8, 293–5;
foreign policies 67–73, 288, 328, 331;
Foreign Trade Council 67, 110, 262, 266;
image in Europe 117–8, 133, 148, 198, 254–5, 259, 262, 296–7, 327;
imperialism 67–8;
import liberalisation 83, 93, 131, 145, 149, 192–3, 201;
import missions 223, 245;
investments in Europe 250, 262, 267, 331;
management styles 197, 259;
market 187–8, 223, 233, 239, 257, 260, 262, 273–4, 279, 283, 290,
    318, 325;
media 107, 150, 181, 227, 244, 259, 269;
military situation 68, 256, 269;
Ministry of Agriculture 62, 228, 232–3, 265;
Ministry of Finance 63–4, 96, 98, 107, 116, 131, 152, 154, 228, 233,
    237, 239, 251, 285, 294–5;
Ministry of Health and Welfare 244, 295;
Ministry of Transport 62–3, 107, 124, 180, 218, 226, 228, 231, 237,
    248;
MITI 60–2, 106, 109, 116, 124, 149–50, 152, 160, 165, 172, 178–9,
    197–8, 200, 218, 223, 225–6, 228–9, 233, 235–6, 255, 264, 273,
    293–5;
Mission in Brussels 241;
Monopoly Tobacco Corporation 221, 226, 228;
Navy 276;
non-tariff barriers 131, 151, 167, 177, 180, 191, 194, 198, 200, 219,
    221, 241, 252, 257, 283, 328;
orderly marketing 88, 104, 155, 159, 166, 176, 192, 201, 222–3, 262;
peace constitution 68, 286;
perception of Europe 90, 94, 97, 105, 108, 114, 118, 125, 148, 199,
    227, 233, 243–4, 253, 261, 295–6, 327, 333;

policies towards Europe 88, 97—9, 104—7, 113—4, 124—5, 132, 149, 153, 162, 176, 200, 237, 241—2;
prime minister 64—5, 68, 72, 227—8, 256, 294;
private economic diplomacy 66, 125, 132;
procurement policies 246;
protectionism 116, 131, 193;
quotas 121, 131—2, 147, 149, 151—2, 227, 237, 239, 283;
raw material supplies 69, 173, 198, 201, 324;
reflation policies 247, 252, 257—8, 261, 320;
relations with China 66, 74, 147, 242;
relations with the Arab world 70—1, 74;
relations with the US 71, 118, 123, 149, 203, 239, 260, 274;
research policy 116;
restructuring 128—9, 159, 188—9, 230, 250, 324, 331;
tariffs 63, 131, 165—6, 192, 198, 222, 226, 237, 239, 241, 243, 249, 283—4;
technological challenge 116, 148, 271—2, 277, 296—7, 331, 333;
trade statistics 277—8;
trade with Europe 125—30, 183—92, 227, 277—84;
war experience 68;
Western integration 147, 198, 327
Japan Inc. 50, 236, 284
Japan Iron & Steel Federation 225
Japan Paris Club 276
JCP 65, 107
Jet engines 264, 286
JETRO 159
Jewellery 281
Joint ventures 197, 264, 282, 286, 333
Juice 283
Jute fabrics 283
JSP 65, 74, 96, 102, 107

Kawasaki Heavy Industries 264, 286
Keidanren 55—6, 66, 99, 106, 113, 119, 122, 154, 157—9, 172, 221—3, 245, 249—50, 298
Keizei Doyukai 56
Ketchup 283
Kobe Steel 158
Komeito 65
Korea 69, 85, 181, 224, 238
Korean War 85
Kurile islands 71, 171
Kyoto confectioners 245

Lancashire 86
Latin America 91, 160, 334
Leather 197, 283, 285
Leisure goods 188
Less Developed Countries 95, 107, 114, 179, 183, 189, 198
Liberal Democratic Party 54—5, 102, 153, 227, 257, 276, 288;
    factions 54, 227, 298
Lighters 110
Light industry 113, 116, 130, 145, 281, 324
Liquor 194, 266, 279—80, 283, 294
Lockheed 165, 219—20
Lomé Agreement 179
Long Term Credit Bank 196
Low politics 1, 72, 169, 199, 288, 293, 317
LTA on cotton textiles 147, 155
Luxembourg 39, 120, 182
Luxury goods 279, 281

Machinery 129, 146, 187—9, 240, 280—1, 324, 331
Machine tools 100, 146, 149, 299, 329
Malaysia 103, 111, 116
Manchuria 85
Marine biology 157
Maritime policy 230
Maritime transportation 194, 201
Matsushita 196, 285
Mazda 267
Meat 228, 232—3, 245, 280, 283
Mechanical engineering 195
Meiji Restoration 327
Metals 187, 280—1
Mexico 189, 276
Microscopes 164, 190, 283
Middle East 182—3, 276, 324—5
Middlesex 285
Midlands 173
Militarism 237
Milk powder 228—9
Mills Bill 153, 198, 202
Mining 197, 285
Mitsubishi 67, 71, 149, 197;
    Heavy Industries 196, 164, 286
Mitsui 71;
    mining 285

MNC 2, 38, 282
Mona Lisa 174
Monetary problems 148, 324
Morocco 85, 89
Most Favoured Nation 86, 92, 96, 104, 120, 130, 328
Moto Guzzi 170
Motor cycles 111, 161, 170, 235–6, 240, 281, 283
Motor Iberica 267
Mullard 240
Musical instruments 187

NATO 276
Neo-mercantilism 319
Nestlé 196
Netherlands 86, 123, 157–8, 167, 181, 224, 230, 232, 269;
    foreign economic policy making 38, 120, 164;
    policies towards Japan 229, 248, 262, 275;
    trade policies 38, 287;
    trade with Japan 183–6, 278–81
New Caledonia 89, 254
New Zealand 94, 156, 289
Nickel 254
NICs 69, 265, 334
Niger 171
Nikkeiren 56, 237
Nippon Electric 285
Nippon Oil Seal Ind. 196
Nippon Seiko 285
Nippon Steel 180
Nippon Tokushu Noyaku Seizo 196
Nissan 267, 272, 275–6, 282
Nissho 56, 123
Nixon shocks 72, 157, 183, 198, 222
Non-iron metals 189
Non-Proliferation Treaty 115, 146
Noritake 285
Northern Ireland 173
North Korea 147
North Sea oil 171, 173, 175
Norway 106, 191, 238
NTBs 148, 170, 262, 333
Nuclear energy 111, 116, 160, 173, 219, 242, 286

OAD 116, 163, 170, 173, 201, 242–3, 246–7, 252, 260, 295

OECD 8, 96, 123, 132, 162, 258, 268, 318, 334;
    DAC 105;
    Japan's admission 93, 96, 100, 104—7, 111, 123, 328;
    trade pledge 182;
    Working Party 6 106, 166, 224, 226, 228, 230, 238, 250, 255
Office equipment 188, 281
Oil 196, 253—4, 261, 266, 270—1, 277
Oil crisis 40, 71, 173—4, 176, 183, 200, 202—3, 263—4, 324, 334
Oil refining 285
Okinawa 226, 281
Olympics 269—70
OPEC 40, 71, 174—5, 198, 217, 285, 324
Optics 187—8
Oranges 239, 241, 283
Overseas travel 194

Pacific Basin Community 69, 295
Pakistan 88, 268
Parliaments 133
Pasta 232
Patronat 119, 158, 222
PCI 249
Peanuts 283
Perfumes 103, 111
Petrochemicals 149, 189
Peugeot 282
Pharmaceuticals 178, 189, 194, 196, 219, 228, 235, 243—6, 257, 262,
    279—80, 283—4
Philippines 69, 254
Philips 161, 164, 196, 240, 267—8, 282, 293, 325
Pig iron 283
Pineapples 283
Plastics 189
PLO 271
Plutonium 117, 160, 286
Poland 220, 276
Political decisions 321—2
Politicisation 217, 227, 297—300, 320, 330, 333
Populism 325
Porcelain 89, 103, 122, 130, 152, 293
Pork 226, 264—5, 281, 283
Portugal 191, 195, 221, 278
Post-industrialism 221, 284
Pottery 97, 282, 285

Power politics 4, 319
Precision instruments 129, 280—1
Price controls 165
Printing machines 146
Processed food 219—20, 226, 232, 235—7, 241, 243, 246, 263
Protectionism 2, 155, 168, 237, 239, 260, 264, 271, 274, 285, 319, 325, 331—4
Public tenders 189, 220, 247, 253, 264, 333

Quartz crystals 240

Rabbit hutches 259—62, 289, 295
Radar 147
Radios 164, 168, 188, 190, 266, 281, 283
Rank 196, 255
Rapier 276
Raw materials 69, 129—30, 149, 179, 187, 265, 280—1, 334
R & D 331
Realist school 4
Record players 168
Renault 222, 293
Reprocessing 286
Research co-operation 170
Rhodesia 116, 147, 268
Rice 283
Roland 269, 276
Rolls Royce 165, 264—5, 286
Roubaix—Tourcoing 93
Royal families 157
Royal Navy 276
Rubber 196

Saar 225
Sacks 283
Safeguard Clause 89, 96, 98, 101—5, 108, 110—1, 121, 124, 148—52, 155—7, 160, 162, 166—7, 198, 201, 251—2, 320
SAJ 165, 221, 224
SALT 256
Samurais 262
San Francisco Peace Treaty 85
Sanitary fittings 252, 257
Scandinavia 86
Seaweeds 283
Sekisui Chemicals 285

Sensitive products 150, 328
Sewing machines 85, 94, 97, 104, 110, 114, 188, 281—3
Shipbuilding 94, 107, 182, 191, 220, 224, 230—1, 238, 250, 286
Ships 113, 159, 165—6, 168, 180—1, 188—90, 195, 220, 222, 228—32, 234, 237—8, 250, 273, 281, 283, 325;
    engines 228, 235, 245, 246—7;
    order sharing 170, 221, 224, 226, 230—2, 255
Shoes 130, 147, 154, 161, 188, 226, 235, 242, 246, 258, 263, 283
Shoguns 262
Showa Oil 196
Silk 65, 90, 103, 129—30, 161, 235, 241—2, 245—6, 283
Singapore 69, 224
SKF 224, 282, 293, 325
Ski boots 222, 235—6, 240, 242, 245—6
SMMT 176, 237, 245, 267, 273
Socialism 235, 242
Socialist International 240
Sogo shosha 67, 131, 177, 223, 266, 327
Sony 285
Sord Computer Systems 285
South Africa 85—6, 189, 255, 276
South East Asia 90, 115, 201
Soviet Union 40, 69, 102, 160, 198, 200, 254, 266, 269, 271, 288;
    fisheries talks with Japan 71—2;
    Far Eastern fleet 69, 254;
    in EC—Japan relations 88, 110, 115, 171, 202;
    peace negotiations with Japan 70
Soy beans 223
Spain 150, 195, 267, 278
Sports equipment 188, 279
Stabex 179
Starch 283
State participation 325
Steel 100, 113, 122, 129, 158—9, 161, 178—9, 182, 188—92, 219—20, 222, 225—6, 229, 233—9, 248—50, 256, 266—7, 271—3, 283, 325
Stockpiling 223
Subsidies 224, 230—2, 250, 283
Sumitomo Electric Inds. 196
Sundry products 88, 117
Suntory 154, 294
Supertankers 230
Sweden 159, 219, 224, 286
Switzerland 157, 191, 286
Synthetic fibres 181, 189, 285

Taiwan 69, 85, 181, 224
Tansam missile 276
Tape recorders 161, 164, 168, 170, 172, 174, 190, 281
Tariffs 333
Tateno Trading Co. 196
Technological co-operation 111, 118, 174, 178, 220, 264, 277, 286
Telecommunications 189, 268, 324, 331
Telematics 268
Terrorism 243
Textiles 89–90, 92, 97, 108, 110, 117, 129–30, 146, 154–5, 161, 181,
    187–8, 192, 218, 271, 280-2, 325;
    industries 72, 85, 87, 99, 100, 118, 120, 237
Thailand 69, 189, 268
Third World 263–4, 276, 333
Thompson–Brandt 268–282
Three pillar theory 95–6, 99, 102, 125
Tiles 283
Titanium 240
TOA 248, 257
Tobacco 129, 226, 228, 246
Tomatoes 232, 283
Toshiba 255, 285
Tourism 201
Toyota 222, 296
Toys 97, 103, 110, 129, 146, 188, 190, 282
Trade 196, 263, 318, 333;
    liberalisation 67;
    marks 177, 243, 246, 247, 260;
    policy 18, 123, 132–3, 181, 201, 234, 236, 266, 287–8, 321, 323,
        327, 333–4;
    unions 219, 222, 235, 261, 267
Tractors 262
Transport attaches 180
Transportation equipment 187–8, 280
Treaty of Commerce and Navigation 86, 93–7, 252
Treaty of Rome 17, 19, 90, 151, 323
Trilateralism 2–4, 165, 170–1, 198–9, 202–3, 244, 253, 265, 276,
    282, 318–9, 324
Trucks 189–90, 237, 267
Tubes 268, 283
TUC 220–1
Turbines 189
Turkey 258, 268–9
TV sets 103, 161, 168, 170, 172, 176, 188, 190, 221, 223, 237, 240,

250, 266—8, 272—3, 281, 283, 285, 324, 329
Typewriters 111, 154, 161
Tyres 283

Ultraimperialism 4—5
Umbrellas 108, 111, 161, 182, 201
Unemployment 220, 222, 227, 235, 242, 267, 273, 287, 332
UNCTAD 41, 219, 324
UNICE 30, 122, 159, 234
United Nations 58;
  Disarmament Council 146
United States 40—1, 86, 105, 108, 115, 134, 160, 174, 179, 182, 189—90,
  200—1, 266, 285, 325;
  foreign policy making 318;
  in EC—Japan relations 84, 92, 111—2, 123—4, 148, 155—6, 161, 174,
    183, 198, 219, 225, 239—41, 243—4, 253, 260, 269, 271, 276, 282,
    286, 288, 324, 330;
  Japan Security Treaty 65, 68, 92;
  Japan textile wrangle 7, 72—3, 114, 124, 145, 151;
  occupation of Japan 85, 281;
  protectionism 153, 183, 202, 219, 238;
  State Department 71, 85;
  technological challenge 116
University of Tokyo 53
Uranium 171, 253, 254, 286

Vans 237
Vermouths 232
Video sets 158, 161, 163—5, 172, 179—80, 192, 220, 222—3, 225, 228—
  30, 235, 239, 250, 253, 255—6, 260, 267—8, 270, 273—4, 277, 287,
  329, 333
Vietnam 115, 151, 160, 202, 324
Volkswagen 275—6, 282

Wales 173
Watches 190, 283
Wheat 223, 283
Whisky 116, 147, 154, 221, 226, 228, 233, 240, 265, 281, 284, 290
Wine 89, 111, 194, 232, 233, 240, 246, 279, 284
Wool 130, 147, 181
Workaholics 259—61
World Bank 123
World car 267
World summits 58, 69, 219, 227, 234, 249—50, 252, 256—8, 263, 271,

318
WW II 155, 334

Yellow submarines 287
Yen 149, 154, 159, 192, 195, 197, 217, 220, 235, 246, 251, 256, 261, 266, 270, 274, 277, 284, 330, 332
Yen bonds 251
Yugoslavia 150

X-ray equipment 324

Zaikai 50—1, 56, 124, 132, 227
Zenno 62, 229
Zimbabwe 41, 242, 268—9
Zip fasteners 201